A
LITERARY
HISTORY
OF
FRANCE

A LITERARY HISTORY OF FRANCE

General Editor: P. E. CHARVET
Fellow of Corpus Christi College, Cambridge

Volume I
THE MIDDLE AGES AND THE RENAISSANCE
by J. P. COLLAS
Professor of French at Queen Mary College, University of London

Volume II
THE SEVENTEENTH CENTURY 1600–1715
by P. J. YARROW
Professor of French at the University of Newcastle upon Tyne

Volume III
THE EIGHTEENTH CENTURY 1715–1789
by ROBERT NIKLAUS
Professor of French at the University of Exeter

Volume IV
THE NINETEENTH CENTURY 1789–1870
by P. E. CHARVET

Volume V
THE NINETEENTH AND TWENTIETH CENTURIES 1870–1940
by P. E. CHARVET

A LITERARY HISTORY OF FRANCE

Volume IV

THE NINETEENTH CENTURY

1789–1870

A LITERARY
HISTORY OF FRANCE

VOLUME IV
The Nineteenth Century
1789–1870

P. E. CHARVET

Fellow of Corpus Christi College, Cambridge

LONDON · ERNEST BENN LIMITED

NEW YORK · BARNES & NOBLE INC

First published 1967 by Ernest Benn Limited
Bouverie House · Fleet Street · London · EC4
and Barnes & Noble Inc. · 105 Fifth Avenue · New York 10003

Distributed in Canada by
The General Publishing Company Limited · Toronto

Printed in Great Britain

FOREWORD BY THE GENERAL EDITOR

IN HIS QUEST for the past, the historian proper deals with a variety of evidence, documentary and other, which is of value to him only for the light it sheds on events and on the men who played a part in them. The historian of literature has before him documents in manuscript or print that exist in their own right, books and ever more books, as the centuries unfold. Within the space allotted to him, his first task must be to give the maximum amount of relevant information about them, but, if he is to avoid producing a mere compilation of unrelated and therefore meaningless facts, he is bound to organize his matter into some sort of pattern.

Time itself does this for him to some extent by keeping alive the memory of those writers and books that retain their relevance, and, often enough, setting one school of writers against another, as successive generations seek to establish their own originality by revolt against their immediate predecessors.

At whatever point in time the historian of literature may stand, he is bound to adopt as a basis of his work the patterns time gives him, although he knows well enough that, just as the tide and the waves may alter the patterns they themselves are for ever imprinting on the sands of the sea shore, time, bringing with it changing tastes and values, will alter these patterns, at least in detail or emphasis.

Within these broad natural patterns come problems of arrangement. Here inevitably a degree of arbitrariness creeps in. Some writers are dubbed precursors, as though they themselves had consciously played the role of prophet in a wilderness, others are marked down as 'epigoni' – poor fellows! Had they but known! – others again are lumped together because they are seen to have in common the characteristics of an age, though they may have had no relations with each other; chronology must often be sacrificed to the need of tidiness. Thus does the historian of literature try to create from the vigorous and confused growth he is faced with, at least on the surface, an ordered garden, where the reader may wander and get an impression to store away in his memory, of neatness and controlled change, an impression helpful, indeed indispensable, as a preliminary to the study of the subject, but not to be confused with the reality.

Nor is this all. Should the historian of literature, need he, smother his personal responses? And if he should (which we doubt and indeed have not tried to do), is this really possible? Within the kindly Doctor Jekyll, recording in detached tones his literary history, seeking to give an objective picture of an age, explaining, elucidating, lurks Mr Hyde, the critic, ready to leap out at the reader on the slightest provocation and wreak his mischief. As in all of us, the levels of his personality that may respond to stimuli are numerous: intellectual, emotional, moral, spiritual; more numerous still the sources of interest whence the stimuli may come: historical and social, psychological, linguistic and stylistic, aesthetic. Literature is a vast catchment area all these streams flow into; a book, a great book is like a burning glass that concentrates the rays of human experience into one bright point; it burns itself into our memories and may even sear the soul.

If he be wise, Mr Hyde the critic will use as his criterium of judgment only the degree to which he feels his own experience has been enriched, his own perceptiveness extended. Thus will he avoid being too rigid or narrow in his attitudes and avoid the temptation of for ever seeking some underlying principle that controls the whole mechanism. Since the corpus of a writer's work is the expression of his experience, since the writer belongs to a given age, a given people, the works may easily become the pretext for an exercise in individual or national psychology. Conversely, the idea of race, the age, the accumulated legacy of history – its momentum, in a word – may be invoked as cause and explanation of the works. Or again, since the works have their place in one or more given art-forms, they may be seen as no more than moments in the evolution of these.

Such ideas and unifying theories have their value no doubt; the people, the society, the age, the art-forms all bear on the question, but who is to assess their impact? They leave the mystery of individual genius and of artistic creation intact; to emphasize them at the expense of the latter is really using the history of literature for other ends. Admittedly books do not spring from nothing, but whether we consider them historically or critically, in the last resort they stand, as we observed at the outset of this foreword, in their own right, and their value depends upon their impact on the individual; every book has three aspects: what the author meant to express, what the book contains, and the image the reader carries away with him; this latter changes with every reader of the book and depends as much upon himself as upon the book and the author.

From its early beginnings in the ninth century down to the present day, French literature can claim a continued existence of 1100 years. What country, beside our own, can boast such literary wealth, such resource, such powers of renewal? The authors of this history, the first of its kind in English, have been only too well aware of the difficulties attendant upon so vast an enterprise. Their hope is that it may give to all readers of French literature a coherent background against which particular periods or writers may be studied and enjoyed in greater depth.

P. E. C.

PREFACE

THE THREE foregoing volumes of this *Literary History of France* have brought the story down to the end of the eighteenth century. To me fell the task of carrying it on from there. Thus, of the two problems that face any chronicler at the outset of his work, namely where to begin and where to end, the first was conveniently solved for me; the decision of my learned colleague, Professor Niklaus, the example of other no less learned writers on French Literature, alike pointed to the French Revolution, where History itself seems to leap across a chasm.

That is no doubt a misleading image, not least in the history of literature, where signs of change in mental attitudes, in beliefs and values, all those imponderables that weigh so heavy in the scales of human life, require from the chronicler a backward look across the chasm, before he turns his face to the future.

The prospect that greets him there is truly one of abundance, albeit of ordered abundance, thanks to the sifting process of time and the work of succeeding generations of critics. 'Embarras de richesses' is an experience given to few, and that many think they would be willing to face, but for me and perhaps even more for my publishers, the abundance of wealth we have been concerned with produced serious dilemmas. For cogent reasons, my publishers finally came to the conclusion that what had originally been designed as one volume must be published as two. Thus volumes IV and V of this *Literary History of France* really form a single work, divided, conveniently enough, at 1870, where History comes to an important turning, and where literary history, too, which so rarely coincides with political events, moves into different or more extreme climates.

Dates play an important part in the patterns we impose on

the past, but the reader will appreciate that where the successive periods are concerned, into which the nineteenth and twentieth centuries may be held to fall, the dates that accompany these in my Table of Contents are intended as no more than a guide, and have nothing definitive about them.

In conclusion, I come to what is the real justification for this brief preface, namely to thank all those who, in one way or another, have helped me in my task: first, on behalf of my colleagues and myself, I desire to thank our publishers for the consideration they have not ceased to show us. In my own particular part of our common work, I desire to record with particular gratitude the names of Professor F. W. Baxter, who has lent me books, provided me with note 60 on page 49 and encouraged me with his kindly interest, of Mrs J. P. T. Bury and Mr Henry Boutflower, both of whom read parts of my text, and gave me excellent advice on matters of style, of Dr A. Fairlie, who helped me locate certain references and lent me an off-print of her valuable paper on Gerard de Nerval, of Professor P. J. Yarrow and Dr T. G. S. Combe, who, busy as they are, were good enough to read my text and give me their invaluable comments, and of Mr J. W. Lucas, who has so generously put at my disposal his wide fund of learning and his technical knowledge of bibliographical and typographical matters, and generously and constantly helped me in numerous practical ways.

P. E. C.

CONTENTS

§ II FROM RESTORATION TO JULY MONARCHY AND AFTER

PART III

THE AUTHORITY OF SCIENCE THE POSITIVIST AGE (1850–1870)

Part I

The Literature of the Revolution
and the Empire (1789–1815)

Chapter 1

EIGHTEENTH-CENTURY LEGACIES
NEW SPIRITUAL FORCES

JEAN-JACQUES ROUSSEAU had died in 1778; but his ideas were to bite deep into the sensibility of the succeeding generations.

This son of a Genevan watch-maker had a harsh experience of life; a social misfit, a wanderer, at times persecuted, at others believing himself to be, he had known the sense of spiritual exile, had found solace in nature and felt himself in intimate communion with it (e.g. *Rêveries du Promeneur Solitaire*, 1776–8). In Nature must be the source of the innate goodness he felt was his and believed to be in man; if men were corrupt, society was at fault for smothering under the artificiality of so-called civilized living the voice of Nature within them.

Dedicated to this doctrine, Rousseau had applied it in different ways: the ideal education (*Emile*, 1762), with Nature as guiding light and a religion hovering between pantheism and deism ('Profession de foi du vicaire savoyard', *Emile*, Bk. IV); passionate love and – after the storm – ideal family relationships (*Nouvelle Héloïse*, 1761), the ideal political structure, destined to ensure the proper integration of the citizen within the body politic and to safeguard the individual within the General Will (*Contrat Social*, 1762).

Rousseau, largely self-taught as he was, knowing unrequited love, clumsy in his social relationships, may have derived some psychological compensation from these lyrical, eloquent, often cogently argued excursions into pedagogy, eroticism, rustic bliss and political philosophy; they could not, however, dispel his burning sense of injustice at the hands of men and the desire to justify himself in their eyes; this *Les Confessions* (posth. 1781–8, 1795) would do; they would present to posterity a faithful unadorned self-portrait of Jean-Jacques.[1] To balk no issue; to dwell with avowed, not to

---

[1] 'Je forme une entreprise qui n'eut jamais d'exemple ... Je veux montrer à mes semblables un homme dans toute la vérité de la nature, et cet homme sera moi.

'Moi seul. Je sens mon coeur et je connais les hommes. Je ne suis fait comme aucun de ceux que j'ai vus; j'ose croire n'être fait comme aucun de ceux qui existent ...' (J.J.R., *Confessions*, Bk. I, opening passage.)

3

say complacent, sincerity on the foibles and idiosyncrasies of his character, on even his pettiest actions; to show himself, in short, as Nature had fashioned him, was the best, the only way to ensure posterity's getting an accurate image of him and being able to judge how ill-intentioned men had misinterpreted and distorted his motives.

Rousseau was, doubtless, too self-conscious, too inward-looking for happiness, but whilst he moved down the treacherous incline from solitude to isolation, from isolation to mistrustful misanthropy, the society that had ill-used him began to find a source of refreshment in his message; beneath the predominantly social role that an aristocratic, cultivated society demanded of its members, was the forgotten or unsuspected store of instincts Nature had implanted in man. Cramped and confined by the brittle rationalism of the eighteenth century, men's awareness of their own emotional potential was to be immeasurably deepened; the secret springs of their being welled up in a flood of feeling, sweeping away the eighteenth-century ideal of social man, leaving in its place the belief in the value of the individual, a creature of instincts, conscious above all of his uniqueness.

In comparison with Rousseau's, the impact of his ardent disciple, Bernardin de Saint-Pierre (1737–1814), though important, is small. He gives a more defined religious character to Rousseau's message, by emphasizing the idea it implies of Providence, and conjures up visions of rich tropical landscapes he had direct experience of (*Paul et Virginie*, 1787); not only did he enrich by this exoticism the emotional desire of escape from the artificiality of society but he stimulated men's interest in a new experience, the pleasure of giving exact descriptive definition to the sights and sounds Nature provided for them in profusion.

Rousseau's attitude to Nature was contemplative, Bernardin's is observant. With Rousseau, man's vague religious aspirations must be satisfied by the emotional emphasis on goodness, the manifestation of the divine spirit working in his innermost part; with Bernardin the notion of God takes on more consistency from the providential theme. In neither does the idea of badness have any reality; at most it is an individual maladjustment, or a distortion of natural values by the temptations of society. From the shadows, however, came a more vigorous reply. The Marquis de Sade (1740–1814),[2] author of, *inter alia*, *Justine, ou les malheurs de la vertu* (1791), *Aline et Valcour* (1795)[3] and *Juliette, ou les prospérités du vice* (1798), which, as the sub-title indicates, is a counterpart to *Justine*,

[2] Donatien-Alphonse-François, Comte de, better known as Marquis de Sade.
[3] Valcour's adventures are founded on the author's own.

grasps the nettle with delight, turns Rousseau and Bernardin up-side down: everything is fundamentally bad; wickedness, not good-ness, is the mainspring of human action; God exists, yes, but he is evil; Satan is God. Thus evil, not excluding murder,[4] as the eman-ation of the true God, at once becomes laudable, and vice should be practised as a matter of religious duty. Justine's catalogue of mis-fortunes arises from her failure to recognize this fundamental truth; her sister Juliette makes no such mistake: 'J'ai suivi la route du vice, moi, mon enfant; je n'y ai jamais rencontré que des roses.'[5]

Juliette and her companions practise vice, not only for its alleged joys, but with 'philosophic' purpose; 'Tout ce qui vient du coeur est faux', declares Saint-Fond (and so much for Rousseau), 'je ne crois qu'aux habitudes charnelles.'[6] Saint-Fond, a Minister of the Crown, no less, sees it indeed as a matter of high policy: 'Le vice fait beaucoup plus d'heureux que la vertu; je sers donc bien mieux le bonheur général en protégeant le vice qu'en récompensant la vertu....'[7]

Rose-strewn though the path may have been for Juliette and company, the reader will be quick to discover that in Sade's pages, at least, it appears stony; he might even draw the conclusion, to Sade's dismay, that vice, practised as a system, is unconscionably dull. But, be that as it may, the powerful attraction of a doctrine that justifies on pseudo-religious grounds the satisfaction of every instinct needs no stressing. From Byron to Baudelaire, from Ro-mantics to Decadents, there were to be writers and poets delighting to bathe in the lurid, sulphurous glare cast up from the Satanic pit; and the theme of beauty persecuted, morally or physically, will take many forms.[8]

Nor is this all, for Sade provides an astringent antidote to the sentimentalism of Rousseau by showing the reverse side of the medal and forcing us to recognize that embedded deep in human nature, rooted in the sexual instinct, lies a streak of cruelty that curiosity may awaken, if circumstances allow, and develop like some hideous cancer; more generally Sade draws attention to the important role of the sexual instinct in human behaviour; from Sade to Freud and his successors the link may be tenuous but it exists.

Rousseau and Sade between them laid bare much that had lain undiscovered or forgotten in the human psyche; beneath the social

---

[4] 'Comme toute destruction, elle (i.e. cette action [murder]) est une des lois de la nature.' See *L'Affaire Sade* (1957), p. 125.
[5] Quoted by G. Apollinaire, Introduction, p. 20, to *L'Oeuvre du Marquis de Sade* (1912).
[6] *Juliette, ibid.*, p. 95.　　　　　　　　[7] *Juliette, ibid.*, p. 91.
[8] See Mario Praz, *The Romantic Agony* (Oxford, 1933), chap. 3.

being, controlled by universal reason, had appeared the individual, with unplumbed depths of emotion, separated from his fellows by the promptings of his own nature.

The influence of the German philosopher Immanuel Kant (1724–1804) accentuated the trend to individualism. Kant subjected the eighteenth-century cult of pure reason to a searching and destructive investigation, but unlike Hume, in whose footsteps he followed, he strove to escape from pure scepticism, to build an indestructible and universally valid basis for faith and ethics on reason, controlled by feeling – a Pascalian alliance. Kant's thought was largely misinterpreted in France, at least at the time of its initial impact. The lesson the Romantics were to draw from it was to reinforce their sense of isolation; since our knowledge of the external world is limited to the realm of phenomena, and our understanding of space and time is no more than the pattern we place on them, in short a projection of our minds, no universal basis for judgment exists, we are prisoners in ourselves, and escape is impossible.

Thus the moral revolution launched by Rousseau gained strength and was to send its shock waves far into the nineteenth century. But in the immediate present French society was to be disrupted by a political revolution, that began in enthusiasm, ended in blood. Here too Rousseau dominates; the men of the Estates General, and those who superseded them, were nourished on his political and moral teachings; with Montesquieu and Voltaire, he was for them a vital member of the intellectual Trinity that was to preside over their deliberations, help them refashion the ancient structure of France, teach Frenchmen the elements of the Social Contract, enshrine their rights in a declaration, force them (if necessary) to be free.[9]

Looking back at the revolutionary years, those who survived the storm must have thought of the Revolution broadly in one of two ways. For some it was a period of massive destruction: destruction of human lives; destruction of an age-old monarchy, which had been a focal point for human loyalties (something men cannot do without), and consequently of the moral unity of France; the destruction of a feudal order; and this meant not merely the murdering of a few thousand aristocrats guilty of no crime other than being the children of their fathers, but the sweeping away of the vast complex of laws and customs that constituted the feudal order, the framework of everybody's life. The Revolution meant the destruction of the Gallican Church as a feudal landowning order in the state, its dispersal as a religious, charitable and educational

[9] *Contrat Social*, Bk. I, chap. VII, 'Du Souverain'.

organization with nothing or precious little to carry on these vital functions, the destruction of all groups or corporations of whatever kind, potential centres of resistance or of independent attitudes to the centralized state; it meant the destruction of the old French provinces by creating new administrative units so as to erase from men's consciousness the fact that the provinces as coherent geographical regions and the cradle of local life and history had been and could again become *foci* for local loyalties against the nation or the republic ... 'une et indivisible'. True, the *ancien régime*, too, had been sensitive to any threat of separation but that was scarcely a live issue by the end of the seventeenth century; centralizing and bureaucratic though the monarchy always was, its demand for uniformity did not extend beyond religion; socially, juridically, economically and even to some extent linguistically, France remained, beneath the uniform structure of the monarchy, a jungle until the Revolution.

For those who thought of the Revolution as begetting chaos, all the destructions we have spoken of spelt the ruin of a France founded upon a religious conception of society and of man's place in it; a God-given order with all men in their appointed stations owing allegiance to someone or some social organism, bound by ties of blood, of belief, of tradition, where men tended to be regarded less as individuals than as members of a group: the family, a corporation, a social order, a people.

The other way in which men thought of the Revolution was as a great liberation. Ruins there may have been, but these were essential before the great work of reconstructing a state on a foundation of justice could be undertaken with every citizen, including what had become a vast submerged majority, a Fourth Estate, able to enjoy moral equality under the law and equality of opportunity. The ruins were necessary before the dynamic of liberty could release the human forces hitherto cramped by a rigid static social structure and weld Frenchmen into a united forward-looking nation. Even assuming the validity of the loyalties and ideals of the *ancien régime*, what a caricature of these French society presented at the eve of the Revolution! The sense of responsibility, if ever it existed, had degenerated into a habit of privilege. 'Qu'avez-vous fait pour tant de biens?', cries Figaro to the irresponsible grand seigneur Almaviva, 'vous vous êtes donné la peine de naître ... voilà tout';[10] an irresponsible government is also the target for his sarcasms: 'Il fallait un calculateur, ce fut un danseur qui l'obtint',[11] he explains, of a job he had applied for, and what an

---

[10] Beaumarchais, *Mariage de Figaro*, V, 3.
[11] The same sort of accusation was to be levelled at democracy under the Third Republic: cf. Faguet, *Le Culte de l'Incompétence* (1909).

indictment of an irresponsible society is provided by Laclos' *Les Liaisons Dangereuses*!

This may be true but the opponents of the Revolution could in their turn point to the phoenix that was claimed to have arisen from the ashes of the *ancien régime* and ask whether it was really as fine a fowl as it was deemed to be. The Revolution's ideal, or more accurately the Jacobin conception of uniformity – Cartesianism *in excelsis* – reduced Frenchmen to administrative units equal in all respects to every other, to 'administrées', standing isolated and unprotected[12] by any secondary social or political grouping, before the majesty of the state.

The men of the Revolution, their opponents could say, may have been liberal idealists but even though liberalism, with its proclaimed respect for the individual and its Declaration of the Rights of Man, has a family likeness with Christianity, in reality it is about as like it as an image in a distorting mirror. The robust characters who stride out of the pages of Balzac or of Stendhal display only too well the canker in liberalism, what Tocqueville was presently to call 'la rouille de la société moderne' – its individualism. Therein lies the fundamental difference between liberalism, the motive power of the new society, and the Christian spirit of the old, and they breed different mentalities: Christianity is outward-looking and speaks in terms of duty, liberalism is inward-looking and insists on human rights; Christianity gives, liberalism demands; Christianity is informed with charity, liberalism consumed by aggressiveness. Built on the former society becomes an infinite complex of reciprocal responsibilities, on the latter a countless collection of autonomous molecules.

Doubtless, neither the opponents nor the upholders of the Revolution were wholly right or wholly wrong; the perfect types of both ideals are images in the mind; the egotism, which is a hallmark of the Romantic period, is to be found on both sides. Yet, that these ideal images should exist is enough for the argument to ring down the century; perhaps the greatest misfortune of the Revolution is to have created this permanent source of division.

On one point, however, all those who had lived through the Revolution could agree: the confirmation it gave of ideas that were already current. Rousseau had emphasized that there were deeper levels in the psyche than the rational one; Kant had destroyed the eighteenth-century belief in pure reason; the Revolution destroyed the aristocratic code of behaviour which in the last

---

[12] True, trade-unionism has altered things. What Frenchman is not now ... 'syndiqué'? But one wonders how well organized the 'syndicats' are or how powerful, financially; further, one may be pardoned for wondering how far the individual's guarantees against excess of police 'zeal' bear examination.

analysis amounted to an insistence upon elegance in living, in
killing,[13] in dying. Be his shortcomings what they may, the aristocrat esteemed as a cardinal virtue the capacity to be master of himself in every situation, for to lose control is supremely inelegant,
the last degree of bad taste or ill-breeding. There are worse ideals.
The Revolution was a grim reminder that beneath this surface
urbanity lay forces in men that a century of elegance had forgotten
about and which, if circumstances like the sorcerer's apprentice
called them forth, were apt to take control. What is unsuspected
cannot be understood and what is not understood is mysterious.
Often enough the Revolution itself was regarded as a mysterious
phenomenon – 'Ce temps horrible qu'il faut considérer comme . . .
en dehors du cercle que parcourent les événements de la vie,
comme un phénomène monstrueux que rien de régulier n'explique
ni ne produit'[14] – and certainly the Romantics in one way and
another were to show themselves very sensitive to the notion of the
mysterious forces governing men's lives.

A soldier untarnished by politics – that was the first impression
Bonaparte made on French society, only too ready, after some
years of Directorial misgovernment, to welcome the appearance of
such a man.

In the closing years of the eighteenth century France must surely
have been a land of opportunity; wealth, position, power – all
seemed within men's grasp. But at such times, when everything
appears to be in a state of flux, men begin to feel more than ever
the need for a solid framework to their lives, a stable aim for their
efforts. Wealth and success rather lose their value if they are felt to
be constantly at the mercy of events and if a man can have little
hope of passing on the former to his children. In short, the need
for stability and security on new foundations was growing and
Bonaparte was to satisfy it.

The Napoleonic reconstructions, administrative, judicial, religious, educational, remain as the foundation of the modern French
state together with the principles, which as heir to the Revolution
Napoleon retained, of equality before the law and equality of
opportunity. These in the eyes of Frenchmen of today constitute his
lasting title to fame; the military glories and conquests are matters
of history. For contemporaries it was different. Napoleon himself
did not regard his military activities as something totally divorced
from his civil activities and conducted on an unrelated plane; all
his activities were different expressions of his personality, different

---

[13] e.g. 'la guerre en dentelles' – 'Messieurs les Anglais, tirez les premiers'!

[14] Mme de Staël, *De la Littérature*, ii, 1.

aspects of the one policy of remoulding France, creating the new Europe, of – who knows? (if fate allowed) – refashioning the world: '... la nation armée de pied en cap ... suit sur le sentier de la guerre, son chef qui est aux prises avec toutes les forces contraires à la Révolution française.'[15]

But the military aspect of Napoleon's total policy inevitably made the greater impact on contemporaries. The fact of hundreds of thousands of men marching and counter-marching over Europe, suffering, dying in pitched battles or long campaigns, was bound to affect the patterns of society and the outlook of individuals.

Once the ancient hierarchy which had kept men anchored to their respective stations in life was swept away, private soldiers could find Marshals' batons in their knapsacks, bourgeois could enrich themselves by lucky or skilful operations on 'les biens nationaux',[16] peasants who had known nothing but their villages, saw European horizons opening before them.[17] Above these personal experiences, moreover, was the towering image of Napoleon himself in the minds of man. Was there not something awesome, in the thought of hundreds of thousands of men, nay, millions if the peoples behind the armies be included, of millions of men, millions of energy units being not only released but increased in power by being given a common direction, fused into an overwhelming thrust by one man, in whom burned the genius of authority, that mysterious complex of mind, will and personality? Something of this demonic force and energy is already apparent in the Revolution – Mirabeau, Danton, Carnot – but these men and the events of their day are dwarfed by Napoleon and his epic.

This moral aspect of the Napoleonic phenomenon, developing and reinforcing some of the effects of the Revolution itself, is not the least of those that impressed themselves upon the nineteenth century especially in the Romantic period.

Napoleon may not have had any positive religious beliefs but he appears to have believed in his star, in some mysterious forces guiding him, in his being the instrument of destiny.

From him as much as from anyone derives the cult of energy, of violence, the cult of the will, of the personality untrammelled by the moral inhibitions and cramping conventions that beset ordinary mortals, the superman in a word; from him too the idea of genius considered as a mysterious subterranean force, suddenly embodied in this or that human vessel, be he warrior, poet, novelist, painter or musician, and erupting with volcanic fury. All these themes are

[15] G. Hanotaux, *Histoire de la Nation française*, vol. V.
[16] Benjamin Constant, see below, p. 50.
[17] Capitaine Gervais, *A la Conquête de l'Europe*, 1939.

at the core of Romanticism. The demonic figure of Napoleon as the genius of war bred a legend that was to become a potent force in politics and to inspire a host of painters, musicians, poets and novelists not only in France.

Chapter 2

POPULAR LITERATURE
REVOLUTIONARY ORATORY. MEMOIRS

IN THE early months of 1789 France must have been tingling
to her farthest extremities with a political awareness, not to be
felt again until June 1848 or the Third Republic. The provincial nobility, the peasants in their parishes with the priest
presiding, the townsfolk by districts or on a corporative basis, all
were assembling to elect representatives to the Estates General to
voice their political ideas and grievances. How rich these gatherings
must at times have been in scenes of comedy and pathos!

From them emerged the *Cahiers de doléances*, a vast book as it
were, composed not by one author but by millions; a disordered
book, full of repetitions, uneven in style and composition, but providing a valuable insight into the mind and mood of Frenchmen
of all classes and from all parts of the country at the threshold of
the nineteenth century – a thirst for liberty, a general desire for a
constitution, for guarantees against arbitrary rule, for regular elections to the Estates General.[1] Side by side with these ideas which
were in the air and which for the peasantry at least may have
seemed theoretical, are cries of distress, urgent personal requests
for relief from heavy burdens: 'Nous avons entendu les voix les
unes après les autres ... moi Deslandes, greffier, je vous demande
la diminution du pain, attendu que nous ne gagnons pas vingt sous
dans les pépinières de sa Majesté étant chargé de beaucoup de
famille qui meurt de faim. Moi Charles Alavant ... je ne saurai
(*sic*) quoi vous demander, car la misère est si grande que personne
ne peut avoir de pain. ...'[2] In contrast to the plain speaking often
to be found in the *cahiers* of the clergy, the nobility and of a
number of big towns, the rural communities speak humbly.[3] But
often too there was such an *entente cordiale* between the three
orders that they agreed to draw up a *cahier* in common.[4]

---

[1] E. Champion, *La France d'après les Cahiers de 1789* (1911).
[2] *Cahier de Rocquencourt*, nr. Versailles. Lavisse, *Histoire de France*,
IX. I.
[3] Lavisse, op. cit.   [4] Champion, op. cit., chap. XVI.

Above all, a wave of enthusiasm and benevolence was launched by the monarch's action in consulting his people, his family as it were. This provoked a revival of loyalty, a touching belief in the power of the king to mend matters, a strong sense of moderation, no egalitarianism, no desire to upset society by sudden changes but to bring in reform with gradual and prudent steps, to act 'avec une extrême prudence par des mouvements très continus, mais très lents et des formes très régulières'.[5]

Here is the authentic voice of the people – a 'Fourth Estate' – who for centuries had stood in darkness without the gate, and who for a moment step into the light.

What a contrast between the modest prudent tones of these people and those of the newspapers, the clubs and the political assemblies once the Revolution has got under way!

The scene shifts; instead of thousands of small rural and provincial *foci* of discussion, a central forum – Versailles, later Paris – where individual competition is harsher, political influences magnified, social reactions quicker, more intense. This is reflected in the evanescent literature of the Revolution: the cacophonous chorus of newspapers[6] that arose after the abolition of the censorship; in the popular songs – always a sensitive pointer to current political attitudes: *La Carmagnole*, the *Ça ira*, the *Chant des Girondins*, above all *Le Chant de Guerre de l'Armée du Rhin* soon to be known as *La Marseillaise*, where Rouget de Lisle enshrined the patriotic ardour of the hour in the current revolutionary vernacular.

> Allons enfants de la Patrie
> Le jour de gloire est arrivé...

Marianne, in Phrygian bonnet, beckons to her children:

> Aux armes citoyens!

The poet has the tocsin ringing in his ears:

> Marchons! Marchons!
> Qu'un sang impur abreuve nos sillons...

-ons!....-ons!....-ons! The syllables hammer out the rhythm like the beats of a native war drum while the tribe whips up the warriors' fervour to the pitch of xenophobic hysteria.[7]

---

[5] Champion, op. cit., chap. XVI.

[6] From the royalist *L'Ami du roi* and *Les Actes des Apôtres* to Hébert's *Le Père Duchesne, le Journal de la Montagne* – organ of the Jacobins, and Tallien's *L'Ami des Sans-Culottes*, with a number of more moderate papers between: *La Quotidienne, L'Avertisseur, La Feuille du Matin*.

[7] At the battle of Wattignies (17 October 1793) while the Austrians were executing their manoeuvres in the prescribed manner, the French troops attacked, against all the rules, singing the Marseillaise – as bad as revoking at bridge.

The new nationalist spirit needed and produced its 'signature tune'; launched into Europe as one of the potent political forces of the nineteenth century, that spirit and the stirring tune rather than any particular poetic merit of *La Marseillaise* itself (who indeed remembers more than the first two lines?) explain the song's survival.

Eloquence is not a new genre in French literature, but whereas under the *ancien régime* the word evokes the majestic figure of Bossuet, now it recalls the great revolutionary assemblies from the Estates General to the Convention and their leading figures: Cazalès, l'Abbé Maury, Mirabeau, Barnave, Vergniaud, Danton, Robespierre, Saint-Just.

Some of their utterances are attached to dramatic moments of the revolutionary saga: thus Mirabeau, with Olympian self-confidence to the Marquis de Brézé:[8] 'Allez dire à votre maître que nous sommes ici par la puissance du peuple et qu'on ne nous en arrachera que par la puissance des baïonnettes'; thus Barnave[9] after 'Varennes': 'La nation française vient d'essuyer une violente secousse...il est temps de terminer la Révolution...' His appeal for the preservation of the monarch's inviolability pre-vailed – for a while – but his belief that the Assembly could put an end to the Revolution by decree suggests the sorcerer's apprentice; thus Vergniaud,[10] attacking Louis XVI for alleged lack of good faith in the opening stages of the war: 'C'est au nom du roi que les princes français ont tenté de soulever contre la nation toutes les cours de l'Europe...' Only a few months later,[11] the monarchy having fallen in the meantime, the same Vergniaud – good Rous-seauist that he is – is pleading that the inviolability of the king's person, guaranteed by the general will of the people, can be lifted only by another solemn plebiscitary action of that will... 'Autre-ment vous usurpez la souveraineté, vous vous rendez coupables de l'un des crimes dont vous voulez punir Louis.' But the time was past for such constitutional niceties; only a few weeks before,[12] 'a new man' had given powerful expression to a revolutionary con-ception of justice that encouraged the extremists : 'je dis que le roi doit être jugé en ennemi... je ne vois point de milieu : cet homme doit régner ou mourir...citoyens, le tribunal qui doit juger Louis n'est point un tribunal judiciaire : c'est un conseil, c'est le peuple, c'est vous....' Thus did Saint-Just, a young man of twenty-five and veritable prototype of Anatole France's sombre Evariste

---

[8] 23 June 1789, when Brézé, as Master of Ceremonies, had brought the King's command that the 'Tiers' should forthwith leave the hall of plenary sessions of the Estates.

[9] 15 July 1791.

[11] 31 December.

[10] 3 July 1792.

[12] 13 November.

Gamelin,[13] first impress his personality on the Convention and hammer home in the minds of its members their collective responsibility, a responsibility they were soon to feel in its most uncomfortable and conspicuous form : a roll call demanding an individually recorded decision.[14]

The fate of the monarchy and consequently of Louis himself was closely connected with the progress of the war which the Girondins had encouraged – unwisely for themselves. Here the dynamic Danton springs to the fore, mounting the tribune as though attacking a fortress; on 2 September 1792, as the news of the Duke of Brunswick's threat to Verdun reached Paris, a patriotic thrill must have run through the Convention as Danton concluded his brief programme for the *levée en masse* with the triumphant peroration: 'Le tocsin qu'on va sonner n'est point un signal d'alarme, c'est la charge sur les ennemis de la patrie. Pour les vaincre, Messieurs, il nous faut de l'audace, encore de l'audace, toujours de l'audace, et la France est sauvée.' That final present tense established the matter beyond any peradventure.

The urgent necessities of war and the threat to the very existence of the Republic were to lead *inter alia* to the Committee of Public Safety and to the development in the mind of Robespierre of the pure revolutionary doctrine: thus, on 25 December 1793, Robespierre gave the intellectual justification of revolutionary tyranny, of terror as a means of crushing disunity and galvanizing the nation into action: 'La théorie du gouvernement révolutionnaire est aussi neuve que la révolution qui l'a amené ... si le gouvernement révolutionnaire doit être plus actif dans sa marche et plus libre dans ses mouvements que le gouvernement ordinaire, en est-il moins juste et moins légitime? Non. Il est appuyé sur la plus sainte de toutes les lois, le salut du peuple; sur le plus irréfragable de tous les titres, la nécessité.'

Apart from the crowd of lesser men, necessity had already claimed Louis XVI[15] and the Girondins[16] as its victims. Soon it was to call Dantonists and Hébertists to account and, when finally too many members of the Convention felt themselves threatened by Robespierre's interpretation of 'necessity', the 'Incorruptible' himself and Saint-Just.

In general, the great speeches of the Revolution (prolix as revolutionary speeches always seem to be[17]) enable the reader to recapture something of the living experience, especially if he remembers

---

[13] *Les Dieux ont Soif.* Below, vol. V, chap. 7. The real model was the painter, Louis David.

[14] Trial of Louis XVI; the document recording the votes is to be seen at the Archives Nationales.

[15] 21 January 1793.

[16] October 1793.   [17] cf. Dr Castro of Cuba.

that the speakers had an audience, that their words must as they were spoken have produced a variety of emotions in their hearers, of which the recording *Moniteur* gives only occasional and vague indications; 'applaudissements d'une grande partie de l'Assemblée ...', 'De violents murmures s'élèvent dans la partie droite...', 'mouvements divers à gauche', etc. The reader is reminded of a playwright's indications to the actors in the printed text of a play. The word play is indeed apposite, for in fact these speeches may well evoke scenes in a play, a play within a play, leading role and stage-audience playing their parts under the eyes of the public in the galleries, and then the whole scene spread out on another stage as wide as the reader's imagination can make it. These speeches are in the first place no doubt evidence for the historian, but, through the historical document as much as through any text of fiction, the student of literature may penetrate to the emotions and character of the men involved, especially at those dramatic moments when an orator, after having perhaps many times enjoyed the euphoric elation of carrying an audience with him, feels the full weight of its hostile silence or is obliged to defend himself against a personal attack.

Thus, Vergniaud on 10 April 1793 under direct attack from Robespierre for the worst offence at such a time, that of being lukewarm: 'J'oserai répondre à M. Robespierre' – no empty formula of politeness, that 'J'oserai', but the expression of a decision taken, perhaps inevitably but in any case in full knowledge of the stakes, and, as the text shows, while Robespierre's bitter ironic tones were still ringing in the ears of the Convention: 'J'oserai répondre à M. Robespierre qui par un roman perfide, artificieusement écrit dans le silence du cabinet et par de froides ironies vient provoquer de nouvelles discordes dans le sein de la Convention; j'oserai lui répondre sans méditation, je n'ai pas comme lui besoin de l'art; il suffit de mon âme...' It did not suffice.

Or Danton on 1 April 1793, with all the impetuosity of his nature, turning defence into attack on his Girondin accusers: 'Appelez le peuple à se réunir en armes contre l'ennemi du dehors [echoes of the *Marseillaise*] et à écraser celui du dedans...l'on verra si je redoute les accusateurs! Je me suis retranché dans la citadelle de la raison; j'en sortirai avec le canon de la vérité et je pulvériserai les scélérats qui ont voulu m'accuser.' His cannon balls of truth did indeed pulverize the Girondins, but just a year later (31 March 1794) the Dantonists, if any were left in the Convention, must have felt their own end was near as Saint-Just apostrophized their leader, arrested that morning: 'Danton, tu répondras à la justice inévitable, inflexible ... Danton, tu as servi la tyrannie...Danton, tu fus donc le complice de Mirabeau...

mauvais citoyen...faux ami...méchant homme.' *Delenda est Carthago!*

Or finally Robespierre, on the eve of his own fall (26 July 1794), inveighs against spies and counter-revolutionaries whom he sees everywhere, apostrophizes the people over the heads of his hearers, whom he knows to be out for his blood, and in the face of danger remains courageous and characteristically self-righteous: 'Peuple ...sache que tout homme qui s'élèvera pour défendre la cause et la morale publique sera accablé d'avanies et proscrit par les fripons; sache que tout ami de la liberté sera toujours placé entre un devoir et une calomnie...que l'influence de la probité...sera comparée à la force de la tyrannie...car que peut-on objecter à un homme qui a raison et qui sait mourir pour son pays?'

The words and attitudes of these men reflect the pressure of events, the responses of their own nature and the influences they have imbibed: classic literature, the heroes of antiquity, the virtues of Republican Rome, Montesquieu, Rousseau. All have in common a sense of urgency, all are charged with a high voltage of passion like an orchestra constantly playing *fortissimo*.

A more subdued note is to be found in the memoirs, stimulated like oratory when events enter a cataclysmic phase and burst in on the personal experience of individuals. The wish to leave some form of spiritual testament, something to survive by, is strong in Madame Roland and Condorcet; in Beugnot, who survived the storm, the impulse is rather to provide an objective record of a life lived at different levels of happiness and misery as the tide of events bore him along from the *ancien régime* to the Restoration.

More than the *Cahiers de doléances*, more than the eloquence of the great orators even when the motive is self-defence, the memoirs bring us close to personal tragedies and suffering; and there is another, a more humble monument to these things that brings us closer still – a personal farewell letter, a kind of memoir in miniature; no attitudes for the gallery, nor self-justification for posterity, just the simplest revelation of a woman matured and tempered in affliction; expressing herself with sincerity; her body imprisoned in the Conciergerie, her mind free of all uncertainties, her inward gaze fixed steadfastly on Louis XVI, her children, her friends, the woman she was writing to and God: 'C'est à vous ma soeur que j'écris pour la dernière fois', writes Marie Antoinette to Madame Elizabeth, 'je viens d'être condamnée, non pas à une mort honteuse, elle ne l'est que pour les criminels, mais à aller rejoindre votre frère...Je suis calme comme on l'est quand la conscience ne reproche rien. J'ai un profond regret d'abandonner mes pauvres enfants; vous savez que je n'existais que pour eux et vous, ma bonne et tendre soeur...' The short and simple sentences follow each other in quick succession as thoughts crowd in, and as if to emphasize that time is pressing: 'Recevez pour eux deux ici ma bénédiction...Que ma fille sente qu'à l'âge qu'elle a elle doit toujours aider son frère...que mon fils, à son tour, rende à sa soeur tous les soins, les services que l'amitié peut inspirer...Que mon fils n'oublie jamais les derniers mots de son père...qu'il ne cherche jamais à venger notre mort!...Il me reste à vous confier encore mes dernières pensées...je meurs dans la religion catholique...Je demande pardon à tous ceux que je connais et à vous, ma soeur, en particulier, de toutes les peines que...j'aurais pu leur causer...'

Only at the end of the letter does a hint of emotion disturb its serenity by an exclamatory statement and the repetition of the word *adieu* : 'Adieu ma bonne et tendre soeur; puisse cette lettre vous arriver[18]...je vous embrasse de tout mon coeur, ainsi que ces pauvres et chers enfants. Mon Dieu qu'il est déchirant de les quitter pour toujours! Adieu, adieu...'.

[18] It did not. Marie-Antoinette entrusted it to Bault, the porter of La Conciergerie; he handed it to Fouquier-Tinville, the state prosecutor, who kept it. When he himself was arrested, the letter was found amongst his papers. It finally came to light in 1816. See Rocheterie et Beaumont, *Lettres de Marie-Antoinette* (Société d'Histoire Contemporaine, 1895), vol. II, p. 441, n. 2.

Chapter 3

'THE REPUBLICAN MOMENT'

THE variety of 'documents' we have been discussing bring us into close contact with the early years of the Revolution and the experience of individuals. Meanwhile, other literary forms follow the traditional patterns, seemingly undisturbed by the massive destructions and violent change that fill the social scene.

Nor is this paradoxical. The men who were writing in 1789 had come to maturity in other – in their view better – times. Why should they, how could they change their tastes and attitudes? Either they must cease writing – some did[1] – or they would continue to use classical moulds. Classical tragedy, thanks to Corneille, Racine and perhaps especially to Voltaire, had acquired a tremendous momentum, not to exhaust itself for some years yet, and no poet worthy the name could hope for recognition unless he had written a five-act tragedy.

Another reason for the survival of the classical forms lies in the distinctive spirit of that brief interlude between Thermidor (1794) and Brumaire (1799) or at any rate the establishment of the Empire (1804), which corresponds to the years of the 'Directory' or the 'Directory and Consulate',[2] an interlude of peace when the chances of establishing a republic seemed strong and the republicans, proud of the Revolution's 'conquests', saw themselves as the heirs of Republican Rome; now was the blossoming of a generation full of civic pride, optimistic patriotism and a moralising self-righteousness that easily justifies (or forgets) revolutionary excesses: 'Jours à jamais célèbres, et à jamais regrettables pour nous', writes 'Monsieur' Thiers, 'A quelle époque notre patrie fut-elle plus belle et plus grande? Les orages de la Revolution paraissaient calmés; les murmures des partis retentissaient comme les derniers bruits de la tempête: on regardait ces restes d'agitation comme la vie même d'un Etat libre . . .'[3]

---

[1] Below, p. 60.

[2] Sainte-Beuve, *Chateaubriand et son groupe littéraire sous l'Empire*, 1e leçon.

[3] *Histoire de la Révolution*, VII, cited by Saint-Beuve, op. cit., 1.

Daunou (1761–1840), organiser of the Institut (1796),[4] and Marie-Joseph Chénier (1764–1811) reflect prevailing moods and attitudes. In his *Tableau historique de l'état et des progrès de la littérature française depuis 1789* (posth. 1816), the latter writes: 'Il se présente à nos regards la poésie dramatique, dont les deux genres eurent tant d'influence sur notre langue, sur notre littérature entière et sur les moeurs nationales.' A staunch republican could indeed find plenty of spiritual nourishment in Corneille and Voltaire. The classical drama in Chénier's view was as though 'built in' to the national tradition; no wonder there was no lack of poets ready to court the tragic muse in succession to the illustrious Voltaire: 'M. Ducis, inventeur même quand il imite, inimitable quand il fait parler la piété filiale, poète justement célèbre, et dont le génie pathétique a tempéré la sombre terreur de la scène anglaise ...' Other poets equally distinguished (*dixit* Marie-Joseph) march close on his heels: Arnault, 'si noble dans Marius, si tragique dans les Vénitiens'; Legouvé, Lemercier, Raynouard, Baour-Lormian, Murville. To each of these illustrious nonentities, the author of the *Tableau* judiciously distributes his meed of praise, and in fairness it should be mentioned that Marie-Joseph himself contributed at least one play – *Charles IX ou le fanatisme* (1789) – not entirely forgotten. On the collective merits of these writers Marie-Joseph writes: 'Sans violer les règles anciennes, ils ont obtenu des effets nouveaux. Du reste, ils ont conservé ce caractère philosophique imprimé à la tragédie par le plus beau génie du dernier siècle ...'[5] The classical canons above all, some Voltairian moralising and, for good measure, new subjects drawn from modern history, 'immense carrière qui promet longtemps des palmes nouvelles'.

How wrong are those who say that tragedy is played out! Sure sign of their own lack of invention: 'heureusement l'erreur est évidente. En quelque genre que ce soit, l'art est semblable à la nature, son modèle: il a des règles, comme la nature à des lois; il n'a point de bornes, puisque la nature est infinie.'

The comic muse too has no lack of devotees: Laujon, Cailhava, François, Fabre d'Eglantine, Colin d'Harleville, Picard, Duval, Roger. The names are numerous, the literary residue nil. Some slight merit might be attributed to that precursor of Eugène Scribe, Picard, author of *La Petite Ville* (1801): 'Une imagination féconde, une gaîté franche, la peinture originale des moeurs', to quote Marie-Joseph. The modern reader would scarcely go all that way with him, especially as the substance of the play is not drawn from 'la peinture originale des moeurs' but from La Bruyère's *Caractères*.

---

[4] See his inaugural speech (4 April), quoted by Sainte-Beuve, op. cit., 1.
[5] Voltaire.

Poetry other than dramatic poetry has the same air of survival from a former age. Marie-Joseph himself, no mean versifier, shows himself an admirable and true successor of Boileau in his *Epître à Voltaire*, or his *Epître sur la Calomnie*, true successor, that is, in the form; less reliable, though, in his critical judgments:

> Au sein du présent même écoutant l'avenir,
> Certain de ses décrets, je veux les prévenir. [Rash fellow!]
> J'aime à voir de Colin la décente Thalie
> Des humains en riant crayonner la folie;
> Parny dicter ses vers mollement soupirés;
> Dans ses malins écrits avec goût épurés,
> Palissot aiguiser le bon mot satyrique;
> Lebrun ravir la foudre à l'aigle pindarique;
> Delille, nous rendant le Cygne armé des Dieux,
> Moduler avec art ses chants mélodieux...

Parny (1753–1814), Palissot (1730–1814), Lebrun (1729–1807), Delille (1738–1813), names that have not been entirely lost without trace; to their number may be added Florian, the fabulist.[6] Lebrun, or Lebrun-Pindare, as he styled himself, is particularly characteristic of these classical survivals. When not occupied by 'the tender passion', which he mostly is, Lebrun-Pindare sings of liberty:

> O Liberté que les Orages
> Ont de charmes pour les grand coeurs[7]

of the heroism (Republican) of the Vengeur's crew:

> Plus fiers d'une Mort infaillible,
> Sans peur, sans désespoir, calmes dans leurs combats,
> De ces Républicains l'Ame n'est plus sensible
> Qu'à l'ivresse d'un beau Trépas...[8]

of the joys of Bacchus and of peace after a famous victory:[9]

> O jour d'éternelle Mémoire,
> Embellis-toi de nos lauriers!
> Siècles! Vous aurez peine à croire
> Les prodiges de nos guerriers:... etc....

The French expression *taquiner la muse* fits well the activities of these skilful versifiers.

Effete classical forms, didacticism, occasional echoes of passing events or current moods and enthusiasms, such are the characteristics of the literature of the 'Republican Moment'; very often too, an undeniable official flavour, in Lebrun particularly, that was sure to please Marie-Joseph: 'nous remarquerons que ses derniers

---

[6] Also remembered for a short poem (11½ alexandrines): 'Le Voyage', which is like a short fable on life: 'Partir avant le jour..., Aller de chute en chute...etc.'

[7] *De l'Enthousiasme* (1792).

[8] 1794.

[9] Marengo (1800).

accents furent consacrés à nos derniers triomphes. Il était digne de les chanter...' *Le Tableau... de la Littérature* which was a report to the 'Institut (Section Belles Lettres)' on the state of The Republic of Letters is itself a mirror of official attitudes, with its condescending Olympian distribution of praise and censure.

The empty husk of classical forms becomes 'Establishment' literature under the Empire. Napoleon regarded Cornelian tragedy as 'l'Ecole des Grands Hommes'; drama, therefore, to be encouraged or tolerated must have that worthy didactic aim.

Both Joseph Joubert (1754–1824) and Jean-Pierre de Fontanes (1757–1821) live for us in the pages of *Les Mémoires d'Outre-Tombe*, as members of the small and lively society that welcomed Chateaubriand on his return to France in 1800. 'Plein de manies et d'originalité, M. Joubert manquera éternellement à ceux qui l'ont connu... M. de Fontanes... était... un poéte irascible, franc jusqu'à la colère, un esprit que la contrariété poussait à bout...'[10] There is in Joubert something faintly reminiscent of Atticus, that skilful pilot of his own bark in the dangerous waters of his time, friend of many politicians, yet refusing all part in their activities.

Some time Justice of the Peace at Montignac (1791–2), later Inspector-General of Schools under Napoleon (1809–15), Joubert was thus on two occasions on the fringe of political life; but, conscientiously though he carried out his functions, his interests lay elsewhere – in literature. The image his friends had of him was a wise, a lucid and self-effacing counsellor, content to scatter his wisdom as moralist and literary critic in his conversation and his letters, apparently unconcerned with creating a reputation for himself, so modest that he published nothing in his own life-time, except a few unsigned articles;[11] 'Je suis comme une harpe éolienne, qui rend quelques beaux sons et qui n'exécute aucun air'.[12]

A reputation such as his founded on hearsay alone could scarcely have lasted to our own day. But a succession of posthumous editions[13] of his work enable us to appreciate all the originality of the man as thinker and critic. On religion, politics, society, on man, on literature (his main passion) and last but not least on himself, Joubert's wisdom is penetrating, often compelling. 'On peut avoir du tact de bonne heure et du goût fort tard; c'est ce qui m'est arrivé.' No matter whether he judges himself accurately in that proposition which, considered in general, reflects so accurately the enriching and refining effect of experience upon a sensitive soul,

[10] *Mémoires d'Outre-Tombe*, second part, book 1, chap. 7 *passim*. Levaillant, Edition du Centenaire.
[11] *Mémoires d'Outre-Tombe*, 2nd part, Levaillant edn.
[12] op. cit., 2nd part.
[13] *Recueil des Pensées* (Lenormant, 1838), down to *Pensées et Lettres* (Grasset, 1954).

the fact remains that Joubert as he appears to us through his *Pensées* and his letters was a man of discerning and eclectic judgment. His love of classical antiquity did not blind him to the potentialities of the literature of his own day: 'Les beaux vers sont ceux qui s'exhalent comme des sons ou des parfums' is a reflection that foreshadows Lamartine; there is even a suggestion of Baudelaire.

Joubert's reputation of gentle philosopher and friend, confined in his own day to a narrow circle, has changed; the distilled wisdom of the moralist has grown stronger like a perfume in contact with the air. His friend Fontanes, on the other hand, is scarcely of the same order. We think of him particularly as a Napoleonic administrator. By contrast the reputation he enjoyed in his own day as poet and critic has faded; we retain of him the impression of someone to whom literature is a secondary, an amateur interest, an unfair impression in the sense that Fontanes cultivated literature and especially the poetic muse with diligence;[14] one of his poems, indeed, *Essai sur l'Astronomie* (1781), launched a vogue soon to be followed by Delille (1738–1813),[15] Chênedollé (1769–1833),[16] Lebrun,[17] and André Chénier.[18] But with all his considerable skill, Fontanes' poetic excursions have little attraction today; they seem nothing more than exercises in versification, dressed up in the classical mode so characteristic of the period, now in melancholic, now in heroic mood according to the promptings of the Muse, so frequently invoked:

> ... Muse, viens m'inspirer
> Un chant majestueux qui te puisse honorer.

With what solace does Fontanes turn from the bleakness of the Revolutionary scene to Ancient Greece. The Revolution in fact gave clear definition to Fontanes' opinions, not only literary but also political. In *Le Mémorial* (1797), the journal he founded with Laharpe and l'Abbé de Vauxcelles, he is unequivocally in favour of the Ancients – what a contrast with the mediocrity of the literature of the hour!

Equally characteristic are his political attitudes. At the beginning of the Revolution Fontanes had been a constitutional monarchist; now he is vigorously reactionary,[19] demanding the recall of the émigrés, defending the clergy, attacking the 'burlesque démence' of the Revolution; Fontanes has joined the ranks of those who, each in his own generation down the nineteenth century, denounce

---

[14] *La Chartreuse, Le Jour des Morts, La Grèce Sauvée, Le Vieux Château.*
[15] *Les Trois Règnes* (1808).
[16] *Génie de l'Homme* (1807).   [17] *Nature* (unfinished).
[18] *Hermès* (fragmentary).   [19] Wilson, *Fontanes*, pp. 150 *et seq.*, 1928.

the Revolution and all its works; his attitude in *Le Mémorial* explains his subsequent decision, once he was convinced that a Restoration was impossible, to turn to the First Consul, in whom he was now[20] prepared to see the Saviour of France; for above all Fontanes hated anarchy; order there must be in the state ... and in poetry. He is at heart an authoritarian: 'Muse, viens m'inspirer ...' A gentle invocation? – rather a command, a summoning of the Muse into the presence of Fontanes!

Le Mémorial also throws light on Fontanes' religious position. In his youth he had admired Voltaire, but had not shared his scepticism.[21] His religious thought is only a vague religiosity, coupled with a conviction the Revolution strengthened, and which is characteristic of an authoritarian, an 'Establishment' man: the Christian religion is essential in a well-ordered society, and in the formation of the future citizen.

As a man of letters, too, Fontanes believed that religion enriched literature: 'L'idée d'un Dieu ... féconde les arts comme elle anime le spectacle de la nature.'[22] Conversely, disbelief desiccates: 'Rien ne fut plus insipide que le langage de l'impiété dans tous les temps.'[23] Here is the source of the idea that Chateaubriand was to develop with force in *Le Génie du Christianisme*.[24]

Fontanes had known Chateaubriand in Paris in the early days of the Revolution. They had not met again until 1798 in London. Chateaubriand, an exile of nearly five years standing, had just published his *Essai sur les Révolutions*; Fontanes was a political fugitive too, as a result of the *coup d'état* of Fructidor (September 1797). The guillotine was by then out of fashion; deportation,[25] the usual compromise solution when fanaticisms have cooled but political enemies remain, was the order of the day and to escape it, Fontanes had fled to Hamburg, thence to England.

In the *Mémoires d'Outre-Tombe* Chateaubriand pays tribute to the influence Fontanes exercised over him during the months they spent together in London.[26]

That influence extended beyond matters of literary form; Chateaubriand makes it plain that Fontanes, whose literary tastes, particularly as a result of the Revolution, had veered so decisively towards antiquity, was not closed to other sources of literary inspiration, admired *Les Natchez* and encouraged its author to persevere with the great prose epic of the New World. Most important

---

[20] January 1800.   [21] Wilson, op. cit., p. 133.
[22] *Magazine Encyclopédique*, 1795, t.v, p. 116, quoted by Wilson, op. cit., p. 134.
[23] *Journal Littéraire*, 25 May 1797, quoted by Wilson, op. cit., p. 134.
[24] Ballanche also stresses this point. See below, p. 65, n. 21.
[25] In this case to Sinnamari, Guiana.
[26] Levaillant, op. cit. Numerous refs., especially Part I, Bk. II, chap. 6.

of all, however, is the fact that Fontanes played a decisive part in Chateaubriand's return to Catholicism, implanted in him his own conviction of the value of the Christian faith for literature and gave him the idea of becoming 'avocat poétique du Christianisme.'

Thus, Fontanes had an indirect but important part in the preparation of a book that was to make a big impact on the contemporary generation.

Fontanes was able to return to France before Chateaubriand and was largely instrumental in arranging for the latter's home-coming – not the least of his services to a friend whose literary genius was so entirely to eclipse his own. As poet and critic Fontanes remains indeed no more than a witness to a particular moment in the evolution of French literary sensibility; his real title to fame assuredly is that he was one of the chief architects of the Imperial 'University', the centralized educational machine willed by Napoleon and built on the ruins left in this domain as in so many others by the Revolution.

The spirit of the 'Republican Moment' burns particularly brightly amongst politicians like Sieyès, Garat and Daunou, critics and journalists like Guinguené, Roederer and Laharpe, great upholder of classical values, amongst intellectuals, notably the Idéologues, e.g. Condorcet, Lakanal, Volney, Laplace, Cabanis, Destutt de Tracy. Their views were reflected in *La Décade philosophique, littéraire et politique*,[27] their stronghold was the newly formed Institut, their influence had made itself felt in the Convention of which some had been members[28] and in the spirit of the new education that was to be dispensed in the schools the Convention intended but had little time to establish. They incurred the professed contempt of Napoleon – 'métaphysiciens nébuleux' – but perhaps he disliked them because he knew them to be against his policy of religious reconstruction and appeasement,[29] for 'métaphysiciens nébuleux' they were not.

In so far as these men can be said to have a common interest it was in the study of psychology, divorced from any metaphysical considerations. They derive from Condillac. 'Notre premier objet', Condillac wrote, 'celui que nous ne devons jamais perdre de vue, c'est l'étude de l'esprit humain, non pour en découvrir la nature mais pour en connaître les opérations . . .'.[30]

Conspicuous amongst the Idéologues is Antoine Caritat, Ms. de Condorcet (1743–94). He had been prominent in scientific and intellectual circles before the Revolution,[31] and was amongst the first

[27] Review, founded by Ginguené in 1794 (floréal an ii). In 1807 it merged with *Le Mercure*.
[28] Notably Condorcet.   [29] Concordat, 1802.
[30] *Essai sur l'Origine des Connaissances humaines*. Introduction.
[31] Elected to Academy of Sciences 1769, to French Academy 1792.

during the Revolution to declare republican sympathies. He had been a member of the Legislative Assembly and presented to that body his Report on Public Instruction. When the Legislative Assembly disappeared in the turmoil and the Convention was formed, Condorcet was again elected but, soon denounced for his opposition to a constitutional project, submitted by Hérault de Séchelles, was forced into hiding; arrested later he committed suicide in his cell. While in hiding and under the threat of the guillotine, he occupied himself with the project for a book he was able to complete only in outline: *Esquisse d'un tableau historique des Progrès de l'Esprit humain* (1794). Published posthumously, it shows that its author, had he lived, would have been in tune with the spirit we are discussing and is a moving tribute to Condorcet's courage.

Its confidence in the capacity of the human intelligence to grasp all the infinite detail of one generation's action upon another in humanity's onward march – 'Ce tableau ... se forme par l'observation successive des sociétés humaines ... Il doit présenter l'ordre des changements, exposer l'influence qu'exerce chaque instant sur l'instant qui lui succède ...';[32] its fanatical attitude to religion; its ignorance of the Middle Ages, dark indeed to enlightened eighteenth-century minds: 'Des rêveries théologiques, des impostures superstitieuses ... l'intolérance religieuse ... l'Europe comprimée entre la tyrannie sacerdotale et le despotisme militaire ...';[33] all these traits show that Condorcet looks back now to Voltaire, now to d'Holbach; on a flood of future tenses, he launches the eighteenth-century message into the nineteenth, where, with ponderous efficiency, Auguste Comte was to take it up.

But with all his cloudy optimism Condorcet has practical abilities; his vision of the progress of equality,[34] his emphasis on the importance to that end of education for the young and for adults,[35] his idea of social security and pensions established on actuarial calculations,[36] on the progressive elimination of national rivalries;[37] in all these ways, Condorcet displays an awareness of social and political problems that points beyond the nineteenth century to the twentieth.

Most prominent of all the writers reflecting the spirit of the 'Republican Moment' is Madame de Staël, whom we shall discuss in the next chapter.

The public of the day knew scarcely anything of André Chénier (1762–94) – two poems[38] and his political articles in *Le Mercure* and *Le Journal de Paris*, no more; the remainder : Idylls, Elegies,

---

[32] *Esquisse* I.
[34] *Ibid.*, X[e] époque.
[36] *Ibid.*

[37] *Ibid.*

[33] *Ibid.*, VIe époque.
[35] *Ibid.*
[38] *L'Aveugle* and *Le Mendiant.*

Odes, Iambics, some of them completed, many only fragmentary, was to lie buried in manuscript form until 1819.

'Mourir sans vider mon carquois...' (*Iambes X*),[39] Chénier himself mourns this lack of fulfilment and plenitude, all the more tragic in that he was so evidently full of joy in creation:

La sainte poésie et m'échauffe et m'entraîne... (*Fragments d'Elégies* ii)

so intent on artistic integrity:

> ... de mes écrits en foule
> Je prépare longtemps et la forme et le moule
> Puis sur tous à la fois je coulerai l'airain:
> Rien n'est fait aujourd'hui, tout sera fait demain. (*Epître* iii)

Thus a poet, the only notable one of his generation, halted in full career and, in many ways so characteristic of the late eighteenth century, finds a special, an isolated place in the nineteenth.

Born in Constantinople of a French father[40] and of a half Spanish half Italian mother, whom he believed to be Greek,[41] Chénier early developed a passion for classical antiquity. His classical scholarship, indeed, sometimes overweights his verse with its top-hamper of classical allusion:

> Plût aux dieux que la Thrace aux rameurs de Jason
> Eût fermé le Bosphore...
> Que Minerve abjurant leur fatale entreprise,
> Pélion n'eût jamais aux bords du bel Amphyse
> Vu le chêne, le pin ses plus antiques fils,
> Former, lancer aux flots, sous la main de Tiphys,
> Ce navire éloquent, fier conquérant du Phase... (*Médée* ii)

and so on. The modern reader – his the loss – is apt to be discouraged by a host of allusions no longer part of his framework of reference.

Other aspects too in Chénier are unlikely to satisfy modern literary taste, e.g. the constant periphrases of the 'style noble'.

> Le lait enfant des sels de ma prairie humide,
> Tantôt breuvage pur et tantôt mets solide
> En un globe fondant sous ses mains épaissi
> En disque savoureux à la longue durci...
> (*Elégies* xxxix 'Aux deux Frères Trudaine')

Why not simply:... a ripe Camembert or Brie? Direct concrete statements are more likely to call forth an immediate response from our experience than circumlocutions, relegated nowadays to the clues of cross-word puzzles.

The eighteenth-century voluptuary is much in evidence:

> Et toi, lampe nocturne, astre cher à l'amour
> Tu fus le seul témoin de ses douces caresses.
> (*Elégies* xxxvii 'La Lampe')

[39] Written in Saint Lazare prison.
[40] French Consul and merchant.   [41] See *Fragments d'Elégies* ii.

Or again :

> ... mon coeur, mon jeune coeur
> Commençait dans l'amour à sentir un vainqueur ...
>
> (*Elégies* xvii 'Au Ms. de Brazais')

A busy cupid, from the pen of Ovid or the brush of François Boucher, must have sent an arrow, indeed many, through the poet's heart as he pursued the Cynthias, the Corinnas, the Camillas, the Amelias and the rest who trip through his poems.

The spirit of the eighteenth century, too, informs the poem: 'L'Invention' where the poet without being unfaithful to classical forms and canons of beauty – 'sur des pensers nouveaux faisons des vers antiques' – proclaims his intention of bringing all the conquests of science into the domain of poetry:

> ... les sciences humaines
> N'ont pu de leur empire étendre les domaines
> Sans agrandir aussi la carrière des vers

Or in the fragmentary poem 'Hermès', where the poet intends to sing man's progress through the ages or in 'L'Amérique', also fragmentary, which was to describe man's gradual conquest of the Globe.

The poet's enthusiasm carries him here to the epic level but we cannot be sure whether these very intellectual enthusiasms would have sustained the poet's flight at the high level he dreamed of as he 'blocked out' his canvas now in prose notes, now launching into verse.

The outbreak of the Revolution aroused André Chénier's latent liberalism; for him Ancient Greece and Rome were not only the source of the arts, they were also the homes of the great virtues because liberty resided there: 'Périssent ceux qui traitent de préjugé, l'admiration pour tous ces modèles antiques et qui ne veulent point savoir que les grandes vertus constantes et solides ne sont qu'aux lieux où vit la liberté!'[42]

Abandoning his career as a diplomat, he hurried back from London to throw himself into political life and journalism. His 'hymne à la justice', his hymn to 'La France libre', his Odes in honour of the painter David (1748–1825) whose constant pictorial references to the virtues of Ancient Rome so exactly mirrored Chénier's own ideas, bear witness to his new enthusiasms. But they were to be shortlived; as the extremists achieve power, joy gives place to the irony and indignation of the 'Iambes', written in the prison of Saint Lazare, or of the Ode to Charlotte Corday: 'Un scélérat de moins rampe dans cette fange...',[43] to the pity,

---

[42] *Fragments d'Elégies* ii.   [43] Marat, 1743–93.

inspired by the sight of a young woman, imprisoned as he was, by the Terror:

> Ainsi, triste et captif, ma lyre toutefois
> S'éveillait, écoutant ces plaintes, cette voix,
> Ces voeux d'une jeune captive...

In fact Aimée de Coigny, who inspired 'La Jeune Captive', more fortunate than the poet, was saved by Thermidor (27 July 1794); Chénier was executed two days before.

André Chénier's appeal, probably limited today, is primarily historical and literary, historical in the sense that he reflects so well the tastes and attitudes of his generation, the voluptuousness, the facile if sincere optimism about progress, perfectibility and the like; the liberal enthusiasms of the Revolution's early stages giving way to generous indignation and disgust at its excesses, the interest in antiquity which, in part at least, is different from that of the seventeenth century. If, on the one hand, a link with Corneille can indeed be found in the enthusiasm for the austere and heroic virtues of Republican Rome – the men of the Revolution flattered themselves they were her heirs, as they admired the canvasses of David,[44] on the other hand, Chénier expresses a new, nostalgic escape to antiquity. The discoveries of Herculaneum and the work of Winckelmann had awakened a strong interest in the outward forms and ways of life of the Ancients; they set a fashion that extended throughout Western Europe and affected less the spirit of the times – except in so far as the paganism of the Ancients might attract eighteenth-century rationalists and atheists – than outward forms: styles in architecture, painting and decoration, dress. André Chénier reflects this atticism admirably.

But for anyone who can bring to his reading of the poet some framework of literary reference, a strong literary interest arises as well; he recalls and foreshadows so much.

> On s'accoutume au mal que l'on voit sans remède (*Elégies* xxvi)

> Qui ne sait être pauvre est né pour l'esclavage. (*Elégies* xvi)

Such weighty moral apophthegms could well have come from Corneille or Boileau or Voltaire; on the other hand, how often within the classical forms does the reader detect Romantic attitudes:

> Douce mélancolie...
> Qui vient...
> Saisir l'ami des champs et pénétrer son coeur (*Elégies* xiv)

suggests the Lamartinian muse;

> Sois satisfait, mon coeur...
> Tu vas dormir en paix dans ton sublime ennui (*Elégies* xii)

[44] e.g. 'Le serment des Horaces'.

has a semi-Baudelairian ring, and are there not suggestions of Mallarmean nostalgia in:

> Partons! la voile ets prête, et Byzance m'appelle (*Fragments d'Elégies* iii)

The ambitious sweep of his big epic fragments are a foretaste of Hugo in conception and spirit; the plasticity of his best verse leads straight to the poetic principles of 'l'Art pour l'Art' and the Parnassians.

Lines such as those just quoted do more than stimulate mere literary reminiscences; their poetic resonance awakens a genuine emotional response in the reader and creates the hope of a poem inspired by some human experience he can share. Often he is disappointed; the poem peters out into a peevish complaint at the heartlessness of Cynthia or Corinna or Camilla or Amelia. Perhaps the complaint was justified but, not knowing the lady, the reader, egotist that he is, loses interest and retains only the memory of the arresting line, a pleasing but fleeting experience.

Occasionally, however, he is not disappointed; the emotion seems to sustain the whole poem; the feeling of frustrated hopes, for example in La Jeune Tarentine, is splendidly rhythmical:

> Pleurez doux alcyons! O vous oiseaux sacrés!
> Oiseaux chers à Thétis, doux alcyons, pleurez! (*Idylles* ix)

Or the anguish of final partings:

> Adieu mon Clinias! Moi, celle qui te plut ... (*Fragments d'Idylles* iv)

But above all André Chénier's merit lies in his plasticity which at its best provides the reader with a rich sensuous experience: azure seas, warm sun, hum of bees, scent of herbs and honey, murmuring waters, cool and shady groves:

> Le souffle insinuant, qui frémit sous l'ombrage
> Voltige dans mes vers comme dans le feuillage,
> Mes vers sont parfumés et de myrte et de fleurs.
> (*Fragments d'Idylles* xxxviii)

The strong emotions excited by the previous years must find other outlets now that the real life dramas of the Revolution were over and a republican peace seemed to be dawning.

Mystery as an emotional stimulant had already been exploited in the 'Gothick' novel initiated by Horace Walpole with *The Castle of Otranto* (1767). No doubt the blood and violence of the Revolution accounts for the popularity enjoyed both in England and France by Walpole's imitators and successors – Ann Radcliffe, 'Monk' Lewis, Maturin, Ducray-Duménil, Ducange.

The tales of horror provided by these writers had their counterpart on the stage in the melodrama, created by Guilbert de Pixérécourt (1773–1844), diversely nicknamed the Shakespeare, the

Corneille, the king of the boulevards. Pixérécourt had emigrated with his father and seen service with the 'Princes' Army'. But he had quickly returned to France, married and at the price of privation and personal risk 'gone to ground' in Paris during the worst of the revolutionary storm. He had begun writing in earnest for the stage in 1795. *Les Petits Auvergnats* (1797), a one-act comedy, was his first success, followed by *Victor ou l'Enfant de la Forêt* (1798), drawn from a novel by Ducray-Duménil. The melodrama was born.

Thereafter and until 1834 Pixérécourt provided the theatres of the boulevard with melodramas – one hundred and twenty of them – mostly from his own pen; not till 1830 did he seek the help of collaborators. Some of the titles, at least, of the plays are remembered, e.g. *Le Château des Apennins ou les Mystères d'Udolphe* (1798), the highly successful *Coelina ou l'Enfant du Mystère* (1800), *Le Chien de Montargis ou la Forêt de Bondy* (1814), *Latude ou trente-cinq ans de captivité* (1834).

As a 'genre' melodrama conformed to a clear-cut pattern which persisted throughout the nineteenth century down to the Lyceum melodramas and the unending cinema serials with Pearl White in the title role, of the early twentieth. Whether weaving its way through forest paths or in the devious corridors of castle and dungeon, whatever its means, dagger or poison, to ensure sudden death, the plot would centre on a young heroine, usually of unknown identity, disclosed only at the end, cruelly persecuted, but saved in the nick of time by the hero, ably seconded by Providence.

Certain typed characters were essential, the innocent heroine, the cowardly and treacherous villain, the good and courageous hero, a 'fool' in the Shakespearian sense, to provide comic relief, now unwittingly traversing the hero's efforts by his clownings, thus prolonging the audience's suspense, now in a flash of lucidity helping to bring the villain to book. That virtue and villainy must in the end receive their just deserts was axiomatic; Providence was in the wings to see to that.

Thus does melodrama capture something of prevailing moods. While the cultivated republican with the image of Rome in mind takes pride in austerity and glibly quotes his Corneille, his unlettered counterpart from the 'boulevard du crime' can frankly enjoy moralising for the masses from Pixérécourt. Unfettered by classical forms, highly coloured in action, highly charged with simple passions, the melodrama as shaped by Pixérécourt was to prove a useful guide and example in dramatic emancipation and crude character delineation to the Romantic dramatists of the next generation.

Chapter 4

I. MADAME DE STAËL

EMIGRATION as an inevitable concomitant of revolution was to have important and valuable consequences for French literature.

Torn from their natural surroundings the *émigrés* were launched on a journey, for some a spiritual journey, a journey of exploration into themselves, for others a journey in the strict sense which for the most receptive, for those who in spite of material difficulties and personal suffering were prepared to look outwards, was one that proved an enriching cultural experience, and this fact in its turn was to extend French horizons.

In this process of widening French horizons, Madame de Staël (1766–1817), though not an *émigré* proper, was to play an outstanding part. For that, her genius is reason enough; but the conjunction of circumstances was favourable to her activity and influence.

Her father, Jacques Necker, had come to Paris from his native Geneva and had made a fortune as a financier. French banking in the eighteenth century was largely in the hands of the Genevese or the Dutch[1] who did not share the inhibitions still existing in Catholic France about possible connexions between banking and usury. Her mother, Suzanne Curchod, was the daughter of a Swiss Protestant pastor. If heredity counts for anything in the moulding of mental attitudes, here in this Germano-Swiss background enriched by the cosmopolitan Protestant tradition of eighteenth-century Switzerland are the makings of a receptive attitude to European influences.

To these natural advantages – advantages, that is, from the point of view we are adopting – Germaine Necker in due course added several others; her marriage to the colourless Baron de Staël, which brought her no happiness but had the merit of conferring upon her a diplomatic status that was a protection during the revolu-

---

[1] C. Herold, *Mistress to an Age*. As late as the eighteen-thirties the finance house in Stendhal's *Lucien Leuwen* is Leuwen, Peters & Cie., which has a distinctly Flemish ring. Balzac's financiers mostly come from Frankfurt.

tionary years and may have assisted her, as she moved about the capitals of Europe even after the Baron de Staël's dismissal from his post, and death (1802). The persecution she suffered at the hands of Napoleon might also be reckoned as an advantage: she could thereby enlist sympathy as the courageous victim of tyranny; moreover, her opposition to the tyrant sharpened her wish, for political and intellectual reasons, to disseminate in France as much knowledge as she could of the culture of other countries. Nor should we forget her wealth, which enabled her to satisfy her intellectual curiosities by constant travel throughout Europe, including Russia and Scandinavia, and not least to make of her château at Coppet the great cosmopolitan stronghold that all prominent people of liberal temper in the intellectual and artistic worlds of Europe and many lesser men, subdued by the basilisk eye of this lion-tamer, were drawn to; thus did Coppet become like a window opened for France on the culture of Europe and a stronghold of resistance to Napoleon.

The word cosmopolitan has unpleasant overtones nowadays; it conjures up the image of a man with no national loyalties. The fortunes of the word reflect the growth of nationalisms in Europe in the nineteenth century. No such disfavour attached to it in the eighteenth century and of the cosmopolitan spirit in the best sense Madame de Staël is a good representative.

But cosmopolitan though she was, be it remembered she was born and brought up in Paris, that her mother was a 'salonnière' of distinction and that, in her formative years, Germaine had experienced and enjoyed the hot-house intellectual atmosphere of the aristocratic Parisian society, liberal and free-thinking as it then largely was. Here she had imbibed the ideas that were current coin: progress, enlightenment, natural goodness; a cult for Montesquieu, father of French liberal thought; an enthusiasm for Rousseau; the habit, at any rate, of French classical literature with all its formalism; the cult of good taste; a passion for 'polite society' with all its urbanity, brilliant conversation and exchange of ideas. And where could all this be found except in Paris? With all the variety of experience she was later to have, she is recorded as saying she would gladly exchange it ... 'pour mon ruisseau de la rue du Bac'.[2] The beauties, the joys of solitude meant nothing to her; only society counted – not an *émigré* perhaps, but no *émigré* could have looked back at the life and scenes he had been forced to leave with keener nostalgia.

The numerous and disparate elements that served to mould her attitudes exist together in her work as best they may. There is another: the sense of isolation – a typical characteristic of the

[2] C. Herold, op. cit.

émigré one will say, so why emphasize it? But, if the result is the same, the source is not. Mme de Staël soon came to believe in the loneliness of genius, more particularly in the loneliness of women of genius. Society will accept, if it must, outstanding men; leadership is essential, inevitable in all spheres; men will be found in every generation to take it by their merit and their courage. Even they may in time come to feel the solitariness of their position – Moses apparently told Vigny so. How much greater will this burden be upon a woman to whom society does not, or did not then, willingly concede a place at the top, not at least in the sphere of intellect or politics. How eagerly will society seize on any pretext at worst to attack and denigrate such a woman, at best to withhold from her any sympathetic understanding, if her enthusiasms or philosophy in the broad sense lead her to flout established canons. That was Madame de Staël's position. A vigorous egotist like all her generation, she will both suffer by her egotism and draw inspiration from her suffering.

Germaine's talents were precocious; at twelve, a comedy: *Les Inconvénients de Paris*; at twenty-two, an encomium, *Lettres sur Jean-Jacques Rousseau* (1788). 'J'ai goûté quelque plaisir', she writes, 'en me retraçant à moi-même le souvenir et l'impression de mon enthousiasme'.[3] Enthusiasm! The word, throughout her life, was to burgeon constantly at the tip of her pen; in *De l'Allemagne*, it was to have a chapter[4] to itself. It gives the key to her attitude to Jean-Jacques. Of *La Nouvelle Héloïse*, she wrote:[5] 'C'est avec plaisir que je me livre à me retracer l'effet que cet ouvrage a produit sur moi: je tâcherai de me défendre d'un enthousiasme qu'on pourrait attribuer à la disposition de mon âme plus qu'au talent de l'auteur'. Note in both these quotations her subjective attitude; she is not assessing the merits of Rousseau, she is recording the impact of Rousseau upon her own sensibility. What chord in her nature responded so vigorously to the touch of Rousseau? Was it not that inward sense of goodness she divined in him and felt in herself, that sense that plucks at the heart-strings, invades the soul with a warmth of feeling as the blood courses round the system and that requires – ah! how delicious and how convenient! – no support, no 'petit-bourgeois' support from our actions? Her advocacy of the morality of *La Nouvelle Héloïse*,[6] and of the character of Jean-Jacques himself, in spite of certain passages in *Les Confessions*, is skilful and in the light of her own later life could be thought of as advance special pleading. Her style may be verbose and lacking in colour (this it always will be, except here and there in *De la Littérature* and *De l'Allemagne* for example, where some

[3] Preface, first edn.
[5] Letter no. 2.
[4] Part IV, 10.
[6] Letter no. 6.

general idea lies particularly close to her personal experience or
sorrows and is suddenly illumined by a lyrical touch), but already
at this early stage in her literary development, the reader may well
be struck by the penetration and delicacy of her moral reflections:
'N'attendez rien de celle qui s'est dégoûtée de la vertu, qui s'est
corrumpue lentement: tout ce qui arrive par degrés est irrémédi-
able';[7] habit, in short, as the most potent force in life; impulse, we
may infer, being as it were the direct thrust of nature, must be
good. The feminine pronoun is also revealing. True, the author is
speaking of Julie; yet the injunction to the reader is so general and
leads to so general and pertinent a moral maxim that the reader
may well think the masculine plural form more appropriate. If so,
he is likely to conclude that though the author is referring to Julie
the image she has in her mind is really of herself.

But Rousseau was not only an apostle of the goodness of Nature,
he was a political thinker. Here a note of criticism is heard...
pianissimo: 'J'oserai blâmer Rousseau cependant...'[8] The author
of these letters already adopts the liberal position she will never
deviate from; she is and will remain a disciple of Montesquieu.

The opening phase of the Revolution was to provide fuel for her
liberal enthusiasms and joy of a personal kind: was not her father,
for whom her devoted admiration knew no bounds, the great man
of the hour?[9]

Mme de Staël's *Considérations sur les principaux événements de
la Révolution française* (posth. 1818) bear witness to the prevailing
euphory; at last the dawn of liberty, a turning point in history –
and, incidentally, an opportunity to play politics, at least in the
wings. Little did she think her liberal friends were helping to
conjure up forces that were to carry away the whole structure
of the society she loved, and set Europe aflame. The next few
years were to provide her with revelations of the human potential
for wickedness that were altogether puzzling to someone steeped in
the urbanity and sentimental beliefs of the eighteenth century.
None the less, her pen was to be active in generous causes: e.g.
Réflexions sur le procès de la Reine (1793) where, with all the
rhetoric, she communicates her own emotion: 'Et ne savez-vous pas
que tout ce qui est écrit en lettres de sang sera lu par l'Univers?' –
an interesting early suggestion of the pressures of international
opinion.

The Thermidorian reaction and the First Coalition War provided further incentives to Madame de Staël as a liberal pamphleteer and publicist on the European stage: *Réflexions sur la Paix*,

----

[7] Letter no. 2.   [8] Letter no. 4.
   [9] 'Le Salut de la France est dans mon porte-feuille', he is recorded as
saying.

adressées à M. Pitt et aux Français (1794) and *Réflexions sur la Paix Intérieure* (1795).

A change of course follows: *L'Essai sur les Fictions* (1796); politics are set aside, the moralist appears; a change more apparent than real, since for Madame de Staël political ideas, ethics, literature are linked together, being no more than different reflections of the human psyche in its constant struggle against the powers of darkness to achieve happiness and its fullest expression in liberty. Unhappiness had already cast its shadow over her; her marriage had brought her no felicity; she had been exposed to virulent attacks in the Parisian press for her political activities – intrigues, her enemies thought them – during the early years of the Revolution; Narbonne, whose life she had saved and whom she had pursued to Juniper Hill in 1793, was proving unfaithful. These personal sorrows added to the general distresses of the hour could account for the melancholy that pervades the *Essai*, these, rather than any metaphysical 'Weltschmerz' in the manner of Werther.

Her aim in the *Essai* is to show the important role that writers have to play as moral guides; the writer's 'mission' in fact – a theme Romantic writers were to exploit.

The problem of human happiness is again at the source of her next work: *De l'influence des Passions sur le bonheur des Individus et des Nations* (1796), of which only the first of the two parts planned was finished and published.

The author examines the various passions that threaten or destroy human happiness and the means whereby the resulting unhappiness may be combated. The personal note is again clearly audible especially when Madame de Staël comes to speak of love! Gone are the frigid tones of the earlier chapters; instead, lyrical sincerity, resulting one may presume from direct experience: 'le dévouement absolu de son être aux sentiments, au bonheur, à la destinée d'un autre ...'.[10] The faithless Narbonne had gone out of her life but there had been Talleyrand – another broken reed – and more particularly there was Benjamin Constant whom she had met in 1794 and was to keep in bondage, now willing now unwilling, for ten years and more.

To judge from the title of the work and the introduction, Madame de Staël's intention was to devote the second part to examining the impact of human passions upon politics. We shall find something of the same sort in *De la Littérature*. That the Revolution was still so fresh in her mind is explanation enough why she should have been led to consider human passions, amongst which significantly she numbers 'l'esprit de parti' – a clear echo of revolutionary times – from the political as well as the individual angle.

[10] chap. iv.

As a moralist she is concerned not, as some philosophers might be, with the nature of our being, but with our conduct both as individuals and as members of society.

The three years and more that were to elapse between the publication of *L'Influence des passions* and that of *De la Littérature* were crammed with events – Madame de Staël's life always was. Most important of these were her early contacts with Bonaparte. The saviour of France, the restorer of order – such was the prevailing opinion of him; she was disposed to share it, but her advances were met with calculated rebuffs; Bonaparte disliked politically-minded women. Here were the seeds of enmity and they were to grow rapidly.

Bonaparte had good grounds for suspecting Madame de Staël's salon of becoming the focus of the liberal opposition taking shape in the Tribunate with Benjamin Constant in a leading role. Bonaparte's answer was to 'purge' the Tribunate of the recalcitrant elements; as for Madame de Staël, a vigilant eye was on her and soon the ever-tightening screw of administrative sanctions was to be applied. In April 1800, however, when *De la Littérature considérée dans ses Rapports avec les Institutions Sociales* appeared, the time for them was not yet.

'Je me suis proposé d'examiner', she writes,[11] 'quelle est l'influence de la religion, des moeurs et des lois sur la littérature et quelle est l'influence de la littérature sur la religion, les moeurs et les lois.' The magnitude of the task is staggering; and quickly her knowledge of literature, let alone the other spheres of learning involved, is revealed as not adequate – whose would be?

Her work is therefore open to criticism both in its statements and in its omissions: 'les Grecs ... laissent peu de regrets ...'[12] ...! They are compared unfavourably to the Romans at least in philosophy;[13] Italian and Spanish literatures are bundled into one chapter.[14] What good, after all, could come from countries either priest-ridden or dominated by 'la tyrannie oppressive et sombre de l'inquisition'? Dante is dismissed in a few lines, Cervantes is not even mentioned; Ossian is hailed as the origin of the northern literatures;[15] her views on Shakespeare are prejudiced by the rigidities of French classical canons; her knowledge of German literature is minimal; in French literature the eighteenth century seems to rank at least as highly in her estimation as that of the seventeenth;[16] in short, debatable value-judgments, and a number of generalizations on flimsy foundations. Madame de Staël has some points of

[11] *Discours Préliminaire.*
[12] I, 4. [13] I, 5. [14] I, 10. [15] I, 11.
[16] Chateaubriand (*Génie du Christianisme*) was the first to combat this view.

contact with Laharpe: her insistence on the canons of ... 'le bon goût', her attachment to the French school of tragedy and on that account her no more than qualified approval of Shakespeare, her moralism.

On the other hand, the seeker after a clearly defined system of literary criticism on the basis of objective criteria will be disappointed, for, as the *Discours Préliminaire*, the most stimulating part of the book, makes plain, that is not her intention.

She proposes to study – is the first to study – a whole corpus of literature, as a kind of living organism rooted in a given soil and slowly developing in time with the society it intimately reflects. Two great groups of literature are claimed to exist, the literatures of the north and the literatures of the south, and this anchoring of literature to geography and climate has led her to look for the specific characteristics of a given people or group of peoples in their literatures: 'Les peuples du Nord n'attachaient point de prix à la vie. Cette disposition les rendait courageux pour eux-mêmes, mais cruels pour les autres ... Leur climat sombre n'offrait à leur imagination que des orages et des ténèbres ... la nature morale de l'homme du Midi se perdait tout entière dans les jouissances de la volupté, celle de l'homme du Nord dans l'exercice de la force.'[17]

But this is only one aspect of the book. Progress! Liberty! To both she holds with passion; literature considered in its broadest sense – fiction, poetry, philosophy – has a vital role to play in progress; liberty is essential to the development of literature. These ideas are developed with brilliance on the ideological plane in the *Discours Préliminaire*; Madame de Staël is always at her best in the analysis of ideas.

To do justice to the wealth of ideas in *De la Littérature* is impossible in a short space. Its scope and depth, its originality and power to stimulate new lines of enquiry or to show a variety of facts in new relationships to each other, are much greater than in any of her previous works, but its wealth is chaotic; the ideas are left to get on together as best they may, and that is not very well. Synthesis is lacking. The reader may in fact become aware of at least three different people in the author: first, the critic making value-judgments. Whenever Madame de Staël is thinking of specific writers, Shakespeare for example, the taste she was brought up to have asserts itself – habit, in a word, than which few stronger forces exist – and she is then led to form opinions that seem often out of tune with those of today; second, the liberal intellectual of the late eighteenth century defending the cause of liberty and progress; third, the forerunner of nineteenth-century criticism scattering a wealth of ideas that have taken root.

[17] I, 8.

She it was that first gave impetus in France to the idea that literature, art generally, is not like a hot-house plant growing up away from outside influences, but is implanted in a given society and should be studied, is in fact best appreciated, only within the framework of that society. Her generalisations about the northern peoples, the southern or Mediterranean peoples and their respective literatures may be debatable, we may reject her conclusions, but we shall retain, as stimulating in itself and enriching to literary studies, her principle of seeking in different literatures a reflection, amongst other things, of national mentalities.

The critic's function is thereby altered; he may not wish to sacrifice the satisfying if risky privilege of pronouncing value-judgments but he will appreciate that his opinions are conditioned by time and place, his standards relative. This may be otiose nowadays; not when Laharpe and Marie-Joseph Chénier were about.

The second of the three selves we discern in the author of *De la Littérature* is the one that claims our attention most, the self that insists the 'Dark Ages' had more light than was currently supposed,[18] that emphasizes the importance of Christianity as an element in medieval mentality, that turns, as it were, the defeat of her eighteenth-century self into victory; as an eighteenth-century liberal Madame de Staël looks upon the Terror not only with horror but with no understanding of how such a thing could come about.[19] Nor could the Revolution be regarded as an argument for liberty's being a prior condition of great literature. Undismayed, her forward-looking self, brushing the Revolution and its works aside as an exception, looks to the future and speculates on the potential progress of literature and philosophy under a republic established on liberty and justice,[20] such progress, particularly in philosophy, being an important factor in promoting human happiness. Her application of Condorcet's ideas on the possible uses of statistical calculations as a means of estimating political opinion in the mass is bold and imaginative: 'C'est une science à créer que la politique ... Les philosophes doivent donc, en politique, se proposer de soumettre à des combinaisons positives tous les faits qui leur sont connus, pour en tirer des résultats certains d'après le nombre et la nature des chances.'[21] Her prophetic self seems to be gazing at a future, our present, of political and market analysts, of behaviourism, of computers.

Intellectual brilliance, shot through with passionate enthusiasms and animosities – anti-Bonapartism, anti-Catholicism – and inspired by personal experience and sorrows, this is constantly evident in

[18] I, 8.
[20] II, 1.
[19] I, 8.
[21] II, 6.

De la Littérature – 'je ne puis séparer mes idées de mes senti-ments'[22] – and is by no means the least attractive part of it.

This combination moreover provides the key to her work both critical and creative. Precisely now Madame de Staël, leaving be-hind her the ideologies of the 'Republican Moment', was to turn her attention to creative writing. Personal sorrows, sentimental misadventures, suspicion and dislike in high places, all these had created a burden so heavy that to unload it into a novel was to be some solace; confessions always are. *Delphine* (1802) takes its place in the 'personal' type of novel so popular in the early years of the nineteenth century.

'C'est un être inspiré que Delphine', writes Léonce, ecstatically, 'sa voix s'animait, ses yeux ravissants regardaient le ciel comme pour le prendre à témoin de ses nobles pensées; ses bras charmants se plaçaient ... de la manière la plus agréable et la plus élégante.'[23]

Did Madame de Staël's own mirror reflect this flatteringly selec-tive image of Delphine d'Albemar, in part confirmed by Benjamin Constant?[24] Like Madame de Staël, too, the unfortunate Delphine, with her goodness of heart, her natural incapacity to act in a calcu-lating manner, flouts the rigid behaviour-norms of society and consequently exposes herself to the censure of public opinion. Léonce de Mondoville, on the other hand, to whom she becomes ... affianced, is particularly sensitive to this invisible tyrant. Thus, in spite of all her advantages: youth, beauty, wealth, yes ... and widowhood, Delphine's happiness turns to ashes, whence rapid decline and death, after which Léonce seeks death, duly granted, fighting in Vendée. Although skilful in construction the novel is unconvincing, the characters wooden, the special pleading – anti-Catholicism, the redemptive quality of great love, justification of divorce – too obvious, and yet to judge from its success it struck a responsive chord in the readers of the day.

With its political aspect *Delphine* was to be the starting point of Madame de Staël's real political tribulations. The peace of Amiens signed (1802), Bonaparte could feel himself firmly established; what further need then to spare recalcitrant political elements? A book that pleaded in favour of divorce just as he was restoring relations with Rome and endeavouring to improve the moral tone of French society was bad enough, but that its author should give the First Consul's political opponents the opportunity of showing their atti-tude by their enthusiastic approval of the book was intolerable. Away with her! Madame de Staël was to quit Paris forthwith and not to live within forty leagues of the capital. Rather than accept

---

[22] II, 9.
[23] Léonce to M. Barton. Letter no. xxiv.
[24] Cf. portrait of Mme de Malbée in *Cécile*, 3e époque.

such a cruelly tantalizing injunction she preferred to depart altogether and take the road to Germany.

Important results were ultimately to flow from this first German tour (October 1803–April 1804); Weimar and Berlin were on the itinerary; the *élite* of German society, social and intellectual, welcomed the authoress of *De la Littérature* and *Delphine*.

In Berlin she met August Wilhelm Schlegel, who was to remain thereafter in her household and was to be of great service to her for the book she already planned to write on Germany.

News of her father's illness brought her post-haste back to Coppet. Too late; Monsieur Necker had died – a crushing blow to his daughter who idolized that most patient of fathers (possibly; he had a great deal to put up with), that greatest of statesmen (no!), that most faithful of husbands.

1804 was also the year of Benjamin Constant's second marriage[25] – another blow. Partly to overcome this sea of troubles and partly to get some 'local colour' for the new novel she had embarked upon, Madame de Staël departed for Italy in November of that year. In June 1805 she was back in Coppet, now at its most brilliant: social gatherings, intellectual jousts, amateur theatricals, amorous intrigues and quarrels, a great deal of anti-Napoleonic talk, much writing withal.[26]

Corinne appeared in April 1807; another personal novel with the authoress in the title role. Forsaking this time the letter form, so popular in the eighteenth century and used by her in *Delphine*, Madame de Staël presents the reader with a triangular love story not unlike that in *Delphine*: Lord Oswald Nelvil has much of Léonce and, be it added, of Benjamin Constant: 'Oswald ... avait, à travers mille rares qualités, beaucoup de faiblesse et d'irrésolution dans le caractère. Ces défauts sont inaperçus de celui qui les a, et prennent à ses yeux une nouvelle forme dans chaque circonstance: tantôt c'est la prudence, la sensibilité ou la délicatesse qui éloignent le moment de prendre un parti et prolongent une situation indécise....'[27] Corinne herself, a more finished portrait, is none the less certainly another Delphine, Lucille Egermond another Mathilde de Vernon.

Much in this work appealed to contemporary taste: a well-contrived eventful plot moving across a European stage: Rome, Naples, Venice, Florence; Germany, France, England, Scotland; characters that are as aristocratic as the readers were or would have liked to be, as cosmopolitan – in the best sense – as Madame de Staël herself, at home, like her, in any European capital, and with such interest as attaches to supposedly national characteristics: the melancholy English 'Milord', the ebullient Italian Castel-Forte,

[25] To Charlotte v. Hardenberg.   [26] C. Herold, op. cit.   [27] XI, 3.

the frivolous Frenchman d'Erfeuil; Roman antiquities... *à trois*:
Corinne, Lord 'O' ... and reader, who, incidentally, may be forgiven if he is tempted at this stage[28] to confuse Corinne with
Baedeker; a touch of mystery, less powerful than in Charlotte
Brontë, less crude than in a contemporaneous *roman noir* but
enough to tease the appetite of Romantic readers. What sombre
weight oppresses the heart and happiness of Oswald? Who precisely is Corinne? If the reader can muster the same patience as the
characters when the author judges the time and place appropriate
– the top of Mount Vesuvius in Lord 'O''s case – for each to reveal
his background, he will learn the answer to these questions. Contemporary readers evidently had it, to judge from the novel's success; for the modern reader, the interest here as in *Delphine* comes
from other levels. As fiction the novel calls forth little response; the
characters have no individual life, either they are conventionalised
shadows or period puppets and too evidently a mouthpiece for their
creator. Our interest goes to her in the first place both because of
the wealth and finesse of her moral, political, social, historical,
archaeological information and reflexions, and of her attitudes to
life in affliction: the isolation of genius, especially a woman of
genius, cruelly misjudged and groping towards the consolation of a
religious belief.[29]

The novel as a whole has the agreeable attractiveness of a period
piece; its Romantic themes are evident: the mysterious harmony
between man and nature; the dark abyss of our inner selves: 'les
âmes capables de réflexions se plongent sans cesse dans l'abîme
d'elles-mêmes et n'en trouvent jamais la fin.'[30] 'Il n'y a plus pour
l'homme que le grand mystère de lui-même.'[31]

And what more Romantic than scenes such as Corinne, harp at
the ready, at the tip of Cape Miseno in the last rays of the setting
sun, her eyes lost in contemplation of an inward vision, her ear
listening for the promptings of the Muse, while Oswald mute with
admiration stands at her side, ready to support her should she
swoon (she does).[32] At a time when inspiration for pictorial art was
so often provided by literature, this scene was duly chosen as a
subject for a picture.[33]

Much to interest the modern reader, yes, but Madame de Staël
has scarcely been successful in fusing into an artistic whole the
diverse elements: personal confession, Italian handbook, cosmo-
politanism, Romantic attitudes.

Expelled once more after the publication of *Corinne*, Madame
de Staël set out again for Austria and Germany. At least Napo-

---

[28] Books IV and V.
[29] e.g. Bk. X, chap. 5; Bk. XX, chap. 5. 'Dernier chant de Corinne'.
[30] XV, 5.   [31] XIX, 5.   [32] XIII, 4.   [33] Girodet.

leon's expulsion order would give her a reason for renewing her impressions and extending her knowledge of the German world. She needed to, because she was engaged upon what was to be her most influential work: *De l'Allemagne*.

The circumstances surrounding the book's publication were dramatic; it was passed by the censor, subject to certain excisions, accepted by Madame de Staël; the first edition was about to be published in 1810 when a sudden police order revoked the previous decision; edition and type were destroyed, but the manuscript did not fall into the hands of the police. Madame de Staël, who had come as far as Chaumont – outside the forbidden radius of forty leagues from Paris – to supervise the preparation of the first edition, was ordered to return to Coppet and placed under police supervision. Three years were to elapse before she was able to get her work published, in London.

'Votre ouvrage n'est point français' – such was the reason alleged by General Savary, Minister of Police, for his action.[34] If he had said the work was anti-Napoleonic he would have been more accurate. Madame de Staël's liberal ideals are very evident and by inference her hostility to the imperial régime.

Her aim was to make Germany, its people, its literature and philosophy, its religious life, better known in France, where at the time the knowledge of what culture existed beyond the Rhine or indeed in any other country must have been scanty; when Madame de Staël was writing *De la Littérature*, her own knowledge of Germany was exiguous. *De l'Allemagne* was therefore to be a work of vulgarization, in the best sense, and no effort of vulgarization on such a big scale had been made before. On that score alone the book deserves a place in any history of French literature.

What of its execution? Any book that sets out to create for its readers an image of a given country is bound to get out of date in time; conditions, attitudes change; data need to be modified and supplemented. Of *De l'Allemagne* we may fairly say it was, at least in part, out of date when published; had it appeared in 1810, it still would have been.

Madame de Staël's image of Germany arose from the impressions and experience of men and things she had acquired in the course of her two visits (1803; 1807–8), supplemented in matters of scholarship by the learning of Charles de Villers and the faithful August Wilhelm Schlegel. The pictures that arise in the mind of the reader, varied as they are, convey these common traits: a people sunk in comfortable and placid inertia: 'Les poëles, la bière et la fumée de tabac forment autour des gens du peuple ... une sorte d'atmosphère lourde et chaude dont ils n'aiment pas à

[34] *De l'Allemagne*, 1813, Preface.

sortir';[35] a society of gentle scholars and grave idealist philosophers gathered in Weimar, Berlin or Vienna – a faithful picture, in 1810, even in 1813; no doubt it still has truth in the nineteen sixties just as there are many small provincial towns in France where a figure from the pages of Balzac may still be expected to appear round a street corner. Eternal Germany? Eternal France? But in 1813 and even in 1810 another and quite different aspect of eternal Germany, or perhaps one should say of eternal humanity, dominated the scene; young Romantic Germany, galvanized into action by the eloquence of Fichte, was girding itself for war. What does *De l'Allemagne* say of this?

Could it be argued that the idea is inherent in the author's reflection: 'Rien de grand ne s'y fera désormais que par l'impulsion libérale',[36] or by her evident sympathy for nationalism: 'le patriotisme des nations doit être égoïste...';[37] 'de nos jours il n'y a de véritable force que dans le caractère national.'[38] What greater example of liberalism, indeed, than a war of liberation – crucible for welding the nationhood of a people. Nationalism is a form of collective enthusiasm that was to have tremendous force in nineteenth-century Europe, nowhere greater than in Germany. French liberals in the wake of Madame de Staël were to welcome its emergence in Germany; not till 1870 were the scales to fall from their eyes. Then only did they begin to appreciate that nationalism could and often did spring from other forces of enthusiasm in the human psyche than those that they and Madame de Staël before them believed in: energy, will, conflict, glory, power, mass hysteria.

Madame de Staël's conception of enthusiasm was indissolubly linked with the conception of human nature she had derived from the eighteenth century: goodness, virtue, sweet reasonableness. Enthusiasm meant a rush of warm feeling to the heart, sure sign of goodness. That there could be other elements in the human potential equally deep and at least as powerful lay beyond her understanding. She had experienced it indeed in the French Revolution, but the violence and cruelty of that time she regarded as a mysterious exception that proved her right in general.[39]

There appears then to be a fundamental confusion between her conception of nationalism, liberal, sentimental, unrealistic, and the blood and iron nationalism that was later to develop in Germany. That she would have condemned it, just as she condemned Napoleon's tyranny, seems a safe bet, and even the War of Liberation, glad though she was to see Napoleon fall, was a grief to her when she recognized it meant the defeat of France also.

The image of Germany Madame de Staël projects is at least an incomplete one; such as it is, it was to fascinate many French

[35] I, 2.   [36] I, 4.   [37] I, 2.   [38] I, 17.   [39] See above, p. 9, n. 14.

writers and intellectuals down the century: Hugo, Michelet, Cousin, Renan, Taine.[40]

Her views on German literature and philosophy were to prove equally stimulating and more enriching. Thanks to Charles de Villers, to A. W. Schlegel, to her own contacts with the great writers of Germany, her knowledge in these fields had expanded greatly since *De la Littérature* and she was to provide a valuable element of cross-fertilization to French Romanticism; yet here too the picture she provided was incomplete. German literature for her meant the world that had its centre at Weimar, with Goethe and Schiller as its chief luminaries. *Sturm und Drang* meant nothing to her; the young German Romantic school: Novalis, Brentano, Arnim, Tieck, Friedrich Schlegel, Kleist receive no mention. On the other hand, her exposition of the philosophy of Kant brought that difficult philosopher within reach of the interested layman in France (possibly in Germany also). Fichte and Schelling also receive honourable mention, though with some reserve. The former, with his emphasis on the will, the latter, establishing his system on nature, are Romantic philosophers. Characteristically, Madame de Staël both places German philosophy as a whole above French materialist philosophy of the eighteenth century, false and debasing to the soul,[41] and, within German philosophy, idealist and universalist, leans towards Kant rather than towards Fichte and Schelling; for Kant's intellectual and spiritual position seems more akin to her own, a position of compromise between reason and feeling, between the eighteenth century and the full flood of Romanticism

In *De l'Allemagne* Madame de Staël adopts for the first time the words classic and romantic.[42] Her idea of the terms goes perhaps beyond the terms south and north of *De la Littérature*; something more than mere geographical location is involved; romantic suggests reverie, sweet melancholy, feeling, 'enthusiasm', yet the term still seems superficial when she uses it; romanticism as a revelation of the deeper levels of human nature lay beyond her ken.

Not the least fascinating aspect of *De l'Allemagne* for anyone interested in Madame de Staël, not exclusively for her literary influence but as a woman passionately involved in the life of her time, is its subjective aspect. Here as always, on all questions she touches she brings to bear not only her brilliant analytical mind but also her passionate nature; 'je ne puis séparer mes idées de mes sentiments'.[43] Thus *De l'Allemagne* is not only a work of popularization about Germany but, like *L'Essai sur les Fictions*, like *De l'Influence des Passions*, *De la Littérature*, *Delphine* and *Corinne*, a further and last chapter in the author's spiritual development; her

---

[40] Taine soon changed his mind and turned towards England.
[41] III, 3, *passim.*   [42] II, 11.   [43] See above, p. 40.

political attitudes, her literary tastes, and not least her religious development are plain for all to see.

The internment at Coppet was scarcely bearable to her, especially when those of her friends, prepared to run the political risk of coming to see her, suffered administrative sanctions in consequence[44] – 'La contagion du malheur'.[45] Her escape in May 1812 into Austria, thence to Poland and Russia, just as Napoleon was launching 'the Grand Army' across the Niemen, is related in the second part of *Dix Années d'Exil*, her fragmentary autobiography (posth. 1821). Amongst the most interesting parts of it are the author's reflections on Russia and the Russian character. Knowing no word of Russian, she yet observed and understood much. If she had had the time, perhaps she could have written a book on Russia, for the West, equal in quality to *De l'Allemagne*. Others in her wake were to do that – Custine[46] and Vogüé.[47] For her there could be no tarrying; Napoleon was close behind; she must hasten on across the vast distances: 'J'éprouvais cette sorte de cauchemar qui saisit quelquefois la nuit, quand on croit marcher toujours et n'avancer jamais.'[48] From Kiev to Moscow; from Moscow to St. Petersburg; hospitality on the Russian scale.[49] Was Russia a despotism? Perhaps, but for Madame de Staël there were at that moment only two sides; Alexander was fighting Napoleon. This lent him charm in her eyes; she speaks of 'la sage liberté qu'on doit au caractère d'Alexandre...ce monarque absolu par les lois comme par les mœurs et si modéré par son propre penchant.'[50]

But England was the goal of her desires, as it was of all liberals in Europe, and in England she landed in June 1813 after eight months' sojourn at Stockholm. From London she witnessed the death throes of the Napoleonic régime; on 12 May 1814 she was back in Paris; in July at Coppet. From Coppet she watched the final gamble of The Hundred Days, her hostility to Napoleon wavering. Surprising? – but like many other people Madame de Staël was caught in a dilemma. If Napoleon were to win, that would mean the end of liberty; if he lost, France itself would be crushed, perhaps subjugated. While Napoleon had been at the height of his power Madame de Staël could well focus her hatred on him alone without reference to France; the Allies certainly entertained the figment of fighting a man, not a country; hence the leniency of the Peace Treaty of 1814. After Napoleon's return from Elba no such illusion was possible; France had apparently espoused the Napoleonic cause and would stand or fall with him. But perhaps Napo-

[44] e.g. Matthieu de Montmorency, Madame Récamier, expelled from Paris to a radius of forty leagues.

[45] *De l'Allemagne*, preface.

[46] See below, p. 186–8.

[47] 1848–1910, *Le Roman Russe* (1886).

[48] *Dix Années d'Exil*, ii, 12.

[49] *Ibid.*, ii, 16 and 18 *passim*.

[50] *Ibid.*, ii, 16 and 17 *passim*.

leon's new profession of liberalism could be trusted? Benjamin Constant seemed to think so.[51] There, perhaps, lay hope of a compromise peace with the Allies that would save all: liberty, France and incidentally Madame de Staël's private interests.[52] Waterloo solved the dilemma.

The two years that remained to her were crowded ones: a second visit to Italy; the marriage of her daughter Albertine to Victor de Broglie (February 1816); a brilliant season – veritable Indian summer – at Coppet; return to Paris, illness, and death (July 1817). She was fifty-one but burnt out like an overloaded high-tension wire.

Madame de Staël's *Considérations sur les principaux evénements de la Révolution française* were originally to be an apologia for the policies of M. Necker but, without neglecting this aspect, the work developed into a record of the author's personal experiences during the Revolution and of her views on the Revolution, on Napoleon, on politics in general – a kind of political testament intermingled with the story of events. Here, as always, speaks the liberal idealist, a daughter of the eighteenth century, looking back to Montesquieu for her political ideas, just as the men of 1789 had done. For them as for her a written constitution was the key to happiness for France; England enshrines all her political ideals, Napoleon's despotism all she detests. What did his power rest on, she asks. On military glory, on his skill in restoring order without harming material interests satisfied by the Revolution.[53] But in spite of his absolute power over eighty million people, she declares: 'Bonaparte maître absolu de quatre-vingts million d'hommes... n'a su fonder ni une institution dans l'Etat, ni un pouvoir stable pour lui-même.'[54] What effrontery! What impertinent misrepresentation! Napoleon, the perfector of the French administrative system, the reorganizer of French education, the architect of a Concordat that was to last over a century,[55] the creator of a civil code that still provides the legal framework of the French citizen's life and has provided a model for similar codes the world over, last but not least the founder of an administrative tribunal[55a] which in the course of time has become the citizen's bulwark against administrative tyranny, and, like the Civil Code, the model for similar institutions throughout the world.

With one stroke of the pen Madame de Staël, liberal idealist

[51] See below, p. 57.

[52] M. Necker had lent the French Government 2,000,000 frs. before the Revolution. On his return from Elba, Napoleon, wanting all the support he could muster, hinted that the debt would be repaid, but it was not repaid until the Restoration.

[53] e.g. purchasers of 'biens nationaux'; *Considérations*, IV, 18.

[54] op. cit., IV, 18.

[55] Until 1905, and still operative in Alsace.　　　[55a] The *Conseil d'Etat*.

that she is, dismisses it all. Napoleon's unforgivable sin in her eyes was his cynical appraisal of humanity: 'Quel est donc le principe destructeur qui suivait ses pas triomphants?...le mépris des hommes et par conséquent de toutes les lois, de toutes les études, de tous les établissements, de toutes les institutions, dont la base est le respect pour l'espèce humaine...il ressemblait...aux tyrans Italiens du quinzième siècle.'[56] Even in her most prejudiced attitudes Madame de Staël may be relied on for some illuminating reflection; Taine was later to develop the theme of the Italian mentality of Napoleon.[57]

How generous in contrast appears Napoleon's opinion of Madame de Staël: 'personne ne saurait nier qu'après tout Madame de Staël est une femme d'un très grand talent, fort distinguée, de beaucoup d'esprit: elle restera'.[58] We can agree, even adding the word genius. Whether she has 'lasted' in the way we may guess Napoleon meant is another matter. Her reputation rests, not on her novels, but on the two central works, *De la Littérature* and *De l'Allemagne*, which made a big impact on her generation and where the modern reader may still find much that is valid and stimulating. He is likely to retain of her the image of a woman inspired by generous enthusiasms, greatly gifted for intellectual and moral analysis, with an open and receptive mind, eager to explore new fields of literature and art, and to disseminate the fruits of her enquiries.

That these rested on an insecure basis of scholarship is no doubt true but the attitude of mind was exemplary. Withal she was as much an egotist as any of her generation. To that some at least of her numerous lovers, certainly Benjamin Constant who probably suffered most from her explosive and possessive temperament, would surely agree.

II. BENJAMIN CONSTANT

Madame de Staël's château at Coppet had been, to quote Napoleon himself, 'un véritable arsenal contre moi; on venait s'y faire armer chevalier...'[59]

Of all the company, habitués or chance visitors that might be met with there: François de Pange, Eléazar de Sabran, Matthieu de Montmorency, Guillaume-Prosper de Barante, Madame Récamier, Bonstetten, Sismondi, the Schlegel brothers – notably August

---

[56] op. cit., IV, 18.
[57] *Les Origines de la France Contemporaine*, Le Régime Moderne, Bk. I, chap. I.
[58] *Mémorial de Sainte Hélène*, II, 7.　　　　[59] *Mémorial*, II, 7.

Wilhelm, Zacharius Werner, Prince Frederick of Prussia, Byron,[60] the Saussures, the Neckers, Victor de Broglie and so on, one in particular is of importance in a history of French literature – Benjamin Constant de Rebecque (1767–1830).

Like many men of his time Benjamin Constant was much given to disclosing his secret thoughts and feelings to that most patient, most silent, yet most indiscreet of confidants – a diary. Thanks to his two short but masterly essays in autobiography – *Le Cahier Rouge* and the recently rediscovered *Cécile*,[61] thanks to his *Journaux Intimes*, now available in their complete and original state,[62] we derive a series of vivid images of him: the gifted child, deprived of a mother's affection,[63] accustomed to the distant spasmodic solicitude of his father; the cynical Cherubino with experience of high life, which he owed to his family background, and low life which he owed to a succession of remarkable tutors; the intelligent and precocious youth whose education had been haphazard but agreeably cosmopolitan (Göttingen, Oxford – very briefly, Edinburgh, where he made some good friends and for a short space of time discovered the joys of scholarship, Paris); the spoilt and irresponsible young man whose crowning escapade was his *fugue* to England with a few louis in his pocket and two ideas in his mind: postpone answering his father's summons to rejoin him in Holland, and see the friends he had made in England, notably in Edinburgh, if he could get there – and he did; the lover, weak-willed, hesitant, tortured and torturing others by his lack of resolution; the ambitious politician; the gamester; the scholar; the writer with as great a gift as any for lucid and unsparing self-analysis; above all and always the egotist for ever measuring and bemoaning the inexorable flow of time that seemed to be leaving him behind, busied only with futile comings and goings.

Constant had known Paris in the years just before the Revolution[64] and to Paris he returned in 1795, the interval having mostly been spent[65] as chamberlain to the Duke of Brunswick. In the previous year he had met Madame de Staël in Switzerland and it was with her that he now came to Paris. The Terror was over, the Thermidorians were in the ascendant, the 'loi du Maximum' had been repealed, prices were rising fast. Liberalism was blowing

---

[60] Byron writes to Miss Milbanke (later Lady Byron): 'Mme de Staël... Do you know her? I don't ask if you have heard her? her tongue is the perpetual motion' – 29 November 1813. *Letters and Journals* – ed. R. E. Prothero, iii (1899), p. 408.

[61] Constant, *Oeuvres* (Pléiade edn., 1957), with Introduction and Notes by A. Roulin.

[62] *Ibid.*

[63] His mother, Henriette de Chandieu, died 10 November 1767, a fortnight after he was born.

[64] In 1785, and again in 1786.   [65] 1788–94.

strongly through the capital – a chill blast for the poor and hungry but an invigorating wind for anyone in a position to grasp opportunities, especially if well furnished – as was Constant – with Swiss francs, to buy 'assignats' with and, before these fell into a bottomless inflation, purchase 'Biens Nationaux' cheap.[66]

Equally this period offered opportunities for the politically ambitious. Constant's correspondence with members of his family in Switzerland shows him much alive to the financial advantages to be had; politically too his appetite was keen, as keen as Madame de Staël's, who intended her salon to be the hub of politics and herself the string-puller of all the puppets on the stage. The prospects seemed bright, as the Directory wobbled from *coups d'état* . . . to *coup de grâce*.[67]

Madame de Staël was at that time enthusiastic for the 'coming man'; Constant was well placed and had friends at court: 'Après le 18 Brumaire, Joseph me tourmenta pour faire nommer Benjamin Constant au Tribunat; je ne voulais pas, mais je finis par céder.'[68] On Christmas Day 1799, his nomination was published in the press. Financially and politically, Constant, after his ill-directed youth, seemed at last to be well launched. His political ambitions, however, were soon frustrated. Prominent in the Liberals' attack against the First Consul in January 1802, he was quickly expelled from the Tribunate. For the next twelve years Constant was out of politics, a touch-line observer, regarded with a suspicious eye by the government. His enforced inaction was anything but idle, however; love, law-suits, sojourns at Coppet, travels with or in the wake of Madame de Staël in France, Switzerland and Germany, not least the pursuit of his intellectual interests.

As early as 1785, Constant had conceived the idea of writing a book on Roman polytheism. His guiding idea at the time, in the line of Helvétius, was to show that paganism was a more satisfying religion than Christianity. This work was published posthumously (1833); he had worked on it sporadically for over twenty-five years and during this time his ideas had changed. This change of attitude is reflected in a more important work on religion: *De la Religion considérée dans sa Source, ses Formes et ses Développements*.[69]

The title has an eighteenth-century ring about it: Montesquieu – *De l'Esprit des Lois*, Madame de Staël – *De la Littérature*; the

[66] See H. Guillemin, *Benjamin Constant Muscadin, 1795–1799* (1958), chap. 1: '1795 ou Benjamin fait des affaires et prend le vent'.
[67] Brumaire (November 1799).
[68] *Journal inédit de Sainte-Hélène*, iii, 133. Quoted by Guillemin, op. cit., chap. V.
[69] Entries in the *Journaux Intimes* indicated that he was occupied with this work already in January 1804; vol. I published 1824, vol. II 1825, vol. III 1827, vol. IV, posthumous, 1831.

great liberal forbear had chosen law as his part; the great contemporary had chosen literature and was shortly to embark on a synthesis of German life and culture. All three works were enquiries into different aspects of human activity; Constant would take as his share in this vast study of man, the domain of religion. In fact he quotes Montesquieu at the very outset: 'L'auteur de *l'Esprit des Lois* a dit, avec raison, que tous les êtres avaient leurs lois, la divinité comme le monde, le monde comme les hommes ...'[70] Religious feeling Constant regards as an indestructible element in man's nature; 'c'est en vain que ses connaissances s'étendent... Les enseignements de l'expérience repoussent la religion sur un autre terrain, mais ne la bannissent pas du coeur de l'homme. ... Ce que les mortels croient, et ce qu'ils espèrent se place toujours, pour ainsi dire, à la circonférence de ce qu'ils savent.'[71]

This indestructible feeling hidden in the inmost recesses of human nature expresses itself in successive religious forms and institutions; the forms themselves, though ephemeral, are good – indeed essential; without them the religious instinct could not express itself from age to age; they become dangerous only when interested parties try to prolong their existence beyond their usefulness.[72] There we may guess speaks the authentic voice of late eighteenth-century Protestant Switzerland, whence all traces of Calvinism and its rigorous attitudes have been melted out, leaving behind a pale rousseauistic deism – enthusiasm Madame de Staël would probably have called it.

But there is more than this, for it follows that if every religious form is good in its own time and clime – 'tout est bon ou mauvais suivant les temps et les lieux',[73] truth has unending forms and an eclectic tolerance is the proper attitude. Thus speaks the authentic voice of Constant, obeying his watered down Protestant instinct, his innate liberalism, keystone of his whole life, always ready to assert itself: 'La persécution provoque la révolte... il y a en nous un principe qui s'indigne de toute contrainte intellectuelle.'[74]

References to *De la Religion* in the *Journaux Intimes* show that Constant thought of this book as the great work of his life, the cornerstone of his reputation, but things were to turn out otherwise. Original though it was in its day, the work had no success, and would by now probably have sunk without trace had it not been by the hand that wrote *Adolphe*. But the author's eclectic attitude to religion is interesting and fits with what his other works reveal of his character.

On 30 October 1806 Constant notes in his diary: 'commence un

---

[70] *De la Religion*, I, 1.   [71] *Ibid.*, I, 1.   [72] *Ibid.*, I, 1.
[73] *Journaux Intimes*, 30 January 1804.   [74] *De la Religion*, I, 1.

roman qui sera notre histoire. Tout autre travail me serait impossible...'. On 10 November a further entry runs: 'Avancé mon épisode d'Ellénore. Je doute fort que j'aie assez de persistance pour finir le roman'. Thus from the evidence provided by the *Journaux Intimes*, it appears that *Adolphe* was originally an 'épisode' in what was to be a longer work drawn from his own relations with Charlotte Du Tertre, née Hardenberg. He had met her first at Brunswick in January 1793. She was then the wife of Wilhelm von Marenholz. Their divorce had enabled her to marry a French *émigré*, the Marquis du Tertre, with whom she had returned to France. This second marriage proved no happier than the first. Early in October 1806, Constant had unexpectedly received a letter from Charlotte whom he had lost sight of. From Rouen, where he had joined Madame de Staël in September, he hurried to Paris to meet her. Letter and meeting revived a passion he had begun to feel for Charlotte in 1793. He was to marry her secretly in June 1808[75] after her divorce from the Marquis du Tertre, but in the meantime his revived love, if it brought some joy to his bleak existence, served to complicate and exacerbate his already complex relations with Madame de Staël. 'Sot animal que je suis', he writes, 'je me fais aimer des femmes que je n'aime pas. Puis tout à coup, l'amour s'élève comme un tourbillon, et le résultat d'un lien que je ne voulais prendre que pour me désennuyer, est le bouleversement de ma vie. Est-ce là la destinée d'un homme d'esprit?'[76]

The original manuscript of the novel has not been found;[77] we are left with 'mon épisode d'Ellénore'[78] and, for those who wish to understand in detail the triangular relationship between Constant, Madame de Staël and Charlotte in all its psychological and material complexities, the autobiographical *Cécile*, probably written between 1809 and 1811 – a masterpiece of narrative where Constant, writing in the first person, provides us with the most revealing character studies of himself, of Madame de Staël, thinly disguised as the imperious Madame de Malbée, and of Charlotte as Cécile de Walterbourg.

Divers entries in the *Journaux Intimes* during November and December 1806 make it plain that Constant both derived greater satisfaction from writing the 'épisode' than from writing the novel, which appears to have become rather burdensome, and appreciated the artistic advantage of detaching the 'épisode' from its 'matrix'. After December 1806 we hear no more of the original

[75] Constant's own first marriage to Wilhelmina von Cramm (May 1789) had ended in divorce (November 1795).
[76] Quoted by Roulin, op. cit., p. 1434.   [77] Roulin, op. cit., p. 1440.
[78] Constant did not call it *Adolphe* until some years later. Roulin, op. cit., p. 1439.

novel; subsequent references in the diary to 'mon roman' clearly refer to the 'épisode', which was destined to remain in manuscript until 1816. In that year Constant, having withdrawn temporarily to London from the French political scene where he had been so prominent during the last act of the Napoleonic drama and the beginning of the Restoration, finally overcame the hesitations that his respect for past affections, long since broken though they were,[79] had caused him; the 'épisode' was published in London and almost simultaneously in Paris with the title of *Adolphe*.

What Constant has revealed of himself in other writings show that the character who gives his name to the book is created, at least partially, in the author's image. He has all Constant's egotism, his capacity already referred to for self-analysis and, perhaps as a result of that (for inward-looking attitudes do not usually produce decisive characters), the same inability to remain firmly attached to a given line of action. Yet if all these traits are evident in Constant's relations with women, another side of his character is not reflected in *Adolphe*; if all we know of Adolphe, not excluding biographical details, is in Constant, not all Constant is in Adolphe, his vigorous ambition for example and the political courage he displayed in pursuit of his liberal ideals, rooted though these were in his egotism.

Ellénore is a more composite and in consequence a less clear-cut portrait but the principal model was Madame de Staël. The situation is banal and for that reason immediately accessible. In accordance with the technique of the 'personal novel' the work in effect consists of a monologue; the central character alone speaks either for himself or reports the speech of others. Yet the reader is scarcely aware of this; the relations between Adolphe and Ellénore are analyzed with such psychological precision, their attitudes and talk reported by Adolphe with such naturalness, such a rigorous economy of means, that the reader is more like a spectator of a classical drama with alternating moments of passionate dialogue and pathetic soliloquy. With nothing to divert his attention from Adolphe and through him from Ellénore, the reader is from the outset imprisoned as it were in Adolphe's mind; as the situation Adolphe is involved in develops along its linear course of cause and effect, no escape is possible for the reader any more than for Adolphe; they are in the toils together. The motivation is clearly expounded and operates with the smoothness of a well-oiled mechanism; at no point can the reader reject as unreal the psychology and attitudes of the characters, reject as improbable the successive actions or inactions that lead them to final tragedy.

These merits are enough to ensure that Adolphe and Ellénore,

[79] He had finally broken with Madame de Staël in 1811.

though in her case more passively, come alive in the reader's imagination; he relives their experience. But as Adolphe relates his story, and reports what he and others thought, said and did, his words often end with a generalization: 'Je ne sais quel instinct', says Adolphe, 'm'avertissait d'ailleurs de me défier de ces axiomes généraux ... si purs de toute nuance'. So much for his own attitude towards the little court society he had come into, and the generalization immediately follows: 'Les sots font de leur morale une masse compacte et indivisible ...'; or again, Adolphe recalls how: 'Nous nous taisions donc sur la pensée unique qui nous occupait ...' and the next paragraph rises to the general proposition: 'la dissimulation jette dans l'amour un élément étranger qui le dénature et le flétrit à ses propres yeux'. Such examples could be multiplied and with them we pass constantly from the psychological analysis of a given character to moral reflexions of universal application. Out of their context they could be maxims from La Rochefoucauld; but in their context they arise so naturally from the story that the reader is unaware of any change in the nature of his interest, on the one hand the reality of Adolphe's world so skilfully conjured up in the reader's imagination, on the other, moral judgments that stem from Constant's broad and bitter experience of the world, providing us with a rich aesthetic and intellectual pleasure by their elegant astringency and their truth that penetrates to the heart. In these moments the author seems to be judging his other self with cold detachment and discreetly revealing direct to the reader his own attitudes on a variety of matters closely connected with Adolphe's predicament: the conquering power of love and Oh! the delight of it – 'charme de l'amour, qui pourrait vous peindre! – ' but also its ephemeral nature: 'l'amour n'est qu'un point lumineux ... il y a peu de jours qu'il n'existait pas. Bientôt il n'existera plus –'; above all, its egoisms – 'comme si l'amour n'était pas de tous les sentiments le plus égoïste ...'; the hypocrisy of society, its callousness, its pressures which men flout at their peril – 'Les lois de la société sont plus fortes que les volontés des hommes. Les sentiments les plus impérieux se brisent contre la fatalité des circonstances.'

Impeccable in its psychological analysis, harsh and pitiless in its moral attitudes, *Adolphe* is a thoroughly satisfying work of art by its perfect balance between these two elements, both of them essential; as readers we like both to forget the author's presence when he creates for us an illusion of reality, and to see where he himself stands as a judge of men and society; like a child wanting both to believe in a conjuror's magic and to see how the trick was done.

Adolphe is conceived on a small scale; it is an episode, as Constant himself originally called it, lacking the rich texture of a full-scale novel, but in its elegant simplicity and rigorous psychological investigation it recaptures the classical tradition.

In 1811 Constant and Charlotte, now his second wife, moved to Göttingen; losses at gaming, a passion shared by his wife, had obliged him to sell his country house in France, Les Herbages; but Göttingen attracted him because of its library where he intended to pursue his work on religion. These studious years were brought to a close by the fall of Napoleon. The *Journaux Intimes* enable us to follow Constant's rising excitement and the reawakening of his political ambitions as events moved to their climax: 10 October 1813: 'Si je veux réessayer de la vie active, c'est le moment.' Literature, scholarship are thrown aside; quick! a postchaise to Hanover; conversations with Bernadotte whom Constant was disposed at this time to see in the role of a William of Orange, borne to the throne of France by the force of French public opinion. The conversations prove abortive; 9 April 1814 – to Brussels; 15 April – on to Paris; surely in the kaleidoscope of men and events after Napoleon's abdication (6 April 1814), something will turn up for a man of parts like Constant? 'Servons la bonne cause', (the Bourbons now) he jots on 16 April and adds significantly 'et servons-nous'. The months of the first Restoration drag on but provide no satisfaction to his political appetite. On 17 July he notes: 'Je ne serai jamais rien dans ce pays; si je ne parviens pas par le gouvernement, et c'est difficile... D'ici à six semaines, il faut que je sois quelque chose...' Alas! the new 'Establishment' seemed reluctant to pass from praise to performance: 15 February 1815 – 'On m'admire, on me loue, mais je ne puis profiter de rien...'. Nor are his amorous advances better rewarded... for Madame Récamier, the new object of his inconstant affections, proves heartless. March brings dramatic news; intelligence of Napoleon's landing on the first in the Golfe de Juan reaches Paris on the sixth as a rumour, and is confirmed on the seventh. Characteristically, Constant immediately assessed the effect of this unforeseen event upon his own position: 'Le gouvernement se rapprochera-t-il enfin de nous? Certes, je ne serai plus un volontaire désavoué.' The next thirteen days against a background of growing panic as Napoleon moves northwards are to witness what from the diary's jottings looks like a dangerous political speculation on Constant's part; while others are abandoning ship in disorder, *he* will make himself indispensable! – 'Quels lâches que ces royalistes si purs', he notes on the tenth, 'qui pensaient me présenter comme un ennemi de ce gouvernement – ils tremblent et je suis le seul qui ose proposer de se défendre', but at the same time he notes that Bonapartist feelers are being put out towards him: on the twelfth 'les buonapartistes m'amadouent...', and on the thirteenth again:

'Avances des buonapartistes comme hier.' Can it be that he has begun to weigh up the chances? Perhaps, but five days later he decides on a final throw: a vigorous philippic against Napoleon, which appears on the nineteenth in the *Journal des Débats*. On the twentieth the desperate gamble seems lost: 'Le Roi est parti. Bouleversement et poltronnerie universelle.' At nine o'clock that evening Napoleon was back in the Tuileries. Constant had taken refuge in the United States Legation, whence he was to emerge a few days later to flee westwards with the idea of seeking refuge or possibly taking ship for England or the United States: 23 March – 'couru la poste toute la nuit'; 24 March – 'couru la poste toute la nuit'; 25 March finds him still in his post-chaise but lo! the direction has been reversed and he is hastening back towards Paris; 26 March – 'couru la poste'; 27 March – he's back in the capital.

With years of hostility to Napoleon behind him, dating back to the Consulate, and culminating in the events just described, Constant's decision to escape is natural enough. Nor must we omit from the debit side of his account with Napoleon the pamphlet he had written in 1813 and which, in the prevailing conditions, had aroused interest throughout Europe; between January and April 1814 it had quickly gone through three editions. *De l'Esprit de Conquête et de l'Usurpation* is much more than merely an anti-Napoleonic pamphlet and does not deserve (any more, be it said in passing, than many of the essays and articles from Constant's pen, which together constitute his *Cours de Politique Constitutionnelle*) the oblivion which is the normal fate of pamphlets once the circumstances that called them forth have passed into history.

As the title of *De l'Esprit de Conquête* indicates, the pamphlet falls into two parts; in the first part the author develops the argument that with Europe advancing into the commercial and industrial age, war and the warlike spirit will soon be out of date: 'Il est clair que plus la tendance commerciale domine, plus la tendance guerrière doit s'affaiblir...' Peace and well-being – a high standard of living we should call it now – replace all other aims; war is too expensive. In these circumstances Bonaparte is an anachronism. In the second half of the pamphlet he contrasts the character of long-established and therefore legitimate governments with that of a usurping régime that can exist only by force and consequently leads society back to 'le système guerrier' or 'l'esprit de conquête' already denounced in the first part.

The value of *De l'Esprit de Conquête* for the modern reader, however, does not lie in the general argument nor, particularly, in the attack, now direct, now oblique, on Napoleon; it lies in the rich harvest of political and moral reflexions that may be garnered from it. The same brilliantly analytical mind is at work as in *Adolphe*.

This anti-Napoleonic record explains Constant's flight; but what motives had he for going back? An entry in the diary for 25 March speaks of bad news. The reference must be to Nantes' having declared for the Emperor and evicted the Préfet, Barante. Nantes, it will be remembered, was one of Constant's possible destinations. He must also have been aware that the Duc de Bourbon's efforts to raise the royalist Vendée was meeting with little success. Here were cogent reasons for a change of course. Would they in themselves explain the return to Paris? Constant, we may suppose, weighed up the various courses open to him at that moment – another port to embark from? Hiding? Paris? – and decided that the last offered him the best chances; it had the further advantage of bringing him back, poor moth, to the ice-cold flame of Madame Récamier.

Apart from this latter consideration, which with Constant's capacity for foolhardy 'coups de tête' may well have had considerable weight, there were solid grounds for his deciding as he did. Against those – and there were certain to be many – who would accuse him of betraying the Bourbons, he could argue that he was not morally committed to them, that despite their cold-shouldering of him, he had done all he could to galvanize their will to stay and fight it out, that since they took such a poor view of their chances, there was no reason why he, unasked, should take a better. On the positive side, he must have been relying on the fact that, as the diary indicates, he had earlier in the month been approached by certain Bonapartists; and there was the more general but equally pertinent calculation that at this juncture Napoleon would need all the support he could get, that just as in the early days of the Consulate he would do all he could, and with more compelling reasons, to gather political support from all quarters; these would oblige him not only to forget men's particular actions in the past but also to consider how to buy their support in the present. For Constant the price would be clear – the promise of a new liberal régime, towards the building of which Constant could see himself as the key man.

If the foregoing in fact reflects the calculations that determined Constant's bold decision to go back to Paris, events proved him right. During the first fortnight of April he is full of doubts and uncertainties but negotiations are obviously going on and lead to his interview with the Emperor on 14 April; 'Longue conversation. C'est un homme étonnant'. Constant was under the spell Napoleon could cast over men. His collaboration was assured and fraught with big consequences.

The *Acte Additionnel aux Constitutions de l'Empire* which was ready for promulgation on 22 April was largely his work and bears the stamp of his political ideas: a two-stage electoral system, a Lower and an Upper House, sharing legislative powers with the Emperor, and having powers of control over ministers by the weapon of impeachment. Dead letter though this constitution was to be, it was none the less destined to have a big impact on Bonapartism as a political factor in the nineteenth century, by justifying the claim in *Le Mémorial de Sainte-Hélène* that Napoleon's real intentions which fate had prevented him from carrying out were liberal. Thus Constant indirectly made his mark on the course of French political history down the century. From his own point of view the consequences of his *volte-face* were to be no less considerable.

The price he paid was first a short period of exile in 1816 while the wave of persecution – la Terreur Blanche – ran its course. This in itself was a minor set-back; when he was able to return to France after the dissolution of 'La Chambre Introuvable' (September 1816) he was to become one of the commanding figures of the liberal opposition under the Restoration and was to have the satisfaction before his death of seeing the triumph of his political ideals – those of Coppet, too, be it added – with the July Revolution and the accession to the throne of Louis-Philippe, Roi des Français.

More serious was the image of him created in the minds of contemporaries and of later generations. Even discounting the attitudes of the Royalists who must have been delighted by the opportunity to discredit him, can we avoid the impression of an unprincipled opportunist, solely interested in the exercise of power, tempted to think that in times of flux there is always a way out or a way round for a skilful politician?

There would seem to be the same dichotomy in Constant as in French liberalism itself; on the one hand, the generous spirit of *Les Trois Glorieuses* which opened the flood gates of enthusiasm and sent its shock waves pulsing through the writings of liberal-minded men: 'dans ces jours mémorables, une grande lumière se fit, et j'aperçus la France',[80] writes Michelet; on the other hand, the narrowest egoism, exemplified by the ruling bourgeoisie of the July Monarchy in the pursuit of its own interests – so at least thought Tocqueville: 'En 1830, le triomphe de la classe moyenne avait été définitif ... Elle se logea dans toutes les places, augmenta prodigieusement le nombre de celles-ci et s'habitua à vivre presque autant du Trésor public que de sa propre industrie.'[81]

Yet, if there are many liberals who would like to gallop off in

[80] *Histoire de France*, Preface of 1869.
[81] *Souvenirs*, NRF edn., 1944, p. 16.

both directions at once, there is really little doubt in which direction Constant faced. His fundamental egotism provides the one unifying theme to the confused discords of his life. Under his liberal ideals lurks the most anarchical individualism. The magnificent attack on despotism,[82] the lucid exposition of the diverse threats in the arbitrary exercise of power to the citizen's personal or intellectual liberty[83] are by-products of it; his religious eclecticism stems from a fundamental indifference to other people's beliefs. What more egotistical than his conception of love? A storm, arising with devastating suddenness and subsiding as abruptly; ecstatic while it lasts, it should leave no bonds, no claims, which, if they exist, betray a weakness of character; marriage is a slavery. Constant's undoubted kindness and courtesy were no more than the good breeding of a man of the world, his cynical attitude to men[84] precludes its being rooted in charity. His diaries and novel, finally, are a constant preoccupation with self.

[82] *De l'Esprit de Conquête et de l'Usurpation.*
[83] See *Cours de Politique Constitutionnelle, passim.*
[84] *Journaux Intimes, passim.*

Chapter 5

I. CHATEAUBRIAND

THE cultivated aristocratic society of the *ancien régime* in its latter day was like a hothouse where the delicate plants of late eighteenth-century literature could flower.

Prominent writers of those closing years who survived the Revolution produced nothing more. Bernardin de Saint-Pierre re-edited his works; that engaging whippersnapper Figaro, after indulging in moments of self-pity ('O! femme, femme, créature faible et décevante . . .'),[1] in impertinent railing at his betters and society ('Vous vous êtes donné la peine de naître . . .'; 'Il fallait un calculateur . . .'[2]), lachrymose effusions (*La Mère Coupable*, 1792), seems stunned into silence; Laclos, as a regular officer and later in the service of the d'Orléans, has no time and perhaps no inclination for literature. However attractive the writings of these men may appear to us now, they belong to a society the Revolution destroyed; in its thunder their voices seem like the twitterings of a canary in a golden cage on a wind and wave-swept shore. Doubtless if Rousseau had survived the Revolution he too would have been awed into silence by human deeds that lay beyond even his sometimes harsh experience.

The destruction of a home involves migration; in terms of what happened, emigration abroad for the most part, but not necessarily; there is also a form of migration inwards into the inner self where undisturbed by the din of events a man may sit like a fakir in contemplation of his navel, pondering on the soul and its destinies.

In contrast with the evanescent literature of the Revolution or the traditional literature of Revolution and Empire, here was an attitude of mind that was to produce something new, as the writings of Chateaubriand and Senancour show.

François-René de Chateaubriand (1768–1848) was the first of three Bretons destined to make a big impact upon French sensibility in the nineteenth century, the other two being Lamennais[3] and Renan.[4] Even those who have never read a line of Chateaubriand are likely to have in their minds the image of him standing

---

[1] *Mariage de Figaro* (1784), V., 3.   [2] *Ibid.*, V. 3.
[3] See below, pp. 107–10.   [4] See below, pp. 362–5.

like a sentinel at the threshold of the nineteenth century, so much is he a part of the legend of literature. Yet if we ask ourselves soberly what remains living today of the massive volumes that constitute his legacy to posterity, what characters created by him remain alive in our minds as people we can understand and identify ourselves with, we are likely to see a discrepancy between the reputation of the man and the permanent achievements of the writer, for Chateaubriand was a writer, yes, but many other things besides.[5] All his activities and dramatic reversals of fortune: the explorer renouncing his intention of discovering the north-west passage (just as well perhaps) and sailing home from the New World to help redress the balance of the old, the one-time exile, penniless and starving, returning as ambassador to the Court of St James, the champion of legitimacy against the assaults of revolution dramatically dismissed in the hour of success by an ungrateful monarch,[6] the victim of ingratitude, the unheeded Cassandra faithful in disaster to the cause he served; these and other big moments in an eventful life, skilfully arranged and exploited, as the readers of the *Mémoires d'Outre-Tombe* will agree, have helped to create and magnify the composite image of the man.

Chateaubriand was fortunate too in that what he had in him to give seemed to suit so well the spiritual and artistic needs of the hour. This as much perhaps as his intrinsic merits, real though these are, explains his success, even though the works that justified it have with a few important exceptions lost their resonance.

If justice had anything to do with this, we would say: this neglect is unjust. The enterprising and diligent reader would indeed find rewards in the *Voyage en Amérique*: night in the virgin forests around the camp fire, moonlight on the savannah, Niagara. Do these evocative descriptions come from the author's direct personal experience? Perhaps not,[7] but for the reader of the *Mémoires d'Outre-Tombe* where they were subsequently to find a place the test of the author's ability as an artist in words lies not in how genuine the description but in the author's power to communicate an experience or evoke a scene. Chateaubriand can do both.

Much the same could be said of that vast amorphous prose epic of the noble savage, *Les Natchez*. Chateaubriand had conceived the idea, in his youthful enthusiasm for Rousseau. One of the reasons why he had set out for the New World was to get genuine local colour for it; no one after Bernardin de Saint-Pierre could presume to choose an exotic theme without some direct experience of what he was writing about. But the voluminous manuscript of

---

[5] See below, pp. 68–9.
[6] The expedition to Spain, to restore Ferdinand VII (1823).
[7] Souriau, *Histoire du Romantisme*, vol. I.

Les Natchez was to lie unknown for many years.[8] In the meantime it was to serve as a convenient quarry whence the author was presently to draw *Atala* and *René*, much descriptive material for *Le Génie du Christianisme* and diverse reflexions for what was to be his first published work: *Essai sur les Révolutions* (1797). Like *Les Natchez*, the *Essai* is an amorphous book; it consists of a series of parallels between the revolutions of antiquity and the various phases and aspects of the French Revolution. It suggests rather an exercise in declamation, and makes no significant or systematic contribution to political thought.

Yet here as elsewhere, in *Le Génie du Christianisme*, in the *Mémoires d'Outre-Tombe* and in forgotten works such as *Les Etudes Historiques* or *L'Analyse raisonnée de l'Histoire de France*, the author scatters carelessly a wealth of penetrating reflexions, political, historical and moral! Its main interest lies in the light it throws on Chateaubriand himself. The author's prevailing mood is one of pessimism: Christianity is in decay, power inevitably corrupts, civil liberty is a vain hope.

Such pessimism is scarcely surprising from a man suffering as Chateaubriand then was in his body and in his affections; it is born more particularly of exile; the feelings of nostalgic homesickness he attributes to Pisistratus[9] may indeed have been the latter's but for readers of *Atala* and *René* they have a familiar ring. Yet he is able to look at the French Revolution with detachment as an inevitable process: 'On pourrait soupçonner qu'il existe des époques inconnues, mais régulières, auxquelles la face du monde se renouvelle. Nous avons le malheur d'être né au moment d'une de ces grandes révolutions.'[10]

The irreligious attitude of the *Essai* is perhaps less evident than it has been made out to be, yet such as it is, within a few years it makes way for a quite different attitude towards Christianity. Can the doubter of *L'Essai* and the Christian apologist of *Le Génie du Christianisme* be one and the same person? Chateaubriand, who foresaw the need to explain the change, ascribes it to the emotional shock he suffered when as a lonely exile in London he received the news that his brother and sister-in-law had been executed and that his mother had died as the result of prison hardships, grieving on the evidence of the *Essai* that her surviving son had deserted the religion of his fathers. 'J'ai pleuré et j'ai cru'.[11] Chateaubriand with his sense of artistic form and his delight in striking attitudes describes his return to the faith in an over-

---

[8] First published *in extenso* in the first complete edition of Chateaubriand's works, 1826–30.

[9] *Essai*, Part I, chap. 9.

[10] *Essai*, I, chap. 9.

[11] *Génie*, first preface.

simplified way – a modern St Paul converted in a trice. Yet the
letter he received from one of his sisters, Madame de Farcy, with
the news of their mother's death, may well have been the first
factor in a change of attitude, if we assume that the religious
detachment of the *Essai* was more the reflexion of a passing mood
than a deep-seated conviction. 'Si tu savais', she writes, 'combien
de pleurs tes erreurs ont fait répandre à notre mère, peut-être cela
contribuerait-il à t'ouvrir les yeux.'

The influence of his friend Fontanes[12] was an added factor in
his resolve to expiate his sin by putting his pen at the service of
the Christian religion. A great opportunity was soon to be vouchsafed to him, in the form of the First Consul's religious policy,
to give a political and social significance to his personal act of
witness.

In emigrating to join the Princes' Army immediately after returning from America (December 1791), Chateaubriand had yielded to
the social and political pressures of his class. These, men usually
but not always very consciously obey, can therefore appreciate and
respect, especially when, as in Chateaubriand's case, they run
counter to a man's wishes and convictions. Chateaubriand disliked
the idea of taking up arms against his country, whatever the
reason, and, more perspicacious than other men of his class and
generation, saw that 'l'armée des Princes' which he describes in
such moving terms in the *Mémoires d'Outre-Tombe*,[13] was a venture without hope unless public opinion within France was over-
whelmingly in favour of it, and Chateaubriand doubted it. A few
years later, the spirit and attitudes of the London *émigrés*, of
those at least who gravitated round Louis XVIII and the Comte
d'Artois,[14] seemed to Chateaubriand equally out of focus, and it
was natural that he should have grasped at the earliest opportunity
to get back to France, even though it meant going under an assumed name and living in hiding until such time as he no longer
figured on the list of proscribed *émigrés*. His removal from that
list [15] was due partly to the influence of his friends at court,[16] but
more especially to the triumph of *Atala* (1801) and the consequent
favour of the First Consul, always ready to secure the services if
possible of men distinguished in whatever field. 'C'est de la publication d'*Atala* que date le bruit que j'ai fait dans le monde', writes
Chateaubriand.[17] Marie-Joseph Chénier confirms the fact: 'Le

[12] See above, pp. 24–5.
[13] Part I, Bk. 9, chap. 10, Levaillant edn.
[14] Twickenham home of the Duc d'Orléans and Juniper Hill, where lived
friends of Madame de Staël, were different propositions.
[15] 21 July 1801.
[16] Notably Fontanes, Madame Baciocchi.
[17] *Mémoires d'Outre-Tombe*, Part II, Bk. 1, chap. 6, Levaillant edn.

petit roman d'*Atala* ... a fait du bruit ...';[18] follows a hostile analysis that delivers some shrewd thrusts at Chateaubriand's story
and compares it unfavourably to *Paul et Virginie*. Chénier's views
show particularly how far he and the effete classicism he represents, the academic official attitude, was removed from contemporary public taste. 'Cette école classique', comments Chateaubriand,
'vieille rajeunie dont la seule vue inspirait l'ennui.'[19] He goes on
to attribute his success with *Atala* to the shock of surprise the story
caused. Even allowing for the genuine merits of Bernardin de
Saint-Pierre's story, it is no more than a charming idyll set against
an exotic background. Chateaubriand was giving his readers a passionate love story; much stronger meat.

We may be tempted now to agree with some of the points made
by Marie-Joseph; the motivation of the characters is not convincing, nor do the little accidents that prevent Atala from discovering
in time that she could be freed from her vows constitute a chain of
circumstance so compelling that, overwhelmed by a sense of tragic
inevitability, we accept her suicide as inescapable. Confound the
girl! Why could she not speak up sooner? Contemporary readers
were less fastidious; what counted first was the mantle of gorgeous
colour the story was clothed in; by comparison, Bernardin's descriptive prose seemed pedestrian. 'La nuit était délicieuse. Le
Génie des airs secouait sa chevelure bleue, embaumée de la senteur
des pins, ... La lune brillait au milieu d'un azur sans tache, et sa
lumière gris de perle descendait sur la cime indéterminée des
forêts...' The descriptions, far from being mere lists of exotic
trees, fruits and plants, as Marie-Joseph insinuates, compel the
reader to create his own images in his mind: '... l'obscurité re-
double: les nuages abaissés entrent sous l'ombrage des bois. La nue
se déchire, et l'éclair trace un rapide losange de feu. Un vent
impétueux ... roule les nuages sur les nuages; les forêts plient ...
La foudre met le feu dans les bois; l'incendie s'étend comme une
chevelure de flammes; des colonnes d'étincelles et de fumée assiè-
gent les nues ...'

Word painting for its own sake soon fatigues; Chateaubriand relates his to the human situation: the sounds of nature prolong those
of men: 'Tout s'endort; à mesure que le bruit des hommes s'affai-
blit, celui du désert augmente, et au tumulte des voix succèdent les
plaintes du vent dans la forêt'; Nature's solitude is the balm of the
passionate heart: 'les grandes passions sont solitaires, et les transporter au désert, c'est les rendre à leur empire'. The lovers are engulfed in the vast silence: 'Atala et moi, nous joignions notre silence
au silence de cette scène'; the full force of the storm orchestrates

---

[18] *Tableau Historique de la Littérature Française*, chap. VI.
[19] *Mémoires*, Part II, Bk. 1, chap. 6.

the lovers' mounting passion; the moon fills the forest not with
light but with melancholy: 'la lune prêta son pâle flambeau à cette
veille funèbre... Bientôt elle répandit dans les bois ce grand
secret de mélancolie, qu'elle aime à raconter aux vieux chênes et
aux rivages antiques des mers.' The secret of melancholy – therein
especially lies the success of *Atala*. Chactas and Atala are flimsy
characters, but into each their creator has breathed his own spirit
of melancholy, the melancholy of the lonely exile: 'Heureux ceux
qui n'ont point vu la fumée des fêtes de l'étranger, et qui ne se
sont assis qu'aux festins de leurs pères'; the melancholy of man in
his journey through life: 'Nous sommes tous voyageurs...'; of his
inconstant desires: 'Connaissez-vous le coeur de l'homme et pour-
riez-vous compter les inconstances de son desir?' Of his transience:
'Homme, tu n'es qu'un songe rapide, un rêve douloureux; tu
n'existes que par le malheur; tu n'es quelque chose que par la
tristesse de ton âme et l'éternelle mélancolie de ta pensée.'

A generation that had suffered heard in *Atala* the echoes of its
own sufferings: its success was to be on a European scale and, extending beyond the bounds of literature, was to provide inspiration
for artists[20] and engravers.

After *Atala*, *Le Génie du Christianisme* (14 April 1802), which
coincided neatly with the promulgation of the Concordat (18
April). While Bonaparte was healing the breach with Rome,
Chateaubriand, encouraged and to a certain extent inspired by
Fontanes, possibly also inspired by Ballanche,[21] entered the lists as
a champion of Christianity. The conquests and progress of science
in the nineteenth century are apt to obscure the fact that it was
also an age of religious revival. Chateaubriand recognizes as an
important factor in the success of his work the general thirst for
change from the long dominion of Voltaire. 'As pants the hart for
the water brooks...' Doubtless another factor was that *Le Génie*
was by the author of *Atala*. Who is to say whether in its turn *Le
Génie* acted as a 'booster rocket' to the religious revival? In any
case the work is indissolubly linked with it. He liked to see himself
in the role of rebuilder of France's religious life: 'A Lyon ... je fus
témoin de la Fête-Dieu renaissante: je croyais avoir quelque part à

---

[20] e.g. Ary Scheffer, *Les Funérailles d'Atala*.
[21] Pierre Simon Ballanche (1776–1847), author of, *inter alia*, *Du sentiment considéré dans ses rapports avec la littérature et les arts* (1801).
Chateaubriand, who mentions Ballanche several times in *Mémoires d'Outre-
Tombe*, may have read this work, cf. in particular Ballanche's chapter
entitled: 'de la mélancolie' and *Le Génie*, Part III, Bk. 5, chaps. 3, 4, 5.
Both authors refer to *Palmyre*. Ballanche's most important work is the unfinished *Palingénésie Sociale* (1827–9) in which, inspired as Michelet in
his own way was also to be, by the early eighteenth-century Italian his-
torian and philosopher Vico, he endeavours to discern the working of
Providence throughout human history. (See J. Buche, *L'Ecole Mystique
De Lyon, 1776–1847*, 1935.)

ces bouquets de fleurs, à cette joie du ciel que j'avais rappelée sur la terre . . . mon nom se mêlait au rétablissement des autels.'[22]

Some museums are known by name but seldom entered; like them, *Le Génie* repays the chance visitor for his courageous curiosity, particularly if he gets beyond the first part of the book. Chateaubriand is neither theologian nor philosopher, his proofs of the existence of God and the immortality of the soul are unlikely to compel assent. He is on much firmer ground when he comes to examine Christianity in its fruits, in its influence on poetry and other forms of literature, on the fine arts, in the impulse it gives to those who, dedicating their lives to it, render service to their fellow men. This approach to the subject is inherent in the title of the work – the genius of Christianity. Rational analysis of a mystery that transcends analysis is irrelevant; the matter must be seen as a force operating in Nature, men, society, as a compelling experience that cannot be dismissed, that gives to all lives touched by it, to all projections of the human soul in art and literature, a quality not to be found elsewhere; without it talent is cribbed and confined: 'L'incrédulité est la principale cause de la décadence du goût et du génie.'[23] To support his thesis Chateaubriand roams far and wide over ancient and modern literatures and shows himself to be a percipient reader in his analysis of texts and quick to detect, for example, attitudes of mind underlying the written word.[24] Nor does he content himself with literature alone. His glance at the fine arts is admittedly cursory but no better example can be found of how his search for the magic touch of the Christian religion has quickened his own sensitivity and given him a fresh eye to see with than his chapter on Gothic architecture,[25] which must have been an important influence in the Gothic revival in France.

The emphasis placed on the mysterious force of the Christian religion operating in and through men enables Chateaubriand to focus attention on the mystery that surrounds human life: 'tout est caché, tout est inconnu dans l'univers. L'homme lui-même n'est-il pas un étrange mystère?'[26] To this sense of mystery Chateaubriand returns constantly after drawing upon his own experiences as a traveller on land and sea;[27] mystery begets awe and awe is a prerequisite of a religious attitude: 'cette immensité des mers qui semble nous donner une mesure confuse de la grandeur de notre

---

[22] *Mémoires*, Pt. II, Bk. 2, chap. 6, Levaillant.
[23] *Génie*, Pt. III, Bk. 4, chap. 5.
[24] cf. for example his analysis of Priam's appeal to Achilles, Pt. II, Bk. 2, chap. 4.
[25] *Génie*, Pt. III, Bk. 1, chap. 8.
[26] *Ibid.*, Pt. I, Bk. 1, chap. 2.
[27] *Ibid.*, Pt. I, Bk. 5, chap. 12; Pt. II, Bk. 4, chap. 1.

âme, ... qui fait naître en nous un vague désir de quitter la vie pour embrasser la nature et nous confondre avec son auteur.'[28] A dangerous suggestion of pantheism? Very possibly, but setting aside the apologetic aspect of Le Génie, its significance in the history of literature lies precisely in its continual emphasis upon the mystery of human destiny and the secret forces of nature man is a part of. Classical literature is in the last resort a human and social literature; in the eighteenth century the fire had gone out of it, it had become desiccated under the parched breath of rationalism; tragedy, and comedy for that matter, were largely filled with moralising abstractions. By discovering or rather re-discovering the sense of mystery Chateaubriand was tapping new springs of emotion, turning man's gaze away from the social, the finite plane, to the infinite: 'Cette immensité des mers ... etc.', giving him a kind of moral vertigo that will make him ready to fall into the lap of nature. Chateaubriand was in fact displaying what was to be the very core of the Romantic inward-looking attitude; he was giving literature and art a new dimension.

'Le Vague des Passions' – such is the title of one chapter.[29] In it the author analyzes the attitude of mind that is engendered by considerations such as the foregoing; 'L'imagination est riche, abondante, merveilleuse; l'existence pauvre, sèche et désenchantée. On habite, avec un coeur plein, un monde vide; et sans avoir usé de rien, on est désabusé de tout.' This chapter was followed in the first edition by the story of René,[30] as an individual example of this attitude of mind.[31] As an improving tale in support of the power of religion to govern and direct men's lives it carries no conviction in spite of René's meditation, in the presence of his dead father, on death as a vision of eternity, in spite of Amélie's withdrawal from the world into the seclusion of a convent, in spite of Father Souël's wise admonitions, in conclusion. Chateaubriand did well to detach the work from Le Génie and publish it separately (1805) together with the definitive edition of Atala.

René is evidently a scarcely veiled personal confession, the first of a series of similar works hovering unsteadily between biography and fiction; there are constant reminders of René's alter ego both in René's character and in his material circumstances: 'Mon humeur était impétueuse, mon caractère inégal ...'; 'chaque automne je revenais au château paternel, situé au milieu des forêts, près d'un lac, dans une province reculée ...; timide et contraint devant mon père, je ne trouvais l'aise et le contentement qu'auprès de ma soeur Amélie ...'

[28] Ibid., Pt. II, Bk. 4, chap. 1.
[29] Ibid., Pt. II, Bk. 3, chap. 9.   [30] Forming Bk. 4.
[31] Like Atala, René originally formed part of Les Natchez.

Here we have Chateaubriand's withdrawal into himself; supreme egotist that he is, he never succeeded in creating a character of fiction (and René is a vivid if rather static character of fiction) otherwise than by contemplating his own image. But there is much more than this; a whole generation saw itself reflected in René, the proud solitary, casting himself with no experience on the stormy ocean of the world, seeking solace for his vague and unsatisfied desires. Travel, the society of his compatriots, solitude – 'un exil champêtre' – are alike of no avail; he longs for death: 'Levez-vous vite, orages désirés, qui devez emporter René dans les espaces d'une autre vie'; suicide seems the only solution: 'Enfin, ne pouvant trouver de remède à cette étrange blessure de mon coeur, qui n'était nulle part et qui était partout, je résolus de quitter la vie.'

Where could one find a better example of Romantic attitudes, of Romantic themes (not excluding the theme of incest) and, one might be tempted to add, if it were not disrespectful to the author – that great artist in prose, 'l'enchanteur' – of Romantic stage bric-à-brac, all things that were presently to move as if by enchantment into the rhythmical verse patterns of Lamartine?[32] Yes indeed, René, after Atala, after Le Génie, is a document of cardinal importance in the Romantic 'dossier', but it has the advantage over them of containing in René the character an element of permanent human truth; not only the Romantic generation but perhaps in every successive generation there are readers who can see something of their own image in him; vast ill-defined desires, a source of pleasure in themselves: 'cet état de calme et de trouble ... n'était pas sans quelques charmes, ...', finding at last with a certain morose delectation, unknown to no one, a genuine cause of sorrow to feed on: 'je sus donc ce que c'était que de verser des larmes pour un mal qui n'était point imaginaire ... je trouvai même une sorte de satisfaction inattendue dans la plénitude de mon chagrin'. To the extent, even minimal, that this discovery of René's about himself evokes an echo in our own hearts, we experience that sense of identification which even if only momentary serves to ensure a place in our memory for René.

By the time René and Atala were published Chateaubriand's life had undergone another change; his first short excursion into diplomacy as a career[33] had come to an end – he had resigned after the execution of the Duc d'Enghien (1804); not, however, before he had had time as First Secretary at Rome to write his 'Lettre à Fontanes sur la Campagne Romaine' (1804), one of those

---

[32] e.g. notably passages from René and Lamartine's 'Isolement' or 'le Crucifix'.

[33] He had been offered and had accepted appointment in the diplomatic service by Bonaparte after the success of Le Génie.

admirable anthology pieces that lie buried, numerous, in Chateau-briand's collected writings.

Les Martyrs (1809) and the *Itinéraire de Paris à Jerusalem* (1811) add nothing in the modern reader's view to their author's reputation. We can scarcely share Augustin Thierry's enthusiasm[34] for the former; the latter, which records Chateaubriand's Near-Eastern journey (1806–7) and put him in the vanguard of Oriental-ism, a fashion that was to make a powerful impact on Romantic literature and art, is less interesting than another famous piece by a man whose European reputation was to equal Chateaubriand's own, Byron's *Childe Harold*.

The fall of the Empire was the signal for Chateaubriand's re-turn to the diplomatic service and then to politics, which were to absorb his energies until his dramatic exit from the political stage as Louis-Philippe stepped on to it (1830). Not till 1833 did he return to his *Mémoires* which he had first thought of undertaking as early as 1803, which he had gathered material for and worked on intermittently ever since; they were now to become the central interest of his life.[35] His only literary diversion from them is the admirable but little known *Vie de Rancé* (1844), which deserves its place in the series of 'Chefs-d'oeuvre méconnus'.

The *Mémoires d'Outre-Tombe* remain Chateaubriand's greatest legacy, his most permanent memorial. Not only are they the in-dispensable source for the study of his life, but they gather within their pages all the impressions, scattered in his other works, of Chateaubriand's rich personality. No doubt Chateaubriand inten-ded the *Mémoires d'Outre-Tombe* to be a great source book for future historians. Like others of his generation, Chateaubriand had lived through dramatic times, had seen the end of a régime cen-turies old and the uncertain beginnings of a new order, but he had been better placed than most to give an account of the abundant material; by turns explorer, soldier, traveller, journalist, polemist, diplomat, politician, a life packed with incident had provided him with contacts with crowned heads, politicians, writers, people in all ranks of society, and at the service of his memory was an acute intelligence.

But the *Mémoires* are much more (or less) than a chronicle. Of this type of work the historian Tocqueville gives us an example in his *Souvenirs*,[36] admirable by their vivid exactitude and imparti-ality. Chateaubriand brought to the writing of his ... exploration of times past, gifts of style greater here than in any other of his

---

[34] *Récits Mérovingiens*, preface (1840).
[35] They were completed in 1841 but the author returned to them con-stantly between 1844–8. Levaillant edn., preface.
[36] See below, p. 245.

works, the imagination of a poet, and his supreme egotism; thus, at once the chronicle is transformed into a vast epic, aflame with colours, sombre or lurid very often. Chateaubriand has not so much written a chronicle as built a temple of memory where the silent multitude of contemporaries he evokes surround him, the symbolic figure of a generation, almost of an age, and listen to his dirge on the vanity of human things.

II. SENANCOUR.
THE ÉMIGRÉS. CHARLES DE VILLIERS

In comparison with Chateaubriand, Etienne de Senancour (1770–1846) is a lesser man, his life obscure and depressing, a record of avoidance, inadaptability, unfulfilment: 'J'interrogeai mon être, je considérai rapidement tout ce qui m'entourait...et je vis qu'il n'y avait d'accord ni entre moi et la société, ni entre mes besoins et les choses qu'elle a faites.'[37] Yet in this melancholy catalogue, one success stands out in contrast, that of *Obermann* (1804). Alone of Senancour's fairly voluminous writings, the letters of Obermann save their author's name from oblivion. They are not an epistolary novel in the eighteenth-century mode but a diary of the author's life from 1789 to 1803, the letters being grouped by years reduced from the fourteen of reality to ten.

At the outset the writer is in Switzerland and we learn in general terms the reason for his taking refuge there. Later he returns to Paris and thence goes to the Forez region. The concluding groups of letters introduce a new character, Fonsalbe, to whom is attributed the conjugal infidelity that embittered Senancour's own life. But the facts of Obermann's life, which are monotonous and often petty, are in themselves of little importance. What gives them significance is the place he takes beside René in the group of characteristic heroes of the first Romantic generation. Steeped in the spirit of the eighteenth century, Obermann has no faith and yet, dissatisfied without one, seeks solace in mysticism, and finds disenchantment. Rousseauist in his attitude to nature, full of a melancholy and a love of solitude that presages Lamartine, Obermann is less substantial as a character than René but is superior to him in the analysis of his metaphysical anguish.

Therein is the secret no doubt of Sainte-Beuve's faithful admiration for him. With the inertia to be expected from someone who has locked himself away from other men in the sanctuary of his own soul, Obermann was at first overshadowed by the equally egotistical but more vigorous René, and was appreciated only by a

[37] *Obermann*, Letter No. 1.

small circle of admirers[38] who identified themselves with his religious anxiety and mystical yearnings, but, thanks to Sainte-Beuve in particular, Obermann came more into his own after 1830 and found in Amaury's[39] distresses of soul and sentiment a hero cast in his own image.

Apart from the 'migration inwards' we must also consider the effects of the emigration, with its two waves: the first in the latter half of 1789 after the so-called 'Grande Peur' (July 1789) when wild rumours of invasion and disasters swept the country, provoking peasants to revolt, to burn feudal charters, sometimes châteaux, and even in a few instances to kill their owners –

> ... force moutons ... et parfois même
> Le berger ... —

the second on a much bigger scale in 1792 and 1793. By then some organized resistance to the Revolution was taking shape, notably 'l'Armée des Princes', and its only result was to exacerbate revolutionary fanaticisms.

The *émigrés* were scattered over the face of Europe: Northern Italy, Switzerland, Germany, England. Some went as far afield as Russia;[40] a future monarch[41] and a future Foreign Minister[42] were for some time in the United States of America.

Little over a century before some 200,000 Huguenots had fled the country after the Revocation of the Edict of Nantes (1685). Since the reason for their going was religious, they could have entertained no hope of return; they went with the idea of settling permanently in some other country, where moreover a common bond of faith gave them the hope of being the more readily welcomed and easily absorbed into a new community. Such men have little incentive to look back at their native country with any wish to exercise influence there, political, intellectual or literary; their energies are absorbed in re-establishing themselves elsewhere. Huguenot exiles, who after the Revocation settled in England and Holland, were indeed a useful channel of information about those countries by their diverse publications that found their clandestine way into France, but the influence was indirect.[43]

The political *émigré* is likely to have a different outlook. The

---

[38] In England the influence of Senancour was particularly marked in the poetry of Matthew Arnold ('Stanzas in Memory of the author of Obermann', and 'Obermann once more').

[39] *Volupté* – see below, pp. 184–5.

[40] The Duc de Richelieu (1766–1822) became Governor of Odessa.

[41] The Duc d'Orléans (1773–1850) the future Louis-Philippe.

[42] Talleyrand (1754–1838).

[43] P. van Tieghem, *Influences Etrangères sur la Littérature française, 1550–1880* (1961, pp. 144 *et seq.*).

chances are he will not regard his enforced sojourn abroad as more than temporary; his hatreds are likely to be directed not against his country, against a whole society that has 'spewed him out', but against some opposing political party that has won the day ... for a time. His whole idea is likely to be to get home as soon as possible especially as, unlike the religious exile, he probably lacks even the consolation of a religious communion with the society he has been thrown into.

These suppositions are in general borne out by the attitudes of the Revolution's *émigrés*. They were not absorbed by the societies they were forced to live amongst; they formed small inward-looking groups, their attention riveted on events in their own country.

A talented example of this type of *émigré* is Antoine Rivarol[44] (1753–1801). Before the Revolution this minor critic and social commentator had at least one passion that did him credit – the French tongue. His *Discours sur l'Universalité de la langue française* (1784) won him the prize offered for an apologia on the theme set by the Berlin Academy – a prize, celebrity and a minor place in French literature. 'Ce qui distingue notre langue des langues anciennes et modernes c'est l'ordre et la construction de la phrase', he writes, 'le français est le seul resté fidèle à l'ordre direct, comme s'il était toute raison ... la syntaxe française est incorruptible', and then follows the triumphant claim: 'C'est de là que résulte cette admirable clarté, base éternelle de notre langue; ce qui n'est pas clair n'est pas français.' Many have repeated the phrase, a little glibly perhaps, without reflecting that what is clear is clear in any language, so that French can claim clarity neither as an inherent quality nor as a monopoly. But could a Frenchman of the late eighteenth century, accustomed to the limpid prose of Voltaire and aware that throughout Europe French was the language spoken in polite society – throughout Europe except in England –, think otherwise?

The Revolution was to make of this literary light-weight, this rather typical eighteenth-century *petit maître*, a vigorous polemist attacking the Revolution and all its works, casting aside his characteristically eighteenth-century irreligion and defending the Catholic Church as an indispensable pillar of the State. 'Il y a un contrat éternel entre la politique et la religion.'[45] From the outset of the Revolution his political articles and commentaries on events,[46] his pen portraits of the leading actors,[47] were incisive. Journalists of

[44] Born at Bagnols, Gard.
[45] Quoted by V.-H. Debidour, preface, p. 29, to *Ecrits politiques et littéraires*.
[46] *Journal Politique National*, 1789–90.
[47] *Petits Dictionnaire des Grands Hommes de la Révolution par un Citoyen actif, ci-devant Rien*, 1790.

varying political shades were busy in the early days but as the drama unfolded and the scene darkened they, or at any rate all but the demagogues, inevitably lost their audience and consequently their influence.

The reasons underlying Rivarol's whole-hearted and unswerving espousal of the counter-revolutionary causes are not obvious; a love of order, an authoritarian attitude, switched from language to politics, the liking for a certain type of life and society, habit in a word, a commendable gratitude to the Bourbons for past favours, there was something of all this perhaps, but whatever the reasons, the result was a consistent attitude of hostility to the Revolution. Rivarol foreshadows another journalist who like him was a Meridional, like him was to conceive of politics as a sum of historical and intellectual forces that could be accurately assessed, and who, like him, was to see salvation for France in uncompromisingly Monarchist terms; his name is Charles Maurras.[48] Rivarol had emigrated in June 1792 and settled in Berlin. He continued his political activity as a pamphleteer[49] but, like a plant torn from its native soil, this Meridional could not adapt himself to conditions, climatic or social, in Eastern Europe, and died at the threshold of the nineteenth century.

Joseph de Maistre and Bonald, on the other hand, lived to see the cause they defended re-established.[50]

For those in whom the nostalgia of home was the overriding force or who became convinced that there was no hope of putting the clock back, or who hated the thought of bearing arms against their own country, the opportunity came with the amnesty (1802) granted by the First Consul. Las Cases (1766–1842) gives expression to these ideas: 'Assez heureux pour ne pas y[51] avoir débarqué, je pus réfléchir au retour sur l'horrible situation de combattre sa patrie sous des bannières étrangères ... est-il rien qui puisse faire oublier le sol natal ou détruire le charme de respirer l'air de la patrie ...',[52] and having after much hesitation taken the decision to transfer his allegiance to Napoleon, he adhered to it unflinchingly.[53]

Chateaubriand, as we have seen, shared these views and in fact returned to France before the amnesty.

Some *émigrés* there were, however, who were adaptable enough in spirit to show an intelligent awareness of the cultural life of the

[48] See below, vol. V, chap. 6.
[49] *Lettres à la Noblesse française au moment de sa Rentrée en France*, 1792.
[50] See below, pp. 84–7.   [51] At Quiberon.
[52] *Mémorial de Sainte-Hélène* (1822–3), preamble.
[53] He remained at St Helena with Napoleon till the end.

societies they had been thrown into: Camille Jordan, Joseph-Marie de Gerando, Lezay-Marnésia, translator of Schiller's *Don Carlos*, Vanderbourg, friend and translator of Jacobi, the German mystic, and most prominent of all, an exception in the sense that he established himself permanently abroad, Charles de Villers (1765–1815).[54]

Charles de Villers may not have been a man of any creative imagination but his assimilative powers, his intellectual curiosity and his intelligent receptiveness for things Germanic made this 'Janus *bifrons*'[55] into a valuable channel of communication between Frenchmen and Germans. It was he who first brought the philosophy of Kant into the radius of French awareness. His book (1801) on the German philosopher was dedicated to the French Institute. It was not 'crowned' by that body, perhaps because of its unflattering contrasts between the intellectual climate of France and that of Germany. His riposte was a pamphlet entitled *Kant jugé par l'Institut* and, with this parting shot, Villers who had come to Paris with his book on Kant returned to Germany.

He was back in France in 1803 with a second book, *L'Esprit et L'Influence de la Réformation de Luther*, on which the Institute looked favourably; internal politics it seemed had something to do with it;[56] the Institute, a stronghold of the Ideologues and therefore of 'liberal'[57] temper, was glad, by placing a crown of laurels on Villers's brow, to register its hostility to Napoleon's ecclesiastical policy, to Chateaubriand's *Génie du Christianisme* and generally to the upsurge of Catholicism.

Encouraged by this success Villers wished to create a focus of German culture in Paris with the help of other germanophile men of letters and scientists: Benjamin Constant, Gerando, Jordan, Stapfer, Cuvier, Laplace. German works were to be published under the general title of 'Bibliothèque Germanique'. Napoleon, however, looked with a suspicious eye on these activities. The chill wind blowing from high places discouraged Villers's collaborators and he, shaking the dust of Paris from his feet, departed once more to Germany, this time for good, to Göttingen where he was appointed to a Chair of Philosophy. Dismissed by the King of Hanover in 1814 – less tolerant be it noted than Napoleon's brother Jérôme, King of Westphalia, who had left him undisturbed – he died broken-hearted in the same year.

Villers's most successful contribution to Franco-German cultural relations was the beacon-light he provided for Madame de Staël's

---

[54] J.-M. Carré, *Les Ecrivains Français et le Mirage Allemand*, chap. 1 (1947); also P. van Tieghem, op. cit.
[55] Goethe applies the expression to Villers in a letter to Reinhardt.
[56] Carré, op. cit.   [57] In the continental, i.e. anti-religious sense.

approach to the German intellectual scene. She had read his articles in *Le Spectateur du Nord*,[58] she adopted[59] Villers's theory of the two great groups of European literatures, those of the north and those of the south; their paths, his to Paris, hers to Germany, crossed at Metz in 1803. Their subsequent relations were never close, but the fact remains that her views on Germany, though in part drawn from her own travel-impressions, were largely coloured by his opinions, and that the workmanlike exposition of Kant's philosophy which was to figure in *De l'Allemagne* is derived from him.

[58] A newspaper appearing in Hamburg and much read by *émigrés*.
[59] In *De la Littérature*. See above, pp. 37-40.

Chapter 6

MINOR NOVELISTS

THE novel is no less old a literary form in France than the theatre or poetry, but in the seventeenth century it had never achieved the same prestige, because its inherent suppleness made it less amenable to the discipline of art forms. While the classical tradition clamped down on the drama and on lyrical poetry, giving the former a rigidity that kept it erect long after life had become extinct and, in effect, killing the latter by suffocation, the novel was much more sensitive to the evolution of eighteenth-century manners and modes.

During the Revolution and Empire, the novel continues to reflect more faithfully than either the drama or poetry the movement of contemporary taste; receiving much sooner than other genres the impact of contemporary events and individual destinies. Particularly important in these respects are the contributions of Madame de Staël, Constant, Senancour, and Chateaubriand, but they did not stand alone; a profusion of minor writers may be cited in whom the conflicting tendencies characteristic in a time of confusion and violent change are reflected: Madame de Charrière (1741–1805), Madame de Flahault-Souza (1761–1836), Count Xavier de Maistre (1764–1852); all these to a greater or lesser extent look back to the aristocratic society of the eighteenth century; the free-thinking Madame de Charrière's *Caliste* (1787) is a minor masterpiece of psychological analysis that compels attention, so well observed is it, so intelligent, a fitting counterpart to *Adolphe* in that respect, though the situation is not parallel, for Caliste refuses an irregular liaison even at the price of abandon and solitude. The direct product of a bitter personal experience indeed,[1] the novel betrays none of the self-justification or the revolt against supposed social injustice often evident in later personal novels. Caliste accepts the social canons of her day. That Madame de Charrière should have fascinated, if only for a short time, Benjamin Constant, can cause no surprise. No better example of her

---

[1] 'Je n'avais pas eu le courage de la relire: j'avais trop pleuré en l'écrivant' – extract from a letter (1800) about *Caliste* from Madame de Charrière to a Dutch friend.

light malicious irony, reminiscent of Beaumarchais, can be found than in an earlier short story (*Le Noble*, 1763) – which offended the social susceptibilities of her entourage.

In novels such as *Adèle de Soulanges* (1794), *Eugène de Rothelin* (1808), *Eugénie et Mathilde* (1811), Mme de Souza gives to a picture, so idealized as to be quite colourless, of the world she had known in her girlhood, something of the charm that was to be found again in the delicate heroines of Musset's comedies.

Xavier de Maistre who, like his elder brother Joseph, emigrated when the French Revolutionary army invaded Savoy (1792), served as a soldier in Russia and died there. He recalls something of the light and agreeably sentimental attitude of Diderot's *Pensées sur ma vieille Robe de Chambre* (1772) in his *Voyage autour de ma Chambre* (1794); with *Les Prisonniers du Caucase* (1815) he may well claim to have written the first good short story in nineteenth-century French literature, foreshadowing the qualities we associate with Mérimée: objectivity, the well-observed and telling detail, a kind of aristocratic detachment in narrating a story of endurance, cruelty and heroism. In *Le Lépreux de la Cité d'Aoste* (1811), on the other hand, the Romantic idea of human solitude and the consolation of external Nature provide the themes of the story: 'La solitude n'est pas toujours au milieu des forêts et des rochers. L'infortune est seul partout ... Lorsque le chagrin s'appesantit sur moi, et que je ne trouve pas dans le coeur des hommes ce que le mien désire, l'aspect des choses inanimées me console ...'; the leper has something of René but a more generous outward-looking attitude.

The works of Madame Cottin (1770–1807) – e.g. *Claire d'Albe* (1799), *Malvina* (1801), *Elizabeth ou les Exilés de Sibérie* (1806) – in no way echo contemporary events; they are an escape from them. 'Le dégoût, le danger, ou l'effroi du monde ayant fait naître en moi le besoin de me retirer dans un monde idéal ...', she writes.[2] A flight from reality, in fact, into her own inner world where she will be free to excogitate stories of illicit passion and heartbreak (*Claire d'Albe*), jealousy and misunderstanding (*Malvina*), touching filial piety (*Elizabeth*), with little or no interference from the tyranny of reality. Yet these works reflect contemporary attitudes. Madame Cottin's harsh experience in the revolutionary years may explain the melancholy that characterizes her heroines.

A strong contemporary flavour is also present in *Valérie* (1803) by Madame de Krüdener (1764–1824). Madame de Krüdener's subsequent excursions into mysticism, her relations with the Tsar Alexander I, her role as a sort of presiding deity to the Holy Alliance gave her a European notoriety, long-since forgotten. Her

[2] Preface to *Claire d'Albe*.

one excursion into fiction has provided her with a more permanent if minor memorial; *Valérie* is an early example of the personal novel with the author cast in the name part. The chief interest however attaches to Gustave[3] through whose love-lorn eyes alone we see Valérie. But Valérie is the wife of another, to whom, moreover, Gustave is devoted; Gustave must therefore love, suffer, fade and die without a word; well, not quite; his letters to the long-suffering Ernest provide him with a derivative and the reader with a record of his torturing and fatal passion to which Valérie remains . . . obtusely? – or in any case obstinately oblivious.[4] Its ascending and descending graph is plotted with some skill; *Valérie* is indeed superior to the work of Madame Cottin and Madame de Souza, not by the slight variant upon an otherwise conventional triangular situation but by Gustave's self-analysis which shows a certain degree of attentive observation and which – this being the important point – reveals him as a typical if minor figure in his generation. The Baltic baroness,[5] with the desolate coasts of Scandinavian seas in her mind's eye, has created a veritable northern René: 'la solitude des mers, leur vaste silence ou leur orageuse activité, . . . le cri mélancolique de l'oiseau qui aime nos régions glacées, la triste et douce clarté de nos aurores boréales . . . ; j'ai changé de ciel; mais j'ai emporté avec moi mes fantastiques songes et mes voeux immodérés . . .'[6]

The impact of the Revolution on the work of Pigault-Lebrun (1753–1835) is different; confusion, violence, unbridled imagination coupled with the coarsest realism of vomit and chamberpot – all these had existed in the popular novel of the seventeenth century:[7] they disappear[8] in the eighteenth century or rather are transmuted into boudoir eroticism and suggestiveness. Now they burst into literature again like a flood, in the chaotic profusion of Pigault-Lebrun's novels: e.g. *L'Enfant du Carnaval* (1792), *Les Barons de Felsheim* (1798), *Angélique et Jeanneton* (1799), *Monsieur Botte* (1802) – picaresque novels in effect, where against a Revolutionary background very often, the characters play out the wildest adventures, and social inequalities are redressed by the hero's marrying above him (*L'Enfant du Carnaval*), or below him

[3] Modelled on the tragic Alexander de Stakieff, one-time lover of Madame de Krüdener and who committed suicide when she threw him over.

[4] Letter xlii: 'Valérie ne m'avait pas compris ou ne voulait pas me comprendre . . .'

[5] Madame de Krüdener, née Vietinghoff, was born at Riga.

[6] Letter ii.

[7] e.g. *Francion* (1622), *Le Roman comique* (1651).

[8] Restif de la Bretonne is an exception. They also cross the Channel – Smollett.

(*Monsieur Botte*) and settling down. The verve is tremendous and is accompanied by occasional moments of repose where the author moralizes and reflects, as it were, on the significance of the scene:

Tout tendait à une désorganisation générale. Le peuple, étourdi par la rapidité des événements ne savait ce qu'il devait craindre ou espérer. Sans gouvernement, sans loi, sans morale, sans pain, il voyait ses bourreaux insulter à sa misère et salir les murs d'affiches, adressées au peuple souverain. Quel souverain, Grand Dieu! On le flagornait, on le trompait... et il ne s'en doutait pas... La crédulité des peuples est le patrimoine de ceux qui savent les tromper.[9]

Pigault is a materialist and a staunch opponent of the Christian religion. He carries over the Voltairian tradition into the nineteenth century; the laborious polemics of *Le Citateur* (1803) were to have an echo in the witticisms of Edmond About[10] or the elephantine jests of Francisque Sarcey, inveighing against the happenings of La Salette and Lourdes;[11] Le Père Jean-François[12] – unworthy Capuchin – can claim a distant relation in Abbé Jérôme Coignard.[13]

Pigault-Lebrun, like the authors of the horror novels,[14] is a forgotten figure, yet his and their influence was considerable; the nineteenth-century giants of the serial novel: Alexandre Dumas, Eugène Sue, Frédéric Soulié, derive from them; nor can the Romantic movement itself disdain a connection inasmuch as mystery and violence have their place in it.

[9] *L'Enfant du Carnaval*, chap. 21.
[10] G. Weill, *Hist. de l'idée laïque en France au dix-neuvieme Siècle*, 1925, p. 235.
[11] *Ibid.*, pp. 236, 237.   [12] *Enfant du carnaval.*
[13] Anatole France: *La Rôtisserie de la Reine Pédauque* and *Les Opinions de M. Jérôme Coignard.*
[14] See above, p. 30.

Part II

The Romantic Era 1815–1850

§ I UNDER THE RESTORATION

Chapter 7

POLITICAL AND INTELLECTUAL BACKGROUND

FRANCE as fashioned administratively and juridically by the Revolution and Napoleon was a stable structure; there was no putting the clock back. Politically, however, the problem remained open; what form of state was France to adopt? Monarchy – and, if Monarchy, what sort of Monarchy? Empire? Republic?

The Romantic era has as its background a succession of régimes between 1814 and 1852 which tried to find an answer to that question: the 'Hundred Days' (March–June 1815), the Restorations (First 1814–5, Second 1815–30), the 'July Monarchy' (1830–48), the Second Republic (1848–52), a succession of régimes destroyed in turn by invasion (1814 and 1815) or revolution – *Les Trois Glorieuses* (July 1830), the February Revolution (1848), the 'June Days' (1848), the *coup d'état* (1851) – not to speak of the abortive attempts during the July Monarchy. The pendulum swings between insurrection and resurrection. Each régime in turn is forced to make a compromise between its own pure doctrine and the spirit of liberalism diffused throughout the body politic by the French Revolution: right of conquest – of genius perhaps? – and liberalism with Napoleon, democratic Caesarism, in short; divine right and liberalism with the Bourbons; 'Juste Milieu', poised on theoretical national sovereignty, with Louis-Philippe; popular sovereignty in practice as well as theory with 'Marianne II', a glorious moment of euphoric political romanticism in Paris (February), soon deflated by provincial realism (June); democratic Caesarism, once more, with Napoleon III.

Napoleon's return from Elba had sent shock-waves of trepidation through Europe, felt as far afield at St Petersburg: 'le retour de Bonaparte est tout aussi miraculeux que sa chute', writes Joseph de Maistre.[1] The word miraculous is not excessive; before the danger was finally dispersed on the plains of Waterloo, Napoleon

---

[1] Letter to 'M le Chevalier de . . .', St Petersburg, 11 April 1815: 'J'avais fermé et envoyé mon paquet aujourd'hui, lorsque la confirmation des fatales nouvelles de France nous est arrivée . . .' Letter No. 97, J. de M., *Lettres et Opuscules Inédits*, 1853.

had had the time to perform what seems indeed a miracle; he stamped his foot and up sprang an army of thousands, munitions, commissariat and all, that nearly won the day![2] The genius of war's image was refurbished, his legend was to grow, and, sheltering within its mantle, Bonapartism, destined to explode like a time bomb later on in the century.[3] Meanwhile liberalism was to profit from Bonapartist sentiments, for the military *coup* – it was scarcely more – of the 'Hundred Days' was too short an interval to develop its potential ethos; only the signs are there in the still-born *Acte additionnel aux Constitutions de l'Empire*, the work of the liberal Benjamin Constant.[4]

The Restoration gave France a charter that was generous, in comparison with what existed elsewhere in Europe; the compromise could satisfy no one for long, however; least of all the 'Ultras', who claimed to represent the pure doctrine of Monarchy and prominent amongst whom was Chateaubriand, more royalist than the moderate Louis XVIII, 'Ce jacobin fleurdelysé', as Balzac called him;[5] they had high hopes, soon frustrated, of better things under Charles X. At least in their opposition to the Revolution, they had champions on the plane of ideas in Joseph de Maistre[6] (1753–1821) and Louis de Bonald (1754–1840), who reflect the pure ethos of the Restoration.

As *émigrés*, withdrawn from events, both could view the Revolution as a whole phenomenon, endeavour to place it in their scheme of things. De Maistre read and admired Burke; from Saint-Martin[7] he derived the idea that providence alone had brought about the Revolution to purify humanity and to prepare the reign of a regenerate Christianity. The impact of divine providence upon human affairs is the central theme of de Maistre's political thought: 'Nous sommes tous attachés au trône de l'être suprême par une chaîne souple, qui nous retient sans nous asservir ...'[8] There, at the outset, the keynote is struck.

Bonald had also emigrated.[9] His first work (of many) also appeared in 1796 – *Théorie du pouvoir politique et religieux dans la société civile, démontrée par le raisonnement et l'histoire.*

Like that of de Maistre, Bonald's system is theocentric. They are

---

[2] 'A' damned nice thing, the nearest run thing you ever saw in your life' – Wellington's comment to Creevey, the day after the battle.
[3] See below, pp. 253–4. [4] See above, p. 58.
[5] *Duchesse de Langeais.*
[6] When the Revolutionary armies under General de Montesquiou invaded his native Savoy (1792), de Maistre emigrated; then only did he discover his talent as a polemist in his *Lettres d'un Royaliste Savoisien* (1793) and *Considérations sur la France* (1796).
[7] Louis Claude de Saint-Martin (1743–1803), 'Le Philosophe inconnu', freemason and mystic. Mentioned by Chateaubriand, *Mémoires d'Outre-Tombe.*
[8] *Considérations*, chap. 1. [9] To Heidelberg (1790).

alike in their loyalties to throne and altar, alike in their condemnation of the Revolution. 'Est-il possible', de Maistre wrote to
Bonald, 'que la nature se soit amusée à tendre deux cordes si
parfaitement d'accord que votre esprit et le mien?'[10] Bonald did
not altogether share de Maistre's opinion, thinking no doubt of
their different approach within the common framework: de Maistre's emphasis on history as touchstone of his political philosophy,
his own appeal to natural order; de Maistre's ultra-montanism (*Du
Pape*, 1819), which in the last resort made him a doubtful ally of
the 'Ultras', his own leaning towards state authority, which made
it at least possible for him to serve – albeit with no enthusiasm –
the Napoleonic régime, and which makes him a Gallican. They are
different also in style; de Maistre, all fire and vigour, not without
lighter touches of irony, Bonald, massive, relentless. Between them
they provided the 'Ultras' with a doctrine that gave that party an
intellectual homogeneity they were not to retain after 1830, and
that the parties to the Left, unorganized at this time, were not to
achieve until the advent of Karl Marx.

Both were the product of their time in that their appeal, to history on the one hand, and the natural order on the other, seemed
to have their triumphant justification in the Restoration. With the
fall of that order of society, however, what becomes of their political
structure? If they be right, humanity is out of step. But though
their political and religious ideas belong to a past era, there is one
work at least of Joseph de Maistre that has not lost its resonance –
Les Soirées de St Pétersbourg (posth. 1821). Whereas Bonald's
powerful mind seems wholly absorbed in problems of power and
the political ordering of society, de Maistre in *Les Soirées de St
Pétersbourg* turns aside from political thought and speaks as a
moralist about problems that concern or may concern the individual at any time: the happiness of the froward, the misfortunes of the righteous ...; crime and punishment; suffering or
the wages of sin; prayer ... 'la prière est la respiration de l'âme';
war.

Nothing in all de Maistre's writings is more characteristic of the
stark unflinching nature of his thought than this long meditation
on war: 'Dans le vaste domaine de la nature vivante, il règne une
violence manifeste, une espèce de rage prescrite qui arme tous les
êtres ... cette loi s'arrêtera-t-elle à l'homme?' Indeed not, for war
is a law of nature and hence divine: 'la guerre est donc divine en
elle-même, puisque c'est une loi du monde.'

From his apocalyptic vision of the Angel of Death encircling the
globe and striking now here now there, de Maistre turns to the
moral factor in war. What, in the last resort, wins or loses battles,

[10] Letter to Bonald, 10 July 1818, Turin. J. de M., Letter No. 157, op. cit.

he asks, only to reply: 'C'est l'opinion qui perd les batailles et c'est l'opinion qui les gagne . . .'; a matter of belief, in fact, of will.

If this powerful soliloquy on war is for the most part placed on the metaphysical and moral planes of Providence, belief, will-power, those mysterious forces impelling men and nations, the author does not on that account fail to think closely and concretely about the physical nature of a battle as it affects the individual: 'possédé tour à tour par la crainte, par l'espérance, par la rage, par cinq ou six ivresses différentes, que devient l'homme? que voit-il? Que sait-il au bout de quelques heures?' Fabrice del Dongo after his experience at Waterloo surely thought the same.

Les Soirées de St Pétersbourg in general and more particularly the Miltonic effulgence of the meditation on war provides further evidence of the theocentric character of de Maistre's thought: men's individual lives, humanity's existence in time, society as built up in history are in the hands of God, a God of justice and wrath, punishing man in his flesh for his sins, by suffering. To that we are all doomed because of human corruption.

De Maistre's faith, like that of the other theocratic thinkers of the day, is full of awe; life is enshrouded in mystery; men, though responsible moral beings, are none the less, like society, impelled by mysterious divine forces; not reason, but the will, that mysterious element that lies on a deeper level of the psyche, wins battles, just as imagination, fear, 'la froide déesse', loses them.

These attitudes have a strong Romantic flavour; like the political philosophy that is an extension of them, they are a brilliant re-flection of the ethos of their time, a period of Revolution, of struggle, of expiation (as de Maistre would say – and how Roman-tic a theme that will become![11]), a period when one man alone – Napoleon, in whom the genius of war with its dynamic of will and energy had become individuated – held Europe in fee. No wonder that de Maistre and Bonald with their polemical power should have been adopted as standard-bearers by the Restoration. The pure stream of their thought became muddied as it flowed into politics; the 'Ultras' were less concerned to grasp the niceties of their intellectual champions' thought on the origins and character of power, on the divine or natural order of things, than to recap-ture material and political positions lost in the Revolution. None the less, these champions created an image of society that Restora-tion opinion gratefully accepted. The aristocracy had toyed with liberalism in the late eighteenth century and had expiated their

[11] cf. Hugo, *Les Misérables* (see below, pp. 299 *et seq.*); Dostoievsky, *Crime and Punishment*.

foolishness. They were the first to return to the Catholic fold. Later in the century, as we shall see, their example will be followed by the upper bourgeoisie. In the meantime we must follow the development of Romanticism in literature during the Restoration.

Chapter 8

I. NODIER

CHARLES NODIER (1780–1844) had wide interests: botanical, entomological, bibliographical, historical, literary – wide rather than profound; his historical writings: e.g. *Souvenirs, épisodes et portraits pour servir à l'histoire de la Révolution* (1833), *le Dernier Banquet des Girondins* (1833), are of dubious value; his name suggests at once the cultivated even the erudite dilettante.

He is chiefly remembered as a sponsor of the Romantic movement. Appointed librarian at the Arsenal Library[1] in 1823, he was in a good position to combine his amiable social gifts and his literary interests. His salon became the headquarters of the *avant-garde* of the day – 'la grande boutique romantique', as Musset called it; the members of the first *cénacle*, many of whom had been contributors to *La Muse française*,[2] were assiduous visitors: Hugo, Vigny, Emile Deschamps, co-founder with Hugo of *La Muse française*, his brother Antony, Sainte-Beuve still in the Romantic camp, Musset; lesser lights such as Ulrich Guttinger, Arvers,[3] Rességuier, Aloysius Bertrand, Pétrus Borel; painters and engravers: Louis Boulanger, the brothers Deveria, the brothers Johannot; the sculptor David d'Angers. At no time was the link closer than in the heroic days of Romanticism between the arts and literature.[4]

Nodier had had a brief acquaintance with Dalmatia in 1813 when for some months he was librarian at Laibach. There he sketched out the story of *Jean Sbogar* (1818), the brigand who under the name of Lothario wins the love of the fair Antonia, is finally captured and shot by the French. In itself the story has little merit; it switches uncomfortably from descriptions that have the stamp of authenticity[5] to the most arbitrary invention where the

[1] See Saint-Beuve, *Portraits Contemporains*, Vol. I. The library was originally founded in the eighteenth century by the Ms. de Paulmy, who sold it in 1785 to the Cte d'Artois. It was confiscated during the Revolution and opened to the public in 1797.
[2] Literary review founded by Victor Hugo, 1823–4; monarchist and Catholic in outlook.
[3] Author of the sonnet: 'Ma vie a son secret . . .', almost better known by the pastiches it became a prey to. See L. Deffoux, *Le Pastiche Littéraire*, 1932, pp. 97–99.
[4] See Théophile Gautier, *Histoire du Romantisme* (1872), *passim*.
[5] e.g. the opening description of the surroundings of Trieste; or the description of sirocco weather at Trieste, chap. 4.

stage trappings of the popular horror novel take the place of direct
personal observation:

> ... elle parcourait les vastes galeries, les escaliers immenses, les salles
> gothiques du château, en se confirmant de plus en plus dans l'horrible idée
> qu'elle était prisonnière à Duino ...

The hero and heroine are no better observed, but as Romantic
figures they are particularly characteristic; the ethereal beauty of
Antonia, the sombre beauty of Lothario Sbogar, a prey to the tor-
tures of disbelief,[6] whose love is as the kiss of death[7] and withal a
truly noble brigand in revolt against society for the most laudable
reasons – at least in his view.[8] In the portrait gallery of Romantic
heroes the Byronic Jean Sbogar has an important place. Interesting
for its period character, the story has little other value.

More interesting is the dream-tale, Smarra[9] (1821). To claim
significance and originality for a tale that is no more than a
confused dream inspired by Chapter I of the Golden Ass of Lucius
Apuleius may seem to need some defending. Have not dreams
appeared often in literature from the Bible to the horror novels?
In Biblical times a man's mind in sleep was presumably thought of
as a screen on to which Jehovah could project his mysterious communications, using pictures to get over the language bar. Dramatists down the centuries – Seneca, Calderón and Shakespeare, Corneille and Racine, all their dreary successors, have used them as a
device in the action of a play or for a dramatic effect of terror or
guilt on a character. Nowhere, however, had the phenomenon
been examined as a psychological process in itself; dreams as related by the characters in question turn out to be a logical if unusual chain of cause and effect of which the character retains a
clear recollection – evidently he must, for the needs of the play and
the benefit of the audience. Nodier's comment is apt:

> Il n'y a pas vingt ans que le songe était de rigueur, quand on composait une
> tragédie; j'en ai entendu cinquante et malheureusement il semblait à les
> entendre, que leurs auteurs n'eussent jamais rêvé.[10]

At this point in the preface, Nodier seems to intend presenting
the phenomenon in a manner more closely related to the reality,
presumably by close attention to his own dream-experience. In fact
he has done no more, as he admits in the preface, than follow his
classical model, mainly with the idea of enriching his story-telling

---

[6] Chap. 9, 'Ma voix le prie, mon coeur l'appelle, et rien ne me répond'.
[7] Chap. 11, 'Mon amour donne la mort'.   [8] Chap. 11, passim.
[9] 'The Sanskrit word for love is smara; it is derived from smar, to recol-
lect; the same root has supplied the German schmerz, pain, and the
English smart ...' (A. R. Oliver, Charles Nodier, 1964, pp. 134, 135).
[10] Smarra, Préface Nouvelle.

from a source so unsatisfactorily tapped, as he thought. Yet the dream of Lorenzo, with its visions of delight and visions of horror melting into each other with kaleidoscopic confusion, has the stamp of authenticity because of the process of free association so characteristic of dreams.

Nodier may thus fairly claim to have been the first French writer in the nineteenth century to exploit the fact that the human mind in a state of sleep is a phenomenon worthy of attention. 'Vous commencez cette vie nocturne qui se passe... dans des mondes toujours nouveaux...'[11] 'Cette vie nocturne...', the phrase is significant. Does it not suggest for Nodier, that sleep is not necessarily a plunging of the mind into an unconscious void but its transference to a different plane of awareness where images and impressions may gain in intensity because they are an inner vision, where exterior sounds – and whose experience would not confirm this? – may be made to slot with ease into the structure of a dream where they had no place at first: 'Le bruit du vent qui pleure ou siffle entre les ais mal joints de la croisée, voilà tout ce qui vous reste des impressions ordinaires de vos sens, et au bout de quelques instants, vous imaginez que ce murmure lui-même existe en vous. Il devient une voix de votre âme, l'écho d'une idée indéfinissable mais fixe qui se confond avec les premières perceptions du sommeil.' As a tale, *Smarra* may not be particularly successful, but it seems to point the way to Nerval, to Proust,[12] to the Surrealists.

With all his whimsicality Nodier had a clear view on the potential of the short story: 'il y a plusieurs espèces d'histoires fantastiques...'[13] *Trilby* (1822), *La Fée aux Miettes* (1832), *Hélène Gillet* (1832), *Trésor des Fèves et Fleur des pois* (1833), *La Combe de l'homme mort* (1833), *Inès de las Sierras* (1837), *Le Chien de Brisquet*... all provide variations on the fantastic theme: 'O fantaisie!... Mère des fables riantes, des génies et des fées!... toi qui te balances d'un pied léger sur les créneaux des vieilles tours et qui t'égares au clair de la lune avec ton cortège d'illusions dans les domaines immenses de l'inconnu...'[14]

The imagination may draw its inspiration from the stage properties of Romanticism – 'les créneaux des vieilles tours', but it may also wander with a kind of investigating mission into the world of the unknown – the world of sleep (*Smarra*), and the world of lunacy – of a gentle sort (*La Fée aux Miettes*): Michel the carpenter is a mythomaniac who believes in the reality of what his imagination has created; illusion and reality in a form parallel

[11] *Smarra*, Prologue.
[12] *Du côté de chez Swann*, Vol. I, chap. 1. 'Un homme qui dort tient autour de lui...'.
[13] *Histoire d'Hélène Gillet*.   [14] *La Fée aux Miettes*, Vol. I.

to that of dreaming and waking, and again with sound observation behind it.

Nodier's whimsical fancy delighted to hover on the borderlands of reality. Dreamland, fairyland, mystery, these were as real to him as normal experience, these were his province.

II. LAMARTINE

In March 1820 a small collection of twenty-four poems was published anonymously under the title *Méditations Poétiques*. A second edition containing two additional poems[15] and bearing the author's name appeared in April; further editions followed each other in quick succession during the year; almost from one day to the next Alphonse de Lamartine (1790–1869) had achieved fame.

An immediate success of this order may be the reward of a work's intrinsic merits or it may denote a favourable conjunction of circumstances, a coincidence, rarely attained, between the work and contemporary sensibility. Both factors were present in the success of the *Méditations*.

In that indeterminate moral region that at any given time governs literary attitudes and taste, the dominant force at this moment, the father figure, was Chateaubriand. His impact, as we have seen, had been tremendous at the beginning of the century with *Atala*, *Le Génie du Christianisme*, and *René*; he had stocked men's imaginations, satisfied their emotions, sentimental and religious, provided the image of a generation in René (Senancour providing a pale shadow with Obermann), and all this in a style that still had enough of the old classical *style noble* to lull readers into thinking they were getting what they were used to, but yet was rich in new sensations: solemn majestic rhythms, nostalgic suggestions, the chiaroscuro of blue moonlight. Chateaubriand had moulded the sensibility of an age, its imagery, style, taste; the Napoleonic years had obscured, not destroyed these, and the return of peace in 1814 seemed to offer them the chance of reasserting their influence. But such effects take time and in any case the tremors of the Napoleonic aftermath – the Hundred Days, Waterloo, the White Terror – took time to subside.

By 1820 the Restoration had weathered its early difficulties, the liberal opposition was in disarray, 'Ultra' society was firmly entrenched, the alliance between throne and altar solid. The murder of the Duc de Berry (1820) was to strengthen the hold of the Right; Chateaubriand's political star, leading figure that he had become in 'Ultra' political circles, was in the ascendant; he was

[15] 'La Retraite' and 'Le Génie'. Levaillant, *Lamartine, Oeuvres Choisies* (1909), p. 103.

still the dominant literary influence, the moral attitudes, the literary images and style he had created between 1800 and 1805 still the literary fashion. Further, the religious sensibility he had stimulated and canalized into Catholic channels had received an impetus, the inevitable one-ness of throne and altar had been strengthened by Lamennais' *Essai sur l'Indifférence*. One thing only was lacking in 1820 – a great poet to give poetic form to the prevailing mood. It was as though some religious sect having contented itself of necessity with minor prophets – Millevoye, Chênedollé, Marceline Desbordes-Valmore – awaited its promised saviour . . . and found him.

Lamartine's family background, religious and royalist, prepared him to express with sincerity the aspirations of the Restoration's social élite; his youthful experience and upbringing had attuned him to Chateaubriand's attitudes; indeed, much in the young Lamartine at Milly and Saint-Point recalls Chateaubriand at Combourg – a youth with no outlet for his energies[16] and filled with vague, as yet shapeless longings, a prey to solitude and *ennui*, filling his time with voracious unorganized reading.

Above all, Lamartine had found a directly personal source of inspiration in a profound emotional experience: his love for Julie Charles whom he had met at Aix-les-Bains in October 1816 and who died of tuberculosis in December 1817; here too, one could establish a parallel with Chateaubriand and Pauline de Beaumont.[17]

In every respect the *Méditations* appealed to contemporary taste; inspiration from the psalms for the high Catholics:

> Je répandrai mon âme au seuil du sanctuaire,
> Seigneur; dans ton nom seul je mettrai mon espoir . . .
>
> ('Chants Lyriques de Saül').

Odes in the classical manner for the devotees of Lebrun-Pindar:

> Muse, contemple ta victoire! . . .
>
> ('L'Enthousiasme').

Rhyming couplets in the traditional manner of the moralists:

> Borné dans sa nature, infini dans ses voeux,
> L'homme est un dieu tombé qui se souvient des cieux . . .
>
> ('L'Homme').

And finally – pearls amongst these classical ashes – a series of elegies with an irresistible appeal for the public as a whole, irrespective of tradition, creed or taste: 'L'Isolement', 'Le Soir', 'Le Vallon', 'Souvenir', 'Le Lac', 'Invocation', 'L'Automne'.

---

[16] Family tradition prevented his serving Napoleon, family status excluded any other form of activity, e.g. commerce.

[17] *Mémoires d'Outre-Tombe*, Part II, Bks. 2–4, *passim*.

All these poems, from 'Invocation' (1816), written at the time of the poet's first meeting with Julie Charles,[18] to 'L'Automne' (1819), are inspired by that tragic episode; all, with exception of 'Invocation', where there is a mood of uncertain hope, express the poet's grief and despair; the very regularity of the alexandrines gives emphasis to this impression in the reader's mind. The poet seeks out places intimately connected with his experience:

> O Lac! l'année à peine a fini sa carrière
> Et près des flots chéris qu'elle devait revoir,
> Regarde! Je viens seul m'asseoir sur cette pierre
> Où tu la vis s'asseoir!

Or he recalls those hours and seasons: sunset, evening, autumn, when Nature's moods reflect and soothe his own:

> ... le deuil de la nature convient à la douleur et plaît à mes regards.
>
> ('L'Automne').

But in spite of the close connexion between these poems and his personal experience, Lamartine, by instinct or by what remained of classical restraint – modesty, Gide would call it,[19] has muted the personal note; the confession element is no more than the source of moods the poet communicates in an immediately accessible form to the reader who responds either from personal experience or, more likely, from imagination drawing on the broadest human experience.

This universalized character of the poems is further emphasized by the general lack of descriptive definition; the reminders of Chateaubriand's idiom are constant; their fusion with the underlying but restrained sincerity of the poet contribute to the immediacy of the communication of mood; no well observed pictures arise in the reader's mind to change the nature of his response.

This small group of poems has a dual claim to our attention. Historically, for all their classical character, they are the fountainhead of the great period of Romantic poetry, of themes that other lyrical poets will take up and develop: the transience of human things, the intimate communion with Nature, the vision of a pure love freed from all the temptations of the flesh.

Whether Julie Charles was anything like the sentimentalized portrait Lamartine painted of her many years later[20] is irrelevant. By fading early she quickly became the ethereal Elvire, that pathetic phantom hovering over the poems, the ideal image of woman for a whole generation. The pallid, faintly anaemic and thereby interesting type who suffered from the vapours, went into a decline and aroused men's protective solicitude. Elvire too has faded, with

---

[18] *Méditations*, Garnier edn., Introduction.
[19] André Gide, *Nouveaux Prétextes* (1911).   [20] *Raphaël.*

much other romantic bric-à-brac; since her day we have known other types: Greta Garbo in the nineteen-twenties, Brigitte Bardot in the nineteen-fifties.

Apart from their period aspect, these few poems – a minority in the *Méditations* – have fixed for all time the Lamartinian image, the poet of elegiac moods, of blurred landscapes bathed in moonlight.

The appeal is perhaps limited and obvious; it remains on the superficial level of our being, but within its limits it is perennial. The impact of the *Méditations* – or rather of this small group of poems – has moreover been so strong that it has tended to eclipse everything else that Lamartine wrote, like a principal actor who likes to draw all the applause to himself. We may be aware, purely as a matter of chronology, that Lamartine lived until 1869, but what could the remaining forty-nine years after the *Méditations Poétiques* have been filled up with? They are far from being the void we are apt to think: an abundant poetic flow, copious prose works, an active political life that led him almost to the summit, only to cast him down with merciless suddenness.

Yet that we forget Lamartine as a literary force after 1820 suggests that his later work either does no more than accentuate the Lamartinian image derived from the *Méditations Poétiques* or belongs to the tastes and interests of an age we have, for the time being at any rate, turned away from. The facts broadly but not entirely confirm that view.

The success of the *Méditations Poétiques* had happy consequences for Lamartine, apart from literary fame. He who for lack of powerful support in high places had been constrained in 1814 to accept, without much enthusiasm for soldiering, a commission in the *Gardes du Corps*,[21] suddenly found doors opening that had till then remained shut. He was offered – and again the parallel with Chateaubriand after the success of *Atala* and *Le Génie* is striking – a position in the diplomatic service, the goal of his desires, and the promise of a post in the diplomatic service in its turn facilitated his marriage.[22]

Lamartine's career as a diplomat was spasmodic: an appointment lasting only a few months as attaché at Naples, in the second half of the year 1820; a second and more important appointment at Florence as secretary in October 1825 was to last over two years.

He had known both Naples and Florence in 1811 during his eleven months' Italian journey, first escape from the narrow provincial life of Burgundy . . . in the footsteps of Corinne. Naples had been the scene of the sentimental adventures later to be re-

---

[21] He resigned his commission in November 1815.
[22] To Marianna-Elisa Birch, June 1820, at Chambéry.

corded in the pages of *Graziella* (1849). The Florence embassy under the benign sway of the Marquis de Maisonfort[23] particularly attracted him; there, as first secretary and for a great part of the time chargé d'affaires, Lamartine became a career diplomat, and showed a hitherto unrevealed aspect of his character: his realistic grasp of politics. None the less, the demands of diplomacy upon his time in the end became irksome, for poetry remained his major interest, and the years since the *Méditations Poétiques* had not been without fruit: the *Nouvelles Méditations* (1823), *La Mort de Socrate* (1823), *Le Dernier Chant du Pèlerinage de Childe Harold* (1825), *Harmonies Poétiques et Religieuses* (1830).

If the *Méditations Poétiques* had had favourable results in the material sphere they had also by their success created pressure for a sequel. The eager expectancy was disappointed when the sequel came, although here was the same mixture as before: a number of love poems – 'Apparition', 'Consolation', 'Le Crucifix', 'Chant d'Amour', 'Ischia', 'Le Poète Mourant', 'Les Préludes', 'Le Passé'; the religious and political themes were also there as before in poems such as 'Les Etoiles', 'L'Esprit de Dieu', 'Bonaparte'; a few earlier poems – 'A El***', 'Sapho', 'Tristesse', etc., were added for good measure.

What then had gone awry? The happy conjunction, whereby different sections of opinion had each for its own reasons been unanimous in praise three years earlier, was no longer present: those who remained faithful to classical forms had deserted to Casimir Delavigne; 'Ultra' opinion found more to their taste in Victor Hugo's Odes – no doubt about his being a 'party' poet, as he plucked his lyre in praise of the Virgins of Verdun or the Martyrs of Vendée, but was this certain of Lamartine?

'Soldat vengeur des rois, plus grands que ces rois mêmes...'[24] ('Bonaparte') was a disturbing line; true, the poet only meant it if Bonaparte had been on the right side, but the very suggestion...

Worse still; soliloquising on the ruins of Rome an apostrophe to liberty had escaped him:

> Liberté! Nom sacré profané par cet âge
> J'ai toujours dans mon coeur adoré ton image...
>
> ('La Liberté'.)

Could a liberal wolf be hiding under the wool? But the keenest disappointment was felt by those who had wanted a second monochrome image, with the same blurred outlines of the ethereal Elvire and of her disconsolate lover. Their wishes received almost

---

[23] 'Philosophie', last of the *Nouvelles Méditations*, dedicated to him.
[24] Garnier, op. cit., Introduction.

no satisfaction; only in 'Apparition' could they recapture something of the old cadences:

> Toi qui du jour mourant consoles la nature,
> Parais, flambeau des nuits lève-toi dans les cieux;
> Etends autour de moi, sur la pâle verdure,
> Les douteuses clartés d'un jour mystérieux . . .

But where is the disconsolate lover of 'Le Lac'? Certainly not in 'Chant d'Amour' or 'Ischia', scarcely in 'Le Poète Mourant' despite the title, or in 'Le Passé'. He is found, to be sure, in 'Le Crucifix', but here another shock awaited the devotees of the earlier Lamartine.

The poem has two themes and is a skilful conflation of them.[25] The part dealing with the crucifix evokes Elvire only incidentally, and apart from one concrete detail: 'sa bouche expirante . . .' scarcely disturbs her delicate image.

But this return to Elvire comes only in the second half of the poem; too late, for meanwhile the first part of the poem evokes a strikingly concrete image before the reader's eyes not of the shadowy Elvire but of Julie Charles on her death bed:

> De son pieux espoir son front gardait la trace . . .
> Le vent qui caressait sa tête échevelée . . .
> Un de ses bras pendait de la funèbre couche;
> L'autre languissamment replié sur son coeur, . . .

What more precise, what more disturbing to those who were not interested as Lamartine was in pathetic – morbid, some might say – details about Julie Charles, but who wanted to recapture under the caress of Elvire's wing a mood of seraphic melancholy?

The exact physical notations in the first part of the poem are in marked contrast with 'Le Lac', for instance. Lamartine derived them from letters he had received,[26] describing Julie Charles' last moments; we know that Lamartine was not present himself in spite of what the poem says:

> Et moi, debout . . .
> Je n'osais m'approcher . . .

Precise observation such as Lamartine displays here is usually the result of a calm, detached attitude of mind; great grief descends like a fog, isolating its victim and obliterating external impressions. Lamartine may have been trying to objectify his grief and rid himself of it, or perhaps time and distance had done their work, for a year or two at least had passed before the composition of this part of the poem, and from the evidence of the second part, a much

---

[25] Levaillant, op. cit., pp. 254 *et seq.*
[26] One from Virieu, one from Doctor Alin. Levaillant, op. cit., p. 254.

longer time had elapsed before the whole poem received its final form:

> Sept fois,[27] depuis ce jour, l'arbre que j'ai planté
> Sur sa tombe sans nom a changé de feuillage . . .

The second half of the poem, where the poet's attention seems mostly turned inwards on his own grief or on the mystery of death, may be the result of a greater emotion than the first part. Small personal objects that have belonged to someone we have loved have a catalytic effect; they concentrate our submerged memories, revive and release our emotions; to throw away such objects, however useless, seems like a betrayal or an unkindness towards the dead that few of us willingly commit.

But the increased attention to physical detail and precise notation is not confined to the first part of 'Le Crucifix'. It is noticeable in a number of poems of *Les Nouvelles Méditations*; contrast for example 'Ischia' with the earlier 'Le Golfe de Baïa'. Lamartine's poetic verve seems to have left its classical chrysalis and flown beyond the point where opinion at that time was prepared to follow it. Yet for the modern reader this change from the *Méditations Poétiques*, this greater definition of reality, is a merit in *Les Nouvelles Méditations*; direct communication of mood floating as it were in the infinite is effective, but if repeated, cloys:

> De Philomèle et du poète
> Les plus doux chants sont des soupirs . . .
>
> ('Adieux à la Poésie'.)

Perhaps, but in moderation.

La Mort de Socrate develops, with a fine balance between Lamartinian suavity and eloquence, a form of philosophical meditation already present in the *Méditations Poétiques*, 'l'Homme' or 'L'Immortalité', which with its salute:

> Je te salue O mort! Libérateur céleste . . .

foreshadows the spiritualist attitude that Lamartine adopts in developing Plato's *Phaedo* into a long meditation on death, skilfully interwoven with the last scenes of Socrates' farewell to his friends and to life. The same abundant vigour of mind – and breath – is to be found in *Le Dernier Chant du Pèlerinage*, more interesting to a modern reader not only for the admiration Lamartine (with his generation) felt for Byron, but also for the development of Lamartine's own philosophy, political and religious. Signs of his moving towards liberalism had not been wanting; now, no doubt remains, fanned as his enthusiasm is by Byron and the cause of

[27] As Levaillant points out, Mme Charles died in December 1817; the *Nouvelles Méditations* were published in September 1823. How does Lamartine calculate seven?

Greek independence, one of liberalism's earliest manifestations on the European scene in the nineteenth century:

> Muse[28] des derniers temps! divinité sublime
> Sentiment plus qu'humain que l'homme déifie,
> Viens seul! c'est à toi seul que mon cœur sacrifie!

The noble Harold is not deaf to the call. With him we embark from Italy, where Byron had left him, and sail for Greece, animadverting as we go on the sorry state of modern Italy:

> ... tout dort!
> Tout, jusqu'aux souvenirs de ton antique histoire,
> Qui te feraient du moins rougir devant ta gloire! ...

The words are Harold's, the thought is Lamartine's.

Greece heaves in sight in Canto xxi; Harold's presence gives heart to the struggle against the Turk, but soon Harold himself is stricken; in the last cantos we listen to his dying soliloquy. The poem ends with a vision of Harold's soul before the Tribunal of the Almighty; as an unbeliever he will be condemned, but the poet appeals for clemency on the grounds that Harold has died a hero's death.

Philhellenism, liberalism, these enthusiasms Lamartine shares with the Byron he portrays; but his hero struggles with religious doubts whereas Lamartine appears now to border on pantheism, a position presently to be found again in *Les Harmonies*.

> Voix céleste, qui parle au bord des mers profondes,
> Dans les soupirs des bois, dans les accords des ondes
> Partout où l'homme enfin n'a point gravé ses pas,
> Harold aussi t'entend ... mais ne te comprend pas!
>
> (Canto xxiii.)

Coming after three magnificent alexandrines, the reference to Harold looks very much like a deliberate piece of bathos and if so it reveals a capacity to become aware of others, a sudden flash of something which to call humour would be exaggerated – for of humour there is no trace in Lamartine – but at least a lightness of touch, much more evident in Byron, incidentally, who often leads the reader to wonder how seriously he is taking himself.

But the impression is momentary; though the work has its origin in Lamartine's sincere admiration for Byron, it becomes the vehicle for the author's own enthusiasms. There are passages of great beauty; particularly striking are cantos xli and xlii where the dying Harold contemplates the beauties of the evening scene:

> Les flots, les vents, les sons, les voix de la nature,
> Sous les ailes du soir tout paraît s'assoupir ...

[28] Liberty.

and addressing his farewell to Nature:

> Triomphe, disait-il, immortelle Nature
> Tandis que devant toi ta frêle créature
> Elevant ses regards de ta beauté ravis
> Va passer et mourir; triomphe! tu survis!

This passage where thought and rhythm are perfectly fused is peculiarly compelling both for its own merits and because the idea it expresses is unexpected in Lamartine. The indifference of Nature, in its immense power and fecundity, to the ephemeral creatures that come and go is a theme, Romantic indeed, but more like Vigny or Leconte de Lisle than Lamartine. Yet the tone is different; no note of fear or revolt at the cruelty and injustice of Nature, rather a mood of resignation; the dying Harold identifies himself moreover with the poet of Le Vallon:

> Plus je fus malheureux, plus tu me fus sacrée!
> Plus l'homme s'éloigna de mon âme ulcérée,
> Plus dans la solitude, asile du malheur,
> Ta voix consolatrice enchanta ma douleur;...

and, at the last, not the indifference but the glory of nature is what he stresses.

The glory of nature recurs as a guiding theme in *Les Harmonies*. Happily married, career and literary ambitions temporarily satisfied by the diplomatic post at Florence and his election to the Academy (1829), Lamartine's cup of happiness was filled in the four years that saw the composition of *Les Harmonies*, and this mood is the main source of the work. The poet sings what in effect are a series of psalms to the glory of God; the splendours of nature proclaim it;[29] the child murmurs it in his waking prayer;[30] the nightingale echoes it.[31] There is a reminder of the spirit and rhythm of Job,[32] something also of traditional Catholic piety,[33] and a suggestion of Lamennais' liberal Catholicism.[34] The mood of the psalmist is not always one of joy; yet even in sadness at the abyss that separates creation from creator the poet's soul soars upwards.[35]

In this chorus of praise with its rich variety of metres and sources of inspiration, other and even discordant notes occasionally creep in: 'Novissima Verba'[36] (October 1829) reflects a moment of uncertainty and discouragement, the poet of the *Méditations* reappears; 'Milly ou La Terre Natale'[37] strikes a note of melancholic nostalgia having only a tenuous link with *Les Harmonies* by the religious inspiration of the conclusion.

[29] *Harmonies*, Bk. I, 3. [30] *Ibid.*, Bk. I, 7. [31] *Ibid.*, Bk. IV, 6.
[32] *Ibid.*, Bk. II, 1. [33] *Ibid.*, Bk. III, 5. [34] *Ibid.*, Bk. III, 5.
[35] *Ibid.*, Bk. I, 10. [36] *Ibid.*, Bk. I, 7. [37] *Ibid.*, Bk. III, 2.

With the development of his liberal ideas Lamartine had no reason in conscience to refuse the oath of allegiance to Louis-Philippe; liberals were acclaiming 1830 as the dawn of a new era. None the less, he decided to resign from the diplomatic service, alleging private reasons – his political ambitions in fact. At forty, he was now eligible to stand for parliament and did so unsuccessfully in 1831.

Another opportunity was to come two years later. In the interval Lamartine decided to respond to the lure of the Near East which had attracted him for a number of years. As in so many other things, Chateaubriand had led the way.[38] The Greek War of Independence and Byron's death at Missolonghi had alike increased Lamartine's desire to go and see for himself. His journey (July 1832–September 1833), which was marked by the tragic loss of his daughter (December 1832), was a turning point in his career. His liberalism has become clearly defined; his religious position, shedding all dogmatic attachments, is now no more than an idealistic belief in humanity and progress.

His 'progressive' ethos also affects the character of the literary output of his middle years. Without abandoning lyrical poetry, his contributions to this form were to be rarer and themselves clearly show the orientation of his thought: Les Révolutions (1832), a long poem of high-pitched eloquence expressing Lamartine's quasi-mystical belief in the tonic social effects of revolution. Recueillements Poétiques (1839), a collection of fugitive pieces often of high quality but that usually belie the promise of intimate lyrical poetry contained in the title, and a political ode: 'La Marseillaise de la Paix', in response to Becker's nationalistic 'Der Deutsche Rhein'. His poetic activity, conforming to the views he himself expresses in the preface to the 1834 edition of his works and in fulfilment of a long cherished interest, turns to the epic, with a social or philosophic message: Jocelyn (1836), La Chute d'un Ange (1836). He takes to prose, first as a descriptive writer in the four volumes of Voyage en Orient (1838), next as a declared historian, but in reality at the service of his political ideals, in L'Histoire des Girondins (1847), then as an autobiographer, direct in Confidences (1849; of which Graziella is an extract), thinly disguised under a cloak of sentimental fiction much in the 'improving' manner of George Sand, in Raphaël (1849), Geneviève (1851) and Le Tailleur de pierre de Saint-Point (1857).

The two epic poems were destined to form part of a much vaster work, entitled Visions, where Lamartine intended to portray the fall of the human soul and its progressive regeneration through ten incarnations chosen from different periods of human history;

[38] His Itineraire de Paris à Jérusalem (1811).

La Chute d'un Ange is thus the first panel in the gigantic scheme and *Jocelyn*, though written first, was to be the ninth. Partly inspired by the story of Lamartine's sometime tutor and friend, L'Abbé Dumont, vicar of Bussière,[39] who became a priest as a result of an unfortunate love affair, *Jocelyn* has self-sacrifice as its theme: Jocelyn renounces his patrimony, thus ensuring a dowry for his sister, and studies for the priesthood. Driven from his seminary by the Terror, he takes refuge in the mountains, falls in love with Laurence, cannot marry her because he accepts holy orders at the hands of the Bishop of Grenoble in order to hear the latter's confession on the eve of his execution, and ultimately becomes vicar of Valneige.

From the period of the Revolution we jump back in *La Chute d'un Ange* to antediluvian times. The poet unfolds the chequered love story of Cédar, the angel become man, and Daïdha.

Both epics reflect not only the literary influences we expect: the Bible, Rousseau, Chateaubriand, but also the evolution of Lamartine's ideas and messianic attitudes; they take their place in the persistent efforts from Chateaubriand[40] down to Sully Prudhomme[41] and Madame Ackerman,[42] through Hugo[43] and Leconte de Lisle[44] to give French literature a great epic poem, with both narrative and philosophic interest.

The critics tell us that both works are full of magnificent poetry; abundantly right they may be,[45] but the poems' abundance is daunting. Our taste for epic and adventure is satisfied by the films; we no longer have the appetite displayed by the Victorians or the Louis-Philippian bourgeoisie, their French counterparts, for romance in verse, and 'improving' quasi-Biblical reading for all ages in the prolific family circle; adventures for the very young, romantic love for the adolescents, optimistic humanitarian philosophy and visions of material progress – strong meat, that – for the mature adults, Virgilian idylls for the elderly, purity for all.

These middle years were also filled by a political career that grew in intensity after 1840. News of his election to parliament had reached Lamartine at Baalbek in March 1833; he had taken his seat as deputy for Bergues in December of that year; three years later he abandoned Bergues in favour of his native town of Mâcon which, with a short interruption in 1849, he continued to represent until the *coup d'état* of 1851. By then, Lamartine was no longer in tune with the times either in politics or literature, and he was left alone to nurse his sorrows, his memories and his debts.

---

[39] Levaillant, op. cit.
[40] *Les Martyrs.*
[41] e.g. 'Le Zénith', 'Le Prisme'.
[42] *Poésies Philosophiques.*
[43] *Légende des Siècles.*
[44] *Qain.*
[45] e.g. the section entitled 'Les Laboureurs', *Jocelyn*, 9ᵉ époque.

To pay off the latter meant literary forced labour: re-edition of his works, histories and particularly the literary journalism of the *Cours Familier de littérature*, conceived as a literary education for the masses. In his political defeat, Lamartine remained faithful to his democratic ideals. Here[46] is to be found 'La Vigne et la Maison', a poem for which inspiration had come to Lamartine on a solitary visit to Milly (autumn, 1857).

This swan song on the theme of family affections is cast in the form of a dialogue between the poet and his soul. With a variety of metres and rhyme schemes it is one of Lamartine's finest poems, rich in thought, concrete observation, texture. The mood is one of resignation as though the ageing poet in spite of his tribulations had achieved some degree of serenity:

> Mais de cette ombre sur la mousse
> L'impression funèbre et douce
> Me consolait d'y pleurer seul . . .

'Jamais, depuis *les Méditations*, vous n'avez donné un tel coup d'archet', wrote Michelet enthusiastically to Lamartine. Sainte-Beuve on his side comments: 'une Méditation d'arrière-saison'. We have seen that Lamartine was sensitive to other forms of inspiration besides personal grief and the intimate communion with Nature, yet the fact that both Sainte-Beuve and Michelet should independently have referred to the *Méditations* confirms that Lamartine's early triumph, forged by that remarkable fusion of classical forms and personal emotion, established him as the first French poet of the Romantic revolution and created of him an image no subsequent work could enrich or modify.

[46] 15th Entretien.

Part II

§ II   FROM RESTORATION TO JULY
TO JULY MONARCHY AND AFTER

Chapter 9

POLITICAL AND
INTELLECTUAL BACKGROUND

IN contrast to the Catholic background of the Restoration, the ethos of the July Monarchy is liberal and Voltairian. Signs are not wanting during the Restoration of this spirit being close to the surface; in political life it is active in the opposition, with Benjamin Constant as the spear-head; in literature what more characteristic of it than Paul-Louis Courier (1772–1825), sometime unenthusiastic Napoleonic officer in the gunners, espousing the cause of the peasantry against the local prefect, not we suspect for any love of rustics (unless they appeared in the pages of Virgil) but because they were good cannon-fodder in his pamphleteering war against the régime. Courier was a bourgeois country squire, not a common species at the time, but they exist in the pages of Balzac; Courier reminds us of no one so much as of Rigau,[1] sometime mayor of Blangy, who plots with his cronies, Gaubertin and Soudry, to oust General de Montcornet from his estate, 'Les Aigues', and, having succeeded, divides the spoils with them.

A more sympathetic example, in a domain lying on the fringes of literature and one in which he reigns supreme, is Anthelme Brillat-Savarin (1755–1826), lawyer by profession, *émigré* during the Terror, but otherwise serving successive régimes with fastidious indifference, determined, as he himself opined, that political revolutions should not upset his digestion, author of the classic *Physiologie du Goût* (1825). 'Dis-moi ce que tu manges', he writes, 'et je te dirai ce que tu es' – what more realist and down to earth? How far removed from the spirit that characterizes the Romanticism fashionable in the early years of the Restoration, the pallid figures that float in the poetry of Chênedollé, of Millevoye, of Madame Desbordes-Valmore, the Elvire of Lamartine.

This down-to-earth spirit will reign supreme after 1830. It was lurking in the wings during the July Revolution ready to kidnap the victory of the Paris mob over Charles X, a victory symbolized in Delacroix's picture of Liberty in the form of a woman striding across the barricades, tricolor in hand. When the revolutionary

---

[1] *Les Paysans.*

storm had spent itself, Orleanism takes the stage, realist, prudential, moderate in all things including generosity; Louis-Philippe is
its living image.[2] It is reflected in the new historical attitudes, those
of Thierry, Guizot and Villemain, in the philosophy of Victor
Cousin (1792–1867)–eclecticism, compromise *in excelsis*: a little
truth, a little beauty, a little good is just the thing–and in the
rather wan philosophy of Théodore Jouffroy (1796–1842; e.g.
Cours de droit naturel, 1835) who had shown his hostility to the
Restoration in an article that made an impact at the time–
'Comment les dogmes finissent' (1823, published in *Le Globe*, 24
May 1825); in the dramatic works of Eugène Scribe. The great
architect Viollet-le-Duc (1814–79) had begun his career during the
July Monarchy and, although his most important work belongs to
a later time, its spirit can without fancifulness be related to that
of the July Monarchy. As the traveller approaches Carcassonne[3] a
splendid medieval vision outlined against the sky arises before him;
on closer inspection it turns out to be a compromise, by no means
unsuccessful, between a great relic of the Middle Ages, historical
romanticism, and a genuine wish to preserve the legacy of the past.

The 'Juste Milieu', personified by the citizen-king, with mutton-
chop whiskers and a physiognomy so fatally like a pear,[4] was not
a bad nor for that matter an unsuccessful calculation; Louis-
Philippe seemed to unite in his own person all the elements for
an essay in eclectic government: royal tradition for the Right,
soldiering and revolutionary patriotism ('the warrior of
Valmy') for Bonapartists and Republicans, Voltairianism and
moral dignity for the liberal bourgeoisie–the compromise seemed
admirable.

Unfortunately the more perfect a compromise, the more surely
will everyone be dissatisfied. The Right could never accept the son
of Philippe-Egalité, the Left soon saw that the promises of the
July Revolution were unfulfilled, the Bonapartists were to hive off,
with a new Napoleonic bee in their bonnets. Far from being welded
together the elements separated out. Orleanist liberals against
democratic liberals, party of resistance against party of movement,
Constitutional Monarchists against Republicans, bourgeois realists
against messianic democrats and 'humanitarians'. We shall have
numerous examples of the messianic urge amongst the writers and
poets of the Romantic age. As the successive régimes try to take
root, become more rigid in self-defence against enemies to the Left,
the Promethean spirit of Romanticism turns away from them; true

---

[2] See the early pages of Tocqueville's *Souvenirs* for an admirable pen
portrait of Louis-Philippe and analysis of the spirit of his age.
[3] Restored by Viollet-le-Duc from 1849.
[4] cf. Philipon's notorious cartoon, 'Le Roi-Poire'.

under the Restoration, this becomes more evident under the July Monarchy, after only a momentary fusion in 1830.

In the intellectual sphere no better examples of the dichotomy can be found than in the tragic figure of Lamennais and in the humanitarian thinkers – Saint-Simon, the great precursor, and lesser men such as Fourier, Cabet and Louis Blanc.

If de Maistre and Bonald reflect so well the ethos of the Restoration – throne and altar, Félicité de Lamennais (1782–1854), less stable in his opinions, at one important moment in his career stands beside de Maistre and Bonald, at another, and equally important, tries to bring Catholicism and liberalism together; in this attitude he was ahead of his time and failed. He had not come early to religion; not until 1816, at the age of thirty-four, did he take orders. His was not an easy or ill-considered decision but, once taken, Lamennais brought to his new life all his vigour of mind and ardour to push his convictions to their furthest conclusion whatever the consequences on the political plane.

In 1817 appeared the first of his works to draw public attention: *L'Essai sur l'Indifférence en matière de religion*, Vol. I.[5]

After *Le Génie du Christianisme* which had made an impact more particularly on the emotional and aesthetic sensibilities of the generation emerging from the Revolution, *L'Essai sur l'Indifférence* was of a higher apologetic quality and was to have a stronger influence in both literary and ecclesiastical circles. 'Ce livre réveillerait un mort', declared Mgr de Frayssinous; Lamartine, Hugo, Sainte-Beuve, de Maistre were all fervent admirers.

Lamennais' thesis starts from the principle that beliefs are at the root of all human activity; absolute indifference would mean the extinction in the human heart of love as well as hatred because of the absence of all judgment, a kind of spiritual death.

Without reaching that stage many men, however, adopt a relative indifference to religion; amongst these Lamennais distinguishes different groups: the atheists, who see in religion only a political institution, deists who accept only natural religion so-called, heretics who pick and choose in the dogma of revealed religion; finally, the indifferent by thoughtlessness and sloth.

To all these groups Lamennais aims to show the importance of the Christian religion in relation to the individual, society, and God Himself. Unlike Pascal who seeks to awaken a sense of awe, and Chateaubriand who tries to excite faith through beauty, Lamennais wants to show that without Catholicism no society is really possible and that to diminish the importance of religion is 'se rendre coupable du crime énorme de lèse-société au premier chef.'[6]

His argument has a certain pragmatism; a doctrine is true, if it

[5] Vol. II (1820); Vols. III and IV (1823).   [6] *Essai*, I, 104.

works; Catholicism must be true because it is essential to society. In 1817 Lammennais' attitude was still authoritarian: 'L'autorité peut tout, soit pour le bien, soit pour le mal; ... on n'agit sur les peuples que par l'autorité.'[7] He stands with de Maistre as champion of absolutism in Church and State, he is a convinced ultramontane. But his pragmatism gives a clue to his line of development.

The subsequent volumes of L'Essai strengthen the theme of the social value of religion; Lamennais becomes more involved in polemics, his natural climate. Not content with defending his position, he takes the offensive; the French state is really atheist; it tolerates false creeds; it finances religion as it does the fine arts, the theatres, the stud farms. It accepts the existence of an educational system (l'Université) that is the product of the Revolution, that corrupts youth. He condemns the Restoration's spirit of compromise with the Revolution, its Gallicanism.[8] Soon he is attacking the Monarchy for enslaving the Church.[9] Let the Church throw off this despotism and demand for itself the liberties guaranteed by the Charter (1814) to French citizens.

This accent on liberty is significant; the people too are oppressed; let Church and people join hands under the banner of Christianity. Of Lamennais' original position his ultramontanism remains, but where before his cry was 'Church and King', it is now 'Church and People'.

By 1830 Lamennais had alienated the 'Ultra' society, both lay and ecclesiastical, of the Restoration, in temper aristocratic and Gallican, but he was not isolated, not yet; he had by the power of his polemical writing gathered round him a band of adherents, laymen and priests[10] from younger Catholic circles. With three disciples, de Coux, Lacordaire, Montalembert, he founded a newspaper – l'Avenir – (October 1830) to defend the ideas of liberal Catholicism. 'Dieu et la Liberté' was the banner. The July Revolution had been no surprise to Lamennais; liberalism was in the air. But again Lamennais had moved beyond the régime. The programme advocated by l'Avenir: religious liberty for the Roman Catholic Church,[11] free Roman Catholic schools, freedom of the press, freedom for the enslaved nations, went much further towards democracy than the prudential ideas of Louis-Philippe and 'le Juste Milieu' policy; Gregory XVI, a new Pope (1831–46) but an old man, and his aged

[7] Essai, I, 1.
[8] cf. La Religion considérée dans ses rapports avec l'ordre politique et civil (1826).
[9] cf. Les Progrès de la Révolution et de la Guerre contre l'Eglise (1829).
[10] E. M. de Coux, M. de Guérin, l'Abbé Gerbet, l'Abbé Lacordaire, Cte de Montalembert, Hippte. de la Morvonnais, Röhbacher, l'Abbé de Salinis.
[11] i.e. separation of Church and State; not freedom of conscience for the individual.

cardinals had not moved at all. They regarded Lamennais with suspicion. The response when the latter announced the suspension of his paper[12] pending a papal decision (15 November 1831) and his pilgrimage to Rome flanked by Lacordaire and Montalembert, was a frigid reception followed by the encyclical *Mirari vos* (July 1832) condemning all the ideas defended by *l'Avenir*.

L'Avenir did not reappear, but under this show of obedience burned the fires of revolt which burst forth in *Paroles d'un Croyant* (1834), a strange mixture of Old Testament prophet condemning the crimes of a stiff-necked, corrupt generation, and of an apostle revealing to the oppressed an apocalyptic vision of a regenerate Christian faith freed of all ecclesiastical or monarchical obstacles between men and God.

L'Essai sur l'Indifférence had been a masterpiece of compelling argument; its impact is understandable; *Les Paroles . . .* are disjointed invective and messianic prophecies. Yet their success, too, was great, because they reflected so well the ethos of that section of the community they were intended for, the industrial workers, the disinherited, sunk in poverty and ignorance:

> Jeune soldat, où vas-tu?
> Je vais combattre pour Dieu et les autels de la Patrie . . .
> Jeune soldat, où vas-tu?
> Je vais combattre pour la Justice, pour la sainte
> Cause des peuples, pour les droits sacrés du genre humain
> *(Paroles, chap. 36.)*

To them, these rhythmical incantatory strophes and dramatic apostrophes, declaimed like the verses of a new Bible by one in their number who could read, must have evoked visions of a new Jerusalem.

But the prophet could no longer remain in the Church; the encyclical *singulari nos* (1834) was his personal condemnation. Thereafter Lamennais' popular influence wanes, unjustly enough; in 1846 Europe was to be startled by the news that the liberal minded Pius IX had ascended the papal throne. For a moment it seemed that the sometime prophet of liberal Catholicism would come into his own, but the democratic explosions of 1848 cured Pius IX of his liberal 'distemper' and though it brought Lamennais momentarily back to the public arena,[13] the *coup d'état* of 1851 sent him back to the oblivion he had sunk into and died in.

Not until the beginning of the twentieth century did the separation of Church and State which *l'Avenir* had advocated come about (1905). Forced upon an unwilling and fearful Gallican

[12] Its financial resources were exhausted.
[13] He sat in the National Assembly on the extreme left, as a deputy for Paris. See Tocqueville, *Souvenirs*, for a splendid pen-portrait of him, at that time.

Church, only then did it and its enemies appreciate that both had been wrong in their assessment of its effects; separation was not to be the death knell of Catholicism in France, but the beginning of its regeneration. Not till then was Lamennais vindicated; the Lamennais who with his tortured features and unquiet mind reflects so well, along with others of his generation – Berlioz, Lamartine, Hugo[14] and even Leconte de Lisle,[15] certain attitudes of the day: struggle, torment, apocalyptic visions and messianism, had seen more clearly than them all.

Without the scientific and mathematical abilities of Condorcet, Claude Henry de Rouvroy, Comte de Saint-Simon (1760–1825), none the less possessed a prophetic vision of the social, industrial and political development of the future. 'Je descends de Charlemagne, mon père s'appelait le comte de Saint-Simon, j'étais le plus proche parent du duc de Saint-Simon . . .', he writes.[16] No details are vouchsafed in support of the first statement which, if correct, makes the Bourbons look like *parvenus*, but it is characteristic of the man, of his magnifying eye that saw everything big and imaginatively, including the family tree.

In a manner faintly reminiscent of Descartes, he had gathered experience from 'the great book of the world' by service in the American War of Independence along with many liberal-minded French aristocrats of the day, by European travel, by consorting with all sorts and conditions of men, notably men of science and the arts whom he entertained on a lavish scale, and ruined himself in doing it. Then he turned to writing and in a series of works dating from 1803 till the year of his death he expounded his interpretation of history and his 'message' to the century: *Lettres d'un habitant de Genève à ses contemporains* (1803),[17] *Introduction aux travaux scientifiques du XIXe siècle* (1808), *Esquisse d'une Nouvelle Encyclopédie* (1809–11); the series was to continue until his death: *La Réorganisation de la Société Européenne* (1814),[18] *l'Industrie* (1817), *L'Organisateur* (1819), *Le Système Industriel* (1820–23), *Le Catéchisme des Industriels* (1823–4), *Le Nouveau Christianisme* (1825).

Saint-Simon saw in history the swing of the pendulum between what he called organic and critical periods; the French Revolution had brought to an end the last critical phase started by the Reformation. Unlike the rationalist Condorcet, the visionary Saint-

---

[14] The Hugo of *La Légende des Siècles*.
[15] cf. *Qaïn*.
[16] *Vie de Saint-Simon, écrite par lui-même*.
[17] After his divorce from his wife (1802) Saint-Simon after visiting Mme de Staël at Coppet was in Geneva for some weeks.
[18] In collaboration with Augustin Thierry, an early disciple.

Simon sees the Revolution as an end rather than as a beginning, as
an element of disorder – what is liberalism but anarchy? – rather
than as an inspiration for the organic society the nineteenth century must build up. Saint-Simon stands on the side of the opponents of the Revolution in the great debate.

His interpretation of the past is a pretext for his vision of the
future, where power must no longer belong to the priesthood or nobility – traditional leaders not in tune with modern society – but
with the industrialists, the men of science, the artists. The first,
with their spirit of enterprise, are capable of developing the full
potential of the globe's wealth; the scientists will provide the requi-
site knowledge, the artists will create the vision of the new Jerusalem, provide emotional outlets for the people by devising fêtes and
ceremonies to maintain morale (as we might say) and create in the
masses the idealistic stimulus, that alone can ensure the necessary
social dynamism; in short they will be the priests of the new
society.

The sense of authority and leadership is strong in Saint-Simon –
a trace of his aristocratic tradition perhaps? – but of a new type;
the authority of scientific truth, the leadership of the experts. The
theme is constant; it appears in the first of his *Lettres d'un Habitant de Genève*: 'Ouvrez une souscription devant le tombeau de
Newton ... Que chaque souscripteur nomme trois mathématiciens,
trois physiciens, trois chimistes, trois physiologistes, trois littéra-
teurs, trois peintres, trois musiciens ... vous donnerez des chefs à
ceux qui travaillent aux progrès de vos lumières.' It is greatly developed in the famous *Parabole*[19] (1819): 'Nous supposons que la
France perde subitement ses cinquante premiers physiciens, ses
cinquantes premiers chimistes, ses cinquante premiers mathématiciens ... etc. ... faisant en tout les trois mille premiers savants,
artistes et artisans de France. Comme ces hommes sont les Français
les plus essentiellement producteurs ... ceux qui dirigent les travaux
les plus utiles à la nation ... ils sont réellement la fleur de la société
française ...'

'Passons à une autre supposition ...' This latter is the sudden en-
gulfment of the royal family, the grand officers of the crown, lawyers, marshals, cardinals and other Church dignitaries, prefects and
other civil servants, etc., etc.; a sad event assuredly; 'Cet accident
affligerait ... les Français parce qu'ils sont bons', continues Saint-
Simon, 'mais ... ne leur causerait de chagrin que sous un rapport
purement sentimental, car il n'en résulterait aucun mal politique
pour l'Etat ...' The parable had a *succès de scandale*; Saint-
Simon was prosecuted ... and acquitted – valuable publicity for
him and his ideas.

[19] Published in the first number of the paper *L'Organisateur*.

But to what purpose this reorganisation of society, this industrial 'exploitation of the globe' – to speak in Saint-Simonian style? As his thought or rather his vision became more defined this question became insistent. The answer is to be found in Saint-Simon's humanitarian doctrine. The aim of the production of wealth is to succour the needy, to root out not heresy but poverty, that is the modern meaning of the Christian injunction to love one's neighbour: 'Les hommes doivent se conduire en frères ... La religion doit diriger la société vers le grand but de l'amélioration la plus rapide du sort de la classe la plus pauvre.'[20]

Saint-Simon's vision extended beyond the social, beyond the quasi-religious and mystical planes, to the political. In 1814, with the Napoleonic political structure in ruins, Saint-Simon vaticinates about Europe.[21] Let France set aside all sense of rancour against England whose political maturity and sense of liberty must become models for the peoples of the continent. Let England on the other hand renounce her balance of power policy which means in effect maintaining a divided Europe, for in the long run a divided and therefore weak Europe will be the ruin of England. Let France and Germany bury the hatchet; England, France and Germany must become the keystone of a European federation with a European parliament having power to raise taxes, control education, direct great enterprises: 'Toutes les enterprises d'une utilité générale pour la société européenne seront dirigées par le grand parlement: ainsi par exemple, il joindra par des canaux le Danube au Rhin, le Rhin à la Baltique etc....' The modern reader may well ask himself whether with England on the threshold of the new Europe, the Common Market will not translate into reality the Saint-Simonian political vision.

Saint-Simon is within certain limits a precursor of modern socialism: his preoccupation with 'social justice', his distinction between the bees and drones of society,[22] his emphasis on planning and leadership by experts foreshadow socialist ideas. So does his suggestion, rather casually thrown out, that liberty consists not in the freedom but in the power to act;[23] from there to the idea of nationalizing the means of production seems but a step. His keywords have a socialist ring about them: 'industriel', 'bourgeois' (in the economic sense), 'prolétaire', 'prolétariat', 'exploitation'.[24]

But his attitude is in reality ambivalent; though opposed to what he thought the anarchy of liberalism, he was not opposed to the enterprising industrialist's reaping his reward. The dominant

[20] *Nouveau Christianisme.*
[21] *La Réorganisation de la Société Européenne.*
[22] cf. *Catéchisme des Industriels*, passim, and *La Parabole*.
[23] *Système Industriel*, Preface.
[24] The French sense is the working or running of a business, a farm, etc.

idea in him is that of developing to its full potential the world's wealth; how the created wealth should be controlled and distributed (a socialist preoccupation) does not concern him, at any rate not in detail nor beyond the duty of helping the poor by education and work. In the last resort the Saint-Simonian ideal would appear to be a technocracy uneasily poised between liberal and socialist conceptions, and inspired by a paternalist humanitarianism.

By the time of his death, Saint-Simon had succeeded in gathering a number of disciples about him: Rodrigues,[25] Enfantin, Bazard, Thierry, Michel Chevalier, Pierre Leroux, Auguste Comte, the brothers Pereire, to name a few of the most prominent. Like the master, they were not egalitarian; 'de chacun selon sa capacité, ...à chaque capacité selon ses oeuvres' was their slogan; they organized lectures to expound Saint-Simon's teaching;[26] they acquired a newspaper;[27] many of them, trained at the Ecole Polytechnique, were destined to play a leading part in the development of banking, the steel industry, the railways, in short the French Industrial Revolution.

'Souvenez-vous', Saint-Simon said on his death-bed to Olindes Rodrigues, 'que pour faire du grand, il faut être passionné.'[28] The messianic ardour of the master communicated itself to the disciples.

Saint-Simon and his followers, other writers in the same field, e.g. François Fourier (1772–1837), Louis Blanc (1811–82), Etienne Cabet (1788–1856), bear the stamp of their age; an age when the modern pattern of industrialization with all its problems was beginning to take shape, proletarian groups with a sense of solidarity beginning to form. Fourier's critique of modern society is more penetrating than Saint-Simon's, though the famous *phalanstère*, his idea of the group organizations that should exist in the harmonious society of the future, is no more inviting than the Saint-Simonian 'family' of Ménilmontant.

These early efforts to meet the challenge of modern society have in common their humanitarian inspiration and to a greater or lesser extent the messianic attitude of Romanticism.

As social consciousness develops, so will the study of society; it will become more scientific. Then imagination will give way to data, the sociologist will replace the visionary in the unending task of building the new Jerusalem. Meanwhile, a Saint-Simon, a Fourier, unhampered by any great load of technical knowledge, are free to escape from reality and take refuge in their visions.

[25] Olinde Rodrigues, editor of Saint-Simon's works, 1832.
[26] *Exposition de la doctrine de Saint-Simon.*
[27] *Le Globe*, founded in 1824, became the organ of the Saint-Simonians in 1831 under the editorship of Michel Chevalier. Ceased publication, 1832.
[28] *Oeuvres de Saint-Simon*, ed. by O. Rodrigues, 1832, Preface.

Their mystical oddity consorts strangely with their practical abilities, and its results were not always happy: the quest for the 'Femme-Messie', for example, in Turkey and Egypt, or the Saint-Simonian 'family' at Ménilmontant founded by Enfantin, prosecuted for immorality and suppressed (1832).

Chapter 10

I. VIGNY

IN 1822 Alfred de Vigny (1797–1863) published *Poèmes*, a modest
collection of thirteen poems, some of which had been composed
as much as seven years earlier ('La Dryade', 'Symétha'). The
most important poem in the collection is 'Moïse'. *Poèmes antiques
et modernes* (1826) are, in reality, a re-publication of *Poèmes*, augmented by a few 'pieces' composed in the interval ('Le Déluge',
'Eloa', 'Dolorida', 'Le Cor'). In 1826, too, Vigny published a
novel in the contemporary historical mode, derived from Sir Walter
Scott: *Cinq-Mars*.

His poetic harvest of the next few years is meagre: a few rather
uninspired poems: 'Madame de Soubise', 'La Frégate la Sérieuse',
'Les Amants de Montmorency', 'Paris', figure in a second edition
of *Poèmes antiques et modernes* (1837), together with a preface
where the author claims the credit of having, by these poems, introduced what amounts to a new dimension in poetry: 'Le seul mérite
qu'on n'ait jamais disputé à ces compositions, c'est d'avoir devancé
en France toutes celles de ce genre, dans lesquelles une pensée
philosophique est mise en scène sous une forme Épique ou Dramatique.' The claim suggests a retrospective attitude, surprising from
a poet, so comparatively early in his career; as he was already re-
publishing earlier work it lends colour to the view that the poet's
creative power was slackening. Admittedly Vigny had turned his
attention elsewhere: another novel, if that be the right description
– *Stello* (1832), the three short stories of *Servitude et Grandeur
Militaires* (1835). The theatre also attracted him: two translations
from Shakespeare: *Romeo et Juliette* (1827) and *Othello* (1829)
with its appended 'Lettre à Lord ***', which is Vigny's contribution to the Romantics' attack on the French classical conception of
drama; a full-blooded historical drama, *La Maréchale d'Ancre*
(1831); a playlet, *Quitte pour la Peur* (1833), and a drama drawn
from one of the episodes in *Stello*: *Chatterton* (1835).

Thereafter, silence, only occasionally broken by the publication
in *La Revue des deux Mondes* of a new poem. In the words of
Sainte-Beuve:

> ... Vigny, plus secret,
> Comme en sa tour d'ivoire, avant midi, rentrait.
> (Epître à M. Villemain.)

Not until 1864 was the public really made aware that the years of silence had not been inactive. In that year Louis Ratisbonne, Vigny's literary executor, published a collection of eleven poems: *Les Destinées*. Here are to be found Vigny's best-known poems: 'La Colère de Samson' (1839), 'La Mort du Loup' (1843), 'La Maison du Berger' (1844), 'Les Destinées' (1849), 'La Bouteille à la Mer' (1858), 'Le Mont des Oliviers' (1862), 'L'Esprit Pur' (1863).

Of all the big figures in the Romantic period, Vigny is the first in whom the didactic attitude is very marked. The claim to be a spiritual and intellectual leader, *qua* poet, will no doubt become more portentous in Hugo; it is discreeter, more aloof in Vigny but clear none the less. *Le Journal d'un Poète* (posth. 1867), where Vigny set down intermittently between 1824 and 1844 his views on current political events, his literary ideas and ambitions, stresses the claim often and in different ways; section ii of 'La Maison du Berger' is an appeal to poets to take their rightful place as leaders of the people, theirs by right of poetry:

> Comment se garderaient les profondes pensées
> Sans rassembler leurs feux dans ton diamant pur,
> Qui conserve si bien leurs splendeurs condensées?
> . . . . . .
> Diamant sans rival, que tes feux illuminent
> Les pas lents et tardifs de l'humaine Raison!

This didacticism, this desire to communicate a message, is as evident in Vigny's fiction and drama as in his poetry. The result is that he propounds a certain number of ideas that may not form a coherent philosophy but are coloured by a fairly consistent pessimism: God and Nature are indifferent to men; man is on trial but ignorant of the charge – Vigny said it before Kafka;[1] men of power are shunned; the poet and the soldier are alike neglected or rejected of society; on whatever plane we like to consider him, moral, political or social, man seems condemned at best to solitude, at worst to isolation. But exile though he be in the face of heaven and on the face of the earth, he has at least the tender companionship of woman – except that she may turn out to be not the Eva of 'La Maison du Berger' but the Dalila of 'La Colère de Samson'.

In contrast to these dark notions, 'La Bouteille à la Mer' offers a crumb of hope to those who can derive comfort from vicarious and gratuitous optimism:

> Jetons l'oeuvre à la mer, la mer des multitudes:
> Dieu la prendra du doigt pour la conduire au port.

[1] 'Il est vrai que vous ne savez pas pourquoi vous êtes prisonnier et de quoi puni; mais vous savez à n'en pas douter quelle sera votre peine: souffrance en prison, mort après.

'Ne pensez pas au juge, ni au procès que vous ignorerez toujours, mais seulement à remercier le geôlier inconnu qui vous permet souvent des joies dignes du ciel.' (*Journal*, entry, 1824.)

In this poem, God has changed in essence; He is no longer the indifferent and unjust God Vigny usually has in mind but 'le vrai
Dieu . . . le Dieu des idées'; knowledge and thought shall inherit
the earth. For the rest man must learn to achieve strength from the
force of example – the dying wolf – and from his own inner resources.

Moralist that he believes himself to be:

Je crois, ma foi, que je ne suis qu'une sorte de moraliste épique. C'est bien
peu de chose.[2] . . . je sens en moi le besoin de dire à la société les idées que
j'ai en moi et qui veulent sortir.[3]

Vigny establishes his code of behaviour on the cult of honour, a
stoic sense of resignation and a proud indifference in response to
the 'silence éternel de la divinité',[4] a sense of pity for human suffering. Those who, like Vigny, can add to this a sense of personal
achievement by making a contribution to the writers' legacy[5] to
humanity, are indeed fortunate:

> J'ai mis sur le cimier doré du gentilhomme
> Une plume de fer qui n'est pas sans beauté.
>
> ('L'Esprit Pur'.)

No one will deny that these are all potent motives in human behaviour, that they can call forth the fullest potential of man's
strength and spirit of sacrifice; they are essential elements in a
worth-while moral code, but they lack completeness, moral repose
and relaxation; they suggest the soldier with his musket for ever at
the ready or the athlete for ever on his toes.

In view of Vigny's own assessment of himself as 'une sorte de
moraliste épique', his moral attitudes may fairly be discussed at the
outset; they provide the dynamic of his work and, often enough,
Vigny's poetry seems little more than the development of a given
moral idea. We are caught in some sort of dilemma here: on the
one hand, Vigny – an uneven poet at the best of times – is usually
flat and uninspired[6] when he is not intent on wrapping up a message in a carefully elaborated symbol; on the other, that very process may so easily fall into rhymed prose. The time may come
again when, as in Vigny's day, that conception of poetry – the
belief that poetry consists merely in the rhythms of a given metre
enclosed in a rhyme scheme, the whole making a greater impact
upon the reader than would the same idea expressed in prose –
may again be in fashion. In the interval we are more likely to

---

[2] *Journal*, entry, 1834.   [3] *Journal*, entry, 1835.
[4] 'Mont des Oliviers' (1862).
[5] 'L'Ecrit Universel . . .' of 'L'Esprit Pur'.
[6] e.g., 'La Dryade', 'Symétha', 'Le Bain d'une Dame Romaine', 'Le Bain',
'La Frégate la Sérieuse', etc.

regard that conception as the negation of poetry, as rhymed eloquence; we are likely to agree with Verlaine's verdict:

> ... prends l'éloquence, et tords lui son cou
>
> ('Art poétique'.)

Fortunately the dilemma is often solved in Vigny's case by the
power of the symbol itself; we are not likely to forget Moses on
Mount Nebo, not because Vigny uses him as a mouthpiece to tell
us about the burden of power, but because by his skilful use of the
Biblical imagery Vigny obliges us to make a new effort of attention; as Moses strides forth to meet Jehovah face to face, an image
of mythical proportions rises in our imagination.

Nor are we likely to forget Christ on the Mount of Olives, and
again, the reason is not Vigny's using him to tell us about the injustice of God but his success in communicating to us the sense of
being present at the playing out of a great tragedy. Vigny was the
first Romantic poet to derive inspiration from the Bible; he did it
well.

He is equally well inspired in two other great symbols: the dying
wolf and the bottle cast on the sea by the ship-wrecked mariner; in
each case the reader's imagination is lit up by a dramatic vision.
Unfortunately in both cases the effect is spoilt; for fear the reader
may not find the golden key to unlock the symbol, Vigny provides
it. The dying wolf speaks:

> Fais énergiquement ta longue et lourde tâche ... etc.
>
> ('La Mort du Loup'.)

and, since the bottle cannot, the poet speaks instead:

> Le vrai Dieu, le Dieu fort, est le Dieu des idées.
> Sur nos fronts où le germe est jeté par le sort,
> Répandons le Savoir en fécondes ondées; ... etc.
>
> ('La Bouteille à la Mer'.)

The result is that the vision is shattered and we are left to go
home, as it were, with a moral tucked away in our pocket.[7] Neither
in 'Moïse' nor in 'Le Mont des Oliviers' does this happen; in the
former Moses himself expresses not a moral, but his attitude to life,
the result of his experience, and the reader is free to give general
significance to what Moses says, or not, as he pleases; in the latter
the moral is quite detached from the poem and the illusion that the
poet has so successfully built up is undisturbed.

'La Maison du Berger' is usually regarded as Vigny's poetic
masterpiece. Probably conceived in 1840,[8] first published in 1844,

---

[7] That the narrative parts of both poems could have been reduced with
advantage is also arguable.

[8] D. Parmée, *Twelve French Poets*, p. 280.

it reflects Vigny's mature thought on a variety of subjects: Nature, society, politics, material progress, the role of women, the role of poets, a rather disparate assortment on the whole successfully interwoven in the poem that takes the form of an address to 'Eva'. In the first two sections Vigny seems to have in mind one particular woman or perhaps a composite picture of a number of women he had known; in the third, however, the figure of 'Eva' is less clearcut; she has become an abstract idea of woman in general.

No finer poetry is to be found in Vigny than some of the stanzas of the first section; thought and image and rhythm have been blended into a wholly satisfying and indestructible unity:

> Les grands bois et les champs sont de vastes asiles,
> Libres comme la mer autour des sombres îles.
> Marche à travers les champs une fleur à la main.
>
> La Nature t'attend dans un silence austère;
> L'herbe élève à tes pieds son nuage des soirs,
> Et le soupir d'adieu du soleil à la terre
> Balance les beaux lis comme des encensoirs.

But here as elsewhere Vigny is not always equal to himself.

In the last section of the poem, when Nature speaks to man, the moralist in verse is clearly . . . in the prompter's box once more, and when the poet replies, why should he assume his personal views to be necessarily significant for the reader?:

> Plus que tout votre règne et que ses splendeurs vaines,
> J'aime la majesté des souffrances humaines;
> Vous ne recevrez pas un cri d'amour de moi.

Then again, after the beautiful opening stanzas of the poem come a number about modern material progress symbolized by the railway; they are pedestrian and at times almost laughable:

> Sur ce taureau de fer qui fume, souffle et beugle . . .

Like most of us, Vigny has turned away from what he dislikes – in this case, modern industrialism – and has not made the necessary effort of attention to understand and assimilate the beauty of a railway engine, that emblem of controlled power. We are confirmed here in a fact that is much in evidence in an earlier poem, 'Eloa': Vigny lacks visual imagination.

None of us has travelled in the realms of heaven or hell and returned alive to tell the tale, but Dante and Milton, by the power of their visionary and magnifying eye, make us believe they have. In comparison, Vigny's endeavour to paint the marvels of divine creation or the vicissitudes of Eloa's journey from Paradise into the arms of Lucifer is pallid; Vigny has, not unnaturally, failed to communicate to the reader the vision of a supernatural landscape that in his own imagination was evidently swathed in fog.

But when Vigny's imagination is stimulated he can be very effective. A case in point is provided by a number of poems that are in effect ballads: 'Dolorida', 'La Prison', 'Madame de Soubise', 'La Neige', 'Le Cor'. Vigny was first in the field here too. Romantic bric-à-brac, some may well call them, but much may be said for Romantic bric-à-brac, if the story has vitality in the telling, because vitality surely means the poet has successfully recaptured in his own imagination an experience of long ago and communicated it to the reader.

The best known of these ballads is probably 'Le Cor', where the poet has placed the telling of a dramatic story within the framework of a personal experience. If he succeeds in getting the reader to share that personal experience he will surely have prepared him to listen to the story; that 'Le Cor' is probably the best known of Vigny's ballads is *prima facie* evidence of his having done it in that poem. Yet on closer examination we may wonder whether the poem's claim to our attention is not a little flimsy, resting as it does mainly on the merits of the first stanza or even – on a stringent appreciation – of the first line:

> J'aime le son du cor, le soir, au fond des bois . . .

The distant sound sets up a chain of reverie in the poet's mind that carries him back to the legendary events of Roncevaux. We may freely admit the line just quoted to be the result of a sincere if fleeting emotional stimulus – the pleasure known to us all of sweet melancholy. The poet's emotion, as the horn's note strikes his ear, is recorded as a personal experience: 'J'aime le son du cor . . .' We are told nothing about the sound, nothing about the evening, nothing about the woods; the barest notation, in fact, of the poet's emotion at a given sound at a given time and place.

Not until the end of the poem does the poet give us some description and indication of the horn's sound, and then only by its effect on the human being who hears it:

> Dieu! que le son du cor est triste au fond des bois!

The slight modification is skilful in that it both recalls the pleasure of the opening line and adds to it the pleasure of variety; after telling the Roncevaux story the poet returns to his original emotional stimulus in a less subjective way, which recalls the tragedy just unfolded. In the interval, if the reader shares the poet's joy, the reason lies not in the descriptive quality of the words used – 'J'aime le son du cor . . .' – but in their leading him to call on his own reserve of experience, partly direct – for what reader will not at some time have walked in the woods at evening? – partly associated – for few readers will have heard the melancholy note of a

French hunting horn in the woods but many will probably have heard a French horn in an orchestra.

The inherent sensuous value of the line is indeed meagre; its effect a little fortuitous and depending largely on its attractive rhythm. The strong tonic accent of the first syllable is as arresting as a rap on the knuckles; it carries us through to the almost equally strong accent – its echo so to speak – on *Cor* and, in the second hemistich, to the accents on *soir*, *fond* and *bois* – every syllable, the hemistich being thus divided into three equal groups.

Rhythm is a valuable servant but a dangerous master because its effect is incantatory and draws the reader's attention away from meaning to organized sound. There is something of this in Vigny's line. Compare it and indeed the whole opening stanza with a sonnet of Verlaine's on a parallel theme:

> Le son du cor s'afflige vers les bois
> D'une douleur on veut croire orpheline
> Qui vient mourir au bas de la colline
> Parmi la bise errant en courts abois . . .[9]

The rhythm of Verlaine's lines are much less obvious, the sensuous suggestions of the words much greater: Le son . . . s'afflige . . ., . . . douleur . . . orpheline, . . . la bise, . . . abois. The personal note (Vigny's 'J'aime . . .') absent.

But then between the date of Vigny's poem (1825) and that of Verlaine (1881) lie nearly sixty years of aesthetic thinking and practice; the direct communication of the Romantics' personal emotions has given way to the search for effect by the impact on the reader of a poem by itself.

II. HUGO

The year 1822 had seen the publication of Vigny's *Poèmes*; Victor Hugo (1802–85) published *Odes et Poésies Diverses*, to give this first edition of the *Odes* their full title, in that year too. Some had already appeared separately, one at least – on 'le Rétablissement de la statue d'Henri IV' – had been crowned by the Academy of Floral Games at Toulouse; the dominant themes of 'throne and altar' ensured the success of the *Odes* in 'Ultra' circles; Hugo received a royal pension; his marriage to Adèle Foucher (October) was assured.

In the ensuing years while new and augmented editions of the *Odes* were appearing (*Nouvelles Odes*, 1824, *Odes et Ballades*, 1826, definitive edition, 1828), literary controversies grew apace. Hugo himself professes detachment – 'Il y a maintenant deux partis dans la littérature comme dans l'Etat, et la guerre poétique ne

[9] *Sagesse*, Section III, No. 9. The whole sonnet should be read.

paraît pas devoir être moins acharnée que la guerre sociale n'est
furieuse ... Pour lui [the author] il ignore profondément ce que
c'est que le genre classique et ... le genre romantique.'[10] But soon
he is in the forefront, leading the Romantics under the banner of
the 'Préface de Cromwell'[11] to the assault on the theatre. From
1827 to 1831 the Romantic battle was at its height and gave great
impetus to Hugo's creative power; lyrical plays – *Cromwell, Marion
de Lorme, Hernani*;[12] poetry – *Les Orientales* (1829); a lyrical
novel – *Notre Dame de Paris*.[13]

Of these, the ballads had already given a foretaste in spirit and
technique (e.g. 'La Chasse du Burgrave', 'Le Pas d'armes du Roi
Jean') but *Les Orientales* revealed Hugo as the supreme metrical
virtuoso (e.g. 'Les Djinns') as he played with a variety of verse
forms and in obedience to the prevailing fashion of Orientalism
switched the interest from the Middle Ages (the ballads) to what
for him were *terrae incognitae*: Greece and Turkey, even Arabia
and Persia. But Hugo, as a child, had been to Spain where his
father was soldiering in the service of Joseph Bonaparte, so that in
bringing Spain (e.g. 'Grenade', 'Les Bluets') with some justification into the orbit of his Near Eastern fantasy, he was drawing on
personal experience, albeit distant, as well as upon the powerful
visual imagination so clearly to be seen in the lyrical works to
come: *Les Feuilles d'Automne* (1831), *Les Chants du Crépuscule*
(1835), *Les Voix Intérieures* (1837) and *Les Rayons et les Ombres*
(1840).

In these works of the middle years, Hugo attains his lyrical
maturity; Romantic bric-à-brac – the medievalism, the Orientalism
– has gone; the political and religious themes of the *Odes* change
and develop in intensity; the poet's philosophy of life takes shape
and, interwoven with these sources of inspiration, are intimate
themes: love, children, Nature, literary preoccupations. 'Olympio's'
every mood – joy and sorrow, anger and anxiety – are reflected in
the great 'symphony'.

In 1840 comes a pause. During the next ten years the public
image of Hugo gradually changes from poet to official personage;
academician (1841), peer (1845). The magnet of politics attracted
him more and more; after the fall of the July Monarchy, he became a deputy and something of a demagogue, haranguing the
crowds at the barricades.

But the *coup d'état* of 1851 drove him into exile,[14] and brought
him back to literature, by the back door of political pamphleteering
(*Histoire d'un Crime*, written 1851–2, published 1877; *Napoléon le*

---

[10] Preface, 1824 edn.
[11] See below, pp. 152–3.
[13] See below, pp. 171–3.

[12] See below, pp. 154 *et seq.*
[14] For nineteen years.

Petit, 1852). Soon 'la corde d'airain' he had added to his lyre much earlier[15] was being plucked vigorously in *Les Châtiments*, and three years later comes Hugo's crowning lyrical achievement: *Les Contemplations*.

None of the Romantic poets had a more developed sense of mission than Hugo. The sense of social responsibility is at first rather passive since his is the soul of crystal reflecting every ray of light, the echo of every sound:

> ... mon âme de cristal,
> Mon âme aux mille voix ...
> ... au centre de tout comme un écho sonore!
>
> (*F.A.*, No. 1.)

A few pages later the poet has become a prophet, a brilliant torch in the gloom that enfolds us all (*F.A.*, No. 13). Here the idea of guidance appears for the first time, to be taken up more emphatically in *Les Voix Intérieures*. In the preface, Hugo speaks of the poet's mission, later of his function: 'le poète a une fonction sérieuse. Sans parler ... de son influence civilisatrice, c'est à lui qu'il appartient d'élever, lorsqu'ils le méritent, les événements politiques à la dignité d'événements historiques. Il faut pour cela, qu'il jette sur ses contemporains ce tranquille regard que l'histoire jette sur le passé; ... il faut qu'il sache se maintenir, au-dessus du tumulte, inébranlable, austère et bienveillant; indulgent quelquefois, chose difficile; impartial toujours, chose plus difficile encore ...' The whole passage deserves quotation from the point of view we are discussing; Hugo has attained a high tableland of sublime self-confidence whence he will not thereafter descend, and, like Moses on Sinaï, he is there to speak with God:

> Des poètes puissants, têtes par Dieu touchées,
> Nous jettent les rayons de leurs fronts inspirés.
>
> (*F.A.*, No. 40.)

Yet another metamorphosis in *Les Rayons et les Ombres*: 'O poète, O maître, O semeur ...'; and at the end of the poem the peoples of the earth are bidden to hearken:

> Peuple, écoutez le poète!
> Ecoutez le rêveur sacré!
> Dans votre nuit, sans lui complète,
> Lui seul a le front éclairé!
> . . . . . .
> Dieu parle à voix basse à son âme,
> Comme aux forêts et comme aux flots!
>
> (*R. et O.*, 1.)

The messianic tone is evident. This role falls to the poet, naturally, because he is a thinker. The words *rêver*, *rêveur*, *rêverie* recur

---

[15] *Feuilles d'Automne*, No. 40.

constantly in Hugo's poetry, and in the course of his reveries the poet sees with the eye of the seer that penetrates to the heart of things; words to do with the idea of sight[16] are also frequent: *oeil, voir, regarder, contempler,* and of course, *contemplation.* Seeing, contemplation, *rêverie* or meditation, thought, the connexion between these seems important as the basis of Hugo's claim to spiritual and moral leadership: Hugo has a powerful visual sense, he is therefore a seer; as a seer he floats into a state of meditative reverie, which he identifies with thought, and because a thinker, it follows he is a guide.

Accordingly Hugo will proclaim the truth to the multitude. But what truths?

Religion and politics are predominant from the outset, but the convictions expressed vary. The young Hugo of *Les Odes* in the wake of Chateaubriand and obedient to the tradition he had learnt in his youth from his mother is imbued with Catholic piety, and derives inspiration from the psalms:

> Voici la vérité qu'au monde je révèle:
> Du ciel dans mon néant je me suis souvenu.
> Louez Dieu! La brebis vient quand l'agneau l'appelle;
> J'appelais le Seigneur, le Seigneur est venu.
>
> (*Odes*, V, 14.)

His imagery suggests the angelic hosts as depicted in pious steel engravings of the period, but this apparatus of piety soon disappears. Thereafter, although the word God recurs constantly in the works of the middle years and *Les Contemplations,* Hugo makes no attempt to maintain a coherent attitude.

> C'est Dieu qui remplit tout. Le monde, c'est son temple!
>
> (*F.A.*, No. 38.)

These lines appear to express an orthodox Christian view; 'The earth is the Lord's . . .'. But the poem is entitled *Pan,* and the God in question is really no more than the force in Nature. God is a personal God when children pray to Him; their innocence is so touching that, in virtue of it, who could doubt that God is?

> Non, si pour la terre méchante
> Quelqu'un peut prier aujourd'hui,
> C'est toi, dont la parole chante,
> C'est toi: ta prière innocente,
> Enfant, peut se charger d'autrui;
>
> (*F.A.*, No. 37.)

---

[16] Hugo, be it noted, was an excellent draughtsman in pen and ink, and sepia washes. No doubt, with his great gifts of visual observation, he could have been a fine artist. Humour quite absent from his lyrical poetry sometimes appears in his drawings.

We are encouraged to pray:

> Espère! et chaque fois que se lève l'aurore,
> Soyons là pour prier, comme Dieu pour bénir
>
> (*C. du C.*, No. 30.)

an activity that seems superfluous if, as in 'La Vache' (*V.I.*, No. 15), Nature, symbolized by the cow, is humanity's universal indulgent provider and God is no more than an image in the mind of the placid ruminant:

> Toi, sans te déranger, tu rêves à ton Dieu.

None the less, Hugo is full of adoration:

> Nous qui ne voyons rien au ciel ou sur la terre
> Sans nous mettre à genoux
>
> (*V.I.*, No. 30.)

and something of a Christian conception appears in 'Dieu est toujours là' (*V.I.*, No. 5):

> Car sur les familles souffrantes,
> L'hiver, l'été, la nuit, le jour,
> Avec des urnes différentes
> Dieu verse à grands flots son amour!

But against this providential view, we must place the indifference that Hugo attributes to the Almighty towards the affairs of men in 'Sagesse' (*R. et O.*, No. 44):

> Que te font, O Très-Haut! les hommes insensés,
> Vers la nuit au hasard l'un par l'autre poussés,
> Fantômes dont jamais tes yeux ne se souviennent,
> Devant ta face immense ombres qui vont et viennent!

At other times again God is love and a very carnal love at that,

> . . . et notre amour, c'est Dieu!
>
> (*C.*, ii, 14.)

or an indulgent fellow:

> Le bon Dieu, qui veut qu'on aime,
> Qui met au coeur de l'amant
> Le premier vers du poème
> Le dernier au firmament.
>
> (*C.*, ii, 18.)

very reminiscent of Béranger's 'Dieu des Bonnes Gens', and we are inclined to agree with Renan's comment on Béranger: 'Mais ce dieu...à qui l'on frappe sur l'épaule, et qu'on traîte en camarade ...m'irrite comme une usurpation de titre de noblesse.'[17]

Clearly Hugo's religious attitudes are conflicting. At times God

---

[17] 'La Théologie de Béranger', *Questions Contemporaines* (1868).

is a personal God whom men can pray to, at other times God is depersonalized and becomes the divine spirit that informs the universe or Nature.

When Hugo contemplates, as he constantly does, the beauties of Nature, the splendours of the universe, the starry heavens by night, then God is there. But when he looks for a meaning in life and surveys its miseries, its cruelties, its suffering, then as often as not, the monster of doubt raises its ugly head. Indeed, at times doubt exists in him, in its own right:

> Je vous l'ai déjà dit, notre incurable plaie
> Notre nuage noir qu'aucun vent ne balaie
> C'est l'âpre anxiété qui nous tient aux entrailles...
>
> (*V.I.*, No. 28.)

And yet the sight of a cross in a cemetery produces a sudden flash of Christian sentiment (*R. et O.*, No. 40), and the idea of a personal God returns when an agony of personal sorrow demands the comfort of a supernatural being and makes the survival of the soul more than ever desirable (*C.*, iv, *passim*). God, in fine, seems to serve as a convenient envelope in which Hugo encloses whatever idea suits his mood of the moment. That is perhaps very human but for a writer who claims to be a beacon light the rays he sends out are wavering.

Hugo's political attitudes change too, but follow a steadier progression down the years. Initially he accepts the traditional link between throne and altar; the same influences were at work – his mother and Chateaubriand. No doubt too, the favour of the 'Ultra' public was flattering, as in the mostly fugitive pieces of the *Odes* the poet invokes the muse and twangs his lyre in honour of some event, past or present, in royalist annals. But like his Catholic piety, his royalism did not long survive; indeed even in the *Odes*, there are faint suggestions of other views. Admittedly the poem entitled 'Buonaparte' expresses no sympathy for Napoleon; the spelling of the name is itself a guarantee of sound royalism, confirmed by the poem's theme – a pious moralization on tyrants; Buonaparte was a scourge sent by the Almighty to bring order out of the Revolution's chaos. Yet there is a revealing detail Hugo must have been unconscious of at that date (March 1822); of Napoleon at St Helena, he writes:

> Là se refroidissant, comme un torrent de lave,
> Gardé par ses vaincus, chassé de l'univers,
> Ce reste d'un tyran...

A figure of rhetoric, no doubt, but we may also detect a beginning of the patriotic attitude so quickly to develop in Hugo, the unwillingness to admit even a momentary superiority in any other nation: 'Gardé par ses vaincus...' In 'Le Retour de l'Empereur', he will make the same point more explicitly:

> Nul homme en ta marche hardie
> N'a vaincu ton bras calme et fort:
> A Moscou, ce fut l'incendie
> A Waterloo, ce fut le sort...
>
> (*R. et O.*, December 1840.)

and again in 'L'Expiation' (*Châtiments*, V, 13): 'Il neigeait. On était vaincu par sa conquête...' The patriotic attitude is not in harmony with the royalist ethos; loyal service to the crown is one thing, patriotism is another, although the results may be the same.

The patriotic string vibrates again and more vigorously in the ode: 'A mon père' (*O. et B.*, ii, 4). No note of personal affection is heard, but the thought of his father, a retired Napoleonic soldier, leads on to the thought of his father's comrades, and with patriotic fervour Hugo recalls their glories:

> O Français! des combats la palme vous décore:
> Courbés sous un tyran, vous étiez grands encore.
> Ce chef prodigieux par vous s'est élevé;
> Son immortalité sur vos gloires se fonde...

Patriotism is the first theme that creeps into the *Odes* to dilute their royalism; Napoleon at first is no more than a side issue; in 'Les Deux Iles' (iii, 1825), admittedly, a sense of awe at the magnitude of the man's destiny appears but the attitude to him is neutral and the theme is really the vanity of power. 'A La Colonne' (iii, 7, 1827) is an explosion of chauvinist wrath.[18]

Both the patriotic and the Napoleonic themes reappear in *Les Orientales*, Hugo's royalist feelings having weakened in the meantime. 'Navarin' salutes the revival of French naval power:

> ...Notre gloire navale
> A cet embrasement rallume son flambeau;

in 'Bonnaberdi' Hugo is fascinated by the isolated grandeur of Napoleon, whilst a month later (December 1828), in 'Lui', no more doubt exists – Hugo (possibly encouraged by the difficulties he had encountered from the royal censorship over *Marion Delorme*[19]) has been won over finally and completely to the cult of Napoleon; scarcely two years later Napoleon has become a god:

> Napoléon ce Dieu dont tu seras le prêtre
>
> (*F.A.*, No. 11.)

---

[18] The invitations to a reception at the Austrian Embassy received by certain Napoleonic marshals had not borne their titles (Napoleonic), only their rank.

[19] August 1829.

and high priest of the cult he was to remain. The patriotic and the Napoleonic themes have fused; of all the writers who were to foster the Napoleonic legend none – unless it be Béranger – has a greater share than Hugo. In itself the legend was not deliberately political and must be distinguished from Bonapartism which was the active element, the partisanship in the cause of Louis Bonaparte, champion of the Napoleonic conception of government: democratic caesarism. But Bonapartism could grow under the shelter of the legend until it was strong enough to scale the heights of power which it partially did in December 1848,[20] and completely in December 1851.[21] Hugo's reply from exile in Jersey was *Les Châtiments*, a series of curses on the viper he had nursed in his bosom.

Hugo's reverence for the genius and the glories of Napoleon, fostered by him and others in the 'Legend', and his patriotic cult were not incompatible with liberalism. As early as 1831 he espouses the cause of liberty everywhere:

> Je suis fils de ce siècle! Une erreur, chaque année,
> S'en va de mon esprit...[22]
> Et, détrompé de tout, mon culte n'est resté
> Qu'à vous, sainte patrie et sainte liberté...[23]
>
> (*F.A.*, No. 40.)

With his liberalism burgeons the mystique of Revolution and consequently of the French Revolution: 'Les révolutions, ces glorieux changements d'âge de l'humanité, les révolutions transforment tout ...' (*F.A.*, preface). This is the line Lamartine was to adopt, the belief in the inherent goodness of revolution in itself, as an instrument of progress, a begetter of liberty, the line, broadly speaking, of 'le parti du mouvement' during the reign of Louis-Philippe. Much later Hugo expresses the same idea:

> Car ce quatrevingt-treize où vous avez frémi,
> Qui dut être, et que rien ne peut plus faire éclore,
> C'est la lueur de sang qui se mêle à l'aurore.
> Les Révolutions, qui viennent tout venger
> Font un bien éternel dans leur mal passager.
>
> (*C.*, v, 3.)

With all this we would expect to find Hugo thumping the democratic drum and we are not disappointed. The theme of the people recurs often. They are thought of as a powerful giant uprooting the towers of the Bastille:

> ...il avait un jour, d'un revers de sa main,
> Déraciné du sol les tours de la Bastille.
>
> (*F.A.*, No. 3.)

---

[20] Louis Bonaparte's election to the presidency.
[21] *coup d'état.*   [22] How nice to know.
[23] Follows a catalogue of countries and places groaning under oppression; the poem concludes: 'La Muse se doit aux peuples sans défense'.

Their prowess in the July Revolution, worthy of the heroes of
Austerlitz, is hailed with enthusiasm:

> Trois jours vous ont suffi pour briser vos entraves.
> Vous êtes les aînés d'une race de braves
> Vous êtes les fils des géants!
>
> (*C. du C.*, No. 1.)

The human scale or at least the idea is still retained in comparing
the people to a giant, who, however dim his intelligence, may still
be presumed to have his own power of decision, control of his own
actions, but when the people are compared to the sea (*C. du C.*,
Nos. 2 and 15), or to a volcano (*V.I.*, No. 1), the poet clearly intends us to lose sight of men altogether and have in our minds
images that convey the idea of mysterious forces beyond human
control.

But with all his developing sympathy for the people, Hugo did
not advance beyond the fringe of a social message, occasional references to rich and poor, to the virtues of charity, to the sufferings
of the disinherited:

> Rois! la bure est souvent jalouse du velours.
> Le peuple a froid l'hiver, le peuple a faim toujours.
> Rendez-lui son sort plus facile.
> . . . . . .
> Le peuple souvent porte un bien rude collier.
> Ouvrez l'école aux fils, aux pères l'atelier . . .
>
> (*C. du C.*, No. 15.)

and even, later, a reference, a solitary but a vigorous one to the
evils of child-labour:

> Où vont tous ces enfants dont pas un seul ne rit?
>
> (*C.*, iii, 2.)

Here are the glimmerings of a social programme, but the social
problems of democracy, some awareness of the impact on the
people of the Industrial Revolution, these sources of inspiration are
to be found rather in some of Hugo's prose works;[24] they must be
sought in the pages of a now forgotten poet, the *Iambes et Poèmes*
(1830) of Auguste Barbier (1805–82):

> Ma mère, que de maux dans ces lieux nous souffrons!
> L'air de nos ateliers nous ronge les poumons,
> Et nous mourrons, les yeux tournés vers les campagnes.
>
> ('La lyre d'Airain'.)

As one of the chief architects of the Napoleonic legend, Hugo
looked favourably towards Louis Napoleon.[25] His innate bourgeois

---

[24] See below, pp. 173–4.
[25] What man of letters was not a journalist in 1848? Hugo wrote in
L'Envénement.

love of order would in itself have been enough to make him welcome, after the horror of the 'June Days', the ascent to power of a
man whose name was inevitably linked with the idea of orderly
government. Moreover, the Prince President had taken office with
the overwhelming approval of a whole people. Order and democracy wedded! Could there be a more auspicious début for the
Second Republic in the eyes of the democratic republican Hugo
had become and the bourgeois he remained?

Hugo also had his own political ambitions; he saw himself in the
part of Minister of Public Instruction; the paltry offer of a leading
role in the administration of fine arts was a disappointment that removed the scales from his eyes; the Prince President was aiming at
dictatorship; 'Quoi! Après Auguste, Augustule! ... Quoi, parce
que nous avons eu Napoléon le Grand, il faut que nous ayons
Napoléon le Petit.' (Speech, 17 July 1851.)

But the thunders of Jove were of no avail. The *coup d'état*
(December 1851) was the graveyard of his political hopes. *Les
Châtiments* are a thunderous re-entry into the poetic lists. The
poet bellows forth his hatred of Louis Napoleon and all his band
of adventurers – Dupin, Saint-Arnaud, Morny, Maupas, Veuillot
and the rest, of Pio Nono and of the Gallican Church, both favour-
ing the new régime. If anyone had supposed the long interval
during which Hugo had published no poetry meant a drying-up of
his inspiration, here was a triumphant refutation; all the stops of
invective are pulled out by turns; vigorous crudities:

> O ruffians! bâtards...
> Nés du honteux coït de l'intrigue et du sort...
>
> (i, 5.)

violent apostrophe:

> Ah! tu finiras bien par hurler, misérable! ...
>
> (iii, 2.)

direct incitement to kill:

> Tu peux tuer cet homme avec tranquillité
>
> (iii, 15.)

Admittedly, in the very next poem, the poet changes his mind:

> Non, ne le tuez pas...

But why? Is it remorse? Or the thought that such an act might
be regarded as murder rather than condign punishment? Not at
all; merely that other means would be more expedient:

> ...Les Piloris infâmes
> Ont besoin d'être ornés parfois d'un empereur.

At times too he achieves epic grandeur – an unfolding scene evoked in such concrete detail that the reader is there himself as an eye-witness, fascinated, horror-stricken, awed; a scene so packed with events that individuals with all their suffering and heroism are dwarfed by the scale of the tragedy: 'Une procession d'ombres sur le ciel noir . . .' and only one man stands out like a giant:

> L'empereur était là, debout, qui regardait.
> Il était comme un arbre en proie à la cognée.
> Sur ce géant, grandeur jusq'alors épargnée,
> Le malheur, bûcheron sinistre, était monté;
> Et lui, chêne vivant, par la hache insulté,
> Tressaillant sous le spectre aux lugubres revanches,
> Il regardait tomber autour de lui ses branches.
>
> (v, 13.)

Here, in 'L'Expiation' the poet has a tale to tell, so awesome in splendour that any mingling of personal animus seems petty and ridiculous; the political lesson he tries to weave into the poem is a discordant element; the reader rejects this effort to prove something irrelevant, as an unworthy attempt to make a sordid little profit from human woe.

But what inventiveness of themes and meter the *Châtiments* provide, what a boxing of the emotional compass from irony to pity, and what bad taste in this prolonged outburst of rough-tongued lyricism! What a contrast too with *Les Contemplations*!

By 1856 the expression of personal emotion in lyric poetry was out of fashion – 'Pas de Sanglots humains dans le chant du poète.'[26]

But in *Les Contemplations* personal emotion is there in plenty; Hugo, in his island exile, is less exposed to the influence of contemporaneous literary movements than he might otherwise have been, more exposed to the love and flattery of Juliette Drouet. The structure given to the work, suggesting that the poems of the first four books belong to the 'forties and are dominated by the memory of the poet's daughter Léopoldine,[27] is largely *trompe-l'oeil*; many of the poems, despite the dates attached to them, are inspired by Juliette and belong to the 'fifties.[28]

In the last two books, on the other hand, the poet, stimulated by the vivid table-turning séances at Marine Terrace, eagerly strides out of the circle of intimate personal experience towards the mysterious shadows enclosing human life. With him we peer into the giddy abyss of the infinite.

Doubtless the prospect unfolded before the reader's eyes is foggy. Yet there is a grandeur about it that intimate lyric poetry cannot achieve, nor wishes to.

[26] Catulle Mendès, *Légende du Parnasse Contemporain*.
[27] Léopoldine, drowned with her husband, Charles Vacquerie (1843).
[28] Souriau, op. cit., Vol. II, pp. 272 *et seq*.

Thus, as the personal note is lost in the thunder of the spheres, the poetry takes on an apocalyptic character, epic in scale, and on the epic level Hugo will remain in his second manner.

With what relief do we turn from Hugo, the spearhead of the attack against the powers of darkness, the high priest of the Napoleonic legend, the champion of liberal nationalism, revolution, progress and democracy, of religiosity rather than true religion, with what relief from all that to Hugo the poet of love, never mind how profane, of children, of a searing grief that all can understand and many experience, of the song of birds, of sunlight and sunsets, of sea and forest, of dusk, of star-flecked skies at night, of all the beauties of Nature in its rich variety of mood and scene, and – in moderation – to the poet of 'the sweet sad music of humanity'; yes, and even to Hugo the versifier of romantic ballads, evoking Middle Ages he must have 'seen' in the pages of Walter Scott, the word-painter of a 'gorgeous (Near) East', 'seen' in the pages of Chateaubriand, Byron and other travellers or borrowed from the canvasses of Delacroix.

Hugo, the 'thinker', is inexhaustibly and exhaustingly eloquent, often orotund and turgid, usually pretentious, always humourless, and often seething with moral indignation. Hugo, the lyrical poet in the best sense, is simple, accurate and concrete in vision, restrained, homely, loving, moving; Hugo, the Romantic in the narrow sense of period décor, is rich in colour and metrical invention, often entertainingly theatrical.

A good example amongst many of the weaknesses attributed in the foregoing paragraph to Hugo the 'thinker' may be found in the poem entitled 'Pensar-Dudar'.[29] In itself the title is admirable; it goes straight to the point with a praiseworthy economy of means; it is a poem in itself; need any more be said? Indeed, yes, and Hugo says it in two hundred lines or more, leaving us exhausted, exactly where we started from:

> Tout corps traîne son ombre et tout esprit son doute.

A lecturer may sometimes begin his lecture with a series of questions on the subject he is about to expound. His audience will readily accept this approach in the confident belief that at some point in the lecture answers will be provided. Hugo often leaves us suspended on question marks over an abyss of doubt. For a poet who claims to give us guidance this is most unfair. The poem entitled 'Le Monde et le Siècle' (R. et O., No. 7) consists of about one hundred lines; in the first forty the poet asks no fewer than eighteen questions: 'Pourquoi...? Pourquoi...? A quoi bon...? A quoi bon...?' The remainder of the poem is made up of long

[29] *Voix Intérieures*, 38.

sentences introduced by the formula: 'Si c'est pour que', repeated no fewer than nine times. These sentences are in no sense answers to the questions, they are a kind of commentary; to achieve the full significance of the questions the commentaries could therefore all be repeated after each question, as it were a chorus: thus

> A quoi bon l'eau du fleuve et l'éclair de l'orage?

Commentaries:

> Si c'est pour qu'en ce siècle, où la loi tombe en cendre,
> l'homme passe sans voir ...
> Si c'est pour que ce temps passe ... etc. (sixty lines);

another question:

> Pourquoi les brouillards d'or et la paix qui tombent des rameaux?

Commentaries:

> Si c'est pour qu'en ce siècle, ... etc. (sixty lines).

The total length of the poem on this basis would be formidable, the effect unendurable. It is eloquence of the worst kind. A speaker who treated his hearers in this way would soon empty the hall.

Yet we must suppose that the readers of Hugo's own day enjoyed this form of accumulation.[30] It occurs frequently in Hugo. How often does a poem begin with some magnificent image only to degenerate into a fatiguing series of variations, one image calling forth another, like bubbling soap-suds.

We turn the page and find some short poem where observation and feeling are nicely balanced, fused into a perfect whole. The four books of poems published between 1830 and 1840 and the *Contemplations* provide a rich harvest of such poems, where the impulse to write them has been picked like a fruit or a flower at the moment of their perfection.

If, on the other hand, we are in the mood for the purely sensuous excitement of colour laid on thick, the intellectual titillation of rhymes rich and rare, skilfully contrived rhythms, or melodramatic scenes – of cruelty, bloodshed and mystery – we know to be of cardboard, we shall be well served in the *Ballades* and *Les Orientales*. Nor are Hugo's technical skills limited to the *Ballades* and *Les Orientales*. With what skill, for instance, by the jerkiness of his metre, does he suggest the irregular flight of a butterfly:

> Mais non, tu vas trop loin! Parmi des fleurs sans nombre
> > Vous fuyez
> Et moi je reste seule à voir tourner mon ombre
> > A mes pieds!
>
> > *(C. du C.*, No. 27.)

[30] 'Escalation' is now the fashionable word.

With evident but justified self-satisfaction, Hugo vaunts his revolutionary services to literature, in *Les Contemplations* (Nos. 1, 7, 8, 26).

> Je mis un bonnet rouge au vieux dictionnaire...
> J'ai de la périphrase écrasé les spirales...
> J'ai disloqué ce grand niais d'alexandrin... etc.

Words, expressions, metres have all been liberated. The last claim is particularly important. The classical structure of the alexandrine with its main caesura after the sixth syllable cuts the line into two equal halves. Within these two hemistiches subsidiary pauses are necessary, which in the strictest classical prosody fall after the third and ninth syllable. The line is thus divided into four equal portions, but the subsidiary pauses may be placed elsewhere within two equal hemistiches; upon this change of position did the French classical alexandrine rely for variety. Hugo added greatly to the variety and suppleness of the alexandrine by refusing to recognize as sacrosanct the need to place the main caesura after the sixth syllable; henceforth it could occur anywhere in the line; there could also be two of equal value. This in fact is the structure of the line quoted:

> J'ai disloqué...

True, Hugo is less of a revolutionary than he claims; there are probably many more regular than irregular alexandrines in his poetry, but if he uses his own dispensation with discretion, it is always with great effect:

> Et que tout cela fasse un astre dans les cieux!
>
> (*C.*, iii, 11.)

This line slightly separated from the rest concludes a short poem where with magnificent imagery and (this time) with economy, Hugo dwells, not for the first time, on the problem of evil and suffering in the world. The line quoted with its quick run of syllables leading up to the one and only caesura after the eighth syllable provides a skilfully calculated metrical climax to the poem and exactly the appropriate cadence.

Within the still moderately conservative limits of his prosody, Hugo is a master of his form. By his verbal and visual power, his technical skill, his abundance, Hugo inevitably dominates the poetic scene in the Romantic period; he is like a quarry where other poets have hewn material they have then fashioned into their own designs: *Les Orientales* are precursors for Théophile Gautier's theories of 'L'Art pour L'Art'; Théodore de Banville could well have been encouraged by the *Ballades* and *Les Orientales* to emulate the verbal and metrical acrobatics of the master; the intimate type of poetry claimed by Sainte-Beuve as his own is to be found,[31] and not least the Parnassian combination of description, skill and objectivity; 'Le Rouet d'Omphale' (*C.*, ii, 3) could have been signed by Leconte de Lisle or Heredia. Baudelaire might not have disavowed the line:

> Oh! par nos vils plaisirs, nos appétits, nos fanges...
>
> (*C.*, vi, 11.)

and from the same poem:

> Sang du coeur, vin des sens âcre et délicieux.

But for all the wealth he may have scattered to others, Hugo remains by his conception of lyrical poetry very much a poet of the eighteen twenties and 'thirties; his is a poetry of mood, impression, ideas, all directly communicated and on a superficial level. The experience of the poet is 'handed out' to the reader who must accept it. There is no effort to stimulate in the reader a more subtle response, no effort to provide him with a means of creating his own experience; such ideas as these belong to a later age.

III. MUSSET

'Lorsque le pélican, lassé d'un long voyage...'[32] Skilful indeed would be the French schoolboy who avoided having the famous 'tirade' embedded in his memory. Linked to it an image, perhaps derived from an educational Sunday matinée at the Comédie Française: a garret, dimly lit by a lamp with bulbous stem and rounded foot, the shade, globe-shaped, in green translucent glass. The lamp stands in the centre of a small table, also round – the curve and the circle, rounded contours, were dominant in furniture design as in women's fashions of the day. Seated at the table is the poet; long hair, flowing Lavallière tie, velvet jacket, check trousers, wide at the knee, narrow at the foot, and fastened with elastic under pointed shoes – Alfred de Musset (1810–57), the 1830 dandy in person; behind him in the shadows stands the Muse – Marie Dorval perhaps? 'Poète', coos the Muse, 'Poète, prends ton luth et me donne un baiser...' Musset in elegiac mood.

But the Romanticism of 1830 also suggests supercharged passions, jealousy, revenge and sudden death; Byronic impertinence and Satanic laughter concealing the heart sob; exoticism and the rich colours of 'the gorgeous East', under the auspices of Hugo, or, alternatively, a flight into the 'Gothic' past; or again, a cortège of amiable Renaissance rakes, rascally priests, black-eyed, olive-skinned hussies, quick to despatch their aberrant lovers and even themselves with dagger or poison. *Les Contes d'Espagne et d'Italie* (1828–30) provide the reader with all this in plenty, especially in 'Don Paez', 'Les Marrons du Feu', 'Portia' and 'Mardoche', not

---

[31] e.g. *Contemplations*, iii, 16.   [32] 'Nuit de Mai', 1835.

forgetting the 'Ballade à la Lune' with the 'polissonnerie' of the last few stanzas, where, with characteristic Romantic irony, the poet thumbs his nose at 'romantic' moonlight and, by inference one may guess, at all the themes that have provided him with the 'stage trappings 'of this first collection of poems:

> Lune, quel esprit sombre
> Promène au bout d'un fil,
> Dans l'ombre,
> Ta face et ton profil.

Signs of personal experience are difficult to find in *Les Contes*.

> Que j'aime le premier frisson d'hiver! Le chaume
> Sous le pied du chasseur refusant de ployer![33]

Here indeed is a suggestion of direct observation. We could have done without the exclamatory 'Que j'aime', for in truth we are not interested in the poet's personal attitude to the cold, any more than we were in another poet's attitude to 'le son du cor le soir au fond des bois',[34] but 'le premier frisson d'hiver', with its transposition of physiological effect to cause, calls forth an immediate response from our own experience, and our own memories of autumn are stimulated by the image of 'le chaume, Sous le pied du chasseur'. But this is only a flash in the pan. For the most part *Les Contes* are a skilful essay in versification with an agreeable period air nourished by literary reminiscences and current mode. A Parisian of the Parisians, the young Musset of 1830 had no thought, as Lamartine then had, of making a pilgrimage to the Levant in the wake of Chateaubriand and Byron, the heroisms and sufferings of the Greeks move him not a whit, as they had moved Lamartine; unlike Hugo he knew nothing of Spain, and even 'Venise la rouge', scene of his later discomfiture, was as yet unknown to him.[35]

The *Poésies Diverses* which contain poems written between 1830 and 1832 have something of the same tone, and yet the mixture is not the same.

There are scattered indications that the poet, beneath the cynical and light-hearted exterior, is discovering a richer vein of inspiration.

> Puisque c'est ton métier, misérable poète,
> ... de faire de ton âme,
> Une prostituée, et que, joie ou douleur,
> Tout demande sans cesse à sortir de ton coeur;
>
> ('Les Voeux Stériles', 1831.)

[33] Sonnet, 1829. [34] See above, pp. 120–1.
[35] 'L'Andalouse' aroused the suspicion at least in the reader's mind that Musset thought Barcelona was in Andalusia, whilst in the first version of 'Venise', Musset had written: 'Pas un cheval qui bouge'. Providentially, the word 'bâteau' also has two syllables.

Here is the first indication of a personal attitude towards poetry
and of what will become the dominant characteristic of his confession. The same idea recurs in 'A mon Ami Edouard B' (1832):

> Ah! frappe-toi le coeur, c'est là qu'est le génie.
> C'est là qu'est la pitié, la souffrance et l'amour;
> C'est là qu'est le rocher du désert de la vie
> D'où les flots d'harmonie
> Quand Moïse viendra, jailliront quelque jour.

Yet with 'Namouna, conte oriental', which for some obscure
reason figures in *Spectacle dans un fauteuil* (1832), the Byron of
'Don Juan' is once more the dominating influence, and in young
'Jacques Rolla' (1833), Musset's *alter ego*, the 'mal du siècle' and
other posturings of the 1830 generation are clearly in evidence:

> Je ne crois pas, O Christ! à ta parole sainte:
> Je suis venu trop tard dans un monde trop vieux

But Musset was now on the threshold of the great sentimental adventure that was to cut through his life like a tornado. He had met
George Sand in June 1833; the Venetian *fugue* followed; but
Musset fell ill and what more unfavourable to romance than illness? Doctor Pagello attended…and supplanted[36] him. Musset,
disconsolate, returned to France alone. A subsequent reconciliation
did not last.

The transformation from the amiable *roué* into the broken-
hearted lover is attested by the cycle of *Les Nuits* (1835–7) and
the 'Lettre à Lamartine' (1836). The emotional conflagration was
also to leave its mark on Musset's plays,[37] inspire his 'personal'
novel *La Confession d'un Enfant du Siècle*[38] and shed its dying
light on 'Souvenir' (1841).

In 'La Nuit de Mai' (May 1835) the Muse upbraids the poet
for his neglect of her:

> O paresseux enfant! regarde, je suis belle

and invites him in this dawn of spring to forget his sufferings by
going with her in search of pastures new:

> Partons, nous sommes seuls, l'univers est à nous.

– the Romantic theme of escape in fact, of 'Invitation au Voyage'
we are all sensitive to. But the poet is too wrapped up in his sorrow
to sing of joy in any form:

> Je ne chante ni l'espérance,
> Ni la gloire, ni le bonheur.

[36] 'Supplanted' is perhaps unfair. See A. B. Walkley, *Pastiche and Prejudice*, 1921, pp. 242 *et seq.*
[37] See below, pp. 161–2.
[38] See below, p. 184.

Indeed under the weight of suffering he cannot sing at all:[39]

> La bouche garde le silence,
> Pour écouter parler le coeur.

To this the Muse, in her confessed aim of arousing the poet from his torpor, replies that of all themes sorrow is the greatest:

> Rien ne nous rend si grands qu'une grande douleur
> Les plus désespérés sont les chants les plus beaux
> Et j'en sais qui sont de purs sanglots.

The poet adopts this advice, and the remaining poems of the cycle reflect various phases of his experience. In 'La Nuit de Décembre' (November 1835), the only one of the four *Nuits* which is not a dialogue between the poet and his Muse, the poet is poring over old letters and other tokens:

> J'enveloppais dans un morceau de bure
> Ces ruines des jours heureux...

They must be returned to their author and donor, who is duly up-braided for her inconstancy, for the suffering she has inflicted. While engaged on this melancholy task he becomes aware of a shadowy presence:

> Mais tout à coup, j'ai vu dans la nuit sombre
> Une forme glisser sans bruit...

It is the spectre of solitude. Ever since his boyhood, in fact, the poet, so we are informed, has objectivized, as it were, the sense of solitude that has come upon him in moments of stress or tribulation. At this great crisis the spectre is with him once more to give him comfort:

> Quand tu seras dans la douleur,
> Viens à moi sans inquiétude...

But perhaps greater comfort may be derived from confession to a fellow poet whose experience, being similar to his own (so he thought), would provide him with understanding sympathy. The 'Lettre à Lamartine' (February 1836) did not in fact produce quite the hoped-for response. Perhaps Lamartine resented as an indiscreet intrusion this evocation of a past he had buried; or perhaps his more resilient nature was genuinely unable to provide the sympathy Musset needed – and felt he had not received:

> Lamartine vieilli qui me traite en enfant
> ('Sonnet au lecteur'.)

The poet turns again to the Muse, but in 'La Nuit d'Août' (August 1836) the roles are unexpectedly reversed: the poet is determined

---

[39] And yet the poem exists!

to shake off his suffering and find consolation in other experience:

> J'aime et je veux chanter la joie et la paresse ...;

the Muse recalls his past sorrow and upbraids him for his neglect. 'La Nuit d'Octobre' (October 1837), finally, reflects a calmer mood. As the poet recalls the treachery of his mistress, a feeling of indignation wells up within him, but the Muse succeeds in the end in inducing a serener and more resigned philosophy – suffering is essential to self-knowledge:

> Et nul ne se connaît tant qu'il n'a pas souffert

which opens up the way to the attitude displayed by the poet in 'Souvenir' (February 1841), a poem recalling two other famous romantic poems: 'Le Lac' and 'Tristesse d'Olympio', where the inspiration is similar, the attitude different. For Lamartine, the scene of his happiness inspires a lament for the ephemeral nature of man; Nature is unchanging, man transient. Olympio, on the other hand, with the memory of his love fresh in his heart, takes the changing dress of Nature as a sign of Nature's indifference to man's sufferings. Musset's attitude is different again; the suffering is over, the memory remains, ineradicable, and is immensely precious:

> J'enfouis ce trésor dans mon âme immortelle,
> Et je l'emporte à Dieu.

Nothing in Musset's later poetry calls for particular mention. If we set aside the agreeable wit, which often reappears in the fugitive pieces of his latter day, and the pleasant period charm, already stressed, of his earlier poems, his title as a significant lyrical poet rests on the *Nuits* cycle; the carefree irreverent 'enfant terrible' of the Nodier salon:

> ... Enfant par hasard adopté
>   Et gâté ...
>   ('Réponse à M. Charles Nodier', 1843.)

is suddenly struck down by sorrow, and expresses its keenness, its changing moods, with urgent sincerity. Who would question Musset's sincerity, the reality of his suffering? The question is rather whether sincerity is enough to achieve what Musset aims to achieve. His main purpose as a poet (apart from such consolation as he could get from writing poetry as a psychological derivative) must be to make the reader share his emotional experience in its intensity.

The fact of suffering, Musset thinks, is the first condition:

> Rien ne nous rend si grands qu'une grande douleur.

The other essential is precisely the poet's sincerity: what the poet feels keenly will be felt equally at the receiving, the reader's end, just as when a rope is shaken hard enough at one end, the impulse will run along it to the other. Musset expresses that idea often:

> Ah! frappe-toi le coeur, c'est là qu'est le génie[40]

or again:

> De ton coeur ou de toi lequel est le poète?[41]
> C'est ton coeur...

and in a letter to his brother[42] Musset writes: 'Quand j'éprouve en faisant un vers, un certain battement de coeur que je connais, je suis sûr que mon vers est de la meilleure qualité que je puisse pondre.' On both these points Musset is in line with the ideas of his day: the belief in the virtues of 'direct communication': in painting as in literature, but, because appealing to the visual sense, the painters may have had more justification,[43] the impact upon viewer or reader is assured by the intensity of the passion (suffering or other) expressed, and the sincerity, the directness therefore, it is expressed with.

But Musset may be regarded as more Romantic than most, and in a deeper sense than was suggested at the outset where the reference was especially to the more superficial aspect of modes and manners. He is peculiarly a Romantic by his belief that love and the suffering it engenders are the only subjects for great lyrical poetry; thus there are some subjects suited to lyrical poetry, others that are not. This is analogous to the cult of the 'picturesque' in (figurative) painting, a cult fashionable in the Romantic period and by no means extinct today: certain subjects, certain landscapes in particular lend themselves to painting, others do not. We believe such a view to be fallacious and prefer to think that good figurative painting may be achieved with any subject: a ship in full sail, a machine, an old boot, provided the colour values and composition are good, the texture of the object selected skilfully suggested.

That love has always been one of the great themes of lyrical poetry is obvious, and there is no denying that some Romantic direct-communication poems still evoke a vigorous emotional response from the modern reader – e.g. 'Le Lac'. We would hesitate to say that Musset ever achieves that height and there are two reasons why: first, his love poetry, in spite of the suffering it records, is sometimes prosaic. The passage in 'La Nuit de Mai', for instance, where the Muse brings a sheaf of suggestions to entice her poet to sing, lacks poetic resonance:

> Chanterons-nous l'espoir, la tristesse ou la joie,...

---

[40] 'A mon Ami Edouard B.', 1832.   [41] 'Nuit d'Août'.
[42] 1831.   [43] e.g. Delacroix, Géricault.

The same applies with greater force to a well-known passage in the 'Lettre à Lamartine':

> Lorsque le laboureur, regagnant sa chaumière . . .

It consists of a string of statements that portray what is indeed a pathetic situation, but it lacks rhythm and the poetic effect is meagre.

The Muse of 'La Nuit d'Août' is also at times very prosy:[44]

> Hélas! toujours un homme, hélas! toujours des larmes! . . .

The second reason raises a matter of taste – what is and what is not appropriate in certain contexts. Thus, for the Muse to place a kiss (of inspiration perhaps?) on the poet's brow could be a suitable, if commonplace image, but a passionate, exchanged kiss

> Notre premier baiser, ne t'en souviens-tu pas . . .
>
> ('Nuit de Mai'.)

changes the whole idea; worse follows:

> Quand je te vis si pâle au toucher de mon aile,
> Et que, les yeux en pleurs, tu tombas dans mes bras.

For Musset to fall into the arms of his mistress is one thing, but for the poet to fall into the arms of his Muse, winged and all,[45] is very like bathos.

> Ce soir encore . . .

exclaims the poet to his spectre of solitude:[46]

> Ce soir encore je t'ai vu m'apparaître
> C'était par une triste nuit.
> L'aile des vents battait à ma fenêtre;
> J'étais seul, courbé sur mon lit.

So far, excellent; a powerful sense of solitude and despair is conveyed, but the impression is destroyed because the poet switches into a different register:

> J'y regardais une place chérie,
> Tiède encor d'un baiser brûlant.

Yet another example of the same sort of thing may be found in 'La Nuit d'Octobre' where the reader is subjected to the story of the betrayal suffered by the poet:

> Tandis qu'à ce balcon, seul, je veille ou je pleure,
> En quel lieu, dans quel lit, à qui souriais-tu?

This is not great lyrical poetry nor even good erotic poetry; neither can survive the very suggestion of beds and bedrooms, suitable perhaps for a novel or a scene of jealousy between a lover and his

[44] This seems particularly true of his alexandrines; his octosyllabics seem more rhythmical.
[45] A winged Muse is, moreover, unorthodox.   [46] 'Nuit de Décembre'.

mistress, on the stage. If the central phrase, 'dans quel lit...', be removed, the reader could well evoke Hermione berating Oreste in the famous scene from *Andromaque*.[47] We discern here the intense egotism of Musset, absorbed with his grief, or more precisely his grievances, intent upon making his poetry authentic... lived, but leaving out of account what is in effect the vital thing, the quality and intensity of the reader's response.

Hitherto we have stressed the Romantic aspects of Musset's lyrical poetry, both superficial and more fundamental. We believe he was by nature thoroughly rooted in his time. Yet he himself might have rejected this judgment. Intellectually he liked to adopt an attitude of detachment. This is clearly indicated as early as 1831 in 'Les Secrètes Pensées de Rafaël:

> Grèce, O Mère des arts, terre d'idolâtrie,
> De mes voeux insensés éternelle patrie

Henceforth he will be a neutralist in the literary polemics of the day: Classics? Romantics? A plague on both your houses:

> Classiques bien rasés, à la face vermeille,
> Romantiques barbus, aux visages blêmis.
> Salut! – J'ai combattu dans vos camps ennemis
> Vétéran je m'assois sur mon tambour crevé.
> Racine rencontrant Shakespeare sur ma table,
> S'endort près de Boileau qui leur a pardonné.

In fact, Musset's attitudes often suggest those of an eighteenth-century free-thinking libertine.

The *Lettres de Dupuis et Cotonnet* (1836) give further proof of his aloofness from his Romantic friends of 'Arsenal' days. There are four of these; Dupuis holds the pen, but the letters claim to reflect the literary preoccupations of the two friends, and behind them those of their worthy little Louis-Philippian circle of La Ferté-sous-Jouarre, anxious to keep abreast of things by reading *Le Constitutionnel*, *Le Journal des Débats* and the most recent books: 'Nous avons dans la rue Marchande un gros cabinet de lecture, où il nous vient des cloyères de livres.' ('Première Lettre'.)

As prototypes of Bouvard and Pécuchet, Musset's two worthies are disappointing, their letters dull; but the first letter in particular serves to show Musset's attitude, agreeably ironical if lacking depth; quite vigorous enough, however, to estrange him from Victor Hugo, to whom a few years later he held out an olive branch:

> On se brouille, on se fuit – Qu'un hasard nous rassemble,
> On s'approche, on sourit, la main touche la main,
> Et nous nous souvenons, que nous marchions ensemble.[48]

---

[47] Act V, 3. 'Qui te l'a dit...' etc.
[48] 'A. M. Victor Hugo', 26 April 1843.

Apart from the quality of Musset's lyrical poetry, a certain dichotomy between his intellectual attitudes and his emotional nature is discernible. It appears more clearly in his plays.

IV. SAINTE-BEUVE

Charles-Augustin Sainte-Beuve (1804–69) had made Hugo's acquaintance in 1827 and fallen under his spell. Not unnaturally, the example of Hugo awakened literary ambitions in his disciple; Sainte-Beuve would not be a mere critic, he would be a poet and a novelist. *Vie, Poésie et Pensées de Joseph Delorme* (1829), *Les Consolations* (1830), *Pensées d'Août* (1837) are his main legacy to poetry,[49] *Volupté* (1834) to the novel.[50] In both Sainte-Beuve largely subscribes to fashion. To Vinet,[51] who had had reservations about his short story *Madame de Pontivy*, he wrote (January 1838): 'Le malheur des natures qui n'ont que des inspirations et des inclinations sans la foi est d'être à la merci d'un souffle et d'une vicissitude.'

The pseudo-biographical note attached to the supposedly posthumous poems presents Joseph Delorme as a latter-day scion of the house of Werther and Obermann. In-breeding has impoverished the blood, but before fading into eternity as a result of phthisis complicated by a heart condition, the poet has sung his song in a minor key, comparing his Muse to a consumptive girl:

> Elle file, elle coud, et garde à la maison
> Un père vieux, aveugle et privé de raison.
> Si, . . .
> Elle chante parfois, une toux déchirante,
> La prend dans sa chanson, pousse en sifflant un cri,
> Et lance les graviers de son poumon meurtri.
>
> ('Ma Muse'.)

The intimate, almost morbid tone is maintained in *Les Consolations* and *Pensées d'Août*; also a religious note is heard, which is a sign of Sainte-Beuve's moral development of those years. Surprisingly perhaps for a poet with such an etiolated muse, he is bold in versification; caesuras are not anchored to the sixth syllable, enjambements are frequent, the liking for 'rimes riches' is marked. To Sainte-Beuve, too, may go the credit of having brought the sonnet back into favour, destined to be the form most affected by the Parnassians.

One at least of his sonnets has become an anthology piece:

> J'étais un arbre en fleurs où chantait ma jeunesse . . .
>
> (*Suite de J.D.*)

[49] Also *Le Livre d'Amour* (posth. 1904).
[50] See below, pp. 184–5.
[51] Swiss critic and Protestant theologian (1797–1847).

and in his 'Epître à Villemain' (*Pensées d'Août*), where in a characteristically prosaic tone he comments on the literary scene of the
day, occurs a passage that has become proverbial:

> ... et Vigny, plus secret,
> Comme en sa tour d'ivoire, avant midi, rentrait.

Nor should we omit to mention an interesting poem, 'Les Rayons
Jaunes' (*Poésies de J.D.*) where, discarding mood as the inspiring
theme, the poet builds his poem on the chain of images suggested
by the word 'yellow'. Sainte-Beuve, in the footsteps of Diderot, has
stumbled on the psychological truth that reverie, uncontrolled by
a given line of thinking, meanders at the whim of fortuitous sense
impressions.[52]

The fiction, however transparent, of posthumous verse from the
pen of an obscure consumptive, had convenience for the *raté*
Sainte-Beuve was, as a poet. He could conveniently re-inter Joseph
Delorme and devote himself to his real vocation, that of the critic
Joseph Delorme had been at heart:

> J'aime rimer et j'aime lire aussi
> Lorsque à rêver mon front s'est obscurci,
>
> O mes amis, alors je prends un livre.
> Non pas un seul, mais dix, mais vingt, mais cent;
>
> C'est mon bonheur.
>
> ('Mes Livres'; *Poésies de J.D.*)

---

[52] 'Une seule qualité physique peut conduire l'esprit qui s'en occupe à
une infinité de choses diverses. Prenons une couleur, le jaune par exemple:
l'or est jaune, la soie est jaune, le souci est jaune, la bile est jaune, la paille
est jaune; à combien d'autres fils ce fil ne répond-il pas? La folie, le rêve,
le décousu de la conversation consistent à passer d'un objet à un autre par
l'entremise d'une qualité commune. Le fou ne s'aperçoit pas qu'il change;
il tient un brun de paille jaune et luisant à la main, et il crie qu'il a saisi
un rayon de soleil. Combien d'hommes qui ressemblent à ce fou sans s'en
douter! Et moi-même, peut-être, dans ce moment.' (20 October 1760,
Lettres à Sophie Volland, 1930, Vol. I, pp. 255, 256.)

Chapter 11

RISE AND FALL OF THE ROMANTIC DRAMA
CLASSICAL REVIVAL
AND 'ECOLE DU BON SENS'

THE debate on dramatic form fought out between Classics and Romantics during the Restoration, in pamphlets, prefaces and petitions, in the columns of the Press and on the stage itself, may, like all the polemics of another age after the dust has settled, seem unimportant; a storm in a tea-cup. Yet significance attaches to it in various ways: it confirms that argument engenders its own heat; from dislike of an opponent's views we come to dislike the man, all the more if he shows skill (obstinacy) and resource (treachery) in defending them. The defenders of tradition ('Les momies', 'les glabres') and the new men ('Les bousingots') came to hate each other. Secondly, it underlines that ever since the great days of the seventeenth century, if not before, the drama had been the pre-eminent literary 'genre'. Lyric poetry was secondary, the novel, despite its long record, almost a 'parvenu'; both had already felt the impact of the new ideas but drama was in a class apart, and when the *Méditations* were kindling poetic enthusiasm, or *Cinq-Mars* and *La Chronique de Charles IX* opening new fields of investigation for the novelist, the weight of inertia acquired by the classical tradition still lay heavy on the drama; naturally therefore the battle became particularly bitter around the citadel of classical tradition, the 'Théâtre Français'. Thirdly, the debate shows how, not for the first time nor the last, political factors entered in and confused the issues.

The background to the Romantic revolution in the drama goes back a long way in the eighteenth century. Voltaire had made innovations in tragedy; comedy, from being comic in the days of Molière, had become serious with Destouches, had verged on the sentimental with Marivaux, dissolved in tears with Nivelle de la Chaussée; a new 'genre' had developed from it, the 'drame bourgeois', in prose instead of verse, stimulated by Diderot, more skilfully practised by Sedaine; later again, and on a lower plane, the melodrama had made its appearance, founded by Mercier. But though the eighteenth century was boldly experimental, tragedy retained its pre-eminence and no dramatic poet could neglect winning his spurs in that 'genre'.

During the Empire it enjoyed official support, the deadliest of stimulants no doubt, but there was no competition; besides, there was Talma! As an alternative to the classical repertoire at the 'Français' and the 'Odéon' there was only the melodrama, immensely popular with the masses, in the boulevard theatres.[1]

After the fall of Napoleon, peace brought renewed contacts with other countries, all the more welcome since France, beleaguered for so many years, had been starved of them. Madame de Staël's influence, hitherto fought off with success by administrative action, was in the ascendant and, through her, German influences, notably A. W. Schlegel, the vigorous critic of French classical traditions,[2] and Schiller. The latter's *Karl Moor* had, indeed, slipped across the frontier before the war and Napoleon had closed it;[3] now his historical plays, much admired by Madame de Staël,[4] were to make a particular impact. Italian influences were to come in with that self-elected citizen of Milan, Stendhal;[5] English influences, especially Byron, Walter Scott and Shakespeare, were to dominate – thanks to translators and adaptors.

All these stimuli created a new climate of opinion. Even the traditionalists felt the need for new sources of inspiration; encouraged perhaps by Marie-Joseph Chenier's admonitions,[6] illumined by Madame de Staël, they followed Schiller and sought new material in national history.[7] Their efforts were no more successful than those of their immediate predecessors under the Empire; who today has heard of A. V. Arnault, Lucien Arnault, Viennet, Jouy, Andrieux, Pichat, Brifaut, to mention only some of the more prominent amongst the dramatic poets who courted the tragic muse and saw themselves as the worthy successors of Corneille and Racine?

Time has dealt only a little less unkindly with another group, the semi-classics or semi-romantics, such as Népomucène Lemercier, Ancelot, Lebrun, Soumet, Casimir Delavigne. Attached to the classical tradition, they sought none the less to revitalize it by more variety of subject, greater freedom of plot, more detail of place and time – the Voltairian formula in fact, with more emphasis. Lemercier's *Pinto*, especially in view of its date (1799), is a remarkable prototype of the historical drama. Pinto, the valet who en-

---

[1] Théâtre de la Porte-St Martin, L'Ambigu-Comique, La Gaîté.
[2] *Über dramatische Kunst u. Litteratur*, a course of lectures, Vienna (1808), attended by Mme de Staël.
[3] Lamartelière's adaptation: *Robert, chef des Brigands* (1792).
[4] *De l'Allemagne*, II, 8.
[5] Martineau, preface to *Racine et Shakespeare*, Divan edn.
[6] See above, p. 20.   [7] e.g., Viennet's tragedy – *Clovis* (1820).

gineers the emancipation of Portugal from the Spanish yoke, is reminiscent of Figaro and foreshadows, but in lighter mood, Hugo's Ruy Blas. 'Notre tragédie nouvelle ressemblera beaucoup à *Pinto*', wrote Stendhal in 1823.[8] Lebrun's *Marie Stuart* (1820) and Ancelot's *Fiesque* (1824) again show the influence of Schiller.

The least forgotten of these dramatists is Casimir Delavigne, the patriotic and liberal poet of *Les Messéniennes* (1818–22) and author of a number of tragedies: *Les Vêpres Siciliennes* (1819), *Le Paria* (1821), *Marino Faliero* (1829)[9], *Louis XI* (1832) and *Les Enfants d'Edouard* (1833).[10] As far as his moderate nature allowed, Delavigne, in the later plays at least, leans towards the Romantics, but like Louis-Philippe in politics, his ideal in the drama was the 'Juste Milieu': 'le mépris des règles n'est pas moins insensé que le fanatisme pour elles', he opined.[11] Neither he nor his friends had grasped that the new dramatic ideas needed a new dramatic structure and, above all, new poetic diction.

In retrospect the contest between the Old Guard and the wild young men seems pathetically uneven, but the former had certain advantages: opponents who were as yet unorganised and unsure of what they wanted; on their own side: entrenched positions at the 'Français' with a bodyguard of actors headed by Talma, and public opinion where diverse currents produced paradoxical if temporary situations. Cultivated opinion, moulded by the habits of over a century, still believed in the classical *bienséances*, there was nothing (on the stage) to make them change their views; the man in the street was apt to form his literary judgments on his politics, liberal and xenophobic, and this, especially after the death of the St Helena exile (1821), meant anglophobic. He may not have been familiar with the opinions of the *Edinburgh Review*, which, conversely, went from literature to politics:[12] the glory of Racine was as nothing compared with that of Shakespeare, *ergo* French intelligence, character, government were inferior; away with the last vestige of French intellectual hegemony! – the French man in the street may have been unfamiliar with all that, but from Wellington and Hudson Lowe to Shakespeare was an easy step.

Thus classical attitudes, liberalism and anglophobia combined to oppose the new ideas. When the Penley troop of English actors came to Paris (August 1822) they were howled off the stage of the 'Porte-Saint-Martin' after two nights.[13]

---

[8] *Racine et Shakespeare.*
[9] Inspired by Byron's tragedy of the same name.
[10] The mediocre painter Paul Delaroche had exhibited a picture with the same title in the Salon (1831).
[11] 'Discours de Réception' at the Académie Française (1825).
[12] Martineau, op. cit.
[13] 'A bas Shakespeare, aide-de-camp de Wellington'!

Stendhal, an early champion of the new dramatic formulae, was, soon after, in the lists. Strong liberal and Napoleonic supporter that he was, imbued with the spirit of Italian Austrophobic 'Romanticismo', he too might have been expected to espouse the French liberal attitude of the day. But Stendhal was years ahead of French liberals nor did he allow his political opinions to interfere with his literary judgments. A passionate Shakespearian, he had paid a visit to London (October 1821) to see Shakespeare performed; the treatment suffered by Penley seemed almost a personal insult;[14] nor to this anti-Bourbon did French national honour appear involved. In two articles (October 1822; January 1823) he expressed his admiration for Shakespeare in preference to Racine, railed at the unities, discussed the impact of the new ideas on comedy. These articles formed the basis of his pamphlet: *Racine et Shakespeare* (March 1823). Articles and pamphlets had little success at the time.

At this point, however, the unnatural alliance between 'ultra' and liberal opinion began to crumble. The conservative *Muse française*[15] perspicaciously divined that in the 'romantic genre' lay hidden a revolutionary principle. What more dangerous! Immediately the conservative forces: Church, Academy, pedagogues, drew together. The Academy's solemn condemnation (1824) of Romanticism was the outcome, a politico-literary decision, well in line with the hardening policies now being pursued by the government.[16]

The Academy's fulmination provoked Stendhal once more. The second and augmented version of *Racine et Shakespeare* (March 1825), full of contemporary political allusions and claiming tragedy should exalt the glory of Napoleon, comedy poke fun at the Bourbon *préfets*, was more successful than the first; for a moment this 'hussard du romantisme',[17] defending a type of drama nourished by history and politics, free of formal rules and alexandrine verse, looked like the leader of a new school. The new school was indeed taking shape,[18] but its development was not what Stendhal wanted; liberal in the broadest sense it was bound to be but its preoccupations were to be literary, not deliberately political. The political confusions of 1822 had melted away. Shakespeare could return to Paris, as he did with Kemble, and be acclaimed at the Odéon (September 1827). Romanticism was on the march towards the citadel of the classics – the 'Théâtre Français'. Talma was dead

---

[14] Martineau, op. cit.   [15] Flourished, July 1823–June 1824.
[16] The Spanish War 1823; 'La Chambre Retrouvée' (1824); the Theatre censorship; the pamphleteer P.-L. Courier and the song-writer Béranger imprisoned.
[17] As *Le Globe* called him.
[18] The first *cénacle* (1824) which met at L'Arsenal (Charles Nodier).

(1826); and here on the Romantic side was a new champion – Victor Hugo. In the prefaces to his early poetic works he had professed a lordly indifference to classico-romantic polemics, but since then he had shaken off the chrysalis of traditionalism. His play *Cromwell* (1827) was too unwieldy for performance at that time but the *Préface* (October 1827), which expressed in lapidary form ideas that were in the air, put heart into the Romantics and Hugo in the forefront of their array.

A valuable ally was revealed in Baron Taylor (1789–1879), the new Royal Commissioner of the 'Théâtre Français', appointed (1824), ironically enough, as a result of pressure from classical partisans[19] – a traitor within the gates! 1829 was to be a crucial year; on 11 February *Henri III et sa cour*, performed with immense success in the presence of the Duc d'Orléans and his dinner guests of that evening, made the reputation of Alexandre Dumas, unknown until then, and thereafter one of Romanticism's most dynamic and prolific forces; in June Hugo wrote *Un duel sous Louis XIII*. Accepted by the 'Théâtre Français' it was quickly censored. Dumas might portray a Valois as he liked but for Hugo to show a Bourbon as a nonentity and a puppet in the hands of his minister was another story – politics again. Yet, shortly before, Charles X had shown himself remarkably liberal; in answer to a petition[20] from the Classics invoking his aid in defence of the National Theatre against the Romantic invasion he had declined to intervene.[21] On 24 October Vigny, who could still at that time almost vie with Hugo as the foremost Romantic poet, scored a minor success with his translation of *Othello – le More de Venise*, following it up on 1 November with a pamphlet: *Lettre à Lord ****, where in more restrained tones the author echoed some of the ideas expressed by *La Préface de Cromwell*. The final blow in the Romantic conquest of the stage was delivered, fittingly, by Hugo. As yet without a performed play to his credit,[22] he wrote *Hernani* in under a month[23] and saw it triumph amidst pandemonium (25 February 1830).

Many years later, Théophile Gautier was to recall[24] the euphoric joy in victory that filled Hugo's supporters, himself so prominent amongst them, on the night of the 'battle of Hernani'. He reflects too the crusading spirit the *Préface de Cromwell* had kindled, the unity of purpose it had created amongst the supporters

[19] Latreille: *La Fin du Théâtre Romantique*, chap. 3.

[20] 'La Pétition des Sept' from the seven signatories. See Le Roy: *L'Aube du Théâtre Romantique*, vi.

[21] 'Messieurs, je ne puis rien pour ce que vous désirez; je n'ai comme tous les Français, qu'une place au parterre'.

[22] His *Amy Robsart* had been performed on 13 February 1828 at the Odéon under the name of his brother-in-law, Paul Foucher. It was a failure. Le Roy, op. cit., xviii.

[23] 29 August–25 September 1828.   [24] *Histoire du Romantisme*.

of the new ideas: '*La Préface de Cromwell* rayonnait à nos yeux comme les Tables de la Loi sur le Sinaï... les injures des petits journaux classiques contre le jeune maître, que nous regardions... comme le plus grand poète de France, nous mettaient en des colères féroces. Aussi brûlions-nous d'aller combattre l'hydre du perruquinisme'.

The Romantics had acquired a unity of purpose thanks to the opposition they had encountered. After 1830 coherence amongst the principals is less easy to see. They had a shared experience behind them and had felt the same influences but each made of these what suited him best.

Alexandre Dumas (1802–70) had come to Paris to seek his fortune in 1822. Meagre employment as a clerk in the service of the Duc d'Orléans enabled him to live during his first efforts at writing for the theatre: two light comedies, in collaboration: *La Chasse et L'Amour* (1825) and *La Noce et L'Enterrement* (1826). In 1827 a real sense of dramatic mission was kindled in him by Kemble's production of *Hamlet*. Hitherto he had known Shakespeare only through Ducis, now he became aware of 'la possibilité de construire un monde' – to quote his own expression.[25] Fired with enthusiasm he wrote a five-act historical drama in verse on the murder of Monaldeschi, a subject suggested to him by a bas-relief he had seen at the 'Salon', representing that event. *Christine* (1827), which, though a historical drama, was classical by its respect of the unities, was not to be performed until 1830. By then Dumas had found fame and greatly helped the Romantic cause with *Henri III et sa cour* (1829).

After the desert with scarcely an oasis the French theatre had presented for a century and more, the enthusiasm aroused by the play is understandable, such are its theatrical merits: Act I: star-reading by astrologer; statecraft – divide to rule! – by Queen; potions by ditto; lady in trance... 'discovered' in closet behind retractable panel; lover (eager), husband (ambitious); discovery of wife's kerchief; jealousy; murder in prospect; curtain (slow) on Duke (scowling), tremolos from the orchestra; all the elements for a pleasant evening's entertainment have been assembled; the spectator is agog to know how the dark deed will be accomplished.

His curiosity will be satisfied, but not until the end of Act V after the trap has been laid and skilful side issues – scenes at court, provocations and prospective duels, council meeting with humiliation of Duke by King – have provided suspense and added fuel to the Duke's desire for revenge, satisfied at last when from the casement of the Duchess' bower he, and the spectators, over his shoulder as it

[25] *Les Mémoires*, ii, p. 420.

were, gaze down on his rival being done to death by a pack of
hired *bravi*.

The tempo of *Henri III* is as nothing compared with that
of *Antony* (1831), where at breakneck gallop the action speeds to
its fearful climax. 'Gallop' fits, for there is something almost symbolical in the sound of galloping horses and carriage wheels that
provide or, to the excited imagination of the spectator, seem to
provide, background music to the vital decisions that have to be
taken in minutes, nay, seconds, to save life or reputation.

Antony is a drama of passion set in the society of the day; in
Act IV, scene 6, one of the rare moments of pause in the play,
Dumas introduces a discussion on modernism; a kind of *Critique
de L'Ecole des Femmes* in miniature which with his accustomed
skill he uses to send the plot on its headlong way. Eugène d'Her-
villy, the young poet, prefers history to modernism; history provides
drama, facts ready-made, which, transposed into modern times,
may invite disbelief.[26] Dumas' own experience had in fact given
him the elements of his play;[27] the sentiments of Antony towards
Colonel d'Hervey had their source in Dumas' own towards Captain
Waldor. But, unlike Eugène, Dumas did not hesitate to court disbelief by embroidering on reality; he did not poignard his mistress;
Antony does, and he follows this up by saving her reputation with
the famous *coup de théâtre*: 'Elle me résistait, je l'ai assassinée.'
Absurd? Undoubtedly. Would the monstrous egotist that Antony
has shown he is, be so solicitous of his victim's reputation in such a
desperate pass? Alternatively, if that were his true nature, could
he ever have allowed such a situation to arise? But the audiences
of the day were less fastidious. The Antony of all but the last words
of the play was the image of what they might have liked to be,[28]
and in the end there is the quixotic flash of generosity – unreal but
no matter – to send them home, their other self satisfied: 'Elle me
résistait . . .' etc.

At least two remarks in *Henri III* have become legends: 'Saint-
Paul! qu'on me cherche les mêmes hommes qui ont assassiné
Dugast (I, 8) and 'serre-lui la gorge avec ce mouchoir; la mort lui
sera plus douce . . .' (V, 3). They give colour to the character (Duc
de Guise), perhaps to an age; theatrically their dynamism is due to
the stimulus they give to the spectators' imagination, the first in
anticipation, the second about what is happening off-stage; neither
produces a *coup de théâtre* because they are in character, whereas
Antony's last words are not; hence the delightful intellectual shock

---

[26] The very argument used by Corneille in the seventeenth century to
justify historical subjects (from classical antiquity of course) in tragedy.
[27] His liaison with Mélanie Waldor, wife of an officer.
[28] See in particular II, 5.

of surprise that stifles criticism and gives them a perennial freshness after all the rest has faded. As a play, *Antony* is less well balanced than *Henri III*; Antony, like a character in Balzac, strides out of his frame; yet, if we can no longer believe in him as his contemporaries did, we can agree with them that with his torrential passion, his bastard's chip on the shoulder justifying his egotism, his Byronic hostility to society,[29] Antony was created, more quintessentially perhaps than any other Romantic hero – Didier, Hernani, Ruy Blas, Chatterton and the rest – out of the stuff of an epoch when Revolution and war had broken down the old structure of society and given free rein to demonic egotisms.

The next twelve years saw most of Dumas' contribution to the Romantic theatre; historical tableaux: *Charles VII chez ses grands vassaux* (1831), historical melodrama: *La Tour de Nesle* (1832), historical comedies contrived with all the skill of *Henri III*: *Mademoiselle de Belle-Isle* (1839), *Les demoiselles de Saint-Cyr* (1843); not the least significant are the plays where Dumas has become fascinated with the typically Romantic theme of energy or genius as a mysterious force personified in a character (usually historical, for greater effect): *Napoléon Bonaparte* (1831), *Richard Darlington* (1831), *Kean* (1836), *Caligula* (1837), *Paul Jones* (1838).

When other inspiration failed, he found abundant material to adapt in his own historical romances: *Les Trois Mousquetaires* (1844), *Monte-Cristo* (1848), *La Dame de Monsereau* (1860).

'...La possibilité de construire un monde...', the flash of intuition Dumas had had when he saw Hamlet was fully realized: Dumas constructed an imaginative world of the theatre mostly from bits and pieces of history, with little regard for accuracy, style or character delineation, but full of zest, passion, energy, and put together with an eye for the elements that keep the spectator's interest alive: a well-motivated and fast-moving plot, suspense, surprise, *coups de théâtre*.

Inevitably the lion's share in Romanticism's conquest of the stage belongs to Hugo. The *Préface de Cromwell*, *Hernani* are great moments in the story; *Marion Delorme* (1831) more doubtfully, *Ruy Blas* (1838) certainly, continue the triumphant record.

In the *Préface* Hugo's aim is to show that the dramatic forms he and his friends are trying to create are in line with the broad development of the human mind as reflected down the ages in art; from the primitive era when art was essentially lyrical and had as its characteristic form the ode, mankind has passed through classical antiquity – the Homeric and epic era, when even tragedy was really epic, to the modern age of which Dante, Milton, Shakes-

[29] e.g. especially in II, 5.

peare above all, are the gods and of which the *drame* is the art form, characterized by a new element, itself the product of Christianity's impact upon man; Christianity showed him his dual nature, whence sprang attitudes unknown to paganism: melancholy and the spirit of enquiry.[30] Ugliness was seen to be inextricably interwoven with beauty and life, evil with good, the grotesque (i.e. all that is comic, ridiculous, unagreeable in life and humanity) with the sublime. The *drame*, as the real poetic form of the modern world, must recognize this truth and show Nature, man, in the round. That does not mean slavish imitation of nature but interpretation and concentration. 'Local colour' must not be superficial imitation of a given period but penetration to its essential character.

Hugo attacks the unities as being out of date and unsuitable for the *drame* which requires only unity of action. Verse, on the other hand, far from being incompatible with art's function of interpreting Nature, gives that interpretation vigour, definition, provided it throws away the traditions of the *style noble*. Hugo's attack on the neo-classical poets – Delille and company, 'L'Ecole de la périphrase' – is masterly. Thus in brief: the *drame* with the grotesque and the tragic together as the art form of the modern world, the unity of action as its only rule, art as an interpretation and concentration of nature, poetry freed from the absurdities of *style noble*, as the ideal vehicle of expression for the *drame*.

Authoritarian, full of confidence in the rightness of the new gospel, the *Préface* was a splendid rallying point for the Romantics. Was it also valuable as an aesthetic code? Its one positive contribution here is the idea that since the comic and the tragic co-exist in life, they should do so in the *drame* – a doubtful proposition, since their simultaneous effects on the spectator, which is the essential consideration, will cancel each other out like a plus and minus sign. With the possible exception of *L'Homme qui rit*[31] Hugo never applied his theory; comic and tragic effects in succession quite often – *Cromwell, Hernani, Ruy Blas* – but not concomitant, and even in these cases he has not, as Shakespeare does, used a comic effect to reinforce a previous tragic one; the scene of the fools in *Cromwell* or the excellent buffoonery by Don Césare in *Ruy Blas* are like cameos inserted in a larger frame, to be enjoyed on their own.

The *Préface de Cromwell* was a brilliant improvisation, quickly put together after the play had been written, more for the good of the Romantic cause, than as a defence of the play it is tenuously related to.

---

[30] cf. *De la Littérature.*
[31] Souriau, *Histoire du Romantisme*, Vol. I, Part 2, Bk. 2, chap. 7. But does the reader really bear in mind the fixed leer of Gwynplaine?

The play itself is simple in plot – will Cromwell become king or not? – but elaborate in presentation, a great pageant. Hugo may reasonably claim to have been faithful to the principle that 'local colour' should penetrate the spirit of the period chosen. Well-portrayed are the Cavalier devil-may-care attitudes (Rochester), the fanatical puritanism (Carr), Cromwell's mixture of piety and political realism, his outward power and domestic subordination to a strong-willed wife and favourite daughter. But in general, the effect is rather of epic scenes on a grand scale than of dramatic action; no wonder, with its sixty characters and more, and the need for a mammoth stage, it did not invite performance. In 1827 the author could do no more than give readings and nearly three years were to elapse before a play from the pen of the young poet, who was now the acknowledged leader of the Romantics and was to confirm his position shortly by the publication of *Les Orientales* (1829), was to be performed.

The 'battle of Hernani' (25 February 1830) has become legendary;[32] the stakes were high; on one side the 'mummies' who felt they were defending a long and proud tradition dating back to antiquity against the biggest danger they had faced to date, a poet of genius; on the other the 'Jeunes-France', a 'happy band of brothers' fighting for freedom in art and for a man they passionately admired. Their victory was not easy; Hugo was obliged to make some sacrifices in his text to overcome the prejudices even of his leading actress, and to meet the demands of the censor; the play was to be amusingly parodied,[33] the critics were not slow to attack the play from the triple point of view of history, psychology and structure. These criticisms remain valid; historical inexactitudes abound:[34] the portrait of Charles V is a caricature, the tomb scene a fantasy, disadvantages arise from placing a prominent historical figure in the foreground of a work of art, the 'pun d'honor' may admit murder, not suicide. Even if we accept Charles merely as a character he is unsatisfactory because of the dichotomy between Charles the King, the irresponsible perfidious rake, and Charles, the magnanimous Emperor; one link only between them – courage. The character himself is aware of the dichotomy and draws Charlemagne's (and the spectators') attention to it:

> Ai-je bien dépouillé les misères du roi,
> Charlemagne? Empereur, suis-je bien un autre homme?[35]

Hugo may have had in mind a vague historical image of Charles V when drawing the character in Acts I and II; in Act IV, scene 5, no doubt remains whom he has in mind – Napoleon. Hugo's

---

[32] Gautier, *Histoire du Romantisme.*   [33] Le Roy, op. cit.
[34] Souriau, *Histoire du Romantisme.*   [35] IV, 5.

Bonapartism had begun to take shape under his monarchism some years earlier; the ode 'A la Colonne' is dated February 1827. The attitude is clearly defined in *Les Orientales*: 'Toujours lui! Lui partout!...';[36] thereafter it will be a constant source of inspiration for him. In *Hernani*, he has sacrificed the coherence of a character to it.

Nor is the character of Hernani any more satisfactory. At least history does not interfere here, only the norms of human behaviour. The man who in Act I, scene 4, is lusting for revenge on the King:

> Nuit et jour ... pas à pas, je te suis.
> Un poignard à la main, l'oeil fixé sur ta trace ...,

and who, after the luck of the draw (IV, 3), refuses to give up the privilege of killing him to Silva, even in exchange for the fateful horn, has two opportunities to despatch him (II, 3 and IV, 4). He takes neither. Why? If he were a *matamore* we should understand, but he evidently is not and, in the absence of any explanation from him of his inhibitions,[37] the conclusion seems inescapable that their only justification is that without them the play would come to an end, before it had run its five acts. Thus the structure of the play is seen to depend on shaky characterization; in any case, the plot and the motivation of the ending stretch credibility to breaking point.

All these defects are in part at least the result of haste. *Hernani* and all Hugo's plays are improvizations,[38] and even to the best of them similar criticisms apply: historical objections where important historical figures are involved (Louis XIII and Richelieu in *Marion Delorme*) with a strong admixture of personal and contemporary politics (Bonapartism, July Revolution), psychology and plot improbabilities (Didier in *Marion Delorme* who invariably prefers a window to a door for entering a room and has a passion for sacrifice; Ruy Blas, the valet of genius, who can dominate a ministry, woo a queen but feels strangely inhibited by his master ... until the last line of the last act).

Without a doubt Hugo's plays do not satisfy the standards of the 'well-made' play as conceived and practised by Dumas *père* or Scribe. Yet the fact remains that *Hernani* did carry the day for the Romantics, that *Hernani*, *Ruy Blas* and even *Marion Delorme* were successfully revived in the 'seventies and inspired the neo-romantic plays of Edmond Rostand, *Cyrano de Bergerac* (1897)

---

[36] December 1828. [37] Hamlet explains his.

[38] e.g. *Hernani*, one month, August–September 1829; *Marion Delorme*, one month, June 1829; *Le Roi s'amuse*, three weeks, June 1832; *Lucrèce Borgia*, eleven days, July 1832; *Marie Tudor*, three weeks approx., August–September 1833; *Angelo*, one month, May 1835; *Les Burgraves*, five weeks, September–October 1842.

and *L'Aiglon* (1900), that even today *Hernani* and *Ruy Blas* are still in the repertoire of the Théâtre Français.

Perhaps after all Hugo had a better sense of dramatic effect than the arm-chair critic, removed from the collective pressure of an audience? Audiences can be brought to overlook the niceties of psychological mechanisms or plot structure if they be moved by broad human effects – truculent bravery (Carlos, facing imminent despatch at Hernani's hands, 11, 3), magnaminity (the Emperor's pardon, IV, 4), searing irony when justly provoked (Ruy Blas to the ministers, III, 1 and 2), pleas for pity (Doña Sol to the Emperor – *Hernani*, IV, 4; Nangis for his son and Marion for Didier to Richelieu – *Marion Delorme*, IV, 7), tragic love (Hernani – Doña Sol, Didier – Marion, Ruy Blas – the Queen), thoughts on death (Didier). All these are moments of human experience everyone can share, if the mood be suitably induced; if it be, then the emotional effect is great and cumulative. And what better way of inducing it, what better way of insulating it from clumsiness of plot or psychological improbabilities than the rhythms and rich sensuous imagery of Hugo's poetry? Examples abound: the love scenes in *Hernani* and *Ruy Blas* too long to quote; Didier's meditation on death (*Marion Delorme*, V, 3).

> Quand le bec du vautour déchire mon étoffe,
> Ou que le ver la ronge, ainsi qu'il fait d'un roi,
> C'est affaire du corps: mais qu'importe, à moi!
> Lorsque la lourde tombe a clos notre paupière,
> L'âme lève du doigt le couvercle de pierre,
> Et s'envole . . .[39]

Rhetoric no doubt, but if dramatic poetry is to make an immediate impact on an audience, it must stimulate the emotions that lie on the surface much as an opera does; Hugo in fact handles his characters as though they were operatic parts. Perhaps that is why composers have found it so convenient to use his plays as libretti.[40]

Hugo's is the lion's share in the rise of the Romantic theatre; his too the lion's share in its demise – *Les Burgraves* (1843) . . . O! what a fall was there. . . . A melodrama, but not the first amongst Hugo's plays. No doubt even Hugo's best plays have something of the melodrama about them: poorly motivated action, exaggerated attitudes. How much more so, his inferior ones: *Le Roi s'amuse* (1832), *Lucrèce Borgia* (1833), *Marie Tudor* (1833), *Angelo, Tyran de Padoue* (1835). Here Hugo's imagination is apt to lose all contact with reality: complex plots, high-tension situations, disguises, incognitos and unexpected recognitions, father killing daughter,

---

[39] This enjambement is particularly effective.

[40] e.g. Verdi's *Rigoletto* (1851), *Le Roi s'amuse*, Marchetti's *Ruy Blas* (1869).

son killing mother, villains as black as pitch, victims as white as snow, antithesis (a favourite idea of Hugo's) between physical beauty and moral ugliness or vice versa.[41] At least these plays are full of action even though the reasons why things happen are as obscure as the stage they happen on. *Les Burgraves*, with its plot complexities and mistaken or hidden identities,[42] lacks melodrama's saving grace – action; it is an epic melodrama full of splendid verse perhaps, at once a return to *Cromwell* without the latter's historical or human interest, and a foretaste of *La Légende des Siècles*. Hugo's incursion into the drama was over.

As a dramatist, Vigny deserves credit, first for spreading the knowledge of Shakespeare in France by his verse translations: *Roméo et Juliette* (1827), *Othello* (1829), *Shylock* (1839). His original contributions to the Romantic stage are meagre, at least in bulk, when compared with that of Dumas or Hugo: *La Maréchale d'Ancre* (1831), *Quitte pour la peur* (1833), *Chatterton* (1835) – a historical drama, a one-act comedy, a domestic tragedy.

Vigny the translator had naturally been concerned with spreading the gospel of Shakespeare, but his *Lettre à Lord* *** also shows his preoccupations at that moment to be those of the other Romantics: the development of the drama, its liberation from the unities, and the chance thereby of character portrayal on a wider canvas, the absurdities of the *style noble* (e.g. Melpomene's ninety-eight years' hesitation before she could bring herself to speak of a handkerchief). Significantly too, Vigny stresses the value of the theatre as a vehicle of communication: a reader can throw a book aside, a spectator is forced to listen: 'La soirée finie, trois mille intelligences ont été remplies de vos idées . . .' Had he waited until after the 'battle of Hernani' he might have wondered whether theatre audiences are always as docile as the *Lettre à Lord* *** suggests, but in any case, Vigny as a dramatist will give particular attention to this point. In contrast to Dumas, whose plays, with all their theatrical skill, have no intellectual content, Vigny, like Hugo, aims at giving a message in his. If Vigny is in many ways an isolated figure in the Romantic movement, he subscribes fully in his plays as elsewhere to the prevailing belief in the poet's role as man's guide and philosopher.

'Si l'art est une fable, il doit être une fable philosophique', he writes in the preface to *La Maréchale d'Ancre*. The story of Concini and Leonora Galigaï, creatures of the Regent Marie de

---

[41] *Lucrèce Borgia*, Preface.
[42] Guanhumara is the long-lost Ginevra; the beggar is the Emperor who turns out to be Donato; Job is the Fosco of yore; Otbert finds that he is really Georges.

Medicis, had dramatic possibilities; ambition, hatred of foreign favourites, adultery, in Dumas' hands these themes, against a dark background of a period where witchcraft was believed in and led Galigaï to the stake, would have produced enough dynamite to blow up the Odéon; Vigny's play is uneasily poised between an undeveloped psychological study vaguely reminiscent of *Macbeth*, and full-blooded Romantic drama; for good 'philosophical' measure he has injected another element. 'C'est la grande voix du peuple', cries Borgia as he listens to a distant crowd.[43] Later,[44] la Maréchale exclaims: 'Ah! courtisans,... vous avez mêlé le peuple à nos affaires; il vous mènera loin!' Such awareness of the potential power of the masses, such prophetic vision, are unlikely to have been present in the minds of early seventeenth-century power seekers.[45] Nor are the final words of the play, echoing the same idea, more convincing: 'What of us?' cries Picard, the bourgeois, to the surrounding workmen. This may fittingly be described in the jargon of the theatrical producer as a good 'pay off line'. What indeed more stimulating to the imagination than a final question mark? With the hindsight that another two centuries provide, the spectator of 1831 could nimbly leap from 1617 to 1789 and even to the 'July Days'; although the theme is not emphasized in the play, left with it at the end, we tend to regard it as the essential message, reflecting as it does Vigny's own preoccupation with the enigma of revolution.

The cult of honour and the destinies of the poet, a 'pariah' like the soldier in society, are two major themes in Vigny's philosophy. The former is echoed, not it must be confessed on a very high level of morality, in *Quitte pour la peur*, the latter in *Chatterton*, the most successful and the best of Vigny's plays. Adapted from one of the episodes in his novel *Stello*, it shows how far Vigny had moved from the Romantic conception of historical drama as held by Dumas and Hugo, and by himself some years before. Gone are all Romantic excesses and posturings, 'local colour' is of the vaguest; the author has even foregone the freedom of time and place. By what is in effect a return to classical concentration and simplicity, he has created a limited number of characters: the vulgarian John Bell, the well-meaning but unperceptive Beckford, the kindly Quaker, the tender Kitty Bell and the over-sensitive Chatterton, with enough individuality to create a developing human situation and consequently dramatic interest that is in the characters first and in the thesis only afterwards. Nor is the thesis an idle one. Judged on scarcity value great poets are more valuable than great

---

[43] III, 7. [44] IV, 12.
[45] Their attitude to the people is probably better reflected in the authentic opinion of Richelieu: 'Il les faut comparer aux Mulets qui étant accoutumés à la Charge, se gâtent par un long repos plus que par le travail.' *Testament-Politique*, I, 4.

scientists; the difficulty is to recognize them for what they are in time to succour their need. What criteria are to be applied and, even if applied successfully, perhaps the poets' creative power might suffer in consequence and their material gain be humanity's loss. Vigny does not solve the problem nor is anyone likely to. It is enough that he should have raised it in a way that is fairly satisfying and points to a return, when the Romantic storm will have blown itself out on the stage, to calmer waters.

Musset's plays are something of a paradox. With two insignificant exceptions[46] they were not originally written for the stage, yet of all French Romantic drama they have held the stage most successfully; they have certain points in common with Musset's lyrical poetry and yet what has dragged down the one has not affected the popularity or the merits of the other.

The plays fall into three categories: *comédies, drames, proverbes*. The *comédies*, from one to three acts in length, comprise: *La Nuit Vénitienne* (1830), *Les Caprices de Marianne* (1833), *Fantasio* (1833), *On ne badine pas avec l'Amour* (1834), *Barberine* (1835), *Le Chandelier* (1835), *Il ne faut jurer de rien* (1836), *Un Caprice* (1837), *Louison* (1849), *Carmosine* (1850) and *Bettine* (1851).

There are two dramas: *André del Sarto* (1833) and *Lorenzaccio* (1834); and two proverbs: *Il faut qu'une porte soit ouverte ou fermée* (1845) and *On ne saurait penser à tout* (1849).

In addition there are two other plays, both written in 1832, *La Coupe et les Lèvres* and *A quoi rêvent les Jeunes Filles*, which Musset grouped together under the title of *Spectacle dans un Fauteuil*, and which may be included in the group of comedies. The title, *Spectacle dans un Fauteuil*, which in the days of television seems so appropriate, marks Musset's resolve, after the failure of *La Nuit Vénitienne*, no longer to expose himself to the insults of the 'ménagerie', as he called the public.

Just as his lyrical poetry, from its light, impertinent beginnings in *Contes d'Espagne et d'Italie*, had gradually become more charged with feeling, so a similar graph can be established for his plays. The insignificant beginnings in *La Nuit Vénitienne*; two years later *Un Spectacle dans un Fauteuil*. The *Dédicace* in verse, with all its elegant badinage, shows that Musset's views about drama or at least his own contribution to it have begun to crystallize: against the critics who have accused him of leaning heavily on Byron, he maintains his own originality:

> Je hais comme la mort l'état de plagiaire;
> Mon verre n'est pas grand, mais je bois dans mon verre;

[46] *La Nuit Vénitienne* and *Louison*.

Yet he indicates his right to choose in whose footsteps he as dramatist will try to follow:

> Mais s'il m'était permis de choisir une route
> Je prendrais la dernière[47] et m'y noierais sans doute.

The two plays of *Un Spectacle dans un Fauteuil* yield little except perhaps the character of Frank;[48] despite Musset's assertion
in the *Dédicace*, Frank has a distinctly Byronic stamp: proud,
cynical, despairing; and at the same time he is a first pale image of
his creator:

> 'Ah! malheur', he exclaims, 'à celui qui laisse les débauches
> Planter le premier clou sous sa mamelle gauche.'[49]

The years 1833 and 1834 yield the richest harvest of Musset's
dramatic achievement: *Les Caprices de Marianne, Fantasio, On ne
badine pas avec l'Amour, Lorenzaccio*. Other good things follow,
notably *Le Chandelier, Il ne faut jurer de rien, Un Caprice, Il faut
qu'une porte soit ouverte ou fermée*, but it may confidently be said
that the four plays Musset wrote in the years 1833 and 1834 provide the reader with all the essential characteristics of Musset as a
dramatist.

'L'amour est tout', Musset writes in the *Dédicace*, 'l'amour, et
la vie au soleil.' The sentiment comes as no surprise from the
creator of Jacques Rolla and the author of *Les Nuits, La Lettre à
Lamartine* and *Souvenir*; he remains faithful to it in his plays.
Love is the central theme, indeed the exclusive theme of the
comedies; admittedly the second part of the quotation does not
wholly apply; the characters may, for the most part, live their
lives in a romantic fairyland, there are none the less sudden total
eclipses of the sun to remind us that 'on ne badine pas avec
l'amour'.

But the fact that love is the essential theme, that Musset has
taken as his subject a human passion, liberates him from considerations of time and space. What his characters do and say has little
relation with where they are: *salon* or *parc*, town or country; for
Musset the barest indications are enough: 'la scène est . . . à Naples,
. . . à Munich, . . . à Paris, . . . une place devant le château', etc., and
as for the position in time, Musset leaves that to our imagination.
The exception to this is evidently the two dramas, where Musset
draws his material from historical sources and aims to portray
historical characters.

The choice of his characters in the dramas has evidently been
determined by the fact that he saw in Andrea del Sarto and in

[47] That of Racine and Shakespeare.
[48] *La Coupe et les Lèvres.*
[49] *Ibid.*, IV, i.

Lorenzaccio something that reflected his own personality; none the less, in both these plays, particularly in the latter, which is the most successful historical play in the whole of French Romantic drama, the characters and the action are rooted in history; the where and when are in consequence essential to the dramatic interest. In both plays too, but the fact is again more striking in *Lorenzaccio*, Musset has taken full advantage of his freedom from stage conditions to throw on to the screen of his reader-spectator's imagination a rapid succession of scenes in obedience to the twists and turns of his plot, inspired perhaps in this technique by the example of Shakespeare's 'histories'.

Setting aside, however, these exceptions which have a freedom of structure of their own, Musset's plays have an almost classical independence of time and space. Another characteristic which the plays—and on this point there is no exception – have in common is that all the central characters are young: Coelio, Octave, Marianne, Fantasio, Perdican, Camille, Rosette, André, Lorenzaccio, Fortunio, Clavaroche, Jacqueline.... At first sight we might be tempted, wrongly, to think this a necessary consequence of Musset's central theme of love; wrongly, for love can choose its victims from older age groups, and dramatists are not wanting who have chosen to portray older characters in love, but Musset's treatment of the theme, which recalls that of Marivaux, necessarily concentrates the main dramatic interest upon youth. The older characters are driven to the periphery: Claudio, Le Baron, Maître Blazius, Maître Bridaine, Dame Pluche, Maître André, Van Buck, La Baronne de Mantes; they are lightly sketched, mostly figures of fun, pantaloons providing the necessary comic relief, original creations certainly in the French theatre but owing something perhaps to Shakespeare's Malvolio, Sir Andrew Aguecheek and Sir Toby Belch.

But there is another reason why Musset's central characters are young, and on this point he parts company from Marivaux and brings his plays into close relation with his lyrical poetry: Musset's young men are reflections of himself; the point was briefly alluded to above in relation to Frank but how much more striking the resemblance with Musset becomes in the more important plays: Coelio, tender but falling so easily into suspicion and jealousy; Octave, the willing victim of drink and debauchery and yet not without occasional flashes of self-appraisal: 'Ma gaieté est comme le masque d'un histrion; mon coeur est plus vieux qu'elle...',[50] the introspective Fantasio and Spark the extrovert: 'Je ne comprends rien à ce travail perpétuel sur toi-même...',[51] Perdican, foreshadowing the Musset of *Souvenir*: 'On est surtout trompé en

[50] *Caprices*, II, 6.   [51] *Fantasio*, I, 2.

amour, souvent blessé et souvent malheureux; mais on aime et quand on est sur le bord de sa tombe, on se retourne pour regarder en arrière, et on se dit: "J'ai souffert souvent, je me suis trompé quelquefois mais j'ai aimé'";[52] Lorenzaccio, that almost tragic figure, divided against himself, imprisoned in his vices: 'il est trop tard. Je me suis fait à mon métier. Le vice a été pour moi un vêtement; maintenant il est collé à ma peau...'.[53]

If the young men, often grouped in pairs, Coelio and Octave, Fantasio and Spark, Fortunio and Clavaroche, are projections of Musset himself, the young women he has created are the images derived from a catholic and, as we know, sometimes stormy experience; the capricious Marianne, the unpredictable Camille, the tender Rosette, the scheming Jacqueline, the serenely innocent but oh so observant Cécile – storm and sunshine. Though the confession element is clearly in evidence in the plays, we do not have, as in Musset's lyrical poetry, that impression of all-pervading and irritating self-pity. The discipline imposed by the dramatic genre proves Musset's salvation. The failure of *La Nuit Vénitienne* had liberated him from the discipline of the stage, not from that of the drama. Drama requires characters; and however much these may be reflections of their creator, their very existence, the fact that a dramatist is bound to see or imagine his characters on the stage, means his being obliged to objectify to some extent his thoughts and feelings, and this in turn implies a certain restraint on personal confession; as he creates his characters his mind will be turned outward upon them instead of inward upon himself.

Musset's characters are not endowed with much independent existence; some of them perhaps make just enough impact to be remembered individually; Lorenzaccio is the best example, nor are we likely to confuse Coelio with Perdican, or Perdican with Valentin. Broadly, however, we remember them in groups: the gay galliards, the tender lovers, the young minxes, the pantaloons. Within their categories they have family resemblances and the first two categories a strong resemblance to Musset: collectively their impact is considerable. Perhaps in the last resort this is because young and old, male and female, they all contribute to a dialogue that has beauty and variety. At times it is delicate and ornate[54] or charged with emotion[55] or with bitter-sweetness[56] and we are tempted to think that Musset's best poetry lies in the poetic diction of his plays; at other times the dialogue has the amiable imperti-

[52] *On ne badine pas avec l'Amour*, II, 5.
[53] *Lorenzaccio*, III, 3.
[54] *Caprices de Marianne*, I, 1. Octave: 'Un mal le plus cruel de tous'.
[55] *Lorenzaccio*, III, 3.
[56] *Les Caprices de Marianne*, *passim*, and *On ne badine pas avec l'Amour*, *passim*; but there is a tendency to declamation here, e.g. II, 5.

nence of Jacques Rolla,[57] or a crispness and speed that is delightful in itself,[58] or again the brilliance of a diamond.

This latter trait is particularly evident in a one-act playlet,[59] or in a *Proverbe*.[60] Neither can give scope for development of character and the latter has the added restriction of the proverb chosen, which the situation portrayed must be related to or lead up to at the end. Here, Musset, master of light dialogue, comes fully into his own; he delights in imagining a situation with two or three characters fluttering round it like moths round a bright light.

The years 1827 to 1843 – if we set Musset aside, the Romantic 'invasion' of the drama fits between these dates. Before 1843, however, signs were not lacking of the invasion's loss of steam; Musset had given up early and his significant contributions were still unknown; Vigny had withdrawn in 1835; Dumas after 1838 contributed only spasmodically; Hugo, it seemed, stood alone to cover the withdrawal. There were also signs that public taste was changing, but before discussing these, the achievements of Romantic drama as a whole need assessing. No doubt its greatest achievement was the destruction of a moribund tradition. The Romantics did not destroy the great French classical drama; indeed they helped indirectly to strengthen it by sweeping from the stage the verbiage in alexandrines that had done service as classical tragedy for so many years. 'Il y a quelque chose de tué à tout jamais: c'est la friperie du bagage littéraire de l'Empire, vieux galons dédorés, ...'.[61]

Before 1830 the classical 'Epigoni' were still active; they do not, admittedly, disappear overnight after 1830 but in retrospect, we can see, 1830 was their *coup de grâce*. Thereafter the dramatist, freed from the unities' dead hand, could cast his plot in the mould he thought best for his subject; no question arises of decrying the three unities and their value for dramatic concentration, but of recognizing other forms and, more particularly, that the efforts of the latter-day tragic poets to invigorate tragedy with subjects from history, for example, was, like new wine in old bottles, a strain on the container.

With the breaking of the old mould comes the liberation of the language from the demands of the *style noble* – an important form of liberation, part of an aesthetic revolution that destroyed the belief in beauty as an objective thing to be achieved only within the limits of accepted canons, and outside which the artist, however

---

[57] *Il ne faut jurer de rien.*
[58] *Le Chandelier*, I, 2, especially the latter part: Jacqueline: 'Toutes ces conditions ...'
[59] e.g. *Un Caprice.*
[60] e.g. *Il faut qu'une porte soit ouverte ou fermée.*
[61] Ponsard, 1840, quoted by Souriau, *Histoire du Romantisme*, II, p. 225.

great, could not hope for salvation. Under the new dispensation the quality of a work of art was to be measured by the impact on the individual – beholder, spectator or listener. The aim of the artist was no longer to achieve beauty by given standards of form but by the highest emotional effect he could achieve.

In the preface of *Hernani*, Hugo defines Romanticism as 'le libéralisme en littérature'. This too is important. Since the beginning of the century Romanticism had taken different superficial forms; with Madame de Staël it seemed to take on a German character, with Chateaubriand it was to be medieval, religious and royalist, now Hugo was putting his finger on its fundamental nature – a form of liberalism.

Apart from these general considerations, what plays of permanent value remain from the movement? One play at least by Hugo which still holds the stage – *Hernani*; two others – *Ruy Blas* and *Cromwell* – which might be produced for a festival or some special occasion and which in any case can still be read with pleasure; that applies to others too in parts: *Marion Delorme, Les Burgraves*; one play by Vigny which can be read with quiet enjoyment – *Chatterton*; none by Dumas. Musset with *Lorenzaccio*, and a number of other plays still in the repertoire of the Théâtre Français, may be accounted the most successful of the Romantic playwrights.

In comparison with the legacy in drama of the previous hundred years and more or with what remains from the rest of the nineteenth-century repertoire, the Romantic drama can claim to have been remarkably successful, and yet – again with the exception of Musset who within the narrow limits he set himself: 'mon verre n'est pas grand, mais je bois dans mon verre', seems to have achieved his full potential – Romantic drama is not fully satisfying. Dumas, with all his theatrical skill and his Byronism, is a hollow shell; Hugo and Vigny, prefaces and all, have little to convey; the former may have seen the need to create a new tragic drama but failed to give his characters universality and a tragic flaw, to his plays a sense of inevitability, all essential if a tragic rather than a merely pathetic impact is to be achieved. We are left with themes that are no longer convincing: the redemptive power of love, the poet as an exile in society, the bastard with a chip on the shoulder, and a number of characters – Didier, Hernani, Antony, Chatterton, Ruy Blas – outstanding, not for their humanity, but their blatant egotism, remembered as portraits in some ducal house might be for their remarkable family likeness.

The failure of *Les Burgraves* showed that Hugo had lost touch with opinion at least in so far as the drama was concerned. Romanticism was not dead; it was to pursue a vigorous life in the novel[62] and was presently to invade the street, become a political revolution. But the theatre-going public, at least, were no longer ready to wing away with Hugo on his wilder flights of imagination. The theatre reflected the general tide of opinion. The Upper Bourgeoisie had asserted itself politically in 1830 and soon after the bourgeois spirit began to invade the arts.[63] The trend is very noticeable in painting; the classical art of David and Ingres had in the eighteen-twenties been largely eclipsed by the power in colour and movement of Géricault and Delacroix; now the influence of Ingres was again in the ascendant; Horace Vernet, Ary Scheffer, Paul Delaroche were the popular painters because this art was a compromise between academic tradition, exact, careful draughtmanship, Romantic interest in history and local colour – compromise, *juste-milieu*! Sculpture in particular, after its Romantic phase with David d'Angers, Auguste Préault, Barye, was brought back by Simart to the School of Antiquity.[64] What could better express the new ethos than the name a small group of anti-Romantics took – 'L'Ecole du Bon Sens'?, obscure poets and playwrights: Jules Barbier, Carré, Henry Thénard, Latour de Saint-Ybars; a critic, Ricourt – a painter, Meissonnier. Meissonnier's skill at reconstituting in paint historical scenes in miniature, down to the last gaiter button, may be recorded, in passing, though without enthusiasm. Apart from him, the most important members of this group are François Ponsard (1814–67), linked with the revival of classical tragedy, and Emile Augier (1820–89), who was later to become with Dumas *fils* the great exponent of the social drama; in the meantime he attempted to revive classical comedy.

The return to favour of classical tragedy was greatly helped by the advent of the great tragic actress Rachel (1820–58), who was as valuable to the classical revival as Talma had been to the classical 'epigoni' of the Empire and the Restoration. The dramatic critics with Jules Janin in the lead 'discovered' Rachel in 1838; soon she was playing the great feminine roles of Corneille and Racine to enthusiastic audiences at the Théâtre Français.

Théophile Gautier, in his efforts to defend Romantic drama, tried to distinguish between the personal success of the actress and the plays: 'Il ne faut pas s'y tromper, l'intérêt qui s'attache à Mademoiselle Rachel ne s'étend pas aux pièces qu'elle joue',[65] but his efforts were unconvincing; popular favour was prepared even to welcome the new tragic poet François Ponsard whose play *Lucrèce* (1843) was being applauded at the Odéon while *Les Burgraves*

---

[62] See below, chap. 12.
[63] See Latreille, op. cit., Bk. III.
[64] Latreille, op. cit.
[65] *L'Art dramatique*, iii; quoted by Souriau, op. cit.

was painfully maintaining itself at the 'Français', and yet what a contrast in poetic talent between them!

What must the author of *La Préface de Cromwell* and of the splendid rhetoric of *Hernani, Marion Delorme, Ruy Blas*, etc., have thought of periphrases like these in the first scene of *Lucrèce*:

> La nuit n'a pas encore fourni son premier quart...
> Je les ferai veiller jusqu'au chant de l'oiseau
> De qui la voix sacrée annonce un jour nouveau...

or shameless padding like this:

> Et qu'un calme sommeil, après ce long voyage,
> *Assouplissant leur corps*, répare leur courage. (I, 2.)

or this:

> On dit que le lion, *qui s'abreuve de sang*,
> Quand il trouve en chemin un cadavre gisant
> Après avoir flairé, *d'une avide narine*
> S'il ne reste plus d'âme au fond de la poitrine... (I, 3.)

or the platitude of this:

> Je n'ai plus qu'une chose à vous dire,
>   et j'achève (III, 2.)

or this:

> J'ai servi mon pays jadis; mais je suis vieux
> Et vous laisse ce soin *à vous qui faites mieux*

or the bathos of this:

> Le guerrier dort souvent sur une froide terre;
> Ses membres sont glacés; il leur faut la chaleur
> Que *d'un bon vêtement lui ménage l'ampleur.*
>   ['Comforts' for the troops!]

On hearing such lines Hugo's heart must have been a prey to conflicting emotions: satisfaction at his own evident superiority, a sense of injustice at the fate of *Les Burgraves*.

Not that everything is bad in *Lucrèce*; in contrast with the plot absurdities of *Les Burgraves* the unpretentious presentation of Lucretia's story, as told by Livy, must have been a relief. Ponsard's success was largely the luck of coming at the right moment – the moment of flight from the Romantic drama and of refuge in moderation in all things, *le juste milieu*! The play reflects that spirit; it is not a genuine classical tragedy but a rather anaemic 'drame' in classical garb, uneven in tone, Lucrèce providing the main tragic element, Sextus Tarquin, a young Roman 'rip', some relief bordering on bathos, abetted by Junius Brutus who, in a manner reminiscent of Musset's Lorenzaccio, hides his political designs under a cloak of frivolous stupidity. But, if diluted Romanticism is apparent in the play, its high moral tone – the virtue of example, self-sacrifice, conjugal fidelity – is in sharp contrast with the egotism of the Romantic drama. On this point too *Lucrèce* appealed to the bourgeois ethos of the day.

No better example of the bourgeois spirit of the July Monarchy could be found than Eugène Scribe (1791–1861). He had begun writing for the theatre as early as 1810 – *Le Prétendu sans le savoir, ou l'occasion fait le Larron*; thereafter, undeterred by Romanticism, he continued writing bourgeois comedies (e.g. *Le Mariage d'Argent*, 1827; *Une Chaîne*, 1841; *Le Puff*, 1848), light comedies (e.g. *La Demoiselle à Marier*, 1826; *Le Diplomate*, 1827), opera libretti (*La Muette de Portici*, 1828; *Robert le Diable*, 1831; *La Juive*, 1835; *Les Huguenots*, 1836) and five-act historical comedies (*Bertrand et Raton*, 1834; *L'Ambitieux*, 1834; *La Camaraderie*, 1836; *la Calomnie*, 1840; *Le Verre d'eau*, 1840).

This last category shows at its best Scribe's skill as a builder of 'well-made' plays. In this art he is if anything more skilful than Dumas *père*, content with one plot, whereas Scribe often cleverly intertwines a major plot with a subsidiary love intrigue, which in due course provides the major plot with an added impetus and precipitates the climax – positively Shakespearian – (e.g. *Bertrand et Raton, Le Verre d'eau*). History in these plays is little more than a pretext; it provides subjects and names – the Danish Court at the time of Struensee (*Bertrand et Raton*), George II and Walpole (*L'Ambitieux*), Queen Anne,[66] Sarah, Duchess of Marlborough, Bolingbroke and others (*Le Verre d'eau*), but the comedy's the thing, the comedy ... and the moral, amusement and edification, surely the perfect combination for worthy bourgeois men of principle. The pattern of the plays is very similar; usually the moral is drawn in the last scene or even the last line. *Bertrand et Raton*[67] is a warning to shopkeepers to keep out of conspiracies:

Marthe: Faites donc des conspirations!
Raton: C'est dit ... désormais je les regarderai passer et le diable m'emporte
    si je m'en mêle!

L'Ambitieux shows Walpole ready for any sacrifice so long as he can get back into power. *La Camaraderie* shows that to get on in life friends and talent are necessary:

Oscar: Eh bien! Vous le voyez par lui, qui refusait notre secours ... on
    arrive quand on a des camarades.
Zoe: Oui, Monsieur, ... mais on reste quand on a du talent!

Worldly wisdom and morality are satisfied!

[66] The mother of thirteen children is portrayed as a young and jealous girl.
[67] cf. La Fontaine, *Fables*, ix, 17. 'Le Singe et le Chat'.

Most characteristic of all is *Le Verre d'eau*, designed to show that in history small causes produce great effects. Bolingbroke is Scribe's spokesman: 'Il ne faut pas mépriser les petites choses, c'est par elles qu'on arrive aux grandes ... Vous croyez peut-être ... que les catastrophes politiques, les révolutions, les chutes d'Empire ... Erreur! ... les grands effets produits par de petites causes ... c'est mon système ... j'y ai confiance, vous en verrez les preuves' (I, 4). The proofs? A glass of water spilt on the dress of the Queen causes the fall of the favourite, which in its turn means the fall of the dominant Tory party, the return of the Whigs to power and this in its turn means the opening of negotiations to end the Spanish Succession War. Who would have foreseen it? Obviously Boling-broke in I, 4 and justifiably he draws the moral as the curtain falls:

Et tout cela grâce à un verre d'eau!

But not only does Bolingbroke provide the audience with a philo-sophy (*sic*) of history; he gives them a policy they could appreciate: 'Il [Marlborough] a pour lui le prince Eugène, la Hollande et cinq cent mille hommes ... j'ai pour moi Swift, Prior et Atterbury ...A lui l'épée, à nous la presse! Nous verrons un jour à qui la victoire ... L'illustre et avare Maréchal veut la guerre, qui épuise le trésor ... moi, je veux la paix et l'industrie, qui, mieux que les conquêtes, doivent assurer la prospérité de l'Angleterre ...' (I, 2).

Louis-Philippe could hardly wish to express himself otherwise. Bolingbroke reflects the spirit of the July Monarchy *in excelsis*. No wonder the Académie Française opened its doors to Scribe (1836). Theatrical skill has not saved his plays from oblivion any more than Dumas', but the tradition of the well-made play was to go on. Dumas *fils*, Augier and Sardou were to carry it on, the former two using the mould for their social crusades.

Chapter 12

THE ROMANTIC NOVEL

1830 was a triumphant moment for French liberalism. It was also a triumphant moment for French Romanticism; its opponents were apparently crushed; the citadel of the 'Français' had been captured; the early blossoms of Romantic lyric poetry were giving promise of the flowering that was soon to come. Even the novel, which had never yet achieved the same prestige as drama and poetry, was soon to become as important an art form as any in the nineteenth century. In Balzac's eyes, not the least service rendered by Walter Scott was that he gave prestige to the novel.[1]

By 1830 a pattern of the novel's development was taking shape. The personal novel which stems from Rousseau's *Confessions* and of which the early years of the century had seen so many examples as 'by-products', from the pen of writers who were not primarily novelists (*Caliste – Valérie – René – Obermann – Delphine – Corinne – Adolphe*), was to have a renewed and long lease of life: *Volupté – La Confession d'un Enfant du Siècle – Elle et Lui – Dominique*. To the list could be added: *Indiana, Jacques, Lélia –* all strongly stamped with the hall-mark of Romanticism.

Equally stamped with the period mark, indeed more strongly since the personal novel had its roots in the eighteenth century, is the historical novel. The most outstanding examples to be noticed among them are: *Cinq-Mars; La Chronique de Charles IX; Les Chouans*; and *Notre Dame de Paris*.

One of the numerous aspects of Romanticism is the greater perceptiveness it gave to historical studies, and this was to lead to a rejuvenation of history as a 'genre' *per se*. Chateaubriand had had a hand in stimulating this chord;[2] Scott was to reinforce that influence by discovering before the fascinated eyes of the public all the romance of history, a land believed hitherto to be arid but now revealed flowing with milk and honey.

The pure waters of historical romance flowing from Scott were to receive a strong admixture from the popular novels and the melodrama and produce a turbid flood where history is drowned in adventure and horror: *Han d'Islande, Bug Jargal*; later the serial

[1] *Comédie Humaine*, Préface.　　　　[2] Especially with *Les Martyrs*.

novel – a highly profitable formula written with gusto, even with conviction and not averse sometimes from conveying a vague message that can be recognized as a distant echo of the Messianic urge: *Les Trois Mousquetaires – Le Comte de Monte Cristo – Les Mystères de Paris – Le Juif Errant.*

But the historical novel is an elastic formula; the present is history in the making. Thus, out of the historical novel or with the historical novel as a foundation, was to grow the work of Stendhal, of Balzac and George Sand too – Romantic in all conscience, all three of them, yet clearly showing other tendencies as well.

First among the Romantics to write a novel was Victor Hugo. If we set aside his poetic juvenilia, *Bug Jargal* (1820)[3] is his first work, and *Han d'Islande* (1823) appeared shortly after the *Odes.* The story of *Bug Jargal* is told round a camp fire during one of the Revolutionary campaigns. The narrator, Leopold d'Auverney, tells his fellow officers of his adventures during the San Domingo slaves' revolt (1791); the firing of the plantations, the wickedness of the dwarf Habibrah, the nobility of soul of Bug Jargal, sometime king in Black Africa, now reduced to slavery under the name of Pierrot, who, as real leader of the revolt, twice saves Leopold's life from the rebels and is finally executed by a firing squad.

From the heat, colour, blood and torture of San Domingo, the author translates us in *Han d'Islande* to the misty landscapes of Scandinavia; the scene is in Norway (1699), the action concerns the plots whereby the wicked Count Ahlefeld endeavours to encompass the death of his rival, the disgraced chancellor Schumacker; but the froward are brought low, virtue and love are rewarded in the long run. In the intricacies of the plot is enmeshed the story of the strange Caliban who gives his name to the book, feeds on human flesh, drinks sea-water out of a human skull – his lamented son's incidentally, whose death he avenges by warring, with commendable impartiality, on society. By any lesser hand, neither of these novels is likely to have survived; they are like a bridge between Ducray-Duménil and Ducange on the one hand, Dumas *père* on the other; their local colour drawn from Hugo's imagination or from literary sources is of the sort that explains Mérimée's later contempt for that particular Romantic fashion.[4] In the figures of Habibrah and Han, Hugo gives a first sketch of a type he liked to portray in his novels and drama – Quasimodo, Triboulet, Gilliat, Gwynplane – and when, as in Han, Quasimodo and Triboulet, he could give them some spark of moral beauty – fatherly affection,

[3] A second edition, revised and partly rewritten, appeared in 1826.
[4] See below, p. 218.

humble love or doglike fidelity – in contrast to their physical re-
pulsiveness, his liking for antithesis as a means of character portrayal is satisfied.

Bug Jargel's and *Han d'Islande*'s contacts with history are flimsy.
Hugo's real contribution to the historical novel is *Notre Dame de
Paris* (1831). A commonplace plot – Esmeralda, the beautiful gipsy,
is loved by Claude Frollo, Archdeacon of Notre Dame, and by the
ungainly dwarf Quasimodo; she in her turn loves the dashing but
heartless officer, Phoebus de Chateaupers. Tragedy awaits them
all: Esmeralda is put to death for a crime she has not committed.
Frollo is hurled to his death by Quasimodo, from the towers of the
cathedral.[5] Quasimodo disappears and his skeleton is found some
two years later embracing that of Esmeralda in the charnel house
of Montfaucon. When touched, the skeleton falls into dust – symbol
of our hopes and vanities? Even Phoebus does not escape . . . quite;
with that elephantine humour, sometimes so successful,[6] Hugo
writes: 'Phoebus de Chateaupers aussi fit une fin tragique, il se
maria.'[7] A flimsy plot indeed, but in itself that is no criticism of
a novel provided the interest lies in the vitality and compelling interest of the characters. Here too, however, the book fails; the
characters are like sea-shells on a beach, lovely or striking to look
at – within, nothing – or at least only the simplest antithesis in
characteristic Hugoesque manner: Esmeralda sings, dances, and
loves her pet goat; the sinister Claude Frollo is a devoted elder
brother; Phoebus is as beautiful in body as he is vacuous in mind,
all are figures of melodrama, of pageantry, of an adventure film in
medieval dress.

Yet, in spite of these weaknesses in characterization, *Notre Dame
de Paris* is an outstanding work of the Romantic period, a kind of
tapestry of the Middle Ages as conceived by the writers of 1830,
often portrayed by the artists and illustrators of the period: Louis
Boulanger, Johannot, the brothers Deveria, Célestin Nanteuil in
particular.[8] Louis XI and his cronies, medieval life with its fat
humour and buffoonery (la Fête des fous[9]), its sordid misery (la
Cour des Miracles[10]), medieval Paris huddled round its cathedral;
all this is much more than a mere *réchauffé* of Walter Scott. He
has indeed a hand in it,[11] but Hugo drew from many sources[12]
and, as he was always to do with his veneer of scholarship,[13] he
threw his gleanings together hurriedly, illuminating them by the
prism of his imagination; only there perhaps did the medieval Paris

[5] A clear reminiscence of Habibrah's fall to death in *Bug Jargal* (chap.
54: 'Habibrah, suspendu sur l'horrible gouffre . . .').
[6] cf. Don César in *Ruy Blas*.   [7] Book XI, 3.
[8] Gautier, *Histoire du Romantisme*.   [9] Book I, 1.
[10] Book I, 6.   [11] *Quentin Durward*.
[12] Souriau, op. cit., Vol. II.   [13] e.g. in *La Légende des Siècles*.

he depicts originally exist. But since 1831 its image has existed in the minds of all Hugo's readers. At the centre of that image the cathedral of Notre Dame rises in majesty;[14] it is in itself a character in the book, the most important; it comes alive like some stone giant: 'il (Frollo) trouva dans l'église une obscurité et un silence de caverne ... les longues fenêtres du choeur montraient ... l'extrémité supérieure de leurs ogives, dont les vitraux, traversés d'un rayon de lune, n'avaient plus que les couleurs douteuses de la nuit, une espèce de violet, de blanc et de bleu, dont on ne retrouve la teinte que sur la face des morts. L'archidiacre, en apercevant tout autour du choeur ces blêmes pointes d'ogives, crut voir des mitres d'évêques damnés ... Il se mit à fuir à travers l'église. Alors il lui sembla que l'église aussi s'ébranlait, remuait, s'animait, vivait, que chaque grosse colonne devenait une patte énorme qui battait le sol de sa large spatule de pierre.'[15]

Hugo is not alone in this habit of endowing inanimate things with a life of their own. Zola too has that magnifying eye under whose contemplative gaze the details of an imagined scene slowly blur, then fuse together and are suddenly reorganized into a gigantic, a collective being.[16] The effect can be powerful and we understand Claude Frollo's fear; for a moment he comes alive. Easily swept aside or crushed, man seems small in comparison with the mysterious, even – who knows? – the cosmic force the Romantic wand has conjured up, for Romantic it is, being another aspect of the belief in the life force inherent in all things.

What reader of Hugo, however, would suppose that the cathedral of Notre Dame is the embodiment of a faith that had set multitudes in motion to build cathedrals, lavishing upon them all their loving skills in stone, glass, metal, whilst they lived in squalid hovels? The Hugo of the *Odes et Ballades* had believed in that faith but by 1830 his Catholicism and the monarchism that went with it had evaporated; his cathedral is an impressive but empty husk, a symbol without a meaning. None the less, for Hugo, with his medieval enthusiasms of the time, it is a precious relic handed down from the past. To Hugo's credit it must be said that, walking here in the footsteps of Chateaubriand, he taught his generation to look with a fresh eye on Gothic architecture; with the rediscovery of a beauty that two centuries and more of classical habits of mind had made men blind to, was born, for our advantage, the wish to protect the heritage of the Middle Ages.

Other signs, besides the eviction, as it were, of Christianity from the cathedral, are not wanting of Hugo's changed attitudes. His anti-clericalism is evident in his portrayal of Claude Frollo, and of Cardinal Bourbon; it is particularly aggressive in the two chapters

[14] Book III, 1.   [15] Book IX, 1.   [16] See vol. V, chap. 2, ii.

of Book V, where any pretence of creating an illusion of past reality is thrown aside while Hugo communicates his hatreds and ideals direct to the reader.

But in spite of these very real blemishes, a vast fresco-like image of medieval Paris and its motley crowds remains in the reader's mind; its epic quality reappears much developed in Victor Hugo's later novels and not only there.[17] In the meantime the two remaining prose works of the early period, *Le Dernier Jour d'un Condamné* (1829) and *Claude Gueux* (1834), deserve brief attention because they are the first indication of Hugo's social preoccupations. More sensitive than any writer of the nineteenth century to current trends and shifts of opinion, Hugo here follows the humanitarian tide that was setting strongly during the July Monarchy. Apart from its effect on early socialism it was sweeping into literature; Auguste Barbier (1805–85) made himself its now forgotten poet and strong echoes are to be found in the work of Lamartine, of Balzac, of George Sand, of Lamennais.

Le Dernier Jour d'un Condamné and *Claude Gueux* are both in effect pamphlets in favour of the abolition of the death penalty. The former is in the form of a diary purporting to be by the hand of the condemned man incarcerated at Bicêtre. It extends over some six weeks, not the last twenty-four hours, and contains two impressive chapters,[18] which might have come from Hugo's *Choses Vues* (posth. 1887); they portray the chaining up and departure of the convict gangs for Toulon. Hugo had witnessed such a scene himself and, as usual when his visual memory or imagination comes into play, the effect is powerful. With Farrabesche's description of life at the Toulon convict station (Balzac's *Curé de Village*) we seem well documented on the subject. Hugo, in company with the anonymous crowd of writers who added to the flood of didactic or 'social' novels[19] so-called that poured out in the middle years of the nineteenth century, may well have helped to create and extend public awareness of social problems, the death penalty being one of them; as an argument in favour of the abolitionists' case, however, *Le Dernier Jour d'un Condamné* scarcely carries weight; nor is it a work of literary significance. *Claude Gueux* has greater merit; in this transposition from reality Hugo has presented in simple terms a short story where there is an authentic clash of personalities leading to the thereby well motivated tragedy. Further, the work gives a vivid reflection of contemporaneous social fervours: 'Le peuple a faim, le peuple a froid. La misère le pousse au crime ou au vice, selon le sexe. Ayez pitié du peuple...Des

[17] See below, chap. 19.
[18] The real Claude Gueux had been executed in 1832.
[19] cf. Philip Spencer: *The Social Novel in France, 1848–1871*, 1949.

écoles pour les enfants, des ateliers pour les hommes.'[20] Here are the ideas and sentiments from which the popular slogans of 1848 will be forged. How different will be the attitudes when the political explosion, so Romantic in spirit, of February that year, has given way to the harsh realism of the 'June days' and after. To Hugo's vibrant pleas for humanitarian reforms, Flaubert gives a douche of cold water: education for the masses? – 'L'instruction gratuite et obligatoire n'y fera rien qu'augmenter le nombre des imbéciles.'[21]

Vigny's achievements in fiction show the same pattern of success and failure, relative at least, as his poetry. His first novel, *Cinq-Mars* (1826), is unsatisfactory both as a historical novel and from an artistic point of view. In his historical romances, Sir Walter Scott provided a formula for the *genre* which Vigny eschewed to his cost. Past time – a wonderful limitless field for the imagination, escaping from the present, to roam in at the invitation of the novelist, provided he give it just enough definition and outline to convince the reader his story is anchored to realities. To derive advantage both from the freedom of fiction and the compulsions of fact, the writer of historical novels must use the known facts of history only as a broad frame-work for his fictional characters, to create the illusion of a faithful representation of a given period. Known historical characters will be discreetly kept in the middle or far distance so that the reader will catch sight of them only out of the corner of his eye while his attention is focused on the main invented characters. Hugo's *Notre Dame* broadly follows Scott's formula. To it there is an alternative: to present some well-known event from the point of view of one or more of the leading characters so that their known actions may become understandable in terms of the psychological mechanisms attributed to them.

Vigny in effect has chosen neither alternative in *Cinq-Mars* and so seems to get the worst of both worlds, the world of history and the world of romance; by choosing as the hub of his story a well-known event, the Cinq-Mars plot against Richelieu, and by focussing the reader's attention, inevitably, upon the great Cardinal, he has sacrificed his liberty of action and exposed himself to the charge of distorting and indeed, in two specific instances, of deliberately falsifying history.[22] Mere accuracy in physical details

---

[20] Hugo, *Oeuvres*, 1950: *Romans*, I, pp. 764–5.
[21] Flaubert, letter to George Sand, 4 October 1871. *Correspondance*, Vol. 6, Conard.
[22] Le Père Joseph, one of the leading characters in the book, died in 1638, Cinq-Mars' plot occurred in 1642; Laubardemont's death is described in the book, whereas in fact he lived until 1653.

can in no way compensate for the unsatisfactory presentation of the character and policies of the great Cardinal, the obviously Romantic sensibilities of Cinq-Mars, the poor motivation of his friend de Thou, the remarkable hindsight of Bassompierre who judges the Cardinal's policies with Vigny's knowledge of the French Revolution. In all these ways the reader's confidence is destroyed, the illusion of reality shattered. The reader sees that the work is nothing more than an unsatisfactory exercise, which the main characters subserve, in Vigny's historical theory about the nobility as a sacrificed class in French society, and he rejects the special pleading of the author's preface: 'Réflexions sur la Vérité dans l'Art' (1827).

As a novel, the intermittent conversations of Le Docteur Noir and his highly-strung patient Stello may not be much more satisfactory than *Cinq-Mars*; these conversations are no more than pretexts to introduce the stories of Gilbert, Chatterton and André Chénier in support of Vigny's thesis that society, whatever its political form – absolute monarchy, constitutional monarchy or republic, is indifferent to the fate of poets. Yet in one respect at least *Stello* (1832) has merit: the analysis of the motives and attitudes of the Robespierristes on the one hand and the Thermidorians on the other, who, if they had been able to overcome their hesitations and launch their action sooner, might have saved Chénier's life, is psychologically sound and artistically effective in the context of the story. The historical awareness too is much sounder than in *Cinq-Mars*.

As a story-teller Vigny's best work is *Servitude et Grandeur Militaires* (1835). The three stories the book contains are, characteristically, intended to exemplify certain truths about soldiers: their dedication to honour, duty, obedience, without thought of reward; yet the narrative skill of the author is such in this case that the stories stand, as it were, in their own right, the main characters persuade us of their existence. The effect of the first story, *Laurette ou le Cachet rouge*, may be thought spoilt by the excess to which the narrator takes the cult of obedience to orders from superior authority; would a sea captain in the circumstances described not have found some way of circumventing the order, of putting his telescope to his blind eye? The reader may well think so, and if he does, he will not feel compensated by the old officer's subsequent life of abnegation.

The other two stories, however, suffer from no such disadvantage; the portrayal of Admiral Collingwood is particularly fine.

Whether in fact the historical novel slipped to an inferior level with the purveyors of material for the novel in serial form is debatable. The master of the historical serial novel is Alexandre Dumas

(1802–70) who for sheer weight of printed pages outstrips all-comers – true, he had collaborators.[23] His ebullient and apparently inexhaustible power allowed him to stride across the centuries in seven-league boots; the sixteenth, the seventeenth, the eighteenth centuries, the Revolution, all provided material for this master-builder, whose reputation is enjoying a certain come-back. A critical edition of *Les Trois Mousquetaires* (1844), one of Dumas' two masterpieces in the serial novel, now figures in the Classiques Garnier nineteenth-century series, rubbing shoulders with the giants – Balzac, Hugo, Flaubert, Zola. ... His learned editor[24] refers to him as 'le magicien de l'histoire'. Dumas's other great serial masterpiece, *Le Comte de Monte-Cristo* (1844–5) – a vast adventure against a background of his own day,[25] already has a critical edition.[26] Truly, as a novelist Dumas can now be said to have received his marshal's baton.

In his historical romances, Dumas, like Hugo, broadly follows Scott's practice; events and historical figures are a background his heroes make contact with just often enough to achieve some sort of historical reality in the imagination of the reader and to gain strength from 'touching down', then to leap off again to the next ad-venture or struggle with villainy. Whichever century Dumas takes as his background, the technique is the same. With his three musket-eers and their friend d'Artagnan, he has created fictional characters who stand out from their background; yet what precisely gives them that distinction? True, they are slightly distinguishable from each other: the aristocratic and melancholy Athos, the grandilo-quent giant Porthos (most akin to his creator?), the pious Aramis, the irrepressible swashbuckling d'Artagnan; these characteristics give them a suggestion, no more, of an inner moral life; Dantès (*Monte-Cristo*), with his determination to avenge his wrongs, and society's, has something of a Balzacian passion, one incidentally that sustains him through all his adventures including immersion in the Mediterranean tied up in a sack – a case of mistaken identity – and gives moral unity to the book. But in general the reader of every generation eagerly responds to their energy – adventure at no cost; a bond of sympathy between reader and characters is created that gives them life in his mind; they mirror something of his escapist self in much the same way as Douglas Fairbanks did in the guise of Robin Hood or the Sheik of Bagdad; they are emanations of Dumas' own dynamism, reflect his own *joie de vivre*, his simple unashamed and devouring egotism. Dumas is a microcosm of ebullient Romanticism, and his characters revolve round him like planets round the sun, full of borrowed light.

[23] 'Nègres', so-called. The most important was Auguste Maquet.
[24] M. Charles Samaran.
[25] From the 100 Days to the July Monarchy.   [26] Garnier.

The serial novel owes its existence in fact not to Dumas *père* but to Eugène Sue (1804–57). The first 'slice' of *Les Mystères de Paris* (1842–3) appeared in *Le Journal des Débats* on 19 June 1842. Unlike Dumas', Sue's characters have not survived. In spite of the phenomenal success of *Les Mystères* and of *Le Juif Errant* (1845–7), his heroes and heroines: Rodolphe de Gérolstein, Rigolette, Le Chourineur – no serial without its convict – Rodin, Dagobert, Morok and the rest, have faded into the shadows of the sordid Parisian scene that was theirs; they have not, like Dumas', not yet at least, been appropriated by film-makers, and if they were, a fair bet is that they would be rudely brushed aside and their creator's fertile inventiveness plundered for ideas useful to the building of a modern thriller; they have not, like Dumas', enough incandescent power to stand in their own right. Our imagination is only too willing to escape to adventure, but the background must itself be acceptable to the waking dream; Dumas' characters will continue to cut their capers . . . *Under the Red Robe*. Sue's have sunk without trace in the Paris sewers. The epic of the poor, which *Les Mystères* was trying in part to be, will have to wait for Jean Valjean, Fantine, Cosette and Gavroche (*Les Misérables*).

Yet with all his moralizing and bad writing, which he was the first to acknowledge,[27] Sue enjoys the peculiar privilege as writer and man of reflecting the attitudes and aspirations of his day better and more faithfully than Dumas;[28] first the elegant dandy of the eighteen-thirties, penetrating at least to the fringes of the aristocratic 'faubourg', enjoying boulevard life, squandering his fortune and creating in his early works (*Atar-Gull*, 1831; *La Salamandre*, 1832; *La Coucaratcha*, 1832–4) a variant on the Romantic image: the Byronic, satanic pirate of impeccable lineage;[29] then, after financial débâcle, the rebuilding of his fortune on the mysteries of Paris; the satanic dandy of the 'thirties has become the advocate of the 'underdog', and, in 1848, will sit on the extreme left of the National Assembly as a deputy of the 'Mountain'; finally, when the Second Republic has made way for the new men, choosing to live and die in exile rather than accept the Second Empire. Contemporaries – Balzac amongst them – were prone to cast doubt on the sincerity of Sue's socialism, and see in his second 'image' a reincarnation of him with a changed personality; but the psychological evolution is continuous. Sue the dandy is an aristocratic individualist in revolt against God or the philistine bourgeois, Sue

---

[27] 'Je ne me cite pas pour example; je n'ai jamais su le français'. *Eugène Sue* by Jean-Louis Bory (Hachette, 1962).
[28] He is also supposed to be the model of Balzac's Lucien de Rubempré.
[29] cf. also Balzac's *La Femme de Trente Ans*.

the socialist is in revolt against a political régime, against poverty; the theme of revolt is the common factor; only, metaphysical despair has given way to Messianic optimism. Not all Romantics followed this evolutionary graph – Hugo's is a parallel, more literary and less individualistic – but it lies within the Romantic potential.[30]

George Sand (1804–76) provides a closer parallel; in her hands more than in anyone's the Romantic novel achieves perhaps its fullest expression as the vehicle for the writer's personal experience, feelings, passions of the moment.

After eight years of married life Aurore Dupin, Baronne Dudevant, decided to cut adrift. The complex skein of personal relationships between the baroness and her husband, later between her and the succession – 'la relève' – of lovers she fell in – and out – with: Sandeau, Musset, Pagello, Michel de Bourges, Leroux, Chopin... could form a chapter, nay a novel, a series of personal novels, apart.[31] Naturally, as she flounced off to Paris there was no doubt in her mind where right lay. 'Sachez qu'en dépit... de ma facilité à pardonner, à oublier les chagrins et les injures, sachez que je viens de prendre un parti violent....'[32]

On 13 January 1831 to the same correspondent she writes: 'Je m'embarque sur la mer orageuse de la littérature. Il faut vivre. Je ne suis pas riche maintenant....' In that month the... collaboration, literary and other, with Jules Sandeau was established, the literary personage 'George Sand' was born. The baroness was nothing if not courageous. Convention? Public opinion? 'Les convenances sont la règle des gens sans âme et sans vertu. L'opinion est une prostituée qui se donne à ceux qui la payent le plus cher...'[33]

The rights and wrongs of the 'fracas' with the baron are in fact of minor significance. George Sand had had what she regarded as a bitter experience of marriage; marriage itself will therefore be condemned, at any rate in its existing forms. Indiana, the aristocratic but penniless creole, has been forced to marry beneath her; Colonel Delmare is a *parvenu*; 'famille obscure et pauvre dont il avait l'air de rougir à force de dire qu'il n'en rougissait pas'.[34] George Sand has these flashes of psychological intuition. Inevitably Indiana's heart is open to suggestion. The brilliant Raymon de Rancière seems indicated, but in due course is revealed as an ambitious egotist with his way to make in the world; Indiana's eyes

[30] J.-L. Bory, op. cit.; comments by Jacqueline Piatier, *Le Monde*, 19 May 1962.

[31] Some of them have in fact been written by herself and others: *Histoire de ma Vie* (1854), *Elle et Lui* (1859), Musset, *Confession d'un Enfant du Siècle* (1836), Maurras, *Les Amants de Venise* (1902).

[32] To Jules Boucoiran, sometime tutor to her two children and life-long friend, 3 December 1830.

[33] To Boucoiran, 13 January 1831.   [34] Chap. V.

are finally opened to the sterling worth – in both senses – of Sir Brown (*sic*)[35] and after the opportune death of Delmare, Sir Brown and Indiana return to the latter's native Island of Bourbon, first with the idea of a double suicide, but on second thoughts to live in secluded, unwedded bliss. Shades of *Paul et Virginie*, brought up to date, with a social message: 'le rapport mal établi entre les sexes par le fait de la société.'[36]

Later in life, George Sand denied that Indiana was a self-portrait: 'On n'a pas manqué de dire qu' Indiana était ma personne et mon histoire. Il n'en est rien'.[37] Maybe, and yet the reader may be pardoned for regarding this 'official' denial as no more convincing than many others. 'Vous, Indiana, profanée à ce rustre [i.e. Delmare] dont la main de fer a courbé votre tête et flétri votre vie!'[38] Surely the baroness animadverting on her own position? Be that as it may, the whole theme of the book springs directly from her experience: the rights of women trampled on in marriage, feminism, a fig for social conventions: 'Madame Delmare profondément blessée par les lois sociales, raidissait toutes les forces de son âme pour les haïr et les mépriser';[39] the sanctifying value of love: 'L'amour c'est la vertu de la femme; c'est pour lui qu'elle se fait une gloire de ses fautes'.[40] In a word: revolt! decked out in shiniest Romantic tinsel.

Jacques (1835), a novel in letter form, is like a sequel to *Indiana*. If wives should revolt with Indiana against the injustice of their subordinate position in marriage, any incompatibility of humour between husband and wife as a result of a triangular situation might most conveniently be put an end to, if only husbands would take their cue from Jacques, a most accommodating man, who will make way for Octave by making away with himself: 'Calme ta douleur, ma soeur chérie... [almost a line from Baudelaire] Quand la vie d'un homme est nuisible à quelques-uns... inutile à tous, le suicide est un acte légitime.'[41] Nor must his sister think ill of the 'guilty pair': 'Ne maudis pas ces deux amants qui vont profiter de ma mort. Ils ne sont pas coupables, ils s'aiment. Il n'y a pas de crime où il y a amour sincère.' The claim of love to be a complete justification for shedding responsibility has no more vigorous champion than George Sand at this stage in her development; in her more than anyone the Romantic flame burns fiercely.

[35] Chap. III, 'Le Colonel et Sir Brown eurent la délicatesse de garder le secret de Moun'. English readers will observe with satisfaction that 'Sir Brown' has the traditional quality of the true Britisher: '... avec un sang-froid vraiment britannique il s'apprêtait à se couper la gorge' (Part II, chap. 13).
[36] Second Preface, 1842.
[37] *Histoire de ma Vie*, Part IV, 15.
[38] Chap. VI.
[40] Chap. XXVII.
[39] Chap. XXVI.
[41] *Jacques*, Letter No. XCVI.

Lélia (1833) completes what might be called her Romantic trilogy. Sham though the characters of *Indiana* and *Jacques* now appear they have at least some connexion with reality, those of *Lélia*
– Stenio, Magnus, Trenmor, le Cardinal, Lélia herself – are purely
symbolic. 'Lélia... où j'ai mis plus de moi que dans tout autre
livre', as the author admits,[42] is a series of dithyrambic outpourings
on Romantic themes of which Lélia-Sand constitutes herself the
high priestess. The lessons? – fortunately George Sand is at hand to
tell us: 'Que la femme, pour échapper à la souffrance et à l'humiliation, se préserve de l'amour et de la maternité, c'est une conclusion romanesque que j'ai essayée dans le roman *Lélia*, non pas
comme un example à suivre, mais comme la peinture d'un martyre
qui peut donner à penser aux juges et aux bourreaux, aux hommes
qui font la loi et à ceux qui l'appliquent. Cela n'était qu'un
poème.'[43]

Lélia is the most subjective of all George Sand's writings. Yet at
the end when the mysterious Trenmor has laid both Lélia and the
luckless poet Stenio in their graves, he rejects the notion that without them his life has become meaningless: 'il y a partout des
hommes qui luttent et qui souffrent, il y a partout des devoirs à
remplir.' As he picks up his stick and strides away along the road
into the future, we may see in his words and action a forecast of
George Sand's own development.

Mauprat (1837) is a clear indication that the change in her
Romantic attitudes has begun. Throughout her long literary career
George Sand was an admirable story-teller; nowhere better than in
Mauprat, a dramatic tale, with a judicious admixture of mystery,
rooted in the eighteenth-century history of the Berry country; the
Romantic novel at its best, with a number of well-drawn characters
whose existence the reader can believe in: the Mauprat brood,
Bernard de Mauprat the narrator, Edmée, Patience the solitary
rustic, Marcasse the trapper.

Mauprat is characteristically Romantic too on the messianic
level. The message is as yet discreet and fits in with the characters.
Thus when old Patience declares to Bernard: 'Suivez mes conseils
... Aimez le peuple; détestez ceux qui le détestent... faites-vous
l'ami du peuple',[44] this is in character, but the attitude is also
George Sand's, and throughout the story the evident warmth of
sympathy for the poor and the simple is true both of late
eighteenth-century Rousseauism and of the humanitarian tendencies stirring in and about George Sand.

Nor should we neglect the fact that Patience and Marcasse are

[42] *Correspondance*, Letter No. CLIV, 21 August 1836.
[43] *Ibid.*, Letter No. CCXVIII, 28 August 1842.
[44] Chap. X.

earlier prototypes of the rustic characters whom George Sand was to portray later on.

By 1840 the full tide of humanitarianism was running. The fact is well reflected in George Sand's novels of the period: e.g. *Le Compagnon du Tour de France* (1840); *Le Meunier d'Angibault* (1845); well-constructed tales where true love in due course conquers social barriers: Pierre Huguenin, honest workman, shall marry the heiress Mademoiselle de Villepreux, Madame de Blanchemon, widowed, shall marry the penniless intellectual Henri Lemor. George Sand has moved a long way from her original attitude towards marriage, but to suggest she seriously puts forward such 'love matches' as solutions to the social problem is unfair; they are part of the romantic tale to help the novel's social message along. The novelist's purpose is to extend awareness of the social problems, to communicate to the reading public her own strong social sympathy for the struggles of the poor by disseminating knowledge about the economic condition of the peasantry, or the pattern of the 'compagnonnage' movements in France and their internecine rivalries, under the Restoration.

Consuelo (1842) and its sequel *La Comtesse de Rüdolstadt* (1843) present a still broader canvas. Into the historical background George Sand weaves the romantic adventures of the singer Consuelo which take her from eighteenth-century Venice to the Castle of Giants in Bohemia, the secret subterranean passages of which are reminiscent of *The Castle of Otranto*, to the court and the prisons of Frederick the Great, to initiation into the mysteries of Freemasonry which was spreading its web of secret societies across Germany and France: 'L'Europe est remplie de sociétés secrètes, laboratoires souterrains où se prépare une grande révolution.'[45] Mystery, mysticism, transmigration of souls, catalepsy, the slavery of marriage without equal partnership – a familiar notion, messianism both revolutionary and anti-clerical – the heroine's adventures enable George Sand to peddle all these wares with generous profusion. Nor must the narrative power of these novels be underestimated; in inventiveness and variety they equal Balzac.

But the time was coming when George Sand would be able to translate her revolutionary and social enthusiasms into action. February 1848 – another royal ninepin had been bowled over, revolution was in the air; Romanticism had spilled over from the moral into the political field. George Sand hurried to Paris to place her pen at the service of the people, as a journalist. Her letters are brimming over with the prevailing euphory: 'La République est la meilleure des familles, le peuple est le meilleur des amis...'[46]

---

[45] *La Comtesse de Rüdolstadt*, Vol. II, chap. XXXI.
[46] *Ibid.*, No. CCLXVII, 6 March 1848.

'Vive la République! Quel rêve, quel enthousiasme, et, en même temps, quelle tenue, quel ordre à Paris!'[47]

But already in Paris a note of disappointment creeps in: 'Hélas! la république est souillée' (17 April). She had begun to understand the criss-cross of conflicting ideas and idealisms, personal rivalries and hatreds that are the realities of politics. By the middle of June she has lost hope: 'Que peuvent faire ceux qui ont consacré leur vie à l'idée d'égalité fraternelle, qui ont aimé l'humanité avec ardeur...que peuvent faire les socialistes...lorsque le peuple méconnaît sa propre cause?'[48] The murderous June days were the crowning blow: 'Je suis navrée...et je ne crois plus à l'existence d'une république qui commence par tuer ses prolétaires...'[49]

For George Sand what was left? To plead as she did not cease to do[50] with the Prince-President in favour of this or that political prisoner, to return to literature and to Nohant like the dove in La Fontaine's fable, bruised in heart. Nohant had always been and was to remain her port of refuge after the storms, whether personal or political: in 1832 after she had broken with Jules Sandeau, in 1834 after Musset, in 1847 after Chopin, in 1848 after the June days, again in 1851 after the *coup d'état*; and Nohant meant the Berry country she loved, not blindly[51] but with intimate knowledge acquired through years of close observation and of experience from childhood onwards, with detailed knowledge of its landscape, its peasants, their lives, attitudes and speech. True it is, and we have noted it, that George Sand had already tapped this golden vein of regional knowledge (*Valentine, Mauprat*), but it had been, as it were, by accident. The writing of books for her had meant primarily (and what more romantic?) direct personal communication of some sort: her ideas on the relations between the sexes as a result of personal experience, her social aspirations largely as a result of her personal relations with humanitarian thinkers – Michel de Bourges, Pierre Leroux, Lamennais. Thus with all her narrative skill there remains a certain dichotomy between the story and the lesson. There are admittedly signs of George Sand's reflecting about the novelist's craft in itself. Thus in the preface of *Le Compagnon du Tour de France* she writes: 'Il y a toute une littérature nouvelle à créer avec les moeurs populaires; elle en sortira brillante...c'est là que se retrempera la muse romantique, muse éminemment révolutionnaire et qui depuis son apparition dans les lettres cherche sa voie et sa famille.' Perhaps she meant the word 'révolutionnaire' to have an exclusively literary meaning in this

---

[47] *Ibid.*, No. CCLXVIII, 9 March 1848.
[48] *Ibid.*, No. CCLXXXII, 15 June 1848.
[49] *Ibid.*, No. CCLXXXIII, July 1848.   [50] *Ibid., passim.*
[51] In 1861 she writes to Dumas *fils*: 'Je trouve le Berry, petit, maigre et laid.'

context, but if so her performance at that date belies her; the people were not to be material for literature, literature was to be at the service of the people.

La Mare au Diable (1846) had been a first excursion, with deliberate intent, into regionalist literature. Thus her disappointments of 1848 did not provide the starting point. Nor did she as a result withdraw from a hostile world; she continued as before, active in good works, closely interested in ideas and events, in contact with people in all walks of life.[52] But her attitude towards literature changes. She sets out, with more conscious artistic intention, to fuse her narrative skill and her deep experience of rustic life into a satisfactory whole;[53] the best results of this matured attitude to her art are seen, after *La Mare au Diable*, in *La Petite Fadette* (1849), *François le Champi* (1850), *Les Maîtres Sonneurs* (1853). 'Dans les arts, le plus simple est ce qu'il y a de plus grand à tenter, de plus difficile à atteindre', George Sand had herself written;[54] in these novels she achieves it. Simplicity of situation is indeed like a wager between author and reader; the problem – how to compel the latter's interest. George Sand's skill in these stories consists in creating initial situations where the main characters are distant from each other in attitude, and bringing them finally together by a series of events that affect their relationships. How will Germain come to recognize that Marie rather than the rich widow is the wife for him? How will Sylvinet's jealous love for his twin brother Lambert come to be reconciled to the latter's love for Fanchon Fadet? How will Madeleine Blanchet come to love François?[55] How will the situation between Joset, Huriel and Brulette work out? The reader soon asks himself these questions and as invisible spectator watches the reorientation of attitude that resolves the problems in joy or sadness; they are genuine human problems because the characters involved are people whose existence he accepts wholly, not intermittently as so often in the author's earlier work.

George Sand's inventive power did not exhaust itself with her rustic novels, but she did not again achieve the same perfection. With them she may claim to have created the regionalist novel and

---

[52] See her letters, *passim*.

[53] See Preface (April 1857) to *La Mare au Diable*; Preface (December 1857) to *La Petite Fadette*; Preface (May 1852) to *François le Champi*; her correspondence with Flaubert; *Histoire de ma Vie*, Part IV, chap. 15— Balzac's opinion. All these are evidence of George Sand's matured attitude to her art.

[54] Preface to *Le Compagnon du Tour de France*.

[55] A serious blemish appears here. Madeleine's attitude to François at the outset is clearly maternal. The shift in her attitude has a disagreeable incestuous suggestion about it, not uncharacteristic of the ambivalence the author herself displayed often enough in her relations with men.

to have given the peasant a status in literature that neither her predecessors nor contemporaries had given him. Mawkish and sentimental? No! Idealized? perhaps. But Balzac (*Les Paysans*) and Zola (*La Terre*) will more than compensate those that think so, by presenting the harsh realities of the war of attrition between peasant and big landowner (Balzac) or the alleged brutishness of peasant life (Zola). Moreover, one important test must be applied in this comparison which is all to the advantage of George Sand – her characters remain in our memory; Balzac's peasants that gather in 'Le Grand I-Vert' to plot the next move against Monsieur de Montcornet are soon forgotten; as for Zola's they are so elemental, so earthy that we are apt to forget, of Jean and César, which is the hero and which the bull.

In comparison with the abundant flood that poured from the pen of George Sand, the contributions to fiction in the Romantic period from other sources are meagre. The woes of Desgenets[56] seem tiresome and declamatory. Musset may have been sincere but sincerity is not enough. Nor do his short stories: *Les Deux Maîtresses* (1837), *Le Fils du Titien* (1838), *Histoire d'un Merle Blanc* (1842), *Mimi Pinson* (1843) contribute much to his reputation which today stands upon his plays.

Sainte-Beuve's contribution to the personal novel, *Volupté* (1834), is interesting if not very moving. The emotional experience the author has transposed into fictional terms[57] was evidently not of the same intensity as the tornado that had cut through Musset's life. Amaury's inclinations, shifting constantly between the shadowy Mademoiselle de Liniers, Madame de Couaën and Madame R., can scarcely be said to go beyond the hamlet 'Assiduity', in the 'Pays de Tendre'. In love as in other spheres – conspiracy, joining the army, poetry – Amaury's actions are half-hearted, remain unfulfilled; life is dust and ashes. But the inward-looking Amaury has at least the compensation of being able to savour his moral bankruptcy with the bitter delectation of an intellectual voluptuary and this delicate analysis extends to the religious sphere, since under the direct influence of an unnamed ecclesiastic, the indirect influence of l'Abbé Carron[58] and the remote literary action of the saintly Port-Royal solitary, Monsieur Hamon,[59] Amaury decides in the end to take orders.

Amaury's inner explorations are not without general validity;

[56] *Confession d'un Enfant du Siècle* (1836).
[57] His relations with Madame Hugo.
[58] 1760–1821. Prominent in *émigré* circles in England and later under the Restoration. Largely through his influence, Lamennais decided to take holy orders.
[59] Port-Royal was shortly to become a major interest in Sainte-Beuve's life. See below, chap. 21.

the reflections of an intelligent man are sure to call forth echoes
in the reader of any generation or at least to win his intellectual
assent. But Amaury is particularly interesting as a reflection of
Sainte-Beuve himself. Amaury claims to see his own image in
René: 'J'ai lu René et j'ai frémi; je m'y suis reconnu tout entier...
Combien d'autres, depuis vingt ans, ont frémi ainsi et se sont crus
en face d'eux-mêmes devant ce portrait immortel'.[60] But with his
usual finesse Amaury has reservations: 'Mon mal était bien à moi
...moins altier et idéal';[61] René is the image of a generation,
Amaury is the reflection of one man, a less incandescent personality; the sounds of the world reach our ears, only muted; events,
experience are no more than a pretext for quiet inner satisfaction;
the egotism is there but more confined, reduced to the 'intimiste'
level that the poems of Joseph Delorme, alias Sainte-Beuve, are
pitched on: 'il y a pourtant dans le lent déclin d'une beauté qu'on
aime... une douceur triste que je pressentais assez pour vouloir la
goûter jusqu'au bout.'[62]

All Sainte-Beuve's intellectual curiosity which was to make of
him one of the greatest critics of the nineteenth century is in being
in Amaury; his attitudes are never clear-cut; both he and his
creator have an almost Proustian sensitiveness to delicate shifts and
shades of mood and thought; both are secretive, velvety, in a word
feline: 'le goût des habitudes intimes... ; l'attrait énervant de
ces molles amitiés...; mon amour serpentait par ces faux-fuyants
sinueux...; ... ce discret parfum...; Ainsi M. Hamon s'emparait
de moi et me pénétrait par mes secrètes avenues.'[63]

The personal novel as a *genre* is at best only a kind of half novel
with the narrator in a sense as both judge and party, judge of the
other characters, whom the reader sees only through his eyes,
advocate for himself. Amaury's advocacy is indeed skilful; yet he
remains remote, unreal, an exercise in analysis with only occasional moments of more than narrow personal significance, a
contribution, interesting no doubt, to a contemporary literary
mode.

Perhaps the best justification for *Volupté* is that it inspired
Eugène Fromentin (1820–76) to write *Dominique* (1862), which
provides some parallels of situation. But parallels are one thing, a
comparison is another, and a comparison between the two novels
is all to the advantage of the latter. In contrast to the shadowy
Amaury floating in an insubstantial world, Dominique, firmly
rooted to the life of the little community he lives in, stands out
against a landscape that Fromentin knew intimately[64] and de-

---

[60] *Volupté*, chap. 12.
[61] *Ibid.*, chap. 12.
[62] *Ibid.*, chap. 12.
[63] *Ibid.*, chap. 21.
[64] La Rochelle.

scribes with the eye of a painter.[65] Only when Dominique has taken shape and substance before the reader's eyes does he become the narrator; only then does he take the reader back in time and breathe life on the ashes of his dead self. Nor is Dominique concerned merely to explore his own ego; he tells a story that, pitched though it is in a minor key, moves to a dramatic climax. Drama requires conflict, and to produce a conflict requires at least two characters or an intense dialogue in his own mind between a man's conflicting selves. Unlike most heroes of personal novels, Dominique is devoid of that egotism that leads them to regard other people as no more than pretexts for the display and analysis of their own sensibilities thus depriving those around him of an independent existence. Not so the characters Dominique evokes; though seen through his eyes, they emerge from his past with lives of their own; Madeleine de Nièvres in particular has a clear-cut moral outline, a will that recalls something of La Princesse de Clèves. Thus in *Dominique* the reader believes he is witnessing an action on a wider stage than the narrator's own ego; the narrow confines of the personal novel have been broken down.

Astolphe[66] de Custine (1790–1858), who for over a century has been no more than a phantom in the glades of Romanticism, has now regained some literary vitality.[67]

Both his grandfather, who had fought in the American War of Independence, and his father, who was a general in the Revolutionary armies, were victims of the Revolution. His mother, Delphine de Custine, figures for good reason in the pages of the *Mémoires d'Outre Tombe*, and gave her name to Madame de Staël's first successful novel. Astolphe, himself a prominent figure in the social circles of his day, friend of Sophie Gay and of Beyle, was both a patron to the Romantics and, in an amateur aristocratic manner, a novelist, in the wake of Chateaubriand's *René*. 'Depuis que je suis au monde mon être est un énigme...',[68] he writes; 'je vis comme un torrent qui au lieu de remplir son lit, creuse un abîme à sa source et s'y précipite en tourbillon. Je suis voué à une tristesse innée...' The sadness finds expression in his first novel, *Aloys* (1829), which, though the personal references are scarcely veiled, made no impact.[69] Custine, betrothed to Mademoiselle de Duras, had broken off the engagement because, so he alleged, he

---

[65] Fromentin was also a painter and art critic – *Les Maîtres d'autre fois* (1876).
[66] The unusual Christian name comes from Ariosto's *Orlando Furioso*.
[67] Custine, *Lettres de Russie*, ed. by H. Massis, 1960.
[68] Custine, *Les Plus Belles Pages*, with introduction by Y. Florenne, 1963.
[69] Other novels include: *Le Monde comme il va* (1835), *Ethel* (1835). Also a tragedy *Béatrice Cenci* (1833).

loved her mother. Aloys, a prey to an unattainable love, becomes
a monk and nurses his grief in the hospice of St Bernard. Madame
de Duras wrote a short story that presents the facts in a different
light and which, though itself unpublished, became the model
through an unauthorized and plagiarized version, entitled *Olivier
ou le Secret*,[70] of Beyle's *Armance*.[71]

Whatever the truth may be about Custine's impotence, his instincts appear to have been aberrant or at least ambivalent; a
Baron de Charlus in embryo, his friendships with men brought him
some unenviable notoriety[72] – Wilhelm Hesse, Edward de Sainte-
Barbe, Ignace Gurowski, not to mention a young soldier, on
account of whom Astolphe received a severe hiding.[73]

But the revived interest in Custine has a sounder basis than his
attainments as a novelist or his peculiar reputation. It derives from
his journey to Russia[74] – undertaken perhaps to straighten out his
friend Gurowski's political position – and the work in four volumes
that resulted: *La Russie en 1839* (1843).

In her *Dix Années d'Exil* Madame de Staël had made a few interesting but cursory reflections on Russia; Custine's letters may
rank as the first illuminating analysis of things Russian – customs,
institutions, Russians and their attitudes. Disliking as he did the
July Monarchy, Custine went to Russia with an open mind, but
with his liberal instincts he disliked much of what he saw in that
autocracy, which he judged to be 'policée' but not 'civilisée' – established on a strong bureaucracy, an effete aristocracy and a suffering religiously-minded people. 'Certes', he writes of himself, 'je
ne suis rien moins que révolutionnaire, mais je suis révolutionné;
voilà ce que c'est que d'être né en France et que d'y vivre.'[75]
From that position he foresees revolution: 'Ou le monde civilisé
passera de nouveau avant cinquante ans sous le joug des barbares,
ou la Russie subira une révolution plus terrible que ne fut la révolution dont l'Occident de l'Europe subit encore les effets',[76] and
approves the Emperor's prudence in making travel both to and
from Russia difficult: 'Plus je vois la Russie, plus j'approuve
l'Empereur lorsqu'il défend aux Russes de voyager et rend l'accès
de son pays difficile. Le régime politique de la Russie ne résisterait
pas vingt ans à la libre communication avec l'Occident de
l'Europe.'[77]

[70] By Hyacinthe de la Touche.　　　　[71] See below, pp. 205–6.
[72] In 1814, Astolfe had the nick-name Guermanges. In that year there
was question of a marriage between him and Albertine de Staël. His wife
was a Saint-Simon Courtomer. All these names have a Proustian ring about
them. Coincidence? or had Proust discovered Custine's story and used the
names or something like them? See Florenne, op. cit.
[73] In 1824, in some stables at Saint-Denis.
[74] In 1839.　　　　　　　　　　　　　[75] Letter No. 13.
[76] Letter No. 10.　　　　　　　　　　[77] Letter No. 11.

Custine was a liberal legitimist, much like Chateaubriand, by his belief in the value of politically powerful and conscious aristocracy, but his desire to understand the underlying mechanisms of the Russian scene and his searching glance into the future recall Tocqueville in America.

Chapter 13

I. BEYLE

'LA manie écrivante d'Henri Beyle[1] semble naître le 18 avril 1801 à Milan', writes Henri Martineau.[2] Thereafter until his death in 1842, but particularly from 1814, Beyle's pen was ceaselessly in motion. The latest complete edition of his works[3] comprises seventy-nine volumes in 16°. If we set aside the numerous fugitive pieces such as the articles Beyle (1783–1842) contributed to divers journals and reviews, also the numerous fragmentary writings, dramatic and other, that are so eagerly sought after by all Beyle enthusiasts, his important works to be discussed in this chapter may conveniently be grouped as follows: the autobiographical studies, a history of art, travel journals, a treatise on the passion of love, the novels.

In the first group a distinction is at once evident between the autobiographical works proper – *La Vie d'Henry Brulard* and the *Souvenirs d'Egotisme,* both intended for publication since the author more than once addresses the reader of the future – 'O lecteur bénévole'! – and the *Journal* which as clearly was not intended for publication. The *Journal* covers the years 1801 to 1815 with a few additional entries for the years 1816 to 1823; with it begins what Martineau calls 'la manie écrivante d'Henri Beyle'. The *Journal* brings us as close as possible to the man himself in his youth and early manhood. But *Brulard* deals with his childhood, and, although the last to be written of the autobiographical works, it offers the best introduction to the author not merely because in its pages, as Beyle puts it, 'je vais naître' but because it is so characteristic of his mental attitudes, in a word, so 'Stendhalien'.

When Beyle began *Brulard* in 1835[4] he was doing nothing that was not the fashion of the day. Yet how different *Brulard* is from the *Mémoires d'Outre-Tombe* for example, much of which was written at the same period. Unlike Chateaubriand, Beyle makes no

---

[1] Beyle used a number of pseudonyms; the most important – Stendhal – appears in 1817. Thereafter all his works are signed Stendhal or 'par l'auteur de' with the name of a previous work signed Stendhal.
[2] *Pensées, Filosofia Nova*, Vol. I, Preface, Le Divan edn.
[3] Divan edn.
[4] Not 1832, in spite of the opening pages. See Martineau's preface, Divan edn.

attempt to strike attitudes or create a carefully composed image of himself for the future; the only justification for writing such a book, he tells the reader, is a rigorous objectivity, an ever alert endeavour to present the facts without embellishment or emotional overtones.

If anything makes Beyle hesitate to embark on autobiography it is the great 'I' inevitably in the centre of the stage, an irritant to future readers: 'cet effroyable quantité de Je et de Moi! Il y a de quoi donner de l'humeur au lecteur le plus bénévole. Je et moi, ce serait au talent près comme M. de Chateaubriand, ce roi des égotistes[5] ... On pourrait écrire, il est vrai, en se servant de la troisième personne *il* fit, *il* dit. Oui, mais comment rendre compte des mouvements intérieurs de l'âme?';[6] changing 'Je' to 'il' is enough – such is the suggestive power of words, even a pronoun – to change the direction of the writer's gaze from the searching inward examination he is aiming to achieve towards an outside character who despite the author's best efforts may take on a life of his own and to that extent no longer be the faithful image of his creator. So, despite the objection of the 'je's' and the 'moi's' – a difficulty Beyle comes back to more than once – the impulse to seek his real self is overriding: 'je devrais écrire ma vie, je saurai peut-être enfin, quand cela sera fini dans deux ou trois ans, ce que j'ai été, gai ou triste, homme d'esprit ou sot, homme de courage ou peureux et enfin au total heureux ou malheureux'[7] ... and on a previous page: 'Je vais avoir cinquante ans, il serait bien temps de me connaître.'

In *Brulard* the mysterious being Beyle is seeking is particularly elusive; the author must leap across the chasm of years to find the child that was father to the man. Can we know ourselves at any time? Does not the effort to achieve such knowledge resolve itself into a list of likes and dislikes, relationships with other people, responses to the outside world?

Sometimes we may discover the image that others have of us; that experience was not foreign to Beyle: 'Encore aujourd'hui toute la société de Mlle Clarke croit fermement que je suis un monstre. Un monstre d'immoralité surtout.'[8] If that happens, as often as not we believe the image to be either embellished or distorted. Who can then decide where the truth lies? How much greater the difficulty of penetrating the mists of time to the personality of the

---

[5] Beyle cannot here be referring to the *Mémoires d'Outre-Tombe* which were not published until 1850; nor was he one of the select band, 'the happy few', as he might have put it, invited to Madame Récamier's salon at l'Abbaye au Bois, to hear 'readings' from the *Mémoires* by the great man.

[6] *La Vie d'Henry Brulard*, I, p. 6, Divan. [8] *Souvenirs d'Egotisme*, p. 75, Divan.

[7] *Ibid.*, p. 6, Divan.

child that looks at us from a faded photo or a portrait? Beyle without these aids (if such they be) was conscious of the problem: 'Si jamais je revois cette femme d'esprit,[9] il faut que je la presse de questions pour qu'elle me dise ce que j'étais alors. En vérité je l'ignore. Je ne puis que noter le degré de bonheur senti par cette machine. Comme j'ai toujour creusé les mêmes idées depuis, comment savoir où j'en étais alors.'[10]

But difficult or even impossible, the game is worth the candle, and what strikes the reader constantly in *Brulard* is Beyle's vigilance to banish prejudice or emotion, his sincerity in search of the boy he had been. The comically clumsy sketches interlarding his pages can be ascribed to the same desire. They recall the detective's method of 'reconstructing the crime'; by reconstituting in his memory the precise plan of this room or that street he will have an accurate picture in his mind and perhaps recapture a fleeting but important sensation, his at that point in his time-stream. Beyle's evident effort to seize the distant truth is a trait of character the reader respects; it inspires confidence.

Beyle's introspective habit may not be the best way to achieve the happiness he so ardently pursued, and believed all men to pursue whether they know it or not. Yet a distinction may be made between objective self-examination as a means of investigating our psychological mechanisms – Beyle's method – and morose delectation, contemplative narcissism which we find neither in Beyle nor in his characters. Beyle does not nurse grievances, thereby encouraging them to grow; he wants to look them squarely in the face, seize hold of them because, as he notes in his *Journal*: 'C'est un moyen de se consoler que de regarder sa douleur de près (surtout avec une tête comme la mienne)...'[11]

With its rather haphazard disjointed presentation, *La Vie d'Henry Brulard* may not be a carefully wrought piece of writing, yet it deserves our attention; it seems so closely akin to modern ideas about psychological mechanisms, and in relation to Stendhal's fiction it is a beacon. Even if it lacked those two qualities, as the record of one human being's boyhood experience, it is loaded with interest: the spiritual loneliness of the little boy after his mother's death comes across to us all the more intensely because unblurred by sentiment. Were his father Chérubin Beyle and his aunt Séraphie the malicious and cruel creatures Beyle makes them out to be? At least once in his reminiscences Beyle relents towards Chérubin.[12] We may indeed suspect Beyle of darkening the picture with emotional colour borrowed from later years. The desire to

---

[9] Madame le Brun, later Marquise de Grave.
[10] *Brulard*, II, p. 227, Divan.   [11] *Journal*, II, p. 145, Divan.
[12] *Brulard*, I, p. 121, Divan. 'J'étais outré et je pense fort injuste...'

protect the boy from all evil communications and physical risks may have been the cause of Chérubin's and Séraphie's severity; but be that as it may, the unimaginative, unintelligent upbringing of the little boy, the habit he acquires through dislike of his father and aunt to adopt (in secret) the opposite attitude to theirs, the joy he found by contrast in the society of his grandfather Gagnon, his hatred of the obsequious and Jesuitical Abbé Raillane – 'cet homme aurait dû faire de moi un noir coquin';[13] the joyful impact that Gros the mathematician made upon the boy's mind after the dreariness of earlier teachers, the plan to make his gift for mathematics the means of escape from the desert of Grenoble, the golden picture in his mind of Paris and his desolation at the first contact with the grey reality, his agonies of shyness in the home of his rich and influential Daru cousins – Julien in the la Môle salon, the authoritarian action of Noël Daru, packing him off without so much as by your leave to work in Pierre Daru's office, his quaint spelling of 'cela' (two l's); all of these and countless other details provide a source of human interest rich in pathos and comedy as fresh today as it ever was; if we knew nothing of Beyle's life we could still read *Brulard* as a novel, carelessly put together no doubt (but what of that?), and recognize in it a family likeness with *Le Rouge et le Noir*, *Lucien Leuwen* and *La Chartreuse de Parme*.

To crown it all the sudden unforeseen liberation – soldiering in Italy! The reader will appreciate all the comedy inherent in Beyle's description of the journey thither in company with Captain de Burelviller, tall, gaunt, hardbitten but not unkindly, long-nosed and long-sabred, a veritable Don Quixote of a man who, thanks to Beyle, steps suddenly into the limelight as guide and mentor, only to disappear as suddenly into the anonymous multitude of 'vieilles moustaches' who followed Napoleon as a God and either left their bones on a European battlefield or returned home to foster Bonapartism and the Napoleonic legend; beside him, Sancho Panza, young Beyle, full of joyful and ebullient ignorance, if a little unsteady in the saddle. For Burelviller crossing the St Bernard was just one, mildly hazardous, event in a soldier's life; for young Beyle it was a liberation, like stepping from darkness into light: 'Je ne dois donc pas me plaindre du destin. J'ai eu un lot exécrable de sept à dix-sept ans, mais depuis le passage du Mont Saint-Bernard (à 2491 metres d'élévation au-dessus de l'océan) je n'ai plus eu à me plaindre du destin ains au contraire à m'en louer.' Why should Beyle bother here to give the height of the pass?[14] Merely his love

---

[13] *Brulard*, I, pp. 94 and 105, Divan. The word 'coquin' is a favourite one of Stendhal's; it recurs frequently, e.g. in *Lucien Leuwen*.

[14] Which, incidentally, is incorrect. It should be 2472 m. according to the guide books. See Martineau's note, *Vie de Henry Brulard* (Divan).

of exact detail? Perhaps; but whether there by chance or design, the detail reinforces the symbolical nature of the event in Beyle's life; the uphill struggle, the lonely eminence, the 'promised land' at his feet. Beyle was about to receive a vision of Italy that remained with him thereafter and was to draw him like a magnet: 'vivre en Italie et entendre de cette musique[15] devint la base de tous mes raisonnements.'[16]

But if Italy[17] remained the goal of all his desires, military life did not. He resigned the second lieutenancy of dragoons[18] he had been commissioned to. In 1802, after a short stay in Grenoble, he is back in Paris, on a niggardly and irregularly paid allowance from his father; but having (in a sense ungratefully) rid himself of the uncomfortable solicitude of the Daru family, he was free to follow his own inclinations, both amorous and intellectual. The *Journal* and more particularly that part of it, bearing no dated day to day entries, that Beyle called his *Filosofia nova*,[19] bear witness to the importance of the next three years in his spiritual and intellectual development.

For a reader in the late twentieth century living in a world tightly knit by speed of communications and power of destructive weapons, where public events intrude upon his privacy and liberty of action, the early pages of the *Journal*, those that cover approximately the same period as the *Pensées*,[20] are noteworthy for the paucity of reference to the public scene, political and military. The renewal of war with England, Trafalgar, Austerlitz which for Pitt meant rolling up the map of Europe for years, the Consulate giving way to the Empire, what had these events to do with this eager young disciple of the Idéologues, exploring his psychological mechanisms, charting the passions, constructing a plan for happiness, theatre-going as often as finance allowed? Napoleon? – an isolated reference, and then only as the basis of an acute piece of

---

Julien Sorel, it will be remembered, when in need of solitude, liked high places. In *Promenades dans Rome* (Vol. 2, p. 141, Divan) Stendhal, alluding to the Carbonari prisoners in the Castle of S. Angelo, writes: 'La vue qu'ils ont du haut de leur prison est magnifique et faite pour changer en douce mélancolie la tristesse la plus colérique.'

[15] Cimarosa's *Matrimonio Segreto*.   [16] *Brulard*, II, p. 311, Divan.

[17] Beyle's epitaph, be it remembered, begins 'Arigo Beyle, Milanese...' etc., composed by himself. Milan, or at any rate northern Italy, was to be his earthly paradise.

[18] A conjunction of circumstances may explain why it was not difficult for him: (a) the peace of Amiens, (b) the fact that his family at Grenoble were royalist in sympathy and consequently did not oppose the step.

[19] Published separately as *Pensées* in the Divan edn.

[20] They cover the period 23 October 1802 to 4 December 1805 (Martineau's Preface, *Journal*, 1; Divan) and are particularly concerned with Beyle's reflections on the authors he was then engrossed in: Helvétius (notably), Cabanis, Hobbes, Shakespeare, Destutt de Tracy.

psychological observation: 'Il salue beaucoup et sourit. Le sourire de théâtre où l'on montre les dents, mais où les yeux ne sourient pas.'[21] Even the contemporary literary scene, which could be expected to have interested him more, receives scant attention; Madame de Staël and Chateaubriand, the giants of the day – the reader of the *Journal* might well forget it – are barely alluded to.

From this vital seed time, the *Journal* carries us on through the years of the Empire. Thanks once more to the Daru family, behold our grocer's assistant[22] transformed into a Napoleonic functionary – *Commissaire des Guerres*, later[23] *Auditeur au Conseil d'Etat*; Brunswick, Vienna, Moscow in 1812; the *Journal* enables us to follow Beyle trundling across Europe. His last mission in Napoleon's service was to Dauphiné in 1814 to organize its defence against the invasion from Savoy.

The latter half of 1814 saw him back in Italy once more having resigned from the public service. He did not return during the 'Hundred Days'. The *Journal* contains a solitary reference: '19 juillet. J'avais lu la capitulation de Paris, tout est perdu même l'honneur.'[24] A few political reflections follow and then a characteristic remark: 'Je n'aime pas les plats Français d'aujourd'hui.'[25]

Throughout the *Journal* the events themselves, not excluding the retreat from Russia, are mentioned very briefly. In themselves they are no more than signposts along the continuous road of experience. The *Journal* is a kind of 'herbarium' where Beyle stores his specimens of sensations, a reference book of experiences that he may later find valuable in his unending investigation of human passions and behaviour: 'les petits détails notés rappellent et rendent présentes toutes les sensations. . . . Un tel journal n'est fait que pour qui l'écrit.'[26] How right he was; how wrong he is! Ever since the 1880s when Beyle's personality was first seen clearly, even more now when we can measure his full stature and appreciate how intimately linked Beyle the man is with his characters, the *Journal* is seen to be not only indispensable for our knowledge of his life in the Napoleonic years but, what is more important, a means of deepening our insight into that incisive mind and sensitive heart.

The *Souvenirs d'Egotisme* take up the chronicle after Beyle's return from Italy in 1821 disconsolate and love-lorn.[27] They are in fact Beyle's first excursion into autobiography proper at a moment

[21] *Journal*, I, p. 166, Divan.
[22] In pursuit of his mistress, the actress Mélanie Guilbert, Beyle had taken a job as clerk to a wholesale grocer in Marseilles.
[23] 1811.
[24] A reminiscence of François I after Pavia 1525: 'Tout est perdu, fors l'honneur.'
[25] *Journal*, V, p. 282, Divan.   [26] *Journal*, V, p. 333, Divan.
[27] Méthilde Dembowska had remained deaf to his passionate entreaties.

where he felt the need of an intellectual occupation: 'Sans travail le vaisseau de la vie humaine n'a point de leste';[28] evidently the consular post he had recently been appointed to (1830) was not exacting, yet the constant interruptions he was exposed to disturbed creative work: 'Je ne puis jamais en prenant mon papier être sûr de passer une heure sans être interrompu. Cette futile contrariété éteint net l'imagination chez moi.'

The *Souvenirs* lack *Brulard*'s wealth of interest; a series of Paris salons with pen portraits of the men and women Beyle met there, the whole loosely strung together into a disjointed narrative. For the enthusiast, however, hot on the scent of any clue to the models of Beyle's fictional characters, the *Souvenirs* provide a fund of interest for 'matching up' the fiction with the reality behind it:

Madame Traversi and Marquise Raversi (*La Chartreuse de Parme*).
Méthilde Dembowska and Madame de Chasteller (*Lucien Leuwen*).
Comtesse Curial and Marquise de Puy-Laurens (*Lucien Leuwen*) and/or Madame Grandet (*Lucien Leuwen*).
Comte d'Argoult and M. de Vaize (*Lucien Leuwen*).
Comtesse Kassera and Madame d'Hocquincourt (*Lucien Leuwen*).
Comte de Sauran and Comte Mosca (*La Chartreuse de Parme*).
Di Fiori and Comte Alta Mira (*Le Rouge et le Noir*) and François Leuwen (*Lucien Leuwen*).
M. de Syon and Marquis de Croisenois (*Le Rouge et le Noir*).
Madame de Saint Aulaire and Madame Grandet (*Lucien Leuwen*).

But apart from this aspect, the *Souvenirs* give a foretaste of the originality of *Brulard*; themes more fully developed there are here too: the enigma of his own personality: 'Quel homme suis-je? Ai-je du bon sens? Ai-je du bon sens avec profondeur? Ai-je l'esprit remarquable? En verité, je n'en sais rien ... Voyons si, en faisant mon examen de conscience, la plume à la main, j'arriverai à quelque chose de positif et qui reste longtemps vrai pour moi.'[29] 'Et qui reste longtemps vrai ...', the phrase seems particularly significant. Does it not indicate that Beyle believed the psyche to be as much the prey of time as our bodies, and like them subject to change? A foretaste of Proust, the belief serves to complicate the quest of self-knowledge and indeed at one point Beyle seems ready to give it up: 'On peut connaître tout excepté soi-même.'[30] Beside the quest of self-knowledge there is also that other quest, so essential to Beyle, the quest for happiness: 'Ai-je tiré tout le parti possible pour mon bonheur des positions où le hasard m'a placé pendant les neuf ans que je viens de passer à Paris?' Then again we find his love of Italy, of Milan in particular; his overriding interest in the analysis of human motivation: 'écrire autre chose que l'analyse du coeur humain m'ennuie';[31] the same bet on future rather than present

---

[28] *Souvenirs d'Eg.*, p. 3, Divan.   [29] *Souvenirs d'Eg.*, p. 4, Divan.
[30] *Ibid.*, Editions Richelieu, 1954, p. 230.   [31] *Ibid.*, p. 160, Divan.

fame: 'Je regarde et j'ai toujours regardé mes ouvrages comme des billets à la loterie. Je n'estime que d'être réimprimé en 1900.'[32]

La Vie d'Henry Brulard, Les Souvenirs d'Egotisme and *Le Journal* provide a detailed portrait of Beyle both moral and intellectual. When the youthful Beyle left Grenoble for the first time, ostensibly to sit the entrance examination for the Ecole Polytechnique, he had already built up in his inner citadel a reserve of hatreds to remain with him for life, and to flow into his characters: family tyranny, priests, throne and altar, hypocrisy in any form, narrow bourgeois provincialism with Grenoble as its focal point.

But his characters like their creator are also endowed with more positive attitudes. The *Journal* and Beyle's letters[33] of the period, especially those to his favourite sister Pauline, give abundant proof that the early years in Paris, the years of his 'apprenticeship', provided him, largely by his reading, with a set of fundamental convictions. To Pauline (6 July 1804): 'Je te conseille donc de chercher une consolation dans la plus belle science qui existe, celle de l'homme'; again to Pauline (1 January 1805): 'La science qui nous occupe, cet épouvantail si terrible aux tyrans, cette science si détestée des charlatans de toutes les espèces, est la chose du monde la plus enfantine, la plus simple. Nous la nommerons idéologie... Locke a trouvé cette science en 1720, je crois. Condillac a commencé à lui donner un corps en 1750. Destutt de Tracy l'a portée à la perfection actuelle, il y a deux ans; tu vois qu'elle n'est pas vieille.' To another correspondent, Edouard Monnier, he speaks of his discovery of Helvétius (15 December 1803): 'J'ai enfin lu un ouvrage qui me semble bien singulier, sublime en quelques parties, méprisables en d'autres et bien décourageant en toutes...' Stendhal seems to have almost resented Helvétius' influence and declares that what he has to offer was plundered from others. To Pauline (7 July 1804): 'Peut-être même tout ce qu'il y a de bon dans son livre est-il copié de La Rochefoucauld, Duclos, Vauvenargues, Hobbes, et Locke. Hobbes étant le plus grand de tous ceux-là.'

The *Journal* in its turn confirms from almost every page what a vital period the early Paris years were for him and how big a part certain English thinkers and eighteenth-century French philosophers played in his moral formation (22 December 1804): 'la grande utilité pour moi de l'idéologie, elle m'explique à moi-même'; 'je suis de l'avis de Tracy: nosce te ipsum... source de bonheur'; 'Ordonner les vertus et leurs contraires, les vices, sur la quantité de bonheur et de malheur qu'ils peuvent produire probablement'; 'Faire aussi l'échelle des vertus suivant leur utilité... construire

---

[32] *Ibid.*, p. 88, Divan.
[33] See *Correspondance de Stendhal*, publiée par A. Paupe et P.-A. Cheramy, 2 vols., 1908.

son âme de manière à ce qu'elle ait le plus grand bonheur possible dans la carrière que je prévois que je parcourrai', and so on.

The fundamental notions he had adopted by intellectual conviction provided him with a supple formula for living – *Beylisme* as he called it. The word occurs at least twice in the *Journal* (Vol. IV, p. 76, Vol. V, p. 176) and in a letter to Félix Faure from Smolensk (24 August 1812); after describing all the irritations that assail him at that time he adds: 'cela pèche contre le beylisme'.[34] Nowhere does Beyle explain the term systematically; the reader must develop it into an articulated structure and see how far Beyle himself and his characters fit into the framework.

Beyle believes he has discovered in Hobbes and Helvétius a satisfactory theory of human motivation; in a letter to Pauline (1804, no month given)[35] he writes: 'le corps et la tête sont les valets de l'âme et l'âme elle-même obéit au moi, qui est désir du bonheur.' The body is the instrument, the head provides the rational control-tower and decides when, how and where to release the physical mechanism; both obey the soul, seat of the passions. The passions in other words provide the motive force, but what finally gives them direction? *Le moi*, that mysterious entity, decides for each of us where the thrust of our passionate motive power will carry us. For every individual the problem is how best to achieve personal happiness, for society how to ensure that these countless egotisms in their inexhaustible variety shall add up in the end to an integrated unified whole.

In the early Paris years Beyle reduces his own ideal of happiness to two passions: *amour, gloire*.[36]

To both ideals he remained unswervingly attached. 'Beyle croyait' writes Mérimée in a perceptive pen portrait of his friend,[37] 'qu'il n'y avait de bonheur possible en ce monde que pour un homme amoureux', and Beyle himself confirms the fact: 'elles ("ces êtres charmants") ont à la lettre occupé toute ma vie. A elles ont succédé mes ouvrages.' Love and literature. There was a moment admittedly when even Beyle seemed to be attracted by the commonplace satisfaction of a successful worldly career. This was the time of his service as *Commissaire des Guerres* and as *Auditeur au Conseil d'Etat* – 'le temps de mon ambition'. What young man at such a euphoric moment would not have felt the pull of the Napoleonic magnet? 'Avez-vous éprouvé, O lecteur bénévole, ce que c'est qu'un uniforme dans une armée victorieuse et unique objet de l'attention de la nation comme l'armée de Napoléon.'[38]

But in due course his passion for writing, never far below the

---

[34] *Correspondance*, I, p. 384.
[35] Op. cit., Vol. I, p. 113.
[36] *Journal*, I, p. 192, Divan.
[37] *Notes et Souvenirs*.
[38] *Brulard*, Nouvelle edn., 1949, Vol. I, p. 448.

surface, re-emerged; during the Restoration and the July Monarchy his *beylisme* achieves its most conscious and diversified form. Fame is still the spur but he has turned away from his early ambition of immediate success by writing great comedies like Molière or a great tragedy like Shakespeare or Alfieri.[39] His eyes are on future generations, those of 1880...1900...1935.

Meanwhile Beyle will cultivate his ego. For a man like him who, because of his early habit of revolt against his family, or for whatever reason, had no religious beliefs,[40] this life, his life, is the only thing that matters; its purpose? – to provide Beyle with intense experience; experience must be maximal. This perpetual seeker after sensations – to use a favourite word of his – aims at a constant enrichment of his psyche at every level. Pen in hand he will collect and record his sensations, convinced as he is of two things: that the sort of books that have any chance of evoking a response from future generations must be the fruit of ripe experience, of true psychological observation, and that the study and observation of one's own sensations is the way to knowledge, both of oneself and other men, to truth, to happiness. Truth and happiness established on knowledge of observed facts, that conviction had admittedly come to him early. The extension of this central conviction, like rings on the surface of a pool, is what we witness in the post-Napoleonic period of his life.

The noblest form of experience for Beyle, excluding the passion of love, was provided by the arts; music the earliest and always the intensest joy. One reason, but not the only one, why Milan held such magic for him was La Scala. He was no musician, only an enthusiastic and in the process of time an informed dilettante. No student of music today is likely to derive benefit from Beyle's *Vies de Haydn, de Mozart et de Métastase* (1814). Carpani, author of the *Haydine*, protested in the open letters to 'M. Bombet', published in the *Constitutionnel*, against the latter's unacknowledged borrowings from his work. Skilfully 'Bombet'-Beyle parried the blow in a reply[41] to the editor purporting to be written by Bombet the younger: 'mon frère, étant à Londres, fort vieux, fort goutteux, fort peu occupé de musique, et encore moins de M. Carpani.' The mettez que je réponde pour lui à la lettre de M. Carpani.' The whole incident does Beyle little credit. Yet, plagiarisms apart, the interest of this work lies in the traces it contains of Beyle's criteria for great music and more generally great art: 'Ils oublient, ces compositeurs, que dans les arts rien ne vit que ce qui donne con-

---

[39] *Journal*, the early years, *passim*.
[40] See Mérimée, *H.B.* Yet, oddly enough, Beyle seems to have liked religious ceremonies, see *Journal*.
[41] 26 September 1816, *Correspondence*, Vol. II, p. 6.

tinuellement du plaisir';[42] 'sans mélancolie, point de musique passionnée';[43] 'le caractère de ce peuple[44] est souverainement mélancolique, c'est le terrain dans lequel les passions germent le plus facilement.'[45]

There can be little doubt that the ten years of opera-going, or, to speak as a *beyliste*, the ten years' collection of musical sensations that separate Bombet's *Vies de Haydn* ... from Beyle's *Vie de Rossini* (1824), had enriched the latter's technical understanding of music, but here again, what he writes of Rossini is less interesting than what he thereby reveals of himself: his love of Italy, 'patrie des Beaux Arts'; his conviction that there is no great art, no great music consequently, without great passion: 'L'aimable petit gouvernement[46] ... est bien plus favorable à l'énergie des passions que les gouvernements plus sages de France et d'Angleterre ... Or les beaux arts ne vivent que de passions.'[47] Beyle evidently saw in Rossini that balance of passion, originality, and clarity of musical outline best calculated to provide him with the intensest pleasure, but is he thinking of Rossini or of himself when he writes: 'Un grand artiste se compose de deux choses: une âme exigeante, tendre, passionnée, dédaigneuse et un talent qui s'efforce de plaire à cette âme et de lui donner des jouissances en créant des beautés nouvelles.'[48]

The technique of painting was if anything more closed to Beyle than that of music but the world of colour called forth a response from him almost as eager as did the world of sound. According to the *Journal* he had decided to write a book on Italian painting in 1811; as a visitor to picture galleries during his Italian journey of that year,[49] he had discovered the inadequacies of Lanzi.[50] There is in consequence a guide book element in his *Histoire de la Peinture* (1817). On that level it is no doubt as inadequate for a modern gallery-trotter as Lanzi had been for him.

Some rudiments about the subject there are, but enthusiasm is no substitute for knowledge; he stuffs out his book with much biographical material, mildly interesting, sometimes even entertaining – 'faits divers' often are; he shows little appreciation of the primitives – 'les tristes mannequins des Giotto et des Cimabue';[51] he fills three books with totally irrelevant material on the ancient and

---

[42] *Vies de Haydn, de Mozart et de Métastase*, p. 20, Divan.
[43] *Ibid.*, p. 61, Divan.
[44] The Italians.   [45] *Vie de Haydn*, p. 63, Divan.
[46] *Sic* – the papal states! Beyle expresses himself rather differently on this subject in *Rome, Naples et Florence en 1817*.
[47] *Vie de Rossini*, chap. 1.
[48] *Ibid.*, chap. 1.   [49] *Journal*, V, p. 80, Divan.
[50] L. Lanzi, 1732–1810, author of a *History of Italian Painting* (1789).
[51] Bk. I, 12. His remarks on Cimabue are probably irrelevant anyway since whether such a man existed is doubtful.

modern ideals of beauty, and, after a final book largely biographical on Michaelangelo, hailed by him as the forerunner of the modern conception of beauty by his sombre violence, bows himself out. Yet sometimes there are pertinent remarks which show Beyle's intelligent perceptiveness in a subject he had no training in[52] and his method of attaching the flowering of the different schools of painting to local conditions, political, social or economic, is interesting.

But what applied to his studies of his favourite musicians applies with even greater force to his history of painting – a valuable piece of evidence for the *beyliste* dossier.

The centuries in Italy that particularly attract Beyle's admiration are the fifteenth and the sixteenth; the reasons are revealing; the fifteenth century was, we are told, a century of passions and exaltation,[53] the sixteenth the only century where intelligence and energy flourished together; its only lack was 'ideology' – 'la science des idées'; war was widespread but what a mistake to believe war to be inimical to the arts: 'les circonstances continuent à favoriser les arts; car la guerre ne leur est point contraire, non plus qu'à tout ce qu'il y a de grand dans le coeur de l'homme...'[54] The three books on the classical and modern ideals of the beautiful, irrelevant though they may be in relation to a history of painting in Italy, show Beyle building up his theory of aesthetics. Both ideals, the classical and the modern, are in his view ultimately anchored to the idea of the useful; but over the centuries and with the different conditions of society, that fundamental idea has changed direction; in the ancient world it led to an ideal of beauty devoid of passions;[55] the modern post-Revolution and post-Napoleonic world may learn anew to value them: 'Depuis deux siècles une prétendue politesse proscrivait les passions fortes et à force de les comprimer elle les avait anéanties... Le dix-neuvième siècle va leur rendre leurs droits.'[56]

What Beyle believed had existed in fifteenth- and sixteenth-century Italy, namely intelligence, exalted passions, energy, with the idea of the useful underlying them all, is about to reappear, *mutatis mutandis*, in the nineteenth. Beyle reveals not only his own aesthetic tastes but seems to foresee the flowering of Romantic art, which makes its impact by its dramatic effects of colour, its violent movement and passion – the art of Géricault, of Delacroix.

A point implicit in Beyle's conception of the modern idea of the beautiful and indeed in his whole *beyliste* idea of the individual's search for happiness, is that the classical objective criteria of judg-

---

[52] e.g. Ghirlandaio and the sense of distance, Bk. II, chap. 28.
[53] Introduction.
[54] Bk. II, chap. 30.
[55] Bk. IV, *passim*.
[56] Bk. VII, chap. 145.

ment fall to the ground; instead there can be nothing but the subjective judgment of the individual arising from the impact made
on him. Beyle does indeed make the point but oddly enough limits
it to music. In the first of his travel journals, *Rome, Naples et
Florence en 1817*, he writes: 'Le degré de ravissement où notre
âme est portée est l'unique thermomètre de la beauté en musique,
tandis que je dis, du plus grand sang-froid du monde, d'un tableau
du Guide: cela est de la première beauté!'[57]

The idea of degrees on a thermometer as a means of measuring
the emotions is characteristic; it occurs more than once in the
Journal and readers of *Le Rouge et le Noir* will recall that in the
last days in prison Julien develops the habit of taking 'the tempera-
ture' of his courage.

Rome, Naples et Florence en 1817 fits in well to the *beyliste*
scheme. A first impression? – random jottings. Beyle the faithful
recorder of his sense experiences is at work as usual. For him the
essential is to set them down; perhaps they may evoke responses in
the reader agreeable to him (for one reader at least, they do); in any
case they will serve that purpose for Beyle. His joy at being in Italy
produces an occasional lyrical outburst rare indeed: 'J'éprouve un
charme, dans ce pays-ci, dont je ne puis me rendre compte: c'est
comme de l'amour; cependant je ne suis amoureux de personne –
[a rare condition for Beyle!]. L'ombre des beaux arbres, la beauté
du ciel pendant les nuits, l'aspect de la mer, tout a pour moi un
charme, une force d'impression qui me rappelle une sensation tout
à fait oubliée, ce que je sentais à 16 ans, à ma première campagne
...' The passage is too long to quote in full but as it stands it serves
to emphasize certain points already mentioned; Beyle is not concerned to do more than give the briefest indications of the objects
he sees: 'l'ombre des beaux arbres', 'la beauté du ciel', 'l'aspect de
la mer' ... the reader is left to imagine, to contribute himself their
inherent qualities; Beyle for his part is concerned to record his own
emotional response; 'un charme' ... 'une force d'impression'; as
he listens to his own emotional vibrations, beneath the layers of
sensations time has accumulated like fallen leaves, he hears a distant and forgotten echo: 'ce que je sentais à 16 ans à ma première
campagne.' The beauties of nature, love, the thrill of danger –
three distinct forms of experience that achieve their significance
for the man by being assessed together, re-expressed (though he
does not say so in this passage) in emotional degrees and measured
off on the 'thermometer' of his soul.

The sensations recorded in the book are mostly musical, but as
Beyle moves from place to place a discernible pattern emerges from
under the random journeys. He makes constant references to the

[57] *Rome, Naples et Florence* (Paris, 1817), p. 5.

existing state of 'moeurs' and the effect they have upon the arts.
Thus what he had done in *L'Histoire de la Peinture* ... for the
past and with specific reference to painting, he here applies to the
contemporary scene. Italy in 1817 is a collection of police states:
Piedmont, the alien Austrians, the Papal Domains, the Neapolitan
Bourbons. Gone the divine fire 'allumé jadis par la liberté et les
moeurs grandioses des républiques au Moyen Age.' What hope
then for the arts, 'produit charmant d'une fermentation générale et
profonde dans un peuple. Imiter ... les signes extérieurs qui couv-
rent cette fermentation, et en attendre les mêmes effets, c'est faire
des académies.'[58] With the exception of one man of genius,
Canova,[59] whose incandescent power is great enough to triumph
over prevailing conditions, the arts are languishing; only music still
has vitality.

For the first time Beyle throws an occasional glance beyond
music and painting towards literature; when he does, a political
note is heard. The emphasis here is not so much on the sum of
energy required in a society to produce great music and painting
but upon liberty, indispensable for great literature: 'L'Italie n'aura
de littérature qu'après les deux chambres ... L'ignorance, la paresse
et la volupté, sont telles parmi les jeunes Italiens, qu'il faut un
long siècle avant que l'Italie soit à la hauteur des deux chambres.'[60]
No literature, in fine, without a liberal régime,[61] no liberal régime
without a revolution in attitudes and for that, in Italy, Beyle foresees a long wait.

'Je supplie qu'à ce mot l'on ne me prenne pas pour un coquin
de libéral', writes Beyle in a different context.[62] The reader, who
had thought so, may be pardoned for his mistake, for what could
a *beyliste* be in politics but ... 'un coquin de libéral'? Not the least
fascinating aspect of many, indeed to a greater or lesser degree, of
all the works of Beyle we have hitherto discussed is their anima-
tion. An unceasing flow of personal impressions and opinions; they
are penetrating, original, ironic, controversial, irritating, sometimes frankly intolerable. The reader's responses are stimulated by
this bombardment, thrust for thrust, until he feels he is engaged in
a vigorous dialogue with a living person. Nowhere perhaps is this
truer than in Beyle's last travel journal, *Mémoires d'un touriste*
(1838), indispensable and entertaining guide to provincial France,
not in space but in time, the time of the July Monarchy at its hey-
day, seen through the eyes of a commercial traveller with all the
intelligence and irony of Beyle: journalism, protectionism and its
impact upon the production of pig-iron, unemployment, over-

---

[58] *Ibid.*, p. 50.
[59] Sculptor, 1757–1822.
[60] *Rome, Naples et Florence*, p. 8.
[61] Echoes of Madame de Staël.
[62] *Histoire de la Peinture*, Bk. VI, chap. 121.

production, poor relief, railways, the provincial *préfets* – 'le gouvernement en province, c'est le préfet' – and another important
figure of the day: 'un superbe capitaine de la garde nationale' (a
cuckold, inevitably); a medley of impressions where the enduring
characteristics of rural and provincial France figure beside problems of the day that have, some of them, a remarkably modern
aspect. Every now and then a comment shows our commercial
traveller was himself a good *beyliste*: 'Aujourd'hui par l'effet de la
Révolution, le peuple est énergique…De là l'énergie qui cherche
à se faire jour dans la littérature de 1837';…'Philippe le Bel,
prince qui pouvait vouloir…'; 'Madame de Nintrey ose faire à
chaque moment de la vie ce qui lui plaît le plus dans ce moment-
là…' He even shares with Beyle a dislike of Gothic architecture,
and, less surprisingly, a fear of bores: 'Une heure de la vue forcée
d'un ennuyeux m'empoisonne toute une soirée.'

One important document in our *beyliste* quest remains: *De
l'Amour*. The book falls into two parts. In the first the author
charts the different types of love and the psychological attitudes
they produce in their ascending and descending phases; in the
second he treats his subject as a social and historical phenomenon.
Here a link exists between *De l'Amour* and *L'Histoire de la Peinture*. . . .

Just as the idea of the beautiful will vary with material conditions at any given time, in any given clime, so will the passion of
love; love in the Italian mode is different from love in the French
mode which in turn differs from the German, the Spanish, the
English. Each is moulded by national social conditions; each varies
in time as well as space. The chapters on the education of women,
on marriage, on virtue, on divorce are in a characteristically ironic
vein; Beyle's way of putting forward quite impossible proposals
with apparent seriousness recalls the manner of Swift on how to
deal with the problem of surplus children. The reader may thereby
be shocked out of his complacency, out of his conventional rut, get
involved in another argument with Beyle, and lo! in the process he
will have been obliged to think.

If that was the intention, it miscarried. Of all Beyle's works, *De
l'Amour* was the completest failure. Even today when Beyle's attitudes and ideas are so much better known than they were to his
contemporaries, no one could say that this disjointed assemblage
of anecdotes and examples, brought together in a good 'idéologue'
manner of inquiry, provides easy reading.

Yet the fascination is undeniable. For some it may lie in recognizing Salviati[63] as the disconsolate and rejected admirer of Méthilde Dembowska; Beyle had at one moment the idea of objectify-
ing his luckless passion by writing a novel about it, but like so

[63] *Extrait du Journal de Salviati*, chap. 16.

many of his literary projects this too foundered. Most readers, however, will not forget the vivid impact of Beyle's original theory of 'cristallisation', founded no doubt upon his own wide experience of the 'tender passion'. We can obtain here a close insight into a vital factor of Beyle's merits as writer and novelist, his capacity both to undergo passionate experience and to conduct a dispassionate investigation of it. How else but by this rigorous introspection could he have obtained so sure a knowledge of the psychological mechanisms of the human being in love? What he is telling us in effect is that, under the impulse of love, we create in our minds an ideal image of the object, to which image we unconsciously attach any or all virtues just as crystals form on a twig left in a salt mine.[64] This image-forming process is surely fundamental, not only in love; it is man's method of making contact with outside reality; once the image is formed in a man's mind, that image becomes the reality for him. Therefore it behoves us, for our own and others' happiness, to ensure that our images conform as closely as possible with the reality behind them, for it takes great commotion to destroy an image once formed and to build up another. This image-forming process is particularly evident, dangerous, almost inevitable in the international sphere. Beyle does not say this but it is implicit in his discovery.

Thus *De l'Amour* with all its imperfections is an important book for the *beyliste*, which in some ways at least we should all be[65] – certainly the main characters in Beyle's novels thought so.

Why did Beyle decide to adopt this form – fit, as he says somewhere, for chamber maids[66] – which, when he took that decision,[67] seemed to please him so little and which nothing in his earlier works or stated ambitions foreshadow? He must have seen it as a convenient mould to pour his feelings of frustration into, after the triumph of the Ultras with its cortège of social, political and clerical hypocrisies. The canvas he chose in *Armance* (1822) – the salons of the Restoration – and the much larger canvas of *Le Rouge et le Noir* – political rivalries in the provinces, 'scenes of clerical life', intrigue, clerical and other, and high life in Paris – gave him immense scope to relieve the feelings of his liberal heart and to indulge his vein of irony which, still muted in *Armance*, is more evident in *Le Rouge et le Noir*, often emphatic in *La Chart-*

[64] Chap. 2.
[65] No. 91 of the *Fragments* is also an important piece of *beylisme*, particularly the last two paragraphs: 'Dans presque tous les événements de la vie, une âme généreuse voit la possibilité d'une action dont l'âme commune n'a pas même l'idée ... On a des devoirs suivant la portée de son esprit ... il est impossible que l'homme ne fasse pas toujours ... ce qui dans le moment est possible et lui fait le plus de plaisir.'
[66] 'A l'usage des femmes de chambre.'
[67] 1826.

reuse ... and *Lucien Leuwen*; in these novels too, the liberal protest against clericalism, political and police tyranny, is insistent.

Here no doubt lies the reason for Beyle's choice of the novel
form, but he who is usually so informative on his ideas, feelings
and intentions gives us no clue, and in the absence of one we must
conclude he had no realization of the importance the novel was to
have in the nineteenth century, or that, apart from his political
feelings, it was to give him the scope he needed for his greatest
qualities. *Armance* owes its existence to an idea derived in all
probability from a novel by the Duchesse de Duras – *Olivier ou le
Secret* – too scabrous in theme[68] for publication.[69]

Here was a subject calculated to please Beyle because the special
physiological condition must evidently produce its own peculiar
psychological motivations; here was an interesting example for the
psychological case-book. The daring nature of the subject may also
have been a reason, or perhaps fairer to Beyle would be to say the
difficulty of getting the daring nature of the theme 'across' to the
reader without offence. In this 'tight-rope' act Beyle manifestly
fails. Mérimée could appreciate the situation, one might almost say
the joke, because Beyle had given him the key,[70] but, being ignorant
of the secret, the contemporary public were unable to grasp the
significance of Octave's unhappiness, or the reason why a young
man with apparently every gift – birth, good looks, courage, intelligence, money – should prefer suicide to marriage with the divine
Armance. The mystery no longer exists but another difficulty arises.
For a novel to achieve its fullest impact, emotional as well as intellectual, the reader must have the opportunity of 'identifying himself' with the hero. Here, for obvious reasons, most readers, be
they in possession of the facts, will inevitably remain on the intellectual plane, unable to measure the passionate content of Octave's
tragedy; the book remains an interesting forerunner of greater
things to come, bearing clear signs of the trait previously mentioned as characteristic of Beyle: the combination of strong passion
and objective analysis, and – of course – of pure *beyliste* principles.

'Il [Octave] oublia de chercher toujours à juger de la quantité
de bonheur dont il jouissait dans le moment présent...';[71] 'Elle
[Armance] sentait cette vérité: du moment que j'ai aperçu le
devoir, ne pas le suivre à l'instant, et sans débats, c'est agir comme
une âme vulgaire.'

The reader will recall No. 91 of the *Fragments* in *De l'Amour*.[72]

---

[68] Sexual impotence.
[69] See Martineau's Preface for the full circumstances of *Olivier* and the
false *Olivier* by Hyacinthe Thabaud de la Touche. Also above, p. 187.
[70] Letter dated 23 December 1826. *Correspondance de Stendhal*, Paupe,
Vol. II, p. 445.
[71] *Armance*, p. 55, Divan.   [72] See above, p. 204, note 65.

What precisely is the moral imperative behind this typically *beyliste* principle that Beyle's heroes and heroines all obey? To resemble 'une âme vulgaire'? – a sorry plight indeed. But in what way is it vulgar not to act immediately, on perceiving where duty – or, to speak in *beyliste* terms, self-interest, that is to say in the last analysis happiness (in relation to the particular matter concerned) – points? It is vulgar, because not to act immediately implies a prudential calculation of chances, a fear of public opinion or conventions, some moral inhibitions, in short the type of weakness the thorough-going *beyliste* does not give way to.

From *Armance* to *Le Rouge et le Noir* (1831) is a big step. From the banal 'fait divers', the Antoine Berthet incident,[73] Beyle has built up a vast novel packed tight with incident. He divides it into two parts but it might be held to fall into four: Verrières, the seminary at Besançon, Paris, and finally Julien's revenge, trial and death; four parts held together by Julien's progress, in what after all is a kind of *Bildungsroman*, through three different worlds – the provinces, the priesthood, Paris, his progress in worldly experience, ultimately achieving his 'moment of truth', the clear realization of where his true happiness lay.

In a critical essay on Constantin Guys Baudelaire writes: 'Le beau est fait d'un élément éternel, invariable, dont la quantité est excessivement difficile à déterminer, et d'un élément relatif, circonstanciel, qui sera, si l'on veut, tour à tour ou tout ensemble, l'époque, la mode, la morale, la passion.' Not everyone would agree with Baudelaire that Guys' charm, whimsicality and all, is a good example of the proposition, in itself impeccable. To *Le Rouge et le Noir*, however, it seems to apply perfectly. The book provides a wealth of period colour in contrast to the almost classical severity of background in *Armance*;[74] mode, moral code, passion are all there, and rooted in the period; they are summed up in one word: Romanticism. Julien himself is cast in the mould of the Byronic hero, a mode if ever there was one, and he has some at least of the physical traits that Beyle lists as the essential components of 'le beau idéal moderne',[75] i.e. Romantic. His moral code, and not only his, is Romantic; all the characters in their several ways from the lowest level of a Valenod to the highest level of Julien and Mathilde are individualists; passion whether it be in the form of intrigue, of love, of lust for power has a motive energy on a Napoleonic scale. Indeed a magnificent 'period piece' with the crowning

---

[73] A murderer executed at Grenoble.

[74] Beyle flattered himself that *Armance* was in the tradition of *La Princesse de Clèves*. This would have been an added reason for the public of the day's lack of enthusiasm. (See *Armance*, edns. Fontaine, introduction by Georges Blin.)

[75] *Histoire de la Peinture en Italie*, VI, 119.

virtue of intensity. This is the projection on to the artistic plane of Beyle's moral gospel of energy; it is at the heart of Romantic aesthetics; to quote Beyle's own definition of art-doctrine: art must contain passion, without it there can be no '... promesse de bonheur', no emotional excitement, no impact therefore, something very akin to what Beyle hated: 'le plat', 'l'étiolé' – favourite words of his.

'Period pieces' have their charm, but it is apt to be a faded, sometimes even a slightly comical charm. *Le Rouge et le Noir* on the contrary retains all its freshness. Why? Two reasons at least may be suggested. First Beyle's skill in the art of dialogue. This calls for an alert and nimble exercise of the capacity to conceive different characters, to place oneself in their shoes and make them speak in character, in accordance with the situation they are placed in at the time – 'faculté de dédoublement'. An excellent example is the short argument between Julien and his father about the post the former has been offered in the Rênal household:[76] 'Réponds-moi sans mentir, si tu le peux, chien de lisard; d'où connais-tu madame de Rênal, quand lui as-tu parlé?'

– Je ne lui ai jamais parlé, répondit Julien, je n'ai jamais vu cette dame qu'à l'église.

– Mais tu l'auras regardée, vilain effronté?

– Jamais! Vous savez qu'à l'église je ne vois que Dieu, ajouta Julien, avec un petit air hypocrite, tout propre, selon lui, à éloigner le retour des taloches.

– Il y a pourtant quelque chose là-dessous, répliqua le paysan malin, et il se tut un instant; mais je ne saurai rien de toi, maudit hypocrite. Au fait, je vais être délivré de toi, et ma scie n'en ira que mieux. Tu as gagné M. le curé ou tout autre, qui t'a procuré une belle place. Vas faire ton paquet, et je te mènerai chez M. de Rênal, où tu seras précepteur des enfants.

– Qu'aurai-je pour cela?

– La nourriture, l'habillement et trois cents francs de gages.

– Je ne veux pas être domestique.

– Animal, qui te parle d'être domestique, est-ce que je voudrais que mon fils fût[77] domestique?

– Mais, avec qui mangerai-je?'

Only some twenty lines, but bringing out vividly the brutality and suspicious nature of the older man, his wiliness too, for note that he does not bring out the real purpose of the interview until after having belaboured Julien with his tongue and so, he presumably hopes, conditioned him to doing what he, old Sorel, wants:

[76] Part 7, chap. 5.
[77] This imperfect subjunctive from an illiterate peasant seems out of place.

'Au fait, je vais être délivré de toi, et ma scie n'en ira que mieux.'
That hope is uppermost in his mind, and so strong is it that he expresses it as a firm fact, 'je vais être délivré...' Perhaps also he
wishes by this show of confidence to avoid an argument he might
be defeated in.

We already know that one of the reasons why he hates his
youngest son is the latter's studious habits: 'il eût peut-être par-
donné à Julien sa taille mince, peu propre aux travaux de force,
et si différente de celle de ses aînés; mais cette manie de lecture lui
était odieuse, il ne savait pas lire lui-même.'[78] We all know the
exaggerated prestige a little learning gives a man, amongst the
unlettered. This motive too may be at work in old Sorel, covering
up his anxiety on that score under a show of brutal authority. And,
if so, perhaps he was right; for once, Julien is in a relatively strong
position; his father is perplexed about how this golden opportunity
of getting rid of his son has occurred, and he cannot in the last
resort force his son to accept. Julien's part in the short dialogue is
very revealing; first, the confidence that comes of knowing oneself
innocent of a given charge: 'd'où connais-tu madame de Rênal,
quand lui as-tu parlé?' Note in passing the dishonest or merely
ignorant way of questioning; the questions are not direct: do you
know? Have you spoken to? But: how do you...? When have
you...? As though rejecting any denial at the outset.

With deliberate or inborn skill Julien rightly divides the question
by his answer: 'Je ne lui ai jamais parlé, ... je n'ai jamais vu cette
dame qu'à l'église.' A confident denial of the latter half of the
question, an indirect denial of the first half; how could he know
her if he had seen her only in church? 'Mais tu l'auras regardée,
vilain effronté?' Note the force of the future here. You *must* have
...Obviously, one might say, if he had seen her he must have
looked at her. And yet this further accusation calls forth an immediate and vigorous 'Jamais!' Clearly, despite their mutual dislike,
father and son are tacitly agreed (and so will the reader be) that
'to look at' has a meaning that extends beyond to see. For old
Sorel, the very idea that the reflection of Madame de Rênal mirrored in Julien's eyes should have given rise in Julien's mind to any
thought, carnal or other, is apparently an impertinence; – 'vilain
effronté', and Julien, on his side, hopes apparently to parry that
thrust by a statement which if it doesn't deceive old Sorel, is highly
revealing of one aspect of Julien's personality. 'Vous savez qu'à
l'église je ne vois que Dieu'; 'maudit hypocrite!' – for once we are
tempted to agree with his father, but let us be fair to Julien; hypocrisy is a defence mechanism forced upon the weaker party by a

---

[78] This passage occurs a page or two before the scene between father and
son we are analyzing.

harsh upbringing; it has become part of his social personality, no doubt, and will often operate; it is not his true nature which appears much more in the rest of the short dialogue. When he hears what the plan is: 'Qu'aurai-je pour cela?' There speaks the realist. His father may try to throw dust in his eyes: 'Tu as gagné M. le curé ou tout autre, qui t'a procuré une belle place.' Maybe, but the cash it is that counts. And yet by no means entirely. His father's reply: 'la nourriture, l'habillement et trois cents francs de gages', evokes a different, an almost opposite response: 'Je ne veux pas être domestique.' The terms offered or at any rate the way they are presented to him suggest something servile to his mind; is it the idea of wearing a livery (*habillement*) or perhaps the word 'gages' instead of for example 'traitement' that produces this effect? Whatever it is, in a flash Julien's pride is aroused and immediately he is prepared, as he will be later on at a far more dramatic moment in his career, to throw over any material advantage, in order to safeguard it. There is more than a hint of resistance to the whole plan in that vigorous: 'Je ne veux pas être domestique'. Old Sorel must appreciate that, for he resorts, in reply, to his usual bluster: 'Animal, ...' followed at once by a rhetorical question, spoken no doubt with appropriate 'hauteur': 'est-ce que je voudrais que mon fils fût domestique?' The conscious (or unconscious aim) of a man who asks a rhetorical question is surely to implant conviction in the mind of the person he is talking to and avoid argument. Why should we adopt this indirect method which is weaker than a categorical affirmation? Perhaps because we are really not so sure of the truth of what we are saying and want our hearer to believe? It may in fact be one of those casuistical evasions situated in that indeterminate region, that no man's land (or everyman's land), between truth and falsehood, that commit us neither to a barefaced lie nor to an unwilling admission.

Surely this fits old Sorel at this very moment. In his previous talk with M. de Rênal no question of status in the household had arisen; obviously old Sorel hadn't thought of it. Thus this sudden weakening, betrayed by the rhetorical question (surely most unwonted in old Sorel's relations with Julien) suggests the old man's momentary fear that his plan for being rid of his son may founder over a silly detail – a fear to which Julien's next question lends further force; brushing aside the pompous rhetorical question, he goes straight to the heart of the matter with realistic precision: 'Avec qui mangerai-je?' Above or below stairs? A vital question indeed, a question that leaves him temporarily master of the field: 'Cette demande déconcerta le vieux Sorel, il sentit qu'en parlant il pourrait commettre quelque imprudence; il s'emporta contre

Julien, qu'il accabla d'injures, en l'accusant de gourmandise, et le
quitta pour aller consulter ses autres fils.'

Whether or not – probably not – Beyle had thought out all the
implications suggested for the above passage, the fact that beneath
the surface dialogue we can, by using our own experience, discover
unexpressed intentions, attitudes of mind, layers of half-conscious
motive, gives depth to the characters, a depth we may not discover
on a first reading. The discovery is progressive and this explains
why *Le Rouge et le Noir* is one of the small number of books we
can return to again and again with a pleasure that grows with
successive visits. Why should it grow rather than decrease with
familiarity? Because the book remains, as it were, a fixed point,
whereas we move along in time, which in this context means we
grow richer in experience. Thus, if in our successive visits to *Le
Rouge et le Noir* we have lost the initial pleasure of surprise and
eager curiosity about what will happen next (except in so far as the
abundant variety of events may have led us to forget some detail),
we more than compensate for that loss by the greater number of
responses stimulated in us by the text and drawn from different
levels of our own experience.

The second reason why this novel retains its freshness is that
Beyle's great characters share his own habit of wanting to see
clearly into themselves. Beyle usually dismisses the external events
quickly with a phrase such as: 'il eut vite fait de'; such and such
an action is described as being 'l'affaire d'un instant'. Evidently
the important thing about them is their inner kernel of thought or
emotion. As the characters debate inwardly what to do, what attitude to adopt and why, they enable us to explore and understand
their psychological mechanisms; we become involved, look out
upon the world through their eyes, move on the same plane of feeling. The time gap is abolished and we take a character's decisions
with him or reject them if we cannot accept his values.

Thus we seem often to stand both inside and outside the characters at one and the same time, identifying ourselves with their
psychological processes but retaining our critical judgment on their
action.

No character in Beyle's novels obliges us to perform these nimble
mental gymnastics so much as Julien Sorel, but the same applies,
mutatis mutandis, to other characters in *Le Rouge et le Noir*, to
characters in *La Chartreuse de Parme* (1839), *Lucien Leuwen*
(posth. 1894) and even to the fragmentary *Lamiel* (posth. 1889), to
all those in fact who practise the two fundamental *beyliste* principles: clear self-knowledge purified of all cant, and the determination to achieve as far as lies within them the immediate goal of
their desires, directly they see it clearly.

Julien is often condemned as a 'go-getter'. There can be no doubt, with Napoleon as his spiritual guide, of his lust for power, but the reason, legitimate enough, is to satisfy his pride, to assure himself that he is not the inferior being society has classed him as, to avenge himself on that society in a variety of ways, including the seduction of women.

The debate about the respective merits of *Le Rouge et le Noir* and *La Chartreuse de Parme* is unending. What the Berthet incident had been for *Le Rouge et le Noir*, the Farnese family chronicles Beyle had found at Palermo in 1832 were to be for *La Chartreuse* – a loose framework to be filled in with his own experience, feelings and philosophy. The result is a work not dissimilar in structure: a catena of events only loosely related to each other by the almost constant presence of the hero.

Transposed to early nineteenth-century Parma, the uninhibited Renaissance adventures of the Farnese chronicles provided Beyle with an opportunity not only to release his liberal feelings by portraying the suffocating atmosphere of the police and Austrian-ridden principality, but to create the high tension characters he delighted in and who are so perfectly in line with his artistic and moral ideals!

Historical anachronism? An 'imbroglio novel'?[79] Such criticisms are insignificant. Fabrice del Dongo's countless ups and downs of fortune are exciting, comic, idyllic and tragic by turns; his experiences before, at and after Waterloo, to quote one example, are a model of evocative narration and of Beyle's technique: placing himself (and us) inside his character and looking outwards, thus creating individual experience. No doubt too, a personal experience of Beyle's at the battle of Bautzen, which brought home to him how limited an individual's range of vision could be in the midst of a battle, had something to do with it: 'Nous voyons fort bien de midi à trois heures tout ce qu'on peut voir d'une bataille, c'est-à-dire rien.'[80]

Fabrice has the advantage over Julien of an assured position in society; his pursuit of happiness does not in consequence require that constant moral struggle, that mistrust of other men always on the alert, that are Julien's lot: is so and so trying to make a fool of me? Ought I to be affronted? and so on. This gives Julien an external harshness absent in Fabrice, who is perhaps more sympathetic as a result. But struggle is spiritually enriching and intellectually stimulating to Julien; his self-exploration is, in consequence, deeper and more acute than Fabrice's, we see more facets of his character. Fabrice is more content to accept men and events as they come but without ever betraying his *beyliste* principle of doing

[79] Sainte-Beuve's view.   [80] *Journal*, V, p. 179, Divan.

what gives him most pleasure at the time; in this way, though in the Citadel,[81] his liberty, perhaps his life, at stake, his cup of joy is full because of his love for Clélia.

La Chartreuse has a gallery of characters almost as rich as that of *Le Rouge*: in addition to Fabrice and Clélia, the Duchess Sanseverina, Count Mosca, Prince Ranuce, Rassi, Countess Raversi; all have vitality. Mosca, in particular, with his experience of court politics, police tyranny, lover's jealousy, is a rich and ironical portrait of worldly wisdom and weakness.

In its unfinished state *Lucien Leuwen* can scarcely compare with *Le Rouge* and *La Chartreuse* but, here too, there are passages of the greatest delicacy – the Lucien-Chasteller theme; others of the richest comedy – Lucien's arrival in Nancy with his regiment; the high society of the town; the political satire in Parts II and III which transform the work into the best political novel in French literature; one passage, however, most inferior, namely the Du Poirier plot to get Lucien away from the town. Beyle evidently found inexhaustible material to draw upon in the society of the July Monarchy, so rich that the reader may wonder whether, if he had had the opportunity of completing the novel, he could have welded its disparate elements into a satisfactory whole. The question almost provides an additional source of attraction: unfinished, the novel stimulates and never satisfies our curiosity.

Lamiel is too fragmentary for that; at most a few characters with some definition, notably Lamiel herself – Julien in woman's form – and Sansfin the Mephistophelian hump-backed doctor whose deformity develops both his sensitiveness and his ambition – another promising phenomenon for Beyle's psychological case book.[82] Beyle appears to have hesitated between relating the fortunes of his ambitious and wholly uninhibited[83] 'demoiselle de Compagnie' or portraying political life in Normandy and the impact of the July Revolution on the peasantry.[84]

After all his other works, which hinge one way or another on the same set of ideas,[85] his novels and their central characters show us *beylisme* in action. To this extent the characters have much in common; reflecting their creator's liberalism, they reject the society they are born into and its values: the aristocratic Octave, the plebeian Julien, Fabrice scion of a great House, Lucien the banker's son, each in his own way refuses to be, as M. Leuwen senior says,

[81] Inspired by the 'Spielberg'.
[82] 'Le Docteur n'eût pas fait de sottise et même eût pu passer pour homme d'esprit s'il eût été sans bosse...'. Chap. I.
[83] cf. the 'Ce n'est que ça' incident.
[84] cf. *Lamiel*, preface by Martineau.
[85] cf. *Brulard*, p. 29, Divan. 'Par instinct ma vie morale s'est passée à considérer attentivement cinq ou six idées et à tâcher de voir la vérité sur elles.'

'assez coquin' for success in this mean hypocritical world; all practise self-analysis, all are self-reliant; they act of their own volition,
remain in control of their destinies; unlike many Romantic characters – e.g. Balzac's – they are never the victims of their own passions; all are young, imprisoned in their egotisms they storm
through their adventures in quest of happiness, but it eludes them.
With all their courage and intelligence they forget one important
factor in life which keeps society together – charity.

II. MÉRIMÉE

Friend and in many ways disciple of Beyle, Prosper Mérimée
(1803–70) appears at the outset of his literary career to espouse
wholeheartedly the Romantic cause. 'Vers l'an de grâce 1827', he
writes in 1840, 'j'étais *romantique*'[86] (his italics). In the battle of
ideas between the classical Old Guard and the young Romantics,
Mérimée was indeed an active participant, something of a leader;
'un génie indépendant et original trace le chemin et, du premier
pas, laisse derrière lui tous les favoris de la Melpomène moderne.'[87]
The first step in question was *Le Théâtre de Clara Gazul* (1825).
Hugo was still no more than the poet of *Les Odes et Ballades*;
neither had Dumas *père* yet appeared on the scene. Local colour,
Mérimée tells us,[88] was the popular cry amongst the disciples of
the new school; wherever the writer might roam in fancy, he must
seize the characteristic details of the society, portray the essential
attitudes of the men he was depicting. Mérimée had as yet no
direct personal experience of Spain – that was to come a little
later[89] – but he knew Spanish, was well informed on the literature
of the 'Siglo d'oro' and in 1824 had contributed four articles on
the Spanish theatre to the *Globe*.[90] On the basis of that knowledge
he was able to write six playlets, attributed to the pen of the mythical Spanish actress Clara Gazul whose portrait[91] appeared as a
frontispiece, and deceived the Spaniards themselves on the authenticity of the work. The literary merits of the playlets are meagre,
yet these glimpses of supposedly Spanish characteristics: patriotic
pride (*Les Espagnols en Danemarck*), ferocious love (*L'Amour
Africain*), 'mésalliance' and the executioner's revenge (*Ines Mendo*),
love, jealousy, poison and dagger play in and out of convents or
the cells of the Inquisition (*L'Occasion, Une Femme est un Diable*,

[86] *La Guzla.* 'Avertissement'.
[87] Article in *Le Globe*, 15 June 1825, quoted by Souriau, *Histoire du
Romantisme*.
[88] 'Avertissement'.   [89] His first trip (of many) to Spain, 1830.
[90] P. van Tieghem, *Influences Etrangères sur la Littérature Française*.
[91] This was a drawing by Delécluze of Mérimée himself attired as a
Spanish woman with mantilla. The name was presumably formed from
Guzla. See below.

Le Ciel et l'Enfer), had enough cumulative effect to set a strong tide of fashion running for things Spanish. 'Le Comte Gazul', as Beyle called Mérimée, showed the way to the author of *Hernani* and *Ruy Blas*.

Two years later Mérimée provided a yet more remarkable proof of his gift for pastiche and hoax: this time his palette was loaded with local colour from Dalmatia. Politics and literature had combined to arouse interest in the Levant: the Greek War of Liberation had quickened liberal enthusiasms, the smoke of Navarino had scarcely cleared; Byron,[92] Chateaubriand,[93] Lamartine,[94] Nodier,[95] had all made contributions to the fashion of orientalism. Under the title of *La Guzla*[96], Mérimée produced a series of alleged prose translations of Illyrian poetry; the themes of murder, and revenge, of heroic chieftains on their white chargers, of flashing scimitars and vampires are supposed to have their roots deep in local history and folk-lore. In fact, one ballad is authentic.[97] With this as his guide, Mérimée invented the remainder, the measure of his success being that the 'translations' were widely accepted as genuine; a German and a Russian translation, the latter by no less a person than Pushkin, appeared.[98] *La Guzla* has at least this merit, that it was a first step towards the Slav world Mérimée was later to discover with enthusiasm in the works of Gogol and Pushkin. Spain and Russia – Mérimée was drawn in spirit to both, and was the first writer in France in the nineteenth century to reawaken French interest in the former, to stimulate interest in the latter. Here he was admittedly less successful; genuine appreciation of Russian literature was not to be awakened in France until much later in the century.[99]

To Mérimée's early interest in Spain may be ascribed two more playlets: *La Famille Carvajal* (1828), a sombre story of incest and murder with little to commend it, and *Le Carrosse du Saint-Sacrement* (1829). Within its narrow framework, the latter is a masterpiece of light comedy. With its delicate delineation of character and well contrived dramatic conflict between Don Andres, the Viceroy and his mistress, Camila Perichole, it stands in surprising contrast with the work of 'Clara Gazul'; one thread links them none the less – Mérimée's irony. That trait in him must have responded eagerly to the current joke of literary mystification; what opportunities it gave that 'pince-sans-rire', in his prefaces to

---

[92] *Childe Harold's Pilgrimage.*
[93] *Itinéraire.*
[94] *Dernier Chant...*
[95] *Jean Sbogar, Smarra.*
[96] One-stringed Dalmatian guitar.
[97] *Triste Ballade de la Noble Epouse d'Asan-Aga.* Souriau, op. cit., II, p. 98.
[98] See Mérimée's 'Avertissement'.
[99] Voguë's *Le Roman Russe* (1886). See below, vol. V, chap. 7.

Gazul and *La Guzla*! His friend Beyle was not averse from it either, but, in his case, a fear of police persecution for a man of such dangerously liberal views may explain his liking for pen names.[100] Perhaps, too, Mérimée's ironical nature enjoyed and hence adopted the Spanish habit of ringing the curtain down on the traditional formula, with variants: 'excusez les fautes de l'auteur'? Traditional courtesy to the audience, in Spain? But for Mérimée no doubt a sure sign he himself at least was not taking his scenes of violence and cruelty too seriously.

The apparatus of notes that accompanies all these plays, whilst admittedly connected with Mérimée's respect for historical exactitude, has an elaboration about it that suggests an ironical emphasis on the authenticity of 'Clara'. The texts themselves, too, reveal occasional flashes of irony that seem less in tune with the characters than with their creator: 'Est-il donc si nécessaire d'être chrétien pour être un inquisiteur', enquires Brother Rafael;[101] 'allons', cries the gouty Viceroy,[102] 'puisque je suis obligé de garder la chambre et que je n'ai rien à faire, je vais m'occuper des affaires de ce gouvernement.' As often as not the irony has an anti-religious bias.

Both the irony and the bias appear again in *La Jacquerie* (1828). Abandoning Spanish scenes for the moment, Mérimée here seeks historical as opposed to geographical local colour; the Romantic mode still holds him, with Walter Scott in the ascendant, reminiscences of Goethe's *Götz von Berlichingen*, and the historical dramas of Schiller, for dramatic technique – the host of characters, the succession of loosely connected scenes, more suitable for the films than for the stage.

Mérimée tells us in his Preface that he wanted to convey an idea of fourteenth-century life and perhaps he is not unsuccessful, but when Frère Jean declares:[103] 'sans miracles, point de religion dans ce temps-ci', we suspect him of speaking for the author.

Much the same criticism may be levelled at Mérimée's one contribution to the vogue of the historical novel: *La Chronique de Charles IX* (1829): 'Je n'aime dans l'histoire que les anecdotes', he writes in the Preface, 'et parmi les anecdotes je préfère celles où j'imagine trouver une peinture vraie des moeurs et des caractères à une époque donnée.' The remainder of the Preface is largely conconcerned with a well-reasoned thesis on the real causes, as Mérimée sees them, of the St Bartholomew massacre – no premeditated plot on the part of Catherine de Medicis and Charles IX, but an explosion of popular feeling. 'Souviens-toi de te méfier' was Mérimée's own device, inherited from his Voltairian mother; a good

---

[100] See Paul Léon, *Mérimée et son Temps*, p. 12.
[101] *Une Femme est un Diable*, scene 1.
[102] *Carosse du Saint-Sacrement*.   [103] Scene 2.

principle for a historian, one to which in this preface he admirably subscribes. The attitude promises well for the novel itself and indeed the author provides us with a series of carefully drawn vignettes of court circles, of Parisian and provincial life, scenes of war and peace that suggest if they do not confirm[104] careful study of contemporary sources.

But Mérimée's sense of period either deliberately or unconsciously goes astray whenever religion enters in; a novel set in the time of the Religious Wars can scarcely avoid religion. 'A plague on both your houses' is the author's evident attitude. 'Je hais les disputes, surtout celles où il s'agit de religion', says Georges de Mergy to his brother Bernard, '... je n'ai pu et je ne puis croire. Croire est un don précieux qui m'a été refusé, mais pour rien au monde je ne chercherais à en priver les autres ...'[105] Throughout his brief soldier's life, his attitude, so unrepresentative we may think of sixteenth-century religious mentality, remains the same. As he lies dying on a hospital bed at La Rochelle, wounded by a shot fired by his brother, he rejects the spiritual comfort offered by minister and monk alike. 'Moine ou ministre, qu'ils aillent au diable.'[106] Georges de Mergy speaks as an eighteenth-century freethinker or a nineteenth-century anti-clerical; he is evidently Mérimée's mouthpiece, and to that extent any illusion of past time the novel might have created is destroyed.

But does Mérimée wish to create an illusion of reality? Chapter VIII, 'Dialogue entre le lecteur et l'auteur', deliberately destroys it and seems to undermine the *genre* of which in some respects *La Chronique* is a model; Mérimée's attitude to Romanticism is plainly ambivalent.

The year 1829 is indeed an important date in Mérimée's literary development, the year of *Mateo Falcone, La Vision de Charles XI, Tamango, L'Enlèvement de la Redoute, Federigo* – all short stories. Mérimée had discovered his true literary vocation.

Linked though they are by their author's irony, which is never far from the surface, Mérimée's stories fall into various groups. In some, against an exotic or unusual background, he portrays a tense situation arising from passions, developing rapidly to a crisis point, as in a Racine tragedy, and ending violently: *Mateo Falcone* (1829), *Tamango* (1829), *Colomba* (1840), *Carmen* (1845). To this category may also perhaps be attributed *L'Enlèvement de la Redoute* (1829), although in this case the underlying conflict of wills – war between France and Russia – is remote and divorced from the action that forms the real subject of the story. Thus, un-

---

[104] Trahard shows Mérimée's documentation to be inadequate. See *La Jeunesse de Mérimée*, chap. ix.
[105] Chap. 4.   [106] Chap. 27.

like the other stories in this group, where passions and situations are intimately linked, *L'Enlèvement*, despite the tense dramatic situation portrayed, has a remote, static quality, peculiar to itself.

The second group consists of tales of developing mystery: *La Vision de Charles XI* (1829), *La Vénus d'Ille* (1837), *Lokis* (1869). A third group uses the formula of the second, but reverses it – an initial mystery turns out to have a commonplace or normal explanation: *Il Vicolo di Madonna Lucrezia* (1846), *La Chambre bleue* (1866), *Djoumane* (1869). A fourth group contains stories that suggest, if they do not greatly develop, some psychological study: *Le Vase étrusque* (1830), *La Partie de Trictrac* (1830), *La Double Méprise* (1833), *Arsène Guillot* (1844), *L'Abbé Aubain* (1846).

Finally there are a number of stories which derive from foreign sources: *Federigo* (1829) – Neapolitan; *La Perle de Tolède, Les Sorcières Espagnoles* (1830), *Les Ames du Purgatoire* (1834) – Spanish; *La Dame de Pique* (posth. 1925), *Les Bohémiens* (posth. 1925), *Le Hussard* (posth. 1925), *Le Coup de Pistolet* (1856), *Les Cosaques d'Autrefois* (1865) – Russian.

The first group probably contains Mérimée's best known stories. Pitiless, uncompromising, told with studied detachment, they remain imprinted on our memories – a sure sign of excellence.

The short story needs rigorous construction; *Mateo Falcone*[107] has it in its neatest form: scene, main character alone described in any detail, action and motive, condign punishment. The ending of the drama, told with rigorous economy, is particularly effective: 'sans jeter un coup d'oeil sur le cadavre, Mateo reprit le chemin de sa maison pour aller chercher une bêche afin d'enterrer son fils.' This concrete detail is inserted as though by chance, but chance has nothing to do with it; the carefully chosen concrete detail, inserted at a moment of high emotional tension, is an essential element in Mérimée's technique; it serves broadly two purposes: either it gives concreteness to the scene; the reader's emotion is all the greater because – as in *Mateo Falcone* – he has a vivid image in his mind to which the detail in question is very relevant, or the concrete detail may be chosen precisely because of its irrelevance. *Le Vase étrusque* ends with a fatal duel; as the hero falls, what does his opponent do? – 'Et Thémines, qu'a-t-il fait? – Oh! Ce qu'il faut faire en pareille occasion. Il a jeté son pistolet à terre d'un air de regret. Il l'a jeté si fort, qu'il en a cassé le chien. C'est un pistolet anglais de Mantou; je ne sais s'il pourra trouver à Paris un arquebusier qui soit capable de lui en refaire un.' The irrelevance is flagrant between the narrator's comment and the tragic death of

[107] For the possible sources of this tale, see M. Kosko, *Le Thème de Mateo Falcone* (1960), and *French Studies* (January 1963), pp. 72–4.

Saint-Clair; what of its effect? Evidently the narrator is unmoved or no longer moved by the tragic death of Saint-Clair. His objective detachment, highly characteristic incidentally of Mérimée, may be shared by the reader; on the other hand, the very inhumanity of it may serve to underline the tragedy and increase the effect by contrast.

Ironic comment is of the same order: 'Ledoux[108] imagina de placer dans cet intervalle d'autres nègres...De la sorte, son navire contenait une dizaine de nègres de plus qu'un autre du même tonnage. A la rigueur, on aurait pu en placer davantage; mais il faut avoir de l'humanité ... les nègres, après tout, sont des hommes comme les blancs.'[109]

Unlike the novel, which is supple and adaptable, the short story has neither time nor space to investigate motive deeply, to build up characters by degrees, until a complete image takes shape in the reader's mind, to place them against a background of secondary characters or elaborate scenes – motives, psychological attitudes must be simple and quickly evident, so that the resultant action can be seen as a natural consequence; in a small house economy of space is essential. 'Il se passa près de dix minutes avant que Mateo ouvrit la bouche'. The reader may well appreciate the tension of those ten silent minutes, but he must (and can) infer what goes on in Mateo's mind from the context. Like Mateo, the chief characters of these stories – Tamango, José, Orso della Rebbia – are men of energy, who as soon as they see what their code of values or their interests dictate, act accordingly without hesitation. Like their author they are all disciples of Beyle but, unlike Beyle's characters, they do not invite us to attend their personal debates: 'Maintenant cet air d'insouciance, ce ton de franchise ... devenaient pour elle un mérite de plus, car c'était la profonde dissimulation d'une âme énergique, qui ne laisse percer à l'extérieur aucun des sentiments qu'elle renferme', and so, in the story,[110] we shall see only the effect of the creature of energy driven by the Corsican code of honour to exact the full price of vengeance.

Such stark characters are more likely to be found in remote or barbaric societies: Corsica, the mountains of Spain, Africa, but there is no self-conscious local colour here as in Mérimée's earlier work, for he had soon come to see the artificiality of that.[111]

The short story as Mérimée conceived it demands such characters to achieve its dramatic effect or, as an alternative, to heighten the sense of the supernatural, which Mérimée exploits in the stories of the second group. Here the characters themselves are of minor importance, they have no will of their own, they are victims of

[108] Note the name, itself an ironic comment!   [109] *Tamango.*
[110] *Colomba.*   [111] See *La Guzla*, 'Avertissement'.

forces which neither they nor we understand. *La Vision de Charles XI* is little more than an eerie situation strongly reminiscent of Hoffman, in which, incidentally, the author touches on the idea of precognition. In *La Vénus d'Ille* and *Lokis*, however, especially in the former, Mérimée carries the reader gradually from the normal to the non-normal; the reader's attention is constantly brought back to the statue, his sense of the evil attaching to it grows, but with each step in the story, alternative natural and supernatural explanations are suggested: was Jean Coll's broken leg merely an accident, did the statue throw back the stone, hitting the thrower on the head or had the stone merely bounced off the metal? Had the ring merely got wedged on the statue's finger, or was Alphonse right in thinking that the statue, of its own volition, prevented him wrenching it off? Was Alphonse strangled as an act of revenge by the Aragonese or was it the statue that...?

In Tirso de Molina's story about the legendary Don Juan, the hero sees the statue of the 'Commander', the man he had killed, walking through the cemetery towards him; the sight must have given him a shock of terrified surprise; the reader, however, does not share it because such an event does not touch his experience at any point; unconsciously, perhaps, he rejects it as legend. In *La Vénus d'Ille*, on the other hand, the reader hovers constantly in doubt; doubt increases his potential of auto-suggestion and, without appreciating the process until too late, he has become psychologically conditioned to accepting as possible – nay more! – to claiming as certain what his own experience would otherwise lead him to reject.

How weak in comparison are the stories where Mérimée reverses the process. The mysterious house in Madame Lucrezia's little street turns out to be a lovers' tryst, the blood oozing from under the bedroom door comes from a bottle of wine spilt by a drunkard,[112] the mysterious and horrifying events in the Saharan cave are the figments of a soldier's dream.[113] In each case, the tension created initially is punctured suddenly, engendering a sense of disappointment, frustration in the reader – Mérimée up to his literary jokes again! A dramatist who gave the audience his play's climax in the first act would run the risk of emptying the theatre before the end of the third.

Nor are the stories in the fourth group amongst Mérimée's most successful but they are interesting in part for that reason. A sense of guilt can, we know, have great dramatic power – witness O'Neill's *Mourning becomes Electra*, Racine's *Phèdre*, *Macbeth*, the Greek tragedies; Mérimée suggests the theme in *La Partie de Trictrac* but it remains undeveloped and the action of the story is

[112] *La Chambre bleue.*   [113] *Djoumane.*

poorly related to it. As a study of sordid realism and the pious effort of a society woman to reclaim a girl from the gutter, *Arsène Guillot* lacks force, though Mérimée's mischievous irony plays with effective cruelty on the character of Madame de Piennes; the study of Saint-Clair's jealousy in *Le Vase étrusque* is superficial.

Of all these stories *La Double Méprise*, with its title so reminiscent of Marivaux, is the most successful; it has much of the latter's delicacy, too, though the handling of the theme and the impermeability, so to speak, of the two main characters to each other have Mérimée's stamp; no character in Marivaux would share Darcy's cynical doubts: 'Voyons... A tout prendre, c'est une très jolie femme... et si je n'étais pas aussi vieux [early 'thirties at most] il ne tiendrait qu'à moi de croire que c'est à mon prodigieux mérite ... Hélas! dans un mois peut-être, mon mérite sera au niveau de celui de ce monsieur à moustaches...' But then Marivaux's characters had not met Mérimée.

La Double Méprise is the most successful because the psychology of the two main characters, Darcy and Julie de Chaverny, are more developed than those of the characters in the other stories, yet not enough to give them much weight. The story remains a kind of 'roman manqué' and confirms, like the other stories of this group, what was said earlier: short stories cannot successfully develop psychological studies depending for their interest on delicate 'nuances'.

This group has the further interest that in two of them at least Mérimée has revealed more of himself and his opinions than elsewhere; his irony, for example, at the expense of Walter Scott: 'Pardon, dit-il; je voudrais bien pour m'endormir le dernier volume de Scott... N'est – ce pas Quentin Durward... ?;[114] at the expense, too, of Romantic exoticism and local colour: 'On dit, poursuivit-elle, que les personnes qui ont vu ce beau ciel de l'Orient ne peuvent plus vivre ailleurs... ce ciel bleu, Madame, Dieu vous en préserve! On finit par le prendre tellement en guignon à force de le voir toujours de même, qu'on admirerait comme le plus beau de tous les spectacles un sale brouillard de Paris...'.

Mérimée's ironic smile appears often on the face of Darcy; his sensitive nature, hidden beneath a mask of cold indifference, is reflected in Saint-Clair: 'Auguste Saint-Clair... ne cherchait à plaire qu'aux gens qui lui plaisaient... il était né avec un coeur tendre et aimant; mais à un âge où l'on prend trop facilement les impressions qui durent toute la vie, sa sensibilité trop expansive lui avait attiré les railleries de ses camarades... Dès lors il se fit une étude de cacher tous les dehors de ce qu'il regardait comme une faiblesse déshonorante.'[115]

[114] *La Double Méprise.*   [115] *Le Vase étrusque.*

Mérimée's letters[116] which, as we should expect from such a precise observer, are a mine of information on society under the July Monarchy and the Second Empire, reveal the same traits: beneath a surface detachment and cynicism, the kindness and loyalty of a true friend.

The last group of stories was to show how broad were Mérimée's interests; his admiration for the Russian writers, Pushkin, Gogol, Turgenev, led him to make translations from them all. Much as Baudelaire was to discover a twin soul in Edgar Allan Poe, so Mérimée found in Pushkin, more akin to him than Gogol or Turgenev, the same artistic ideas as his own: themes of violence and cruelty, reflecting men's energy or passions, 'Car l'énergie, même dans les mauvaises passions, excite toujours en nous un étonnement et une espèce d'admiration involontaire.'[117] There too speaks Beyle's disciple! Such is Mérimée's remaining link with Romanticism. His liking for mystery does not derive from any Romantic belief in mysterious forces governing our lives, of oneness with the infinite; it is an artistic technique, and how skilfully exploited – for making an impact on the reader.

His Romanticism, such as it is, is severely disciplined by precise observation, and a rigorous control of form that makes no concession to personal feeling. Thus Romantic, Realist and Classical elements are nicely balanced in his art, just as they are, in a sense, in his life; the historical novel writer becomes the historian of Don Pedro I of Castille (1848) and the dedicated Inspector of Historical Monuments; the dabbler in exoticism becomes the Russian scholar; reality and facts in the past or the present, take priority over fancy; balance, moderation, self-control are his ideal; Mérimée becomes a man of 'le juste milieu'.

[116] *Correspondance Générale*. Etablie et annotée par Maurice Parturier, 1941.
[117] *Vénus d'Ille*.

Chapter 14

BALZAC

HONORÉ DE BALZAC[1] (1799–1850) did not begin to make an impact upon the public or even the critics until 1829. Until then, life had provided him with a varied fund of experience: a harsh schooling, which amounted to nearly six years' exile from his family (1807–13), legal studies and apprenticeship in Paris (1816–19), followed by several years of literary endeavour partly on his own and partly in collaboration (1819–24), but in neither case with any success; then a launching into business (1825–7), first as publisher and, when that venture failed, as a printer – no less disastrously.

Balzac then took up writing once more to pay his debts, and as his only hope of achieving success, a will o' the wisp that had hitherto eluded his ambitious if ill-organized strivings.

1829, the date of *Les Chouans* and *La Physiologie du Mariage*, is like a boundary line, on one side the early novels,[2] largely conceived in the prevailing fashion of the *roman noir*, with a vague reminiscence of Sir Walter Scott thrown in, produced with only two ends in view: success, money;[3] on the other, the mass of novels and short stories to which in the first collected edition of his work (1842) Balzac gave the name of *La Comédie humaine*.[4]

The goal is still the same: money, success; Balzac labours un-

---

[1] The Balssa family (orig. spelling) came from the village of Nougayrié (Tarn). Bernard-François, Honoré's father (1746–1829), one of eleven children, came to Paris aged sixteen; married Anne-Charlotte-Laure Sallambier.

[2] e.g. *Sténie*, *Argow le Pirate*, *L'Héritière de Birague*, *Clotilde de Lusignan*.

[3] An exception may be made for Balzac's earliest (unfinished) novel, in letter form, *Sténie* (from Stephanie de Formosand, the name of the heroine, 1819–20). With all its derivativeness (e.g. *Werther*, Rousseau) and Romantic conventionalism, the story is not without merit, the characters have some individuality. The discussion in the first two letters between the hero Jacob Del Ryès, spiritualistically inclined, and his friend Vanehers, the materialist, shows Balzac's early interest in philosophy, which was to reappear in *La Comédie humaine* (e.g. *Louis Lambert*, *Séraphita*; his interest in Swedenborgism, magnetism). Much else that will emerge in *La Comédie humaine* is here too in embryo: his love of Touraine, his descriptions of Tours, his social and political interests.

[4] The idea of this title may have been due to an English acquaintance, Henry Reeve in 1835, or to a friend, Auguste de Belloy in 1841.

ceasingly to pay his debts, keep creditors at bay – and, when necessary, elude them – find the money to satisfy his voracious appetites:
high living and high society, mistresses and museum pieces, journalism and sporadic political ambitions. To all this feverish social
activity carried on at the same time as his creative work his voluminous correspondence,[5] itself no mean burden, bears witness.

But in contrast to his earlier efforts, Balzac as a writer has now
found his way; whereas *Les Chouans* is still derivative, leaning on
contemporary taste for historical romance, *La Physiologie du
Mariage*, mediocre though it may be and no novel, is a product of
social awareness and looks forward to the novels of contemporary
life.

The year 1829 is indeed a turning point; thereafter, the years
from 1830 to 1845 inclusive and again 1847 yield their quota of
works, novels and short stories. Long pent-up pressures had burst
open the flood-gates and released a powerful creative force that
was to carry Balzac along a tumultuous course for nearly twenty
years.

La Comédie humaine owes its existence as a coherent structure
to an original idea of Balzac's that took clear shape in his mind in
1833: the characters he had hitherto created, those in his mind and
those as yet unborn, would henceforth be conceived not merely as
characters in a number of stories or novels and their sequels, but as
forming collectively a human society connected as men are in reality by all sorts of ties – family, social, business, and professional –
growing more or less prosperous, more dug into their habits, their
faces more furrowed by the passions that consume them, as they
move down the years from the Revolution to the July Monarchy –
often to the very year of the book Balzac was engaged on – , as they
move in and out of the reader's view, in the streets, in the houses,
boarding houses, salons and offices, on the highways, the fields and
battlefields of *La Comédie humaine*.

Balzac invites us to think not so much in terms of books as in
terms of different scenes in a vast pageant of French society, a
pageant with nearly a hundred scenes and some two thousand
characters. Gigantic as it is, the conception remains only partially
realized, but, as it was, it needed a structure to mould it into the
organic whole Balzac intended.

The preface Balzac wrote for the 1842 edition is a valuable guide
to his ideas and intentions. Its doctoral tone is in line with the
spirit of the period, but unlike for example the pompous and pretentious prefaces Hugo attaches to *Hernani* and *Ruy Blas*, it can
claim some relation to the performance.

Two main points emerge: first that *La Comédie humaine* has a

---

[5] *Correspondance, Textes réunis, Classés et annotés* par R. Pierrot.

background of naturalist and mystical thought rooted in the period, and secondly the debt Balzac owed or thought he owed to Walter Scott.

With the great naturalist Geoffroy Saint-Hilaire, and Buffon before him, with philosophers such as Leibnitz, mystics such as Charles Bonnet, Swedenborg and Saint-Martin who wrestled with the problem of how to bring the natural sciences into proper relationship with the infinite, Balzac is fascinated by the idea of the unity of all species. 'Le créateur', writes Balzac, 'ne s'est servi que d'un seul et même patron pour tous les êtres organisés'. Differences between species arise from conditions and milieux: 'L'animal est un principe qui prend sa forme, dans les milieux où il est appelé à se développer. Les espèces zoologiques résultent de ces différences' – 'transformism', in a word, forerunner of 'evolution'.

Balzac believed the same principle to apply to human society, albeit on an infinitely more complex scale. Here was the intellectual starting point for Balzac's unifying conception, so evident in *La Comédie humaine*, of society as a vast co-ordinated zoological organism – men in their environment, acting and reacting on each other. Buffon had brought the whole animal kingdom within the compass of a single work; Balzac would do the same for men. But not until he read Walter Scott, he tells us, did he understand how the novel – 'genre de composition injustement appelé secondaire' – might be used as a vehicle to provide society with a complex and varied image of itself. Walter Scott had indeed raised the status of the novel, in Balzac's view: 'il y mettait l'esprit des anciens temps, il y réunissait à la fois le drame, le dialogue, le portrait, le paysage, la description: il y faisait rentrer le merveilleux et le vrai, ces éléments de l'époque, il y faisait coudoyer la poésie par la familiarité des plus humbles langages.' Inspired by Scott's example, Balzac would do for French society what Scott had done for the Middle Ages: 'La société française allait être l'historien, je ne devais être que le secrétaire'. In one particular only did Balzac think he could improve on Scott, namely in giving a co-ordinated and therefore a more systematic image than Scott had thought of doing.

Doubtless the general titles of the six groups of the 'Etudes de Moeurs'[6] indicate well enough the facets of French society each is intended to portray; the reader may well accept Balzac's claim: 'Mon ouvrage a sa géographie comme il a sa généalogie et ses familles, ses lieux et ses choses, ses personnes et ses faits; comme il a son armorial, ses nobles et ses bourgeois, ses artisans et ses paysans, ses politiques et ses dandys, son armée, tout son monde enfin.' There is one important omission, two even – the industrial toilers, who had scarcely emerged as a definable social group in Balzac's

[6] See below, pp. 376–7, bibliog. for this chap.

day and who will have to await Zola to achieve a footing in literature, and the servant class who in fact do appear in Balzac's pages but are mere cyphers; Proust will give *them* life.

Although the *Etudes de moeurs* form the biggest part of Balzac's elaborate and systematic structure, the *Etudes philosophiques* as a group have their own importance. The majority are short stories and in the usual manner of short stories are built around an incident developing quickly to its conclusion. Although they deal with a wide variety of subjects they have one noticeable feature in common; all have as their subject characters or incidents that stand only on the fringe of everyday life; two of them, *Le Chef-d'Oeuvre inconnu* and *Gambara*, deal with the private tragedy of artists who are possessed, the one by a world of colour, the other by a world of sound, both so intense that they cannot master them, nor give them shape; others, notably *Jesus-Christ en Flandre, Melmoth réconcilié, L'Elixir de Longue Vie,* touch on the supernatural; others again, like *Adieu, Le Réquisitionnaire, Maître Cornélius,* deal with mysterious psychological phenomena; mental disturbance, telepathy, sleep-walking; others finally, like *Les Marana, El Verdugo, Un Drame au Bord de la Mer, L'Auberge Rouge,* portray violent incidents arising from human passions driven to paroxysm: revenge, pride, remorse.

The remaining works comprised in the *Etudes philosophiques* are longer works: *La Peau de Chagrin, La Recherche de l'Absolu, Sur Catherine de Médicis, Louis Lambert, Séraphita.* If we except the study on Catherine de Médicis, which is a political study, the others share with the short stories the fact that they deal with the extraordinary or abnormal: Raphaël (*Peau de Chagrin*) is destroyed by the occult power he accidentally comes into possession of, Claës (*Recherche de l'Absolu*) is the victim of his scientific passion, Louis Lambert goes mad, Séraphita is a mysterious Swedenborgian figure.

The *Etudes philosophiques,* so Balzac claims, show the underlying laws operating within society; we are invited to draw from them, dealing as they do with the abnormal, the supernatural, the traumatic, the mystical, lessons of general and fundamental social significance.

Thus the *Etudes philosophiques* amount to a general affirmation that for good or ill our lives, the whole of society, are governed, driven, we may say, by mysterious forces, that reveal themselves in human passions. Evidently in the *Etudes philosophiques* Balzac has escaped from the sway of the naturalists to pass under that of Swedenborg and the mystics.

In the *Etudes analytiques* Balzac intended to analyse the inner mechanisms of the forces themselves, but he had found little to say about these before death relieved him of any further difficulty, and that little is not illuminating. We may therefore safely neglect the *Etudes analytiques,* and devote our attention mainly to the *Etudes de moeurs.*

Abundance of background detail both of places and people is a marked characteristic that must soon strike and sometimes fatigue the reader of Balzac. His characters must not float on air; they must be anchored to the place they live in by a strong cable of precise circumstantial detail: 'En entrant à Nemours, du côté de Paris, on passe sur le canal du Loing, dont les berges forment à la fois de champêtres remparts et de pittoresques promenades à cette jolie petite ville. Depuis 1830, on a malheureusement bâti plusieurs maisons en deçà du pont.'[7] Or again: 'Au milieu de la rue Saint-Denis, presque au coin de la rue du Petit-Lion, existait naguère une de ces maisons précieuses qui donnent aux historiens la facilité de reconstruire par analogie l'ancien Paris.'[8] Not always do the stories open as in these two cases with a description of the town; often the reader is first located in time rather than in place: 'Vers le milieu du mois de juillet de l'année 1838';[9] 'Au commencement de l'année 1826 ... '.[10] But whichever way the story starts we may be sure the framework of place and time is securely set as a preliminary. Usually too, in a manner that anticipates the roving eye of a camera, Balzac discovers for us first the larger prospect of the town, then takes us into the street either at once or at an early stage of the story, holds our gaze on a given house, the intimate scene of the drama: 'la maison à M. Grandet, cette maison pâle, froide, silencieuse, située en haut de la ville ...'; or again: 'La maison où s'exploite la pension bourgeoise appartient à Madame Vauquer. Elle est située dans le bas de la rue Neuve-Sainte-Geneviève à l'endroit où ...'.[11]

Nor is that enough; the characters themselves must be presented to us with their detailed *curriculum vitae:* 'cette maison, louée d'abord, fut plus tard achetée par un nommé Sauviat, marchand forain, qui de 1792 à 1796, parcourut les campagnes dans un rayon de cinquante lieues autour de L'Auvergne ... Dès la troisième année, Sauviat joignit à ce commerce celui de ... En 1793, il put acquérir un château... il avait, en 1797, épousé... etc.'[12]; and usually in their physical characteristics and dress: *La Cousine Bette* provides a good example,[13] *Le Cousin Pons* an even better.

[7] *Ursule Mirouët.* Ribbon development!
[8] *Maison du Chat-qui-pelote.* As he wrote this passage, Balzac must, characteristically, have been thinking of the palaeontologist reconstructing a prehistoric animal from the evidence of a fossilized tooth.
[9] *La Cousine Bette.*   [10] *Le Curé de Tours.*
[11] *Le Père Goriot.*   [12] *Le Curé de Village.*
[13] But unlike so many of Balzac's stories, *La Cousine Bette* introduces the reader at once into the action, postponing the detailed background until after the opening scene.

The modern reader may be tempted to find this wealth of extraneous matter burdensome. He has grown lazy, habituated as he is by the camera, the cinema, the television, to registering, subliminally, images of persons and places without the effort of attention and imagination required to digest a text and project the image on to his inward screen. But where textual descriptions are successful (Balzac excels in the sordid[14]), where, that is, they have compelled the reader's attention and forced him to make the effort, their impact is all the greater because the reader will in fact have created a vision of his own; he will have taken full possession of what the author offers.

To appreciate the imaginative power Balzac shows in all this, let the reader try for himself the experiment of creating one character, picturing and describing him, his features, colouring, facial expressions and resemblances,[15] other physical characteristics, dress, habits. Let him then invent for his character an appropriate background of place, of personal events and human relationships, so that his character can be woven into the texture of his time and society. In doing this the reader will pass from the receiving and critical to the creative end of literature; and if he do this not merely once but hundreds of times without repeating himself, he will measure Balzac's power all the better.

Background description on the Balzacian scale implies immense knowledge; Balzac's seems inexhaustible. His stories take us all over France to the small towns where provincial life as opposed to country life is concentrated: Alençon (*La Vieille Fille*), Angoulême (*Illusions Perdues*), Arcis-sur-Aube (*Le Deputé d'Arcis*), Fougères (*Les Chouans*), Le Havre (*Modeste Mignon*), Issoudun (*La Rabouilleuse*), Limoges (*Le Curé de Village*), Nemours (*Ursule Mirouët*), Provins (*Pierrette*), Saumur (*Eugénie Grandet*), Tours (*Le Curé de Tours*) and so on; one is tempted to wonder how many letters of the alphabet could be used in naming the towns where Balzac's stories unfold; Balzac knows and describes them, often with topographical exactitude and an inborn understanding of provincial life. Nor is his geographical knowledge restricted to the provinces; of all the towns that play a background part in *La Comédie humaine*, Paris takes pride of place.

The information we can derive about French social history from the Revolution to almost the end of the July Monarchy is no less, in range and variety: interesting if trifling material details first –

---

[14] e.g. la Pension Vauquer; on a small scale the stairs leading to Fraisier's office (*Le Cousin Pons*). Many examples could be given. His descriptions of 'high life', on the other hand, both in Paris and in the provinces lack the same stamp of authenticity.

[15] Balzac is fond of comparisons with birds or beasts of prey – vulture, tiger, wolf, boa-constrictor, etc.

'une fausse bûche en terre cuite',[16] the equivalent of the modern electric wood fire was apparently known in Balzac's day! 'Le joyeux dîner fut terminé à 5 heures',[17] the hours at which succeeding generations sit down to eat is an interesting and revealing social study; in 1817 we learn that tilburys,[18] in which all Balzac's dandys ride usually with a groom or 'tigre', had only recently been imported from England; magic lanterns already existed under the Restoration, for children to enjoy;[19] 'unie comme la rainure d'un chemin de fer';[20] were rails at this date[21] really made with a groove, or is Balzac's knowledge or observation, like Tennyson's,[22] for once at fault? The poetry of Chénier, recently published,[23] had penetrated as far as Angoulême;[24] already under the Restoration the Avenue des Champs Elysées was the fashionable Sunday rendezvous for carriage folk, and we are reminded that the 'Arc de Triomphe' at that time stood unfinished;[25] advertisement posters appeared on the walls of Paris for the first time under the Restoration[26] and horse omnibuses in its streets at the same time. Carlos Herrera proposes to launch a company of them, make the shares rise by distributing big dividends from the capital subscribed, and sell out quickly;[27] company law must still have been rudimentary since Carlos had borrowed the idea from that much respected member of *Comédie humaine* high financial circles, Baron de Nucingen.

More important than trivia of this sort is the valuable insight we so often derive from Balzac into mentalities, social or political attitudes, all of which tend to bring the facts of history into an understandable human pattern: the immense land confiscation of *Les Biens Nationaux* must, we can guess, have weighed upon French society in diverse ways for generations; we find illuminating allusions to the question in Balzac: 'je vous jure qu'une demande en restitution des bois de Navarreins par le domaine extraordinaire sera chaudement appuyé auprès de l'empereur.'[28] Here is a clear indication of what happened: the State, unable to find immediate buyers, was left with large tracts of land on its hands; their administration would require a special service – 'le domaine[29] extraordinaire'; so much for the material facts, but the political value of this land in the hands of Napoleon is also evident, as a means of coaxing, bribing or forcing *émigrés* away from their Bourbon alle-

---

[16] *La Bourse.*
[17] *Une double Famille.*
[18] *Ibid.*
[19] *Ibid.*
[20] *La Peau de Chagrin.*
[21] 1830.
[22] cf. *Locksley Hall:* 'Let the great world spin for ever down the ringing grooves of change'!
[23] 1819.
[24] *Illusions Perdues.*
[25] *Ibid.*
[26] *Ibid.*
[27] *Splendeurs et Misères.*
[28] *La Paix du Ménage* (1830).
[29] 'Le domaine' is the expression to this day of state-owned property.

giance, back to France and into Napoleonic service.[30] The paragraph, too long to quote, that follows the sentence just given,
indicates another possibility; we learn that a shabby bargain is
being proposed whereby the Navarreins woods might be handed
back not to the elder branch of the family, their rightful owners,
but to the younger. Admittedly this detail is not history, it is of
Balzac's invention. Invention? May we not suppose it to be in its
turn rooted in history? Such things may well have happened many
times over, as a matter of deliberate calculation by government, or
by someone's dishonesty or by chance, and what a paradise of litiga-
tion was thereby being prepared for the lawyers, with conspiracies
woven round the existence or destruction of deeds or conveyances
and the like, the sort of conspiracies that are, incidentally, of the
very stuff of *La Comédie humaine*.[31]

Little imagination, too, is required to guess at the opportunities
provided by the *Biens Nationaux* and indeed by the Revolution
generally for anyone with an eye to the main chance and not too
scrupulous. On this point the career of M. du Bousquier,[32] recorded by Balzac with the usual wealth of detail, is illuminating:
'Au commencement de la Révolution, il s'était mis dans les affaires.
En dépit des républicains, qui sont tous à cheval sur la probité
révolutionnaire, les affaires de ce temps-là n'étaient pas claires. Un
espion politique, un agioteur, un munitionnaire, un homme qui
faisait confisquer, d'accord avec le syndic de la commune, des biens
d'émigrés pour les acheter et les revendre; un ministre et un général
étaient tous également dans les affaires. De 1793 à 1799, du Bousquier fut entrepreneur des vivres des armées françaises ... eut ...
un magnifique hôtel ...'. Even assuming unimpeachable actions,
when the Restoration came, owners of *Biens Nationaux* might and
surely did have a difficulty to reckon with of an imponderable but,
as Balzac knew and as we all know or may at any moment discover
to our cost, a very real kind: the pressures of society. Mademoiselle
Sophie Gamard[33] had inherited a fine house in the heart of Tours
under the very shadow of the cathedral; her father had bought it
as *Bien National*; the fact, known of course – for what is not known
in a provincial town? –, might have been most uncomfortable for
Mademoiselle Gamard, had she not with her characteristic skill
found a safe bulwark against public opinion: 'Quoique ce bien eût
été acquis de la nation, pendant la Terreur, par le père de Mademoiselle Gamard, comme, depuis vingt ans, cette vieille fille y logeait
des prêtres, personne ne s'avisait de trouver mauvais, sous la

[30] A further reference to this incident is to be found in *Splendeurs et
Misères des Courtisanes*, Part I, p. 109, Calmann Levy edn.
[31] e.g. *Ursule Mirouët, Illusions Perdues, Splendeurs et Misères, César
Birotteau, Le Contrat de Mariage*.
[32] *La Vieille Fille*.   [33] *Le Curé de Tours*.

Restauration, qu'une dévote conservait un bien national: peut-être les gens religieux lui supposaient-ils l'intention de le léguer au chapître, et les gens du monde n'en voyaient-ils pas la destination changée.'

We have taken *Les Biens Nationaux* as one amongst innumerable illuminating details the reader comes across in the pages of *La Comédie humaine*; they lead him into the very heart of French life during the Revolution, the Empire, the Restoration, the July Monarchy. 'Seul dans le monde,[34] jeté dès l'âge de vingt ans dans cette tempête d'hommes au sein de laquelle vécut Napoleon ...'. The phrase, which might so well fit the situation of Stendhal's hero Fabrice thrown into the mêlée at Waterloo, suggests in a flash the heroic measure of Napoleonic times, after which, as many Romantics bear witness, the calm of the Restoration and its politics seemed so flat, even sordid. Clericalism was now in the ascendant; Balzac knew it as well as Stendhal: 'Comment, diable! Vas-tu te mêler de faire la guerre aux prêtres? ... j'ai su que tu parlais fort légèrement d'un certain abbé Troubert simple vicaire général, mais le personnage le plus important de la province où il représente la Congrégation ... Monsieur mon neveu, si tu veux faire ton chemin, ne te crée aucune inimitié sacerdotale.'[35] Thus warned by his uncle, the deputy, what could Baron de Listomère – a mere naval lieutenant with his way to make in the world – do but drop the cause of poor Birotteau, like a hot potato? And Balzac provides us often with a picture of the provincial nobility[36] who, submerged rather than destroyed by the tidal waves of Revolution and Empire, bob up in 1815 with their network of family alliances (a great source of strength for getting on in the world), and their suspicions of the moderate Louis XVIII, 'Jacobin fleur de lysé'.[37] Backbone of the 'Ultras', they come into their own under Charles X and the Ministry of Villèle, but by their own rigid pride sow the winds of social hatred and reap the storms of 1830: 'Il est facile de concevoir combien l'esprit de caste influe sur les sentiments qui divisent Angoulême et l'Houmeau. Le commerce est riche, la noblesse est généralement pauvre. L'une se venge sur l'autre par un mépris égal des deux côtés ... En dessinant la position de la noblesse en France et lui donnant des espérances qui ne pouvaient se réaliser sans un bouleversement général, la Restauration étendit la distance morale qui séparait ... Angoulême de l'Houmeau ... De là procédaient des haines sourdes et profondes qui donnèrent une effroyable unanimité à l'insurrection de 1830 et détruisirent les éléments d'un durable état social en France.'[38]

<hr />

[34] Armand de Montriveau, *Histoire des Treize.*   [35] *Le Curé de Tours.*
[36] e.g. in *La Femme abandonnée, Le Curé de Tours, Illusions Perdues,* Part I, *La Vieille Fille* and *Le Cabinet des Antiques.*
[37] *Duchesse de Langeais.*   [38] *Illusions Perdues,* Part I.

Balzac's thorough understanding of his own times and its mechanisms is accompanied by a prophetic vision matched in his own day only by Chateaubriand[39] and by Tocqueville:[40] 'Notre siècle reliera le règne de la force isolée, abondante en créations originales, au règne de la force uniforme, mais niveleuse, égalisant les produits, les jetant par masses, et obéissant à une pensée unitaire, dernière expression des sociétés.'[41]

Balzac is indeed both an inexhaustible mine of information about the France of his day and a valuable guide to our understanding of it on the political level. His aim is to be more. He lays great emphasis in his *Préface* on the scientific character of *La Comédie humaine*; the classifications he indulges in have a veneer of scientific method; method is an indispensable preliminary to any investigation, and no doubt he would have liked to see that word – investigation – used to describe his work.

Balzac lights a candle, as we have seen, at the shrine of Geoffroy Saint-Hilaire, from whom he got the idea that men, no less than animals, are inseparable from their environments. For the first time in French literature we come across an idea that the Naturalists will develop later to extremes; hitherto the interest in the human psyche had remained on the individual plane.

The interdependence of the individual and the society he lives in, like an amorphous cocoon that seems to leave him entirely free and yet exerts constant pressures on him, was undiscovered as a factor in the interpretation of men's caperings. *La Comédie humaine* is shot through with this idea: the young Parisian Gaston de Nueil[42] is sent by his doctors to recuperate in the country: 'Après les légères souffrances de cette transition, s'accomplit pour l'individu le phénomène de sa transplantation dans un terrain qui lui est contraire, où il doit s'atrophier et mener une vie rachitique.' The importance of 'milieu' is strongly emphasized in *Le Curé de Tours*: '"Abandonner Tours!" s'écria le vicaire avec un effroi indescriptible. C'était pour lui une sorte de mort. N'était-ce pas briser toutes les racines par lesquelles il s'était planté dans le monde . . . Birotteau était . . . devenu semblable à quelque végétal: le transplanter, c'était en risquer l'innocente fructification. De même que pour vivre un arbre doit retrouver à toute heure les mêmes sucs . . .' Who today would deny the psychological soundness of the ideas underlying these metaphors, or the validity of the reciprocal thrust, as it were, of an individual's action on his environment? The nature of the soil may encourage the growth of certain types of tree and when these have grown into a forest, the forest will in its turn

[39] *Mémoires d'Outre-Tombe*, last chapters.
[40] *De la Démocratie en Amérique.*
[41] *L'Illustre Gaudissart.*   [42] *La Femme abandonnée.*

affect the environment. Balzac often emphasizes this point too: 'Cependant, cet appartement si misérable lui apparut dénué des poésies de l'amour . . . il le vit sale et flétri, le considéra comme la représentation d'une vie intérieure sans noblesse, inoccupée, vicieuse. Nos sentiments ne sont-ils pas pour ainsi dire, écrits sur les choses qui nous entourent.'

One 'milieu' Balzac knew well, from direct experience: the world of Paris journalism. His opinion of it was low: 'Le journalisme est un enfer, un abîme d'iniquités, de mensonges, de trahisons . . .';[43] 'ces mauvais lieux de la pensée appelés journaux';[44] thus do the 'incorruptibles' of *Illusions Perdues* – d'Arthez, Michel Chrestien and their friends – express themselves – and we are given ample opportunity in the novel of assessing the effect of the profession upon the men who exercise it, Emile Blondet, Lousteau, Nathan – a sorry lot of 'hand-to-mouthers', servile pen-pushers, because their work conditions those attitudes of mind.

The idea of man in his environment leads on to Balzac's oft repeated suggestion that given sectors of society have their underlying laws which, being constant, may be studied; provincial life has its laws, Paris has its laws. This is surely the beginning of a sociological attitude which in Balzac betrays itself particularly in his tendency to regard Paris as an organism endowed with a mysterious life of its own: 'Ces deux parties formeront alors une même histoire qui, par une loi particulière à la vie parisienne, avait produit deux actions distinctes . . .'[45] In *Splendeurs et Misères* he speaks of 'l'agitation quasi marine de cette grande cité'; at the end of *Le Père Goriot*, Rastignac sees Paris as a hive: 'il lança sur cette ruche bourdonnante un regard qui semblait par avance en pomper le miel'. Paris, with its underlying laws, Paris an ocean, Paris a hive; Paris throughout the *Comédie humaine* acts like a huge magnet attracting to itself all ambitious adventurers. The opening pages of *La Fille aux Yeux d'or* is like a little sociological essay on the struggle for life in Paris, which Balzac offers us as a contribution 'à la science des moeurs'. It is revealing in relation to Balzac but poorly integrated with the story that follows.

Yet with all his pretentions Balzac is primarily neither chronicler nor scientist, he is a novelist for ever staking out claims for himself in these other fields, and as a novelist Balzac's first concern is to portray passions in action.

Within the provincial or the Parisian setting then, and at the periods Balzac has chosen for his characters, we are to see them playing out their dramas. Very soon we become conscious of one important fact: Balzac's characters are of two distinct kinds. In *Le*

[43] *Illusions Perdues*, Part II.
[44] *Ibid.*, Part III.
[45] *Une Double Famille.*

Curé de Tours, after describing Sophie Gamard's house standing silent under the shadow of the cathedral, the author writes: 'Cet endroit est un désert de pierres, une solitude pleine de physionomie, et qui ne peut être habitée que par des êtres arrivés à une nullité complète ou doués d'une force d'âme prodigieuse.' Either . . . or . . ., the alternative is clearly intended to prepare us for the nonentity Birotteau, moulded by his surroundings, enmeshed in all the little habits and creature comforts that form the texture of his life, facing the two monsters, Sophie Gamard and l'Abbé Troubert, whose inner strength enables them to resist the process of incrustation by local forces. But the alternative is constantly applicable in the *Etudes de moeurs* between the characters of giant moral stature, and the others. On one hand, Grandet, Goriot, Hulot, Troubert, Vautrin, Minoret-Levrault,[46] Sophie Gamard, la Cousine Bette, Valérie Marneffe, Sophie Rougon, to whom might be attached a sub-category: giants who lurk in the shadows of the *Comédie humaine* and are therefore less well defined although their potential is as great: the 'go-getters' like Nucingen, Du Tillet, Gobseck and the other financial sharks; Rastignac, for whom everyone has his price;[47] the equally cynical Marsay, that political manipulator of skill – his name often recurs but he is usually behind the scenes; Lucien de Rubempré who, though well in the foreground of *Illusions Perdues* and *Splendeurs et Misères des Courtisanes*, bathes in a strange Romantic mystery that tends to blur the outlines; he is fascinated as we are by the basilisk eye of the Satanic Herrera, Vautrin, alias Jacques Collin, in disguise, and becomes a kind of projection of his will; a go-getter Lucien would like to have been, but he lacks the inner incandescence, and in Balzac's Paris, where 'la stratégie des intérêts' is a romantic war to the knife, the price of failure is death. Frédéric Moreau, Lucien's reincarnation in a later age, will merely sink into the mud of frustrated inertia.[48]

On the other side are the numerous, lesser characters, some of whom are successful living characters of life size: l'Abbé Birotteau, César Birotteau, David Séchard, Crevel, Pons, Schmucke, for example; but many of whom are inert: Madame Grandet, Eugénie Grandet, Ursule Mirouët, Pierrette . . . and trail off into the background. On the one hand the powerful, the successful, the cruel, the amoral, a kind of rogues' gallery . . . 'doués d'une force d'âme prodigieuse', on the other the weak, the foolish, the kindly, the vulgar and the multitude of mice who fade out into that anonymous mass called society.

[46] *Ursule Mirouët.*
[47] 'Il n'y a pas de vertu absolue, il n'y a que des circonstances' was an axiom of his.
[48] See below, pp. 283 *et seq.*

This moral dichotomy in the society of *La Comédie humaine* is in line with the general message Balzac seems to give in his *Etudes philosophiques*, namely that men are governed by mysterious forces.

From an early age Balzac was interested in the mysterious, the occult, the mystical; it was a taste he seems to have inherited from his mother. On the religious plane, the Swedenborgian ideas of the ultimate unity of all religions and the communion that may be established by feeling, with the ultimate life force, appealed to him; he was attracted both by Mesmer's theories on the mysterious waves and currents of communication between individuals whereby they can acquire information in an occult way or influence each other, and by Gall's ideas on the spiritual and intellectual significance of the configuration of men's skulls. All these ideas were means of exploring the supernatural force itself and of its action on or through individuals.

These beliefs have left a clear mark on *La Comédie humaine*. Certain individuals acquire a mysterious power over their fellows – magnetism at work! Of the young artist Schinner,[49] Balzac writes: 'En le voyant, on se sentait porté vers lui par une de ces attractions morales que les savants ne savent heureusement pas encore analyser, ils y trouveraient quelque phénomène de galvanisme ou le jeu de je ne sais quel fluide, et formuleraient nos sentiments par des proportions d'oxygène et d'électricité.' The 'heureusement' of this quotation is, incidentally, revealing. It suggests that Balzac – good Romantic that he is – prefers to remain on the plane of mystery than to see this source of emotion dissipated by scientific formulae. How different will be the attitude of a Taine or a Zola some thirty or forty years later![50] In *Une Fille d'Eve* Marie-Eugénie de Vandenesse throws an 'electrifying' glance at Raoul Nathan: 'Quant à Marie ... elle attacha sur lui ce regard violent et fixe par lequel la volonté jaillit de l'oeil, comme du soleil jaillissent les ondes lumineuses, et qui pénètre, selon les magnétiseurs, la personne sur laquelle il est dirigé. Raoul sembla frappé par une baguette magique ...' What characters in Balzac from the early and rather obscure ones in *Scènes de la Vie Privée* down to the sublime Vautrin do not flash an eye that is variously described as 'magnétique' or 'électrique' or simply 'mystérieux'. The story in *Ursule Mirouët* turns on certain occult phenomena which providentially restore the balance between the froward and their victim. The worthy Gaudissart[51] for his part roundly declares his faith in signs revealed by a client's physiognomy: 'Bah! Il y mordra, c'est sûr, il a un front bombé, tous les fronts bombés sont idéologues.'

But the dominating characters are those whose inner responses

[49] *La Bourse.* [50] Below, pp. 360–2. & Vol. V, ch. 2. [51] *L'Illustre Gaudissart.*

we come to recognize as thrusting always in the same direction, in whom the mysterious force reveals itself as a devouring passion, the monomaniacs; Balzac himself uses the term,[52] but may they not better be described as the 'possessed'? The word monomania is neutral; it describes objectively a given mental condition; the word 'possessed' suggests an interpretation of that condition, the interpretation that the Balzac of the *Etudes philosophiques* believes in: these characters are like human vessels in whom emanations of the mysterious force have become individuated, singling them out from the ordinary run of men and women, raising them to a higher power; we have left ordinary society behind, with its sociological laws Balzac laid such emphasis on, and where ordinary mortals have their being. Balzac's vocabulary itself is indicative of the change; words such as *feu, brûler, dévorer*, expressions such as *passion dévorante, passion qui lui dévore l'âme* recur constantly in reference to the 'possessed'.

The word 'possessed' has a further advantage in connexion with Balzac, namely the sense of evil it conveys. Evil cannot be dissociated from its cognate term – good; and a writer who uses them or who evidently places his main characters between the poles of good and evil has abandoned the scientific attitude he may have had, he has become a moralist. This, in the last resort, Balzac undoubtedly is, even though his moral system is incoherent. He rejects Rousseau's ideas and declares his belief that society exercises a good influence on man: 'la société, loin de le dépraver, comme l'a prétendu Rousseau, le perfectionne, le rend meilleur...'[53] Yet Paris, for example, is a haunt of wickedness, egoisms lurk in every corner: 'Paris est un singulier pays, dit Lucien, en trouvant l'intérêt accroupi dans tous les coins',[54] yet society is sunk in materialism, money its motive power. The odious Crevel[55] is not alone in thinking that 'au-dessus de la Charte il y a la Sainte, la vénérée, la solide, l'aimable, la grâcieuse, la belle, la noble, la jeune, la toute-puissante pièce de cent sous'; Balzac comes back to the subject again and again,[56] Balzac believes in Swedenborgian mysticism as a means of apprehending the divine spirit,[57] which must surely be the source of the mysterious force that governs men's lives, yet the emanations from this force that possess his great characters and burn them up seem wholly evil. Whatever Balzac may say in his preface, his general moral attitude as it emerges from *La Comédie humaine* is pessimistic; the only hope lies in the strong moral bulwark provided by the twin forces of the Roman Church and Mon-

[52] e.g. in *Eugénie Grandet* and in *Le Curé de Tours*.   [53] Préface.
[54] *Illusions Perdues*, Vol. II.   [55] *La Cousine Bette*.
[56] e.g. *inter alia*: *La Peau de Chagrin, La Fille aux Yeux d'Or, Louis Lambert, Melmoth réconcilié, Illusions Perdues*.
[57] *Séraphita*.

archy.[58] Here again we may well ask how Balzac reconciles his profession of Catholic belief with his Swedenborgian mysticism.

His political attitudes, on the other hand, can be seen to be in line with his central belief as expressed in the *Etudes philosophiques* of the mysterious force governing our lives. Some contemporaries[59] of Balzac derived an exactly opposite position from religious views akin to his, so that the latter's political ideas cannot be regarded as arising inevitably from his philosophy, but they do at least fit in. No more vigorous opponent of democracy can be found than he; 'J'éprouve un immense plaisir', says Henri de Marsay,[60] 'd'échapper à la stupide juridiction de la masse'. In *Les Paysans* and in *Le Médecin de Campagne* too, Balzac provides us with a number of characters evidently his spokesmen.[61] Democracy gives equal weight to the vote of the nonentity and of the genius, democracy breeds individualism, egoism – 'notre lèpre actuelle';[62] democracy grinds individuals into uniformity. How could Balzac favour such a system, he who believes in the mysterious life force taking possession of certain individuals and making them so manifestly 'more equal than others'.[63] In *Le Médecin de Campagne* Doctor Benassis transforms a little village in the Isère, near Grenoble, from a miserable collection of hovels into an active prosperous community of which he becomes mayor and to whose inhabitants he is guide, philosopher and friend. The lesson? Ideal society is authoritarian. Must it necessarily be monarchist? It has been suggested that Balzac's monarchism had much to do with the flattering welcome accorded to him by the Faubourg Saint-Germain in the early 'thirties, especially by certain 'grandes dames'; Balzac may indeed have been flattered but in fact his monarchist views had emerged earlier and in any case his monarchism neither blinded him to the defects of the aristocracy nor prevented him from stating with cogency the only conditions on which the aristocracy could claim political and social leadership.[64] On the other hand, in later years Balzac drifted away from the royalist camp, without in any way departing from his opposition to democracy.[65]

---

[58] See *Préface*, also *Le Médecin de Campagne* and *Les Paysans*.

[59] Lamartine, Hugo, Michelet, Lamennais.

[60] *La Fille aux Yeux d'Or*.

[61] See also *La Peau de Chagrin*, *L'Illustre Gaudissart*, *La Duchesse de Langeais*, *Louis Lambert*, *La Vieille Fille*, *Illusions Perdues*, for other references to democracy and other aspects of Balzac's political opinions. Balzac also wrote for royalist newspapers.

[62] *La Peau de Chagrin* – cf. Tocqueville's: 'la rouille de la société'.

[63] Balzac made a very similar remark before George Orwell: 'Aristocrates par inclination, ils se font républicains par dépit, uniquement pour trouver beaucoup d'inférieurs parmi leurs égaux' – *Madame Firmiani*.

[64] *La Duchesse de Langeais*.

[65] n.b. *Les Paysans* first appeared in 1844. He appears to have had some leaning towards republicanism in 1848, but it was only momentary.

He remains with an authoritarian attitude and perhaps we may
see in the picture he paints of the peasants listening to Le Père
Goguelat[66] recounting his Napoleonic campaigns a prophetic image
of his own later views. What, one wonders, would have been his
attitude to Louis Napoleon's *coup d'état* of December 1851, if he
had lived to see it?

Chronicler, sociologist, moralist, political thinker, Balzac adopts
all these roles in *La Comédie humaine* and the final question that
must be asked is how successfully has he as a novelist welded these
disparate elements into an artistic whole? If, to decide this question, we take as our criteria the principles of integration, propor-
tion, perspective, our answer will surely be that Balzac's art as a
novelist is uneven. His framework descriptions, for example, are
artistically justified, when they help us to situate, to 'see' and
understand the characters. In such cases they are well integrated
and numerous are the examples both long and short that measure
up fully to this criterion: 'la maison à M. Grandet', 'la Pension
Vauquer', Baronne Hulot's decayed drawing room;[67] the description of Sophie Gamard's house,[68] the sordid staircase leading to
Fraisier's office;[69] or again, with what skill does Balzac lead us un-
suspectingly in the wake of Raphaël de Valentin from the realistic
sordid gaming house to the twilight world he is to live and die in,
where reality and magic merge.[70]

The same may be said of Balzac's scientific attitudes; they are
artistically justified when they subserve the aim of the novelist. The
character of l'Abbé Birotteau, the intensity of his sufferings at the
hands of the odious Sophie Gamard, are illuminated for us by the
ecological idea of man like a plant drawing sustenance and indeed
life itself from his surroundings; we see at once that the poor little
man's tragedy is inescapable, and that sense of inevitability ensures
the fullest impact of a story, whatever the size of the canvas or the
stature of the characters.

But beside these successful cases of artistic integration stand
numerous instances where the reader has the impression that the descriptions or the information imparted are there in their own right.
An excellent example of this occurs in *Illusions Perdues*: 'A cette
époque, les galeries de bois constituaient une des curiosités parisiennes les plus illustres. Il n'est pas inutile de peindre ce bazar
ignoble; car, pendant trente-six ans, il a joué dans la vie parisienne
un si grand rôle, qu'il est peu d'hommes âgés de quarante ans à
qui cette description, incroyable pour les jeunes gens, ne fasse encore
plaisir.' Could an author admit more engagingly that what he is

[66] *Le Médicin de Campagne*: chapter entitled 'La Veillée'.
[67] *La Cousine Bette.*
[68] *Le Curé de Tours.*
[69] *Le Cousin Pons.*
[70] *La Peau de Chagrin.*

putting down has a purpose other than that of creating the reality his characters are going to move in? We have already noted what an immense fund of interest Balzac provides from a historical angle, but this type of interest must be recognized as lying outside the artistic effect of a novel; Balzac's descriptions, whatever their inherent interest, are often more like a backcloth the spectator of a play forgets about when the play begins than a background skilfully interwoven into the texture of a character's experience.

The same lack of integration and perspective is evident in those novels where the action is dominated by one or more of Balzac's 'possessed': Monsieur Grandet, Le Père Goriot, La Cousine Bette. The dominant characters stride out of their frames which become too small to hold them. The illusion of life is shattered; the proportions are distorted; the word caricature springs to mind. In these cases, however, we may question whether our previously chosen criteria any longer apply. The illusion of normal life may be shattered but in some cases at least Balzac provides us instead with a vision of intenser incandescent power. *Eugénie Grandet* and *Le Père Goriot* probably provide the best examples; in both novels the action at the outset is firmly rooted in reality; gradually the passion in question grows like the crescendo of an orchestra and builds up to a climax. The moribund Grandet with his gold: 'Serre, serre ça, pour qu'on ne me vole pas . . ., veille à l'or . . ., mets de l'or devant moi . . ., ça me réchauffe . . .'; Goriot on his death-bed alternately blessing and cursing his daughters: 'Elles vont venir . . . Je les connais. Cette bonne Delphine . . . Nasie aussi . . . Non, elles ne viendront pas! Je sais cela depuis dix ans. Je me le disais quelquefois, mais je n'osais pas y croire . . . Mes filles, c'était mon vice à moi . . . Envoyez-les chercher par la gendarmerie, de force! la justice est pour moi, tout est pour moi, la nature, le code civil! Je proteste . . .' Scenes such as these force their own reality upon us; like some tremendous personal experience of pity and horror, they make us forget our own surroundings; we ourselves become eye-witnesses like Nanon and Eugénie, like Bianchon and Rastignac.

These experiences quite destroy the idea of caricature, because with a caricature we never lose the sense of normal reality which is our standard of comparison; here we do. And there are other scenes in Balzac of which the same may be said: César Birotteau trying to stave off financial disaster and being refused a loan by one banker after another; the false teutonic bonhomie with which Nucingen shows him the door is particularly telling; or again the scene in *Illusions Perdues*, where Lucien de Rubempré, alone and friendless in Paris, wanders up the Champs Elysées and sees Madame de Bargeton who has thrown him over and Madame d'Espard in the latter's carriage: 'Des jeunes gens à cheval, parmi

lesquels Lucien remarqua Marsay et Rastignac se joignirent à la
calèche pour conduire les deux cousines au Bois... La calèche
passa. La rage, le désir de vengeance, s'emparèrent de cet homme
dédaigné: s'il avait tenu Madame de Bargeton, il l'aurait égorgée;
il se fit Fouquier-Tinville pour se donner la jouissance d'envoyer
Madame d'Espard à l'échafaud; il aurait voulu pouvoir faire subir
à Marsay un de ces supplices raffinés qu'ont inventés les sauvages.
Il vit passer Canalis à cheval, élégant comme devait l'être le plus
câlin des poètes, et saluant les femmes les plus jolies.

– Mon Dieu! de l'or à tout prix! se disait Lucien, l'or est la
seule puissance devant laquelle ce monde s'agenouille.' Lucien is
fully alive in this scene – he isn't always – and we can appreciate
his bitter humiliation, understand the compensating psychological
process that makes him think himself into the part of Fouquier-
Tinville.

But the margin of error between convincing magnification and
caricature, between a scene that enforces its own truth on us and
one that strikes us as unreal, is narrow. Balzac is not always on the
right side of it. We accept the magnification of Grandet and
Goriot, of Sophie Gamard and even Bette. Hulot, on the other
hand, has a rigid insistence on his monomania that makes us suspect him of playing a part and exaggerating it; he is, or at least becomes, a caricature; the scenes of *Le Curé de Tours* are wholly
successful; many of those in *La Cousine Bette* – the soirée at the
Marneffes for example – and in general Balzac's scenes of 'high
life' are not; Parisian society life in Balzac's rather naïve portrayal
seems to consist of carriage exercise in the Bois, a box at the opera
and 'Les Italiens', or a ball. His banquet scenes, of which there
are a number, are interchangeable, such is their dreary sameness. The artistic weakness of these orgiastic all-night sittings, like
that of many scenes in Balzac, arises from their being neither
accurately observed nor illuminated by his powerful imagination.

The art of the novel in Balzac is uneven; at its best hallucina-
ting, at its worst unconvincing, even ridiculous. But to use 'the
art of the novel' as a yard-stick in Balzac's case may well be unfair.
'The art of the novel', with the awareness it implies of the technical
problems involved in creating the illusion of life is a later development. Balzac in fact is not so much a novelist as a story-teller. A
story-teller may sometimes successfully create the illusion of life,
force the reader, in other words, to forget his own place in space
and time, to become a contemporary of the action being unfolded
for him; but in the main the story-teller remains master of his own
creation; he does not bother to conceal his own presence, does not
hesitate to intervene personally, or to interrupt the time-flow, by

'flash-backs', if it suits his purpose.[71] Balzac does all these things constantly. Another favourite gambit of Balzac's is to introduce at once 'un inconnu'. How can he be 'inconnu' to his own creator? This obvious fact destroys the very illusion it is intended to foster. There is no question of his trying by 'the art of the novel' or 'the craft of fiction' to hide that there are inevitably three permanent parties to the contract of fiction: author, story, reader.

Balzac in fact would reject the criteria we have applied in assessing the artistic merits of his work. For him the novel-form is not an art *per se*, it is a means, just as politics or journalism[72] are means, of acting on society, of expressing one's views, one's interpretation of life, in a word oneself. What could be more Romantic? Balzac made of the novel a vehicle of direct communication, a vessel into which he might pour anything he cared without concern for the proportions of the mixture. His vast knowledge of French society, his scientific pretentions, his mystical beliefs, all are thrown into the witches' cauldron whence gradually emerges the splendid vision, the chaotic saga of *La Comédie humaine*.

[71] After setting his scene Balzac almost invariably proceeds: 'Pour comprendre l'importance de . . . il faut que . . .'; the flash-back, often long and complex, follows.
[72] He used the latter and at one time thought of standing for parliament.

Chapter 15

HISTORIANS AND CRITICS

INTEREST in the past has always existed but it received a great impetus during the Romantic era. Chateaubriand's *Les Martyrs* was an important influence in the 'escape to the past', just as *Atala* and the *Itinéraire* were, in the 'escape to exotic lands'. Walter Scott's novels provided an even more vital stimulus; from historical romance to the romance of history is an easy step. Thanks to both writers, too, their generation became more discerning than previous generations had ever been, in their taste for history, more sensitive to the changing face of men and things from age to age; a sense of period develops which may not then have gone beyond the superficial liking for 'local colour' but is a first step in removing the study of the past from that idealist 'no man's land', situated in neither space nor time, where abstract passions alone may have truth, the first effort to see history as a study of past reality rather than as a storehouse of moral lessons.

Augustin Thierry (1795–1856), one of the architects of French historical studies in the nineteenth century, was well aware of the vital importance of individual or period differences: 'Le grand précepte', he writes, 'qu'il faut donner aux historiens c'est de distinguer au lieu de confondre; car à moins d'être varié l'on n'est point vrai. Malheureusement les esprits médiocres ont le goût de l'uniformité; l'uniformité est si commode! Si elle fausse tout, du moins elle tranche tout, et avec elle aucun chemin n'est rude.'[1]

The response to the romance of history is in the narrative school of historians of which Augustin Thierry is the founder. His *Lettres sur l'Histoire de France*[2] (1827) are full of pertinent criticisms, such as the passage just quoted, of earlier professional historians; his grasp of the nature of historical study makes it plain that in this field all previous work could be swept away without loss and that nineteenth-century historians must build anew.

His own historical vocation had been revealed to him by the enthusiasm he felt on reading *Les Martyrs*.[3] In contrast to the

---

[1] *Lettres sur l'Histoire de France*, No. II.
[2] Originally published in *Le Courrier français* from 1820.
[3] *Récits Mérovingiens*, Preface.

desiccated recital of facts he had been used to, here was a magician in words whose wand gave life to the dry bones, and evoked a period of history before his eyes. Thierry would do the same. His *Histoire de la Conquête de l'Angleterre par les Normands* (1825) and *Récits Mérovingiens* (1840) are the results of that decision and show – particularly the latter which are his masterpiece – his effort to produce a dramatic narrative, faithful in detail and period colour, established on original sources.

But what better method could be found to give narrative history the sense of period than to piece the ancient chroniclers together, intervening only to ensure a coherent narrative? This is the formula adopted by one of Thierry's disciples, Prosper de Barante (1782–1866), in his *Histoire des ducs de Bourgogne* (1824–6).

The narrative historian is likely to be attracted by historical moments where the accelerated tempo of events has particular dramatic and epic value; such periods lay close at hand: the Revolution, the Consulate and Empire. Apart from their dramatic value these periods had other advantages: they were close enough to make first hand evidence available, and yet, cut off by the violent changes that began and ended them, they seemed both out of the flow of history and aloof enough in time to allow for objective treatment; illusions, no doubt, but attractive to a succession of historians[4] down to this day, drawn as by a magnet to this mysterious volcanic eruption that divides the classical idyllic eighteenth-century landscape from the busy mercantile nineteenth-century scene. The attraction is evident for the narrative historians: Mignet (1796–1884), *Histoire de la Révolution Française* (1824) and Thiers (1797–1877), *Histoire de la Révolution Française* (1823–7) and *Histoire du Consulat et de l'Empire* (1845–55). None of these survives except as a name in the museum of literature, but the works of Thiers are interesting because so characteristic of the intelligent self-assured journalist and politician – Thiers was both – who strips every question, diplomatic or financial, from its contingencies and treats it as an intellectual problem to which, with the hindsight time has given him, he has no difficulty in finding the answer. Add to this the *petit bourgeois* delight in arm-chair strategy and a dish suited to the financial and martial tastes of the Gobsecks of the Garde Nationale or the zealots of the Napoleonic Legend was served.

Apart from the impact of Romanticism another reason giving impetus to historical studies under the Restoration was politics. Both the Monarchy itself, with its 'Ultra' supporters, and the constitutional opposition looked towards history; what could the former set against the glories of Napoleon if not the right of long possession conferred by history? This was part of the romance of

[4] Daniel Halévy, *Histoire d'une Histoire.*

history with the mystical religious admixture provided by Chateaubriand. The Opposition needed a more searching study of history to find – and some searchers always find what they are looking for – a justification, in the processes of history, for their political position. At this point we pass from the narrative to the interpretative school of history: Guizot, Tocqueville and Quinet. Thierry too had certain affinities with them.

Across the gulf separating nineteenth-century historians from their predecessors, this school has a connection with those who saw some purpose or meaning in history: a Bossuet, a Montesquieu, a Voltaire, a Mably; same attitude, different conclusions, each in tune with the temper of an age or a group. Guizot and Thierry, champions of the middle classes they sprang from, see these as carried inexorably by the tide of French history to political power; hidden within the folds of history from the beginnings was the 'Glorious Revolution' which appeared at the appointed hour – 1830. 'Whiggism' *in excelsis*! The titles of some of Guizot's works are in themselves illuminating: *Essais sur l'Histoire de France*[5] (1823) – not history but essays on history; *Histoire de la Civilisation en Europe* (1828), *Histoire de la Civilisation en France* (1828–30)[6] – facts are significant only when put into a meaningful pattern, which is the civilizing process.

But although Guizot and Thierry had a given perspective, this led them to the sources. Guizot's analysis of the early institutions of the French Monarchy in the *Essais* is masterly, as well as being the first; it is a model that Fustel de Coulanges was to follow later.

Nor does Guizot's contribution to the exploration of the 'terra incognita' of French history stop there. Such exploration depends on making the sources available to scholars. Here Guizot was helped by circumstances; 1830 was not only the triumph of Orleanist liberalism; it enabled Guizot from his position of power to organize the publication of historical documents,[7] thus setting an example followed by numerous learned societies and reviews,[8] to revivify existing institutions (e.g. l'Ecole des Chartes, founded 1821, and l'Ecole des Langues Orientales, founded 1795), to found others (e.g. l'Ecole d'Athènes, 1846) and to give a more powerful thrust to scholarship, controlled by the state, itself controlled by scholars of the Establishment.[9] The year 1830 appeared as the fitting conclusion of the French historical process to liberals of the

[5] Destined to be a complement to Mably's *Observations sur l'Histoire de France*.
[6] Both were courses of lectures given at the Sorbonne, 1828–30.
[7] *Documents inédits relatifs à l'Histoire de France*, 1835.
[8] Julian, *Historiens Français du 19e siècle* (1910), Preface.
[9] e.g. (besides Guizot) Thiers, Villemain, Cousin, Barante.

Guizot and Thierry stamp. Further movement must cease; Guizot's politics were the cutting edge of his historical attitude. Give the people education (e.g. his law on Primary Education, 1833); but only those paying a minimum of 200 frs., in short the bourgeoisie, those who, in the words of a later publicist,[10] have something in reserve, shall have the vote.[11] Not all the interpretative historians shared Guizot's allegiance to the 'parti de la résistance', e.g. Quinet (1803–75), a historian of revolutions (*Les Révolutions d'Italie*, 1848–52, *La Révolution*, 1865), determined to reveal their chain of cause and effect, but also a politico-historical polemist for whom 1830 was not an end but a beginning, the dawn of liberty, darkened only by those wanting to keep the people in tutelage (e.g. *Les Jésuites*, 1843), and a prophet of humanity on the march (e.g. *Ahasvérus*, 1833), much like the Lamennais of *Paroles d'un Croyant* and the Hugo of *La Légende des Siècles*.

At least the equal of Guizot amongst the interpretative historians, Tocqueville (1805–59) is far from sharing either Guizot's or Quinet's enthusiasms for 1830. He has been called 'the prophet of the Mass Age';[12] a prophet he is indeed, but without enthusiasm; the advance of democracy is irresistible, despite Guizot, and unwelcome, despite Quinet; democracy is a social phenomenon, the result of the equalization of social conditions. This process, at a greater or lesser tempo, is constant throughout the Christian world. Since we cannot arrest, we must understand the mechanism. The United States offered the perfect site for field study; there, planted in a virgin soil by self-governing Christian communities, the democratic ideal had been allowed to grow without the burden of distorting historical traditions or outside interference. Tocqueville spent a year in America (1831–2) accompanied by his friend Gustave de Beaumont, officially enquiring into the American penitential system but also studying American democracy on his own account. The result was *De la Démocratie en Amérique* (Part I, 1835, Part II, 1840), one of the great books of the nineteenth century and a permanent memorial to its author.

Part I provides a detailed analysis of American democracy, Part II discusses democracy in general. The great danger facing a mass of equal citizens is subjection to the power of one individual. This arises from centralization, which a variety of causes in a modern democracy conspire to produce: war, revolution, industrialization, above all individualism – 'rouille de la société moderne' – which,

10 André Siegfried.
11 This idea is admittedly not Guizot's own; it is already present in the First Constitution of the Revolution, where the distinction is made between the 'Citoyen actif' and the 'Citoyen passif'. It was adapted by the Restoration and July Monarchy. It is a facet of bourgeois paternalism.
12 J. P. Mayer, *Tocqueville*, 1939.

inward-looking and preferring equality to liberty, abdicates so willingly to the power seekers.[13]

The American miracle is precisely to have avoided that danger, because although social conditions are more equal there than anywhere, society remains fragmented in small semi-autonomous groups where the individual is obliged to take his share of the public weal; thus the sovereign people in American democracy is a reality. If the democracies, taking shape in Europe, are to avoid the dangers inherent in the process, decentralization is vital.

Nor did Tocqueville remain a theorist; like Guizot, but in opposition to him, he entered political life and, during the eight-year 'condominium' of Louis-Philippe and Guizot (1840–8), endeavoured to shake the régime from its complacent torpor, by warnings of the looming revolution. Though judging severely the inanity of the February Revolution,[14] he continued in political life during the Second Republic. Only when this first genuine French experiment in democracy had gone the way he had described in *De la Démocratie*... and made way for Louis Napoleon, was Tocqueville forced to abandon politics.

Of his experiences in and out of office during the years 1848 and 1849, Tocqueville has left a record in his *Souvenirs* (written 1850–1, published 1893) – an indispensable document for anyone wishing to get an insight into the period, nay more, an understanding of many permanent elements of nineteenth-century French politics. How far removed the *Souvenirs* are from the subjective attitude of a Chateaubriand! No reader can fail to be impressed by the integrity of the writer, a historian to the marrow, determined above all to carry out his declared intention of setting down an objective record of what he himself saw and did. Here is the ideal of the 'realist' period; as we stand looking over Tocqueville's shoulder at some of the street scenes he witnessed during the June Days, we expect Flaubert's Frédéric[15] to appear round the corner.

But the great work of Tocqueville's last years was *L'Ancien Régime et la Révolution* (1856), the first and only existing part of a work wherein he aimed to show the impact of the Revolution on nineteenth-century France. In *De la Démocratie* Tocqueville is a sociologist and political thinker, in *Les Souvenirs* the ideal chronicler, in *L'Ancien Régime* the historian; in all three the theme is democracy; democracy at its best; democracy consuming itself and falling into the pit; democracy emerging from the decay of an aristocratic society. First amongst the nineteenth-century historians of the

[13] For the analysis of individualism as a phenomenon of democracy, see especially *De la Démocratie*, Vol. II, Part ii, chap. 2.
[14] *Souvenirs*, chap. 1.
[15] *Education Sentimentale* – below, pp. 284–5.

Revolution to do so, Tocqueville shows how, beneath the violence and bloodshed, the continuity of French institutions largely remains.

The lucid analytical power is as evident here as in *De la Démocratie*. Unlike Guizot, who tends to see history as a series of intellectual problems, the solution of which is to be sought in documents, Tocqueville, whether studying a living society (America) or a vanished society (the *ancien régime*), studies primarily the psychology of the individual within the framework of his society. On the basis of the psychological mechanisms, he builds up a coherent view of a given society's fortunes. Thus in Tocqueville history merges with sociology. The result is impressive by its solidity, but the individuals by or through whom the forces of history, whatever they are believed to be, operate, and who for the narrative historian are in the centre of the stage, tend to become social units.

How different this is from the work of Jules Michelet (1798–1874): narrator, interpreter, philosopher, in a sense so broad as to be meaningless, he has a foot in every camp and stands at the peak of his generation's historians. The adversity of Michelet's early years was to colour his whole attitude to history.[16] Life had been a struggle and, in spite of the various stages in a successful career – 1822: entry into the teaching profession, 1827: lectureship in history and philosophy at the Ecole Normale Supérieure, 1831: Appointment as Director of the Historical Section, National Archives, 1838: chair of History and Ethics at the Collège de France – Michelet, with his ardent nature and vigorous imagination, saw life and history in those terms; history was the struggle of humanity – but for or against what?

Here too his early years were vital. From the ardent old republican who taught him to read Michelet imbibed a burning faith in the idea of liberty, the glory, therefore, of the French Revolution and the French nation which had delivered the message.

Two other influences reinforcing each other must also be mentioned: the Neapolitan historian-philosopher Vico (1668–1744), whom Michelet discovered in 1824 and whose *Scienza Nuova* he translated (*Principes de la Philosophie de l'histoire*, 1827), and Herder (1744–1803). Interest in Germany had been kindled in Michelet and his friend Quinet by Victor Cousin. Together they went to Heidelberg in 1828, discovered the Germany of Romanticism and scholarship, fell under its spell, which was to keep Michelet in thrall until 1870.[17] Herder in his *Ideen zur Philosophie der Geschichte der Menschheit* confirmed Vico.

---

16 *Le Peuple*, first chaps.
17 Quinet revised his views earlier: J. M. Carré, *Les Ecrivains Français et le Mirage Allemand*, chap. 6 (1947).

Thus before 1830 Michelet had the faith he was to live by, and his conception of history: a synthesis of all the factors that have moulded a people down the ages: soil and climate, men as individuals and in the mass, beliefs, legends, arts, philosophies.[18] Modern nations are the sum of all these factors, combining, reinforcing, neutralizing each other in an inextricable complex; they work through the living people who, in a sense therefore, may be regarded as an organism ceaselessly modifying itself, in time: 'Le mot de la *Scienza Nuova* est celui-ci: l'humanité: l'humanité est son oeuvre à elle-même. Dieu agit sur elle, mais par elle... Ce radicalisme historique ne va pas jusqu'à supprimer les grands hommes. Il en est sans doute, qui dominent la foule... Ils ne sont pas d'une autre espèce; l'humanité peut se reconnaître dans toute son histoire, une et identique à elle-même.'[19] History is not isolating and analyzing certain problems, tracing the growth of given institutions, or narrating events, which is like a diagram in two dimensions. The historian must see the past in the round, see history as a vast continuum of life sweeping the past into the present, the present into the future; his task is nothing less than... 'une résurrection intégrale du passé'.[20] In 1831 Michelet published two works: *Introduction à l'Histoire Universelle* and *Histoire de la République Romaine*. The first is an essay where, faithful to his philosophy, he gives history a meaning: humanity struggling against fate, the dead weight of matter, the powers of darkness, call it what you will, towards the light... of liberty, each nation in turn bringing its contribution, the last and greatest being that of the French Revolution; the second shows him already evoking early Roman history in its totality.

Like Quinet, Michelet saw the July Revolution as a glorious dawn – 'Dans ces jours mémorables', he writes, 'une grande lumière se fit et j'aperçus la France'.[21] What greater work for Michelet than to give France her history, which none had done hitherto, so that with a clearer understanding of herself, of the forging of her centralized unity, she could the better carry out her civilizing and liberating mission? His appointment at the National Archives nourished his ardour to release the life-force hidden in this wealth of documents: 'Ces papiers, ces parchemins... ne demandaient pas mieux que de revenir au jour.'[22]

With bold strokes, Michelet first paints his 'Tableau de la France'[23] – a people's history cannot be divorced from the soil it

[18] Carré, op. cit., chap. 5.
[19] Michelet, *Oeuvres choisies de Vico*, 1835, Introduction.
[20] *Histoire de France*, 1869, preface; it gives a good picture of his conception of history.
[21] 1869 preface, *Histoire de France*.   [22] 1833 preface, *ibid*.
[23] *Ibid*., Vol. II, and in Vol. I he describes the racial elements.

takes place on. Against this backcloth evoking the provinces, Michelet presents something like a vast pageant, the first part[24] of which carries the story from the beginnings to the death of Louis XI (1483).

Then the sequence of the pageant is suddenly interrupted. As the curtain rises again the spectator finds the scene has switched to the Revolution.[25] Michelet has become involved in the polemics of his own day; the July Monarchy has frozen into political immobility, the bourgeoisie are conspiring with the Church to enslave the people anew, perfidious Albion is in the way of French liberal nationalism's onward march; *Les Jésuites* (1843),[26] *Le Prêtre, la Femme et la Famille* (1845), *Le Peuple* (1846) reflect these species of wickedness in the face of which Michelet feels compelled to sacrifice the normal order of events and show the people of France their 'Greatest Hour', the whole epic of their coming of age from the Sack of the Bastille to Thermidor.

As the spectacle draws to a close, current events again take a hand; the Second Republic, almost smothered at birth by the 'June Days', falls before the sinister Bonaparte. Republicans are expelled from the 'Establishment'. Michelet's bitterness bursts out in the third part of his pageant,[27] which becomes a bitter attack on kings, emperors, prelates, monarchy, Catholicism. History has become propaganda. Michelet's cup of bitterness overflowed in 1870. His dream of the fraternity of nations under the leadership of republican France was shattered; the fourth part of his pageant[28] remains unfinished.

The pageant is as chaotic as life itself; without a prior knowledge of history, the motley crowd passing across the stage may be full of vitality, its movements are mere confusion. In the broadest sense Michelet has striven to show the complex processes whereby the French people achieved nationhood, in liberty. The task, as conceived under the guidance of Vico and Herder, is so vast that Michelet inevitably relies much on quickly moving scenes (e.g. a battle, Crécy) or objects (e.g. Gothic cathedrals, Dürer's 'Melancolia') or historical characters (e.g. Joan of Arc, Saint Louis, Louis XI, Danton, Robespierre) as symbols destined to give us insight into an age or event. So long as Michelet's personal feelings are not aroused, the method may be powerful or moving. It is at its best when Michelet evokes the Middle Ages, the people's religious aspirations made flesh in St. Louis, their patriotism in Joan of Arc,

[24] *Histoire de France*, Vols. I–VI, with first Preface, 1833–4.
[25] *Histoire de la Révolution*, 1847–53.
[26] In collaboration with Quinet.
[27] *Histoire de France*, Vols. VII–XVII, 1855–67. Complete edition with second Preface 1869.
[28] *Histoire du XIXe siècle*.

their cunning in Louis XI. But as the people march on to nation-hood and Michelet's feelings are aroused to enthusiasm or aggres-siveness by the events of his own day, the symbols become projec-tions of his own views, he is an apostle launching a message that was to colour the ideas of his countrymen for a long time: the mystique of the French Revolution. As manichean in his judgments as Lamennais or Hugo, he may still be, by his power and energy, at the peak of his generation's historians, but the peak has become eruptive, sulphurous... Romantic.

Critics had existed before the nineteenth century, but criticism as a separate art-form, with writers devoting themselves exclu-sively to it, discussing its problems and functions, as well as chart-ing the ever-broadening literary scene, is a nineteenth-century departure, provoked by a variety of causes: the steady growth of the reading public, and the consequent demand for guidance; the growth of journals both daily and monthly, itself the response to this increasing public appetite for news and reviews; last but not least, the development of historical studies themselves, which spilt over from national and political events to other spheres where the processes of development and change in a given society's life could be traced; literature for example. Literature became a recog-nized branch of humane studies; academe staked out a large claim, that of literary history in the new domain of criticism.

Even in the storm of the Revolution, and under the cramping conditions of the Empire, critics were not wanting: Laharpe and Marie-Joseph Chénier, the Classical rear-guard; Joubert, Fontanes, Julien-Louis Geoffroy (1743–1814), 'Establishment' figures but re-ceptive of new ideas; Chateaubriand, no mean critic when so minded, Madame de Staël, in whom opposition to Napoleon and liberalism conspired to produce a critical relativism, destined to exercise some influence on later critics.

The Romantic era saw critics of many different allegiances; divers members of the 'Arsenal' circle and others, all rallying to the defence of the new literary school, from Nodier himself to Ulrich Guttinger (1785–1866) and Emile Deschamps (1791–1871), from Théophile Gautier to Stendhal; journalists such as Jules Janin (1804–74), Gustave Planche (1808–57), and the Catholic legitimist Alfred Nettement (1805–69); a number of university scholars: Claude Fauriel (1772–1844), Guizot, Abel Villemain (1790–1870), Saint-Marc Girardin (1801–73), Désiré Nisard (1806–88), some of whom adopted clearly diversified critical positions; Villemain the historical relativist (e.g. *Tableau de la littérature au dix-huitième siècle*, 1828–9), Saint-Marc Girardin the moralist (e.g. *Cours de littérature dramatique*, 1843), Nisard the defender of the classical tradition (e.g. *Histoire de la littérature française*, 1844–9) and, like Saint-Marc Girardin, hostile to Romanticism.

Great in their own day, the reputation as critics of most of these men has faded; the names of some of them are remembered for other reasons. The only critic of the Romantic generation to retain vitality is Sainte-Beuve, who achieved a dominant position under the Second Empire and whom we shall accordingly return to later on in this book.

Part III

The Authority of Science

THE POSITIVIST AGE (1850–1870)

Chapter 16

POLITICAL AND INTELLECTUAL
BACKGROUND

THE 'June Days' (1848) had shown France to be mistrustful of the messianism that had infected the Republicans in Paris. The old adage, 'Paris makes revolutions and France accepts them', was no longer true; the provinces had taken their revenge; thereafter the Republic would pursue a prudent conservative course. The Red peril had changed bourgeois attitudes: Voltairian in the early days of the July Monarchy, they were ready now to return to the Catholic fold. As early as February 1848, Victor Cousin, symbol if ever there was one of the Louis-Philippe 'Establishment', had said to Rémusat: 'Courons nous jeter aux pieds des évêques; eux seuls peuvent nous sauver.'[1]

The Church too had ended its flirtation with liberalism. The 'Loi Falloux' (1850), which greatly increased its power in state secondary education as well as giving virtual freedom of education to Catholic schools, was the sign of the new orientation.

But the Republic was soon divided against itself; no cohesion in the centre, on the left the 'Mountain', on the right the Monarchists in disarray, and a new menace in the person of the President of the Republic, Louis Napoleon, elected (December 1848), like the National Assembly itself, by universal suffrage, and consequently with as good a mandate.

The Napoleonic Legend had been a powerful factor in his rise. Napoleon himself in *Le Mémorial de Sainte-Hélène* had been a skilful advocate in his own cause, establishing himself before posterity as the heir of the Revolution, the defender of equal opportunity: 'La Révolution eut pour but principal de détruire tous les privilèges ... elle proclama l'égalité des droits. Tous les citoyens purent parvenir à tous les emplois, selon leurs talents et les chances de la fortune';[2] of constitutional liberty: 'La paix dans Moscou accomplissait et terminait mes expéditions de guerre ... De retour en France ... j'eusse proclamé ses limites immuables; toute guerre

---

[1] A. Dansette, *Hist. religieuse de la France contemporaine*, Bk. VI, 3.
[2] Cte de Las Cases, *Mémorial de Sainte-Hélène* (1842), Vol. II, pp. 205, 206.

future, purement défensive; tout agrandissement nouveau, anti-national. J'eusse associé mon fils à l'empire; ma dictature eût fini, et son règne constitutionnel eût commencé...'[3]

The Restoration, by contrast, had provided the best culture for the germs to grow – in a spirit of dissatisfaction. The tricolor replaced by the white flag; 'the eighteenth year of the reign'; a char-ter... 'granted'... ('octroyé'); a spirit of inequality, privilege, reaction; the 'Holy Alliance'; 'the milliard of the émigrés'; and that fatal phrase 'les fourgons des alliés' that seemed to fasten the shame of defeat and the treaties of 1815 irrevocably on the Bour-bons – with all these pin-pricks, how easily could past hardships, conscription, political tyranny be consumed in the fire of present discontents.

On the moral plane we have already observed[4] how Napoleon, genius of war, Prometheus chained to his rock, could symbolize the cult of energy, of wild instinct, of individualism and revolt.

Thus already by 1830 there were two aspects of the Legend, the political – Napoleon, heir of the Revolution; and the moral – Napoleon, symbol of demonic energy.

The July Monarchy was to do its best to appropriate the former,[5] literature was to exploit the epic potential of the latter. Drama, poetry, fiction, history were all affected. What writer from Dumas *père* to Hugo, from Beyle to Balzac, from Béranger (1780–1857) to Thiers did not feel the spell. Béranger has three strings to his lyre: love, God, Napoleon.[6] Characteristically, he vulgarizes all three: love is no more than sentimentalized naughtiness in the Murger vein; God becomes 'Le Dieu des bonnes gens', Napoleon 'le petit caporal'. We are tempted to recall Hindenburg's habit of referring to Hitler as 'der Feldwebel'. But what a world of difference between the aristocrat's understandable dislike and tragic mis-judgment of the 'jumped-up' corporal and Béranger's technique of endearing familiarization; he, if anyone, created the carpet-slip-pered image of Napoleon in which guise he could shuffle so easily into the hearts of humble folk, especially the peasantry.

Long before the end of the July Monarchy the Legend, as a political force, had detached itself from Orleanism, because it had found a champion in Louis Bonaparte. He alone of the family be-lieved in their 'star' and skilfully drew its light and magic upon himself by pamphleteering; his *Idées Napoléoniennes* (1839) re-furbished, in a more accessible form, the ideas of the *Mémorial*,

---

[3] *Ibid.*, Vol. II, pp. 144, 145 (note special use of imperfect here with conditional force: would have accomplished, and would have terminated... The imperfect has greater persuasive force).

[4] See above, chap. 1.   [5] See above, chap. 9.

[6] When he was safely out of the way; during the Empire, Béranger had been anything but enthusiastic; cf. *Le Roi d'Yvetot*.

and the potential of democratic caesarism: in contrast to the existing order in France – a narrow bourgeois hegemony, and its foreign policy of immobility, lest the balance of power be disturbed, the reigning dynasties overthrown – a strong democracy within the framework of nationalism! Nor did he forget the social preoccupations of the day; his *Extinction du Paupérisme* (1844) promised war on want by a programme of public works on a big scale.

Louis Bonaparte's sword was less skilful[7] than his pen. None the less, by 1848 the Legend had grown into a political force; the proof was in the five million votes and more that carried Louis Bonaparte to the Presidency.

By keeping aloof from the National Assembly, Louis Bonaparte was able to create an image of himself as the bulwark of peace and of strong, efficient government; thus little regret was felt at the virtual demise of the Republic (December 1851), especially as the pockets of resistance Louis Bonaparte met with in some parts of France (e.g. Lyon and the south) enabled him to present his *coup d'état* as a protection of society against subversive elements.

In December 1852 the Republic was dead and the Bonapartist experiment in democratic caesarism began, supported at the outset by the majority: Monarchists and Catholics, bourgeoisie and peasantry. Such unanimity was not to last long; the one time carbonaro was pledged to promote Italian nationalism which was a threat to the temporal power of the papacy; the French garrison in Rome was not enough to reassure French Catholic opinion; the Emperor's efforts to compensate this by liberalizing the régime from 1860 onwards alienated conservative opinion without winning over republicans and democrats. Yet, but for the final and disastrous adventure of the war against Prussia, for which the régime revealed itself to be woefully unprepared, despite the 'last gaiter button', Napoleon III might have established his dynasty on the solid basis of material prosperity created by the industrial revolution, which was then getting into its stride; the 'fête impériale' was to be no vain term.

What gives the new age its particular *cachet* is the idea of authority. To it may be ascribed the political unity, albeit fragile, that set the Second Empire on its way; it had appealed to monarchists who in the absence of unity in their own ranks between 'Henriquinquistes' and Orleanists, were content, 'faute de mieux', with the authority of a strong government; it had appealed to ultramontane Catholics and their doughty champion Louis Veuillot (1813–1883), editor of *L'Univers*, to the bourgeoisie who had seen in it a guarantee of social order against socialism – had not that bogey-man

---

[7] cf. The Fiascos of Strasbourg, 1836, and Boulogne, 1840; the Prisoner of Ham, and his escape (engineered by the government?), 1846.

Pierre-Joseph Proudhon (1809–65), with his genius for lapidary phrases, so much more violent than his systematized ideas, dared to declare: 'La propriété, c'est le vol'?;[8] it had appealed, finally, to the peasantry for whom it had meant goodbye to the threat of 'la loi agraire'.[9]

The intellectual justification for an authoritarian régime resides in its claim to a monopoly of truth in the science of government. How far such a claim was valid for the Second Empire need not concern us; the important point is that the claim is rooted in a new ideal – science, with its twin poles of truth and falsehood to be set up as standards of value in place of the old ones derived from Rousseau (and Sade) of goodness and badness.

Sainte-Beuve, always sensitive to shifts of intellectual climate, was right, when, commenting on *Madame Bovary*,[10] he wrote: 'en bien des endroits et sous des formes diverses je crois reconnaître des signes littéraires nouveaux: science, esprit d'observation, maturité, force, un peu de dureté'. Sainte-Beuve was thinking only in terms of literature but the scientific spirit informs the age, and the intellectual force behind it is Auguste Comte (1798–1857).

Many of his ideas go back to the eighteenth century, to Montesquieu, Turgot, Condorcet. In Comte's systematic mind, ideas, submerged by the Romantic flood, take their place and, in orderly array, battle against what Comte regarded as the anarchic aftermath of the French Revolution. The desire to create an ordered and stable society remains the ultimate goal of all Comte's thought, an aim he has in common with thinkers only a little older than he but who remain Christian in inspiration (de Maistre and Bonald) whereas Comte retains from his Catholic upbringing in Montpellier only the Catholic attitude of mind that accepts no compromise; truth is one, not various.

Unlike other thinkers, however, Comte believed that to deal successfully with political and social problems was impossible without first re-examining intellectual attitudes. Institutions (i.e. politics) were built on custom, customs on beliefs; any plan for the first is futile without a previous survey of the second, itself futile without a general alignment of attitudes. 'Je regarde toutes les discussions sur les institutions comme de pures niaiseries jusqu'à ce que la réorganisation spirituelle de la société soit effectuée ou du moins fort avancée'.[11] Science will provide the common mould for beliefs.

---

[8] *Qu'est-ce que la propriété?* (1840).

[9] Originally, any law in Ancient Rome, designed to safeguard the right of poor citizens to a share in lands, annexed by conquest. The expression since the French Revolution was used loosely to mean the equal division of the soil.

[10] *Causeries du Lundi*, Vol. 13.   [11] Letter to Valat, 1824.

As early as 1822, when he was employed by Saint-Simon as secretary,[12] Comte establishes the close interrelation between science
and society in his *Plan des travaux scientifiques nécessaires pour
réformer la société*. Thereafter Comte's whole life was dedicated
to the methodical development of his early programme. The lack
of uniform ways of thinking about phenomena, which is at the root
of social anarchy, is summed up in what Comte regarded as an
important discovery about human mental processes – 'la loi des
trois états.' The habit of seeing all human development in a given
number of stages, which at the time of writing has reached a final
one alterable only in degree not in nature, is a habit nineteenth-
century writers and thinkers from Hugo to Karl Marx seem particularly prone to; Comte is no exception. There are three types
of mental attitude: the 'theological', the 'metaphysical', the 'positive'. Adumbrated in the *Plan des travaux* ... the law is developed
in the *Cours de Philosophie Positive*[13] (1830–42) and shown to
correspond with different stages in human development. Comte believes man began to emerge from the 'theological' state only with
the advent of Protestantism, from the 'metaphysical' only with the
French Revolution. In the past, men have slipped easily into ambivalent attitudes – a scientific or positive approach to natural phenomena with, for example, a belief in miracles – unaware that these
two positions are unrelated and irreconcilable; the Cartesian compromise will not do; the three mentalities still coexist. The great
hope for the future is that thanks to Comte's law men will be
aware of the different types of attitude and may slowly be brought
to a uniform, positive way of looking at the whole range of phenomena. To this end Comte undertakes a systematic review of all the
branches of science, placing them in relation to each other, allotting
to each a specific function, ensuring that everywhere the proper
and uniform attitude of mind is in control. The hierarchy of the
sciences starts from the most general and abstract, the furthest removed from the human level – mathematics, and ends at the most
complex, the most integrated, the most vital to man – sociology,
what Comte calls 'la physique sociale';[14] Comte was the first to
establish it as a science on its own.

The vigour and encyclopaedic breadth of Comte's mind is impressive. In the manner of Descartes but on a much bigger scale,
he sets out to bring order into the seemingly inextricable complex
of phenomena; Comte's chart of scientific knowledge, where every

[12] They quarrelled in 1824 and accused each other of plagiarism.
[13] Lesson 1. The terms 'theological' and 'metaphysical' are used by
Comte in a particular sense, the former to mean the attitude that attributes
natural phenomena to the independent will of gods, the latter to mean
attributing them to invariable forces.
[14] Mathematics, astronomy, physics, chemistry, biology, sociology.

known science is allotted its position in relation to all others, shall give humanity a guide, his method a compass, in nature. Comte seems familiar with every branch of science; he speaks with the authority of knowledge and system. Originality may not be the keynote of Positivism, but to bring system, to create order in the chaos of acquired knowledge has its value as much as to be original which is to be different, to create disorder in fact! The systematic nature of Positivism accounts in part for its impact; Comte's ponti-fical tones, calm assurance, his almost naïve optimism must have contributed to it too, in spite of the ponderous stodginess of the style![15] M. Comte knows everything, has an answer to everything; the infinite complexities of the factors bearing on human societies have no terrors for M. Comte. In the end we derive the impression that his mind is rigid, pitched on the register of absolute certainty, uninhibited by doubts or appropriate scientific humility. If the characteristic trait of the scientific mind is to be self-critical and always on the edge of doubt, Comte, who thought himself scientific in a supreme degree, seems a victim of theoretical ideas, no longer verified by the touchstone of experiment.

This is particularly true in the *Système de Politique Positive* (1851–4). With all the preliminary work done, with the chaos of 1848 as an added spur, Comte now approaches the peak of his endeavour: society must be thought out anew on a scientific basis.

The task inevitably brought him up against the moral question: how will the supreme designer of society ensure that men at all levels will show that essential 'altruism',[16] without which no society can hang together? Comte had no better answer than to invent his own religion, with the example of great men as the spur to human endeavour – the religion of humanity under another name.[17]

Comte's attitude is authoritarian; liberty consists in understand-ing the laws of nature and in obeying them,[18] scientists and gov-ernment are at one. Yet Comte originally welcomed the establish-ment of the Second Republic. Why? Because the July Monarchy appeared to him and others like him to have become, in its turn, a bastion of interests and privilege, inimical therefore to progress; surely a republic would eschew sectional interests and be governed

---

[15] 'Si je m'abandonnais à mon goût personnel, je serais peut-être aussi peu favorable que vous à M. Auguste Comte qui me semble le plus souvent répéter en mauvais style ce qu'ont pensé et dit ... en très bon style, Des-cartes, d'Alembert, Condorcet, Laplace.' Renan, *Réponse à M. Pasteur* (1882).

[16] Comte coined the word.

[17] *Système de Politique Positive, instituant la Religion de l'Humanité* (1851–4).

[18] *Catéchisme Positiviste* (1852), 4e entretien.

by disinterested knowledge? Comte did not long retain that hope; he shed no tears at the shipwreck of 1851. By then he had come to believe power should be concentrated in the hands of one man, advised by experts. Louis Bonaparte with his formula of democratic caesarism seemed the answer.

Chapter 17

THE NOVEL
REALISTS AND OTHERS

THE early manifestations of Realism, so-called, appear before the full impact of Positivism was felt and accord well with the prudential middle-of-the-road attitudes of the Louis-Philippian bourgeoisie, but, in the new climate, Realism was bound to thrive; science means knowledge, knowledge implies the assembling of data; what if not the recording of data was the artistic aim of the Realists? That ideal is fully reflected in the art of Gustave Courbet (1819–77), just as the ideal of Romanticism had been reflected in the art of Delacroix; in the latter, violence, passion, cruelty, action, depicted and suggested by the artist's lurid and sombre palette, dark reds and greens predominating; in the former, dispassionate statement of observed facts. The difference in attitude between the two artists accounts also for the different sources of their inspiration; in the latter, history (e.g. *Entrée des Croisés à Constantinople*, or *Massacre de Scio*), literature (e.g. *Dante et Virgile aux enfers*), politics (e.g. *La liberté guidant le peuple*), wild animals (e.g. *Chasse au tigre*); in all of them Delacroix' imagination could and did reign supreme. Where it could not (e.g. the scenes taken from life on his Algerian journey), how dull he often is! Direct observation, far from stimulating, seemed to bore him.

In Courbet the position is reversed; he is at his best when subjected to the 'authority' of what he sees around him in nature or the contemporary scene (e.g. *Enterrement à Ornans*, *La Rencontre*); his art is faithful recording, but as a result it is static, in contrast to the vitality of Delacroix.

The Realist novelists claim as their precursor Henri Monnier (1805–77), author of *Scènes populaires* (1830), of which Joseph Prudhomme is the hero. They could with at least equal justification have pointed to an earlier one – Restif de la Bretonne (1734–1806) who, in his voluminous writings, reflects the very characteristics – down-to-earth sincerity, harsh facts, even documentation[1] – the writers of 1850 claimed as theirs, under the rallying cry of Realism. The word is so general that it can cover a multitude of meanings

---

[1] See Maynial, *L'Epoque réaliste* (1931).

from Boileau's ideas of 'le vrai', i.e. the normal or average, to the egocentric sincerity of the Romantics.

New schools seek to define their position against their immediate predecessors. The Realists of the 1850's are no exception; the lyrical effusions of the Romantics were anathema, so, incidentally, were the contemporaneous doctrines of the protagonists of art for art's sake, and for the same reason: both offended against the principle of sincerity as the Realists understood it. Invoked by every successive school, sincerity for the Realists meant the exact registering of life around them; the emphasis is on objective observation, with rigorous exclusion of any 'slanting', to borrow from journalese, for 'slanting' means selection either to inject subjective comment or to achieve some effect inherent in the object but not apparent without the artist's intervention; objective, unimaginative daguerreotype was the ideal.

This results in pushing the selective process a stage further back, namely to the choice of scenes to be recorded. Here again the Realists were reacting against the Romantics; to scenes of 'high life' in Romantic fashion, they would oppose scenes of 'low life'; the more sordid the scene, the more vulgar the characters or commonplace the dialogue and style, the greater the sincerity. Often the scenes presented were from direct experience, but where this was lacking, documentation would take its place.

The impact of Balzac on all this is evident enough, but the theorist and founder of the Realist school was Champfleury[2] (1821–89) – 'le Courbet de la littérature', as he was called. Champfleury draws the lessons he had derived from Courbet's art: 'sérieux et convaincu, ironique et brutal, sincère et plein de poésie';[3] he applies it in a series of novels: *Les Aventures de Mlle Mariette* (1853), *Les Bourgeois de Molinchard* (1854), *Les Souffrances du Professeur Delteil* (1856), *La Succession Le Camus* (1858). The preface of *Mlle Mariette*, which is in the form of an article purporting to come from the pen of a critic hostile to the Realist school, also gives, by inference, the principles Champfleury and the school stand for: 'Mais la vie moderne n'est pas instructive. Est-il rien de plus facile que de copier les individus qui se promènent devant nous, de les écouter causer, de reproduire leurs conversations, comme par la sténographie? Il ne manquerait plus que de dessiner en tête leur portrait au daguerréotype!' Precisely.

Henry Murger (1822–61) is chiefly remembered, thanks largely to Puccini, for his *Scènes de la vie de Bohème* (1849), a vein he had found within his own youthful experience and, with its coating of

---

[2] Real name – Jules Husson.
[3] The quotation comes from his critical study of Courbet in *Souvenirs et portraits de jeunesse* (1872).

sentiment, so successful that he exploited it further in *Scènes de la vie de Jeunesse* (1851), *Le Pays Latin* (1851), *Les Buveurs d'Eau* (1853). Only in his *Sabot Rouge* (1860), a sombre peasant story, does Murger leave the conventional setting of the Latin Quarter.

Founder of an ephemeral review, *Le Réalisme* (1856), Duranty (1833–80) published three realist novels: *Le Malheur d'Henriette Gérard* (1860), *La Cause du beau Guillaume* (1862) and *La Canne de Mme Desrieux, époque de 1822* (1862). He was also the author of a *Théâtre des Marionnettes du jardin des Tuileries* (1862) which is the source of many of the puppet shows that are the joy of children to this day in the Tuileries Gardens and the Champs Elysées. His later novels written in collaboration with Paul Alexis belong properly to the Naturalist period.

Between 1860 and 1870 Edmond and Jules de Goncourt wrote in collaboration a number of novels which by their aim to be so many physiological or social studies, by their documentary character, fit into the Realist pattern. On the other hand they stand closer to the Naturalists and will accordingly be discussed later.[4]

Ernest Feydeau (1821–73), friend of Flaubert and Théophile Gautier, was both archaeologist, in a superficial way, and novelist. His *Histoire des usages funèbres et des sépultures des peuples anciens* (1857–61) was a valuable stimulant to the imagination of Gautier for his excursions into classical antiquity, and to Ancient Egypt; the author of *Le Roman de la Momie* was not to see Egypt himself until 1869. Feydeau's first novel, *Fanny* (1858), followed by *Daniel* (1859), enjoyed unmerited success, thanks perhaps to the support of Sainte-Beuve. A comparison between *Fanny* and *Madame Bovary*, which it apes, soon reveals the flimsy pretentiousness of the former. Why these novels which are more in line with the personal type of novel and full of romantic episodes should have been hailed as fine examples of Realism is not easy to see.

In a much higher category than Feydeau, by his intellect and his artistic integrity, stands Jules Barbey d'Aurevilly (1808–89). No immediate relation appears between him and Realism which he condemned. In his youth as a law student at Caen, Barbey had indeed caught the democratic fever; it was short lived. Thereafter as critic, which he remained by harsh necessity, he speaks of democracy as 'la souveraineté de l'ignoble'; high Catholic and monarchist, he admires de Maistre, Bonald, Chateaubriand, Lamennais.[5] The critical attitudes, often penetrating,[6] remain uncompromisingly within the framework of those ideas;[7] evidently he remains outside

---

[4] See Vol. V, chap. 2, i.
[5] *Prophètes du Passé* (1851).
[6] He was an early admirer of Baudelaire.
[7] *Les Hommes et les Oeuvres*, 26 Vols. (1860–1909).

the political and literary worlds of his day; his spiritual home is the aristocratic 'faubourg St Germain'.

As a writer of fiction, again on a first impression, the reader would be tempted to class him as a late Romantic, which in part he is. His story-tellers[8] – Brassard, Ravila, Torty – are all aristocratic, aloof, cynical, in a word dandies, the image of their creator. What more Romantic than the series of historical tales, *L'Ensorcelée* (1854), *Le Chevalier des Touches* (1864), *Un Prêtre Marié* (1865), which form a veritable Norman cycle in their evocation of local adventures and tragedies at the time of the Revolution? – in the manner of Walter Scott. Or again his evident delight in extremes – cruelty, valour, adventure, passion, fidelity in adversity, his belief as an artistic principle that extremes in character and theme alone can produce the desired impact; this too puts him in the same bracket as the author of *Les Misérables*, and *L'Homme qui rit*. Furthermore it puts him at the head of a line of story-tellers from Villiers de L'Isle Adam and Léon Bloy down to Georges Bernanos in whose work cruelty and suffering, passion and religion combine to martyrize hero and reader.

Yet beneath it all a strong residuum remains that shows him to be at least a contemporary of the Realists. A comparison between Balzac's *Les Chouans*, Hugo's *93* and Barbey's *Le Chevalier des Touches* is instructive here. *Les Chouans* is written with verve; it is reminiscent of an early adventure film with opposing forces marching, counter-marching, skirmishing at such breathless speed that the spectator loses the thread of what the film is about though in the end he may feel he's had his money's worth; *93* begins, characteristically, in darkness and ends with a concomitant execution and suicide. Scarcely any relation exists between the action and reality, much with Hugo's artistic formula (antithesis) and his political ideas.

In contrast with both of these, *Le Chevalier des Touches* is rooted in historic reality – the characters were figures of Barbey's childhood; even the hero existed and survived as a human wreck whom the narrator had found, in a home for the aged. The action is lucid and develops against a background Barbey knew intimately and loved. The same applies, *mutatis mutandis*, to the other stories. Barbey may not like the reality of the Realists but he likes reality. 'Ah, les plaisirs de l'observateur, que j'ai toujours mis au-dessus de tous les autres', exclaims Doctor Torty;[9] evidently Barbey's mouthpiece. If we except the Goncourt brothers and still more Barbey, only recently coming into his own, none of the Realists of the strict obedience deserves much individual attention, but, with their claim

[8] *Les Diaboliques* (1874).
[9] *Les Diaboliques*; 'Le bonheur dans le crime'.

to objectivity, their choice of subjects, they are as a group a sign-post of the time.

On the artistic level their principles had certain results. Their vaunted objectivity tends to produce novels where plot is reduced to a minimum; the reader is offered a succession of static scenes, whence a risk of monotony compensated for – the reader after all needs to be considered – by sentiment; a new sugary romanticism is born that leads to the novelette, about love in the attic (e.g. Murger).

Another compensatory factor is the taste for farce and caricature – an exaggeration in a new direction. The age, be it noted, is not only that of the Realist novelists and painters but also a great age of caricature: Daumier (1808–79), Gavarni (1804–66), Cham (1819–79), Philipon (1800–62).

Finally the emphasis on the visual leads to a fading of the inner life of the characters; they must be seen from the outside only, to look beneath the surface means creating a mentality, which in turn means the writer's own imagination coming into play and by definition he has foregone that right. Thus individual characters merge, lifeless, into the scene; the emphasis is on social groups, scenes, society – Balzac again! But, as we have seen, that is only one side of him. In so far as the individual character retains any personality, it is representative of his social group (e.g. M. Prud-homme) or his profession.

Barbey condemns all this, yet his obsessive hatred of the 'bour-geoisisme' of the Realists gives him a relation with them by oppo-sites. By it also he stands close to the author of *Bouvard et Pécu-chet*. Flaubert would turn in his grave if in this age we followed the example of his own and thought of him as a Realist, albeit the greatest. He rejected them; yet no more than Barbey can he be divorced from them; he transcends categories but is well planted in his age.

If success in an author's own day justifies a place, be it never so small, in a history of literature, mention must be made of Octave Feuillet (1821–90), the popular purveyor of idealist novels for the upper classes during the Second Empire and early years of the Third Republic. Characteristic of his style is the ineffable *Roman d'un jeune homme pauvre* (1856), an improving tale about how the scion of a noble house, orphaned and ruined, restores his for-tunes and those of his young sister by honest work and impeccable moral sentiments. The Romantic idealism running through the story like a cloying stream of synthetic honey, emphasized by the stylistic and moralizing clichés of melodrama ('les détestables hasards de la Bourse'; 'le digne vieillard...'; 'soutenu par les mains pieuses de sa petite-fille ...'; 'le noble visage ...'; 'au milieu des bruyants plaisirs'; 'la source de ces larmes sacrées ...' etc.), almost sticks the pages together and is in no way corrected by the supposedly realistic picture of contemporaneous 'high life'. False sentiment and lack of genuine observation combine to make what Huysmans justifiably described as 'les juleps de Feuillet'.[10]

Less pretentious and more entertaining are the stories of the journalist Edmond About (1825–85), e.g. *Le Roi des Montagnes* (1857), a story of Greek banditry 'moderne-style' – stripped, that is, of all Romantic exoticism and attuned to a commercial age that would appreciate the joke of bandits plying their trade on the basis of a limited liability company; essays in the fantastic: *Le cas de M. Guérin* (1862), *L'Homme à l'oreille cassée* (1862) and *Le nez d'un notaire* (1862). Much verve, often anti-clerical – e.g. *La Question romaine* (1859), compensated for by touching tales illustrating democratic patriotism and the virtues of 'la morale laïque' – e.g. the stories with the general title *La vieille Roche*, notably *Le Roman d'un brave homme* (1874).

More sympathetic are the once highly successful tandem Emile Erckmann (1822–99) and Alexandre Chatrian (1826–90), whose collaboration began in 1847. Alsatians, both of them, they had but to dip into their memories of the tales they had heard in their childhood, from local peasants and workmen, of the allied invasion, following the collapse of the First Empire. These eye-witness accounts formed the basis of their best fiction, which is both Romantic and Realist: *Le Fou Yégof* (1862), *Madame Thérèse* (1863), *L'Ami Fritz* (1864, dramatized 1876), *Histoire d'un conscrit de 1813* (1864), *Waterloo* (1865), *Histoire d'un paysan* (1868) – a broad canvas of the Revolutionary and Napoleonic Saga, and the impact of invasion painted with fidelity to realistic detail: fire and carnage, dead and dying, smell of corpses; no concession here to sentiment. Zola applauds this realism, which, as he notes,[11] was condemned at the time by some critics; his reservations[12] lay not with the social picture but with the credibility of the characters. The optimism, natural to the authors, and reflected in the bonhomie of the characters, with, here and there, an unconvincing villain, could not satisfy Zola's Naturalistic conception of human motivation. But the smiling sentiment notwithstanding, which after the loss of Alsace in 1870 helped to create sentimental images of the lost province in French minds, there is in stories such as *Le Fou Yégof*, *Madame Thérèse*, in some of the *Contes populaires* (1866), notably in the charming *Confessions d'un joueur de Clarinette* or

---

[10] *Là-Bas*, chap. 1.
[11] Zola, *Mes Haines*.   [12] *Ibid.*

Un Juif polonais (dramatized 1869) – a study in the sense of guilt, much human truth.

.   .   .

That the scientific enthusiasms of the Positivist era should have found an outlet in fiction was characteristic of the age and the creator of science fiction deserves to appear in a catalogue of lesser writers of the Second Empire, by his inventive verve and massive production. Jules Verne (1828–1905) may rank as a Dumas *père* of the new age. The latter's characters, by a quick change of clothes, by 'crash courses' in science (elementary grade) and geography, could well have been members of the balloon party of *Cinq semaines en ballon* (1863), or dug their way into the bowels of the earth (*Voyage au centre de la Terre*, 1864) or signed on as members of gallant Captain Némo's crew in the *Nautilus* (*Vingt mille lieues sous les mers*, 1870) or displayed the inexhaustible resourcefulness of Passe-Partout (*Le Tour du Monde en quatre-vingts jours*, 1873); in short, Romantic energy transposed from the imaginative realms of history to the no less Romantic unknowns of the earth and the universe.

Comte Arthur de Gobineau (1816–82) was a widely travelled diplomat (Europe, Western and Eastern, Persia, the Americas). Some of his writings are the product of his journeyings, e.g. *Trois ans en Asie, 1855–58* (1859), *Les Religions et les philosophies dans l'Asie centrale* (1865), *Histoire des Perses d'après les auteurs Orientaux* (1869). To these may be added the collection of Oriental stories in *Souvenirs de Voyage* (1872) and *Nouvelles Asiatiques* (1876).

Besides being an observant and scholarly diplomat, interested, as few men in the France of his day were, in the mentalities of eastern peoples as reflected in their history and culture, Gobineau was a political philosopher whose ideas are to be found in his *Essai sur l'inégalité des races humaines* (1853–55); they also inspired one at least of his fictional works, *Les Pléiades* (1874).

Influenced by the Positivism of his generation and the ideas of Taine, he emphasized particularly the notion of race, proclaiming the superiority of the 'Aryan' races in general and the Nordic type in particular. Houston Stewart Chamberlain, a Germanized Englishman, popularized Gobineau's ideas in Germany where in due course they were adopted as the philosophic justification for Hitler's racial and 'Herrenvolk' policies. But Gobineau's racialism developed into an individualistic authoritarianism, reflected in *Les Pléiades*,[13] which is both a sentimental novel with discreet autobiographical elements[14] and a political novel.

---

[13] Re-edited by Plon with introduction by M. Jean Mistler, 1963.
[14] His friendship with Comtesse de la Tour, whom he met at Stockholm in 1872. See Introduction.

The story of the three young men, a Frenchman, Louis de Laudon, an Englishman, Wilfrid Nore, and a German, Conrad Lanze, and their respective affairs of the heart, is conventional, the characters wooden. The interest of the work arises from the author's political ideas, his authoritarian conservatism, his aristocratic pessimism at the progress of democracy. The enthusiasm of the day for material progress, Positivist optimism, touched him no more than Baudelaire; his faith foreshadowing Nietzsche was pinned to the successive emergence of the 'élites', of the heroes, the *Pléiades* of the title through whom alone human progress can be achieved; humanity for the most part is made up of fools, pretentious asses and cads – on that point the three friends are agreed; but from this grim multitude arise in infinitesimal numbers, so Lanze says, 'des êtres lumineux, entrecroisant leurs pas dans des courbes célestes...; constellations, réunions, groupes, soit fixés, soit errants, cela seul est digne d'admiration et d'amitié...'.[15]

This aristocratic attitude, which is like a later nineteenth-century transposition of the Romantic idea of genius, is very different from the determinism inherent in racialism; Gobineau grafts the former on to the latter by the tenuous link of purer heredity working in what he calls 'fils de roi', but the expression has no class nor ultimate biological significance, it is a question of individual character: 'je suis fils de roi', declares Nore, 'ne veut nullement dire – mon père n'est pas négociant, militaire, écrivain, artiste, banquier, chaudronnier ou chef de gare ... cela signifie je suis d'un tempérament hardi et généreux ... l'indépendance de mon esprit, la liberté la plus absolue dans mes opinions sont des privilèges inébranlables de ma noble origine.'[16]

Laudon, Nore and Lanze had become friends because each had recognized that the other two were 'sons of kings'. But the word heredity used in this way has no meaning except that a man is the son of his parents, and cannot be used as a 'herrenvolk' argument; rather could it be seen as a forerunner, through Nietzsche, of the heroism to be found in the 1920's in the work of Saint-Exupéry and Malraux.

[15] Bk. I, chap. 2. [16] Bk. I, chap. 2.

Chapter 18

FLAUBERT

THE works of Gustave Flaubert (1821–80) fall into two separate groups: the early writing, the works of his maturity. The former he never published; no doubt he looked upon some of them at least as sources to draw on if need be and to be destroyed ... some time. They never were; had they been, later generations would have been the poorer, for they give a valuable insight into the development of Flaubert as a writer, with precocious literary gifts.

The early writings comprise, *inter alia*: *Opuscules Historiques* (1835 and 1836); *Rêve d'Enfer* (1837) and *Smarh* (1839); an essay entitled *Une leçon d'histoire naturelle, Genre Commis* (1837); a number of short stories; two autobiographical fragments, *Mémoires d'un fou* (1838), and *Novembre* (1842) a full scale novel: *L'Education Sentimentale*, first version (1845).

With their wide variety of subject the juvenilia reflect the literary fashions of the day ... 'Expansions dernières du Romantisme arrivant jusqu'à nous et qui, comprimées par le milieu provincial, faisaient dans nos cervelles d'étranges bouillonnements...',[1] writes Flaubert of himself and his friends at school. The romance of history, ecstatic visions, pseudo-sociological analysis in the manner of the popular ... 'physiologies', romantic tales that recall at every turn Hugo and George Sand, Balzac and Musset. 'Nous méritions peu d'éloges ... Mais quelle haine de toute platitude! Quels élans vers la grandeur! Quel respect des maîtres![2] Flaubert was to remain faithful throughout his life to some at least of his youthful idols: Hugo, Balzac; he was to become a devoted friend and correspondent of George Sand.

Already something of the pattern and characteristics of the mature works is apparent; the cruelty and violence of *Salammbô* in the historical sketches, the chaotic visions and temptations of St Antony in those of *Smarh*,[3] inspired by Edgar Quinet's *Ahasvérus* (1833); an early image of Emma Bovary in the heroine of *Passion et Vertu* (1837), a mentality that sours every experience: 'Elle pen-

---

[1] Flaubert: Louis Bouilhet, *Dernières Chansons*, Préface.
[2] *Ibid.*   [3] Could the name have been suggested by Nodier's *Smarra*?

sait aux sensations qu'elle avait éprouvées et ne trouvait en y pensant rien que déception et amertume. "O ce n'est pas ce que j'avais rêvé" disait-elle'; in the *Genre Commis* the irony that was to play about the ineffable Homais and that pathetic couple Bouvard and Pécuchet.

Most important of all the early works, however, are the autobiographical pieces and the first novel. The corrosive scepticism of later years is apparent in the seventeen-year-old author of *Mémoires d'un fou*. What a compelling indictment of man, of life's futility! The escape to art as the only compensation is already developed: 'S'il y a sur la terre et parmi les néants une croyance qu'on adore, s'il est quelque chose de saint, de pur, de sublime, quelque chose qui aille à ce désir immodéré de l'infini et du vague que nous appelons âme, c'est l'art.'

Into this background of romantic anguish is entwined, like a delicate thread, the story of Maria. This is the first allusion to Elisa Foucauld,[4] whom Flaubert met at Trouville in the summer of 1836 – a brief encounter, but the impression made on the youthful Gustave is apparent: 'Elle partit le matin, nous le soir; elle partit et je ne la revis plus. Adieu pour toujours! Elle partit comme la poussière de la route qui s'envola derrière ses pas...' The sadness of the parting gathers force by the repetition of 'elle partit...'; first the fact, then the result for himself, and then, the emotion resolves itself in a simile. This probably softened the writer's pain; similes have that cathartic effect on the emotions; they relieve tension. To the reader, the image conveys the sense of desolation forcibly. Already Flaubert the stylist is alert; already he understands what the reader of *Madame Bovary* in particular will understand so well, how to create a vigorous image in the reader's mind, and stimulate *his* emotion.

Flaubert was to meet the Schlésingers again in Paris; Elisa's memory was to remain with him throughout his life and have important consequences for his work.

If the *Mémoires d'un fou* recall Flaubert's adolescent years, *Novembre* offers us the image of him on the threshold of manhood. The title of this compelling piece of self-analysis scarcely suggests that divine moment, which Flaubert seems to have enjoyed as much as others, but it is symbolic of his melancholy dissatisfaction engendered partly perhaps by his dislike of the legal studies he had just embarked on in deference to his family's wishes,[5] partly by the lusts of the flesh.

[4] Although living with Maurice Schlésinger at the time and passing as his wife, she was not able to regularize this situation until after the death of her first husband, Emile Judée, in 1840.
[5] He pursued them with disgruntled conscientiousness and not entirely without success from 1841 to 1843.

The first version of *L'Education Sentimentale* (February 1843–January 1845) is a veiled confession. In the character of Henry Gosselin, the young provincial, who comes to Paris without enthusiasm to study law, the reader recognizes Flaubert. Henry's love for Emilie Renaud, their New York escapade, the taste of harsh reality that killed romance, their return to France and to the even flow of their respective lives have little or no relation with Flaubert's personal experience; that little may or may not reflect the truth of his relationship with Elisa Schlésinger whom he had met again in 1843.

Be that as it may, Flaubert has obeyed the almost inevitable law that obliges the young novelist[6] to draw upon his own fund of ideas and feelings for want of the broad experience of life that time, observation and percipience alone may give. The element of confession is to be sought in the analysis both of Henry and of his friend Jules. As a novel, the work serves to show by comparison the strides Flaubert was to make as an artist in the years separating this version from the second, and, incidentally, the artistic standards that forbade him to publish a work many other authors would have thought worthy. But in the attitudes of Henry and Jules towards life, in the development of their artistic ideas, we can see much of Flaubert's own progress from youth to maturity, his sentimental education in the broadest sense.

Starry-eyed provincial at the outset ('Mais Henry... croyait encore... à toute la réalité du bonheur de la vie, époque d'illusions, où l'amour bourgeonne dans l'âme'), Henry learns that love is transient; he becomes a man of the world, cynically indifferent to events and happier in consequence: 'il se résigna à la perte de sa belle passion évanouie... comprenant bien qu'il entrait alors dans une autre période de sa vie et que l'amour aussi est un drame complet... qui a son premier acte... et son cinquième enfin, où il doit mourir... pour faire place ensuite au vaudeville ou à quelque autre comédie plus sérieuse et tout aussi bouffonne.'[7] He develops, in short, into a society hedonist with artistic ideas as shallow as the attitudes of the Parisian circles he moves in.

Jules's narrower provincial life provides him with parallel disappointments. Deceived by the actress Lucinde, frustrated in his ambitions as a playwright, he becomes harsh and embittered: 'il s'était endurci.... s'était presque pétrifié le coeur...'[8] His reflections lead him to a determinist philosophy but he finds an abundant compensation in art: 'n'y a-t-il pas au monde une manière quelconque d'arriver à la conscience de la vérité? Si l'art était pour

---

[6] Flaubert was only twenty-two when he began writing *L'Education Sentimentale* (I).
[7] *Oeuvres de Jeunesse*, Vol. 3, p. 227, Conard.
[8] *Ibid.*, p. 43.

lui ce moyen, il devait le prendre. Et même aurait-il eu cette idée
de l'art ... sans les douleurs préparatoires qu'il avait subies?'

From this point, the novel develops into a comparison between
the artistic attitudes of the two friends. As an essay in analysis
it is searching and gives a foretaste of the pitiless dissection Emma
Bovary will be subjected to, but in the process the illusion of
reality, in so far as the novel had succeeded in creating it for
the reader, fades. Only the incident of the stray dog that attaches
itself to Jules, in spite of the latter's efforts to drive it away,
provides a momentary and brilliant flame of vitality by its precision of detail. Yet in relation to the story the incident seems
gratuitous and the reader looks for some symbolic purpose; with
the hindsight provided by a knowledge of *Madame Bovary* he may
see a parallel in the case of the beggar whose three separate ap-
pearances are like some grotesque commentary at a moment of
emotional tension, as unwelcome as a worm in an apple or a leering
skull in the background of a beautiful young woman's portrait. But
the beggar incidents are skilfully interwoven; they serve to underline now Emma's attitude of defiant desperation (her last five-franc
piece thrown to him), now the smugness of Monsieur Homais;
even his last appearance, as Emma lies dying, contrived though it
is, is motivated by the offer Homais had made to him in an un-
guarded moment of 'une pommade antiphlogistique de sa composition', and his croaking song has a hideous relevance to Emma's
tragedy.

If specific proof were needed of development in Flaubert's skill
between 1845 and 1857 these parallel cases would provide it. In
fact the incident of the dog, however excellent in itself, has no other
purpose than to make Jules reflect more deeply than hitherto, to
look with more attention beyond the surface of things at their
inner significance and relationships: 'dans tout ce qui s'était passé
entre lui et le monstre, dans tout ce qui se rattachait à cette aven-
ture, il y avait quelque chose de si intime, de si profond, de si net
en même temps qu'il fallait bien reconnaître une réalité d'une autre
espèce et aussi réelle que la vulgaire cependant, tout en semblant
la contredire. Or ce que l'existence offre de tangible, de sensible,
disparaissait à sa pensée, comme secondaire et inutile et comme
une illusion qui n'en est que la superficie.'[9] Jules's conceptions about
art as a reflection of life are now transformed; away with Romanticism and its tawdry trappings! Salvation must be found in objective observation of detail, in rigorous analysis, not in personal emotion but in knowledge.

At this stage the comparison between Henry and Jules is all to

[9] See particularly *L'Education Sentimentale* (I), pp. 258, 267–9, 279.
Oeuvres de Jeunesse, Vol. 3, Conard.

the advantage of the latter; Flaubert, ceasing to identify himself with Henry, has evidently migrated into the skin of Jules; or more precisely there is something of him in both their attitudes: the cynical pessimism that leads Henry after the bankruptcy of his relationship with Emilie to expect from life 'quelque autre comédie plus sérieuse et tout aussi bouffonne . . .' and Jules's new percipience.

None of the other characters is subject to the same exercise of intellectual dissection as Henry and Jules. But in a narrow compass some of them have a certain vividness: the worthy M. Renaud, concerned above all with the good name of his coaching establishment, Emilie, at least in the early part of the book, and Morel – a first sketch of the circumspect Martinon of the second version.

Alvarès and Mendès and the plodding German Shahutnischbach, whose name suggests a prodigious sneeze and the sort of grotesque joke Flaubert enjoyed, are all figures of fun with little significance. Yet they, like the others, are all neatly pigeon-holed at the end, so that the reader is not left wondering what becomes of them. This neatness in tying up all loose ends is very marked in *Madame Bovary* and *L'Education Sentimentale* (II); it is part of Flaubert's technique for creating in a reader's mind the illusion of, as it were, 'falling in with' a given number of people whose lives, relationships and fortunes he witnesses for a space. At the end, no abrupt cutting off but a gentle fading out; reader and characters lose sight of each other as though in a mist, and the reader returns to his own point in time without a sense of discontinuity. Some characters sink, inevitably (Charles Bovary, Dussardier), most go on, as we do, with the motley – 'quelque autre comédie plus sérieuse, et tout aussi bouffonne'.

But the real significance of *L'Education Sentimentale* (I) is its bearing on Flaubert's own development. Here is the record of the moral and intellectual transformation that occurred in Flaubert between 1842 and 1844, the period of his legal studies and of his sojourn in Paris, of the first attack of his nervous illness, whatever that was. The Romantic pessimist of the early works is transformed; behold him now, all thoughts of the law or any other 'useful' career set aside, ready to enter the priesthood of art – not without trepidation: 'O l'Art, l'Art, quel gouffre et que nous sommes petits pour y descendre . . .'[10]

Circumstances abetted him. After the deaths[11] in quick succession of her husband, the renowned Rouen surgeon, and of her daughter Caroline in child-birth, Madame Flaubert, with her grand daughter, also Caroline, withdrew to the seclusion

---

[10] Letter to Louise Colet, October 1847. *Correspondance*, Vol. 2, Conard.
[11] January and March, 1846.

of Croisset,[12] seldom to leave it;[13] Gustave went to live with them.

Thereafter, apart from occasional trips to Paris where he kept a flat, a walking tour in Brittany (1847)[14] with his friend Maxime Du Camp, his tour in the Near East, also with Maxime Du Camp (November 1849–May 1851), the journey to North Africa (April–June 1858) and other minor trips (London, September 1851, Brussels, 1871, Brittany, 1875), nothing, save the brutal if short interlude of the war of 1870, was to interrupt the hermit of Croisset in his titanic struggle with words and metaphors, phrases, periods, paragraphs, seeking, in the quiet watches of the night, to give formal perfection to his visions of the past or the present. 'J'arriverai peut-être un jour à produire une belle chose! car tout cède, n'est-ce pas, à la continuité d'un sentiment énergique. Chaque rêve finit par trouver sa forme...';[15] or again, quoting Buffon, 'bien écrire est tout parce que "bien écrire, c'est à la fois bien sentir, bien penser et bien dire".'[16]

Not unnaturally, perhaps, the provincial hermit he had become and was so determinedly to remain began by creating a hermit after his own image, assailed with temptations, some of them not dissimilar from those of the author of *Novembre,* with visions like those of *Smarh;* perhaps naturally, his friends, Maxime Du Camp and Louis Bouilhet, found this lyrical effusion tedious. Du Camp records[17] that they advised him to burn it. Flaubert did not, and many years later he was to publish a third and final version;[18] in the meantime he did adopt their other suggestion, namely to look for material in contemporary life; not however before satisfying a long-cherished wish, that of visiting the Near East, whither he departed in the company of Maxime Du Camp. Emma Bovary, as yet anonymous, went too, for when the two travellers were at Wadi-Halfa on 22 May 1851, Flaubert suddenly remarked: 'J'ai trouvé! Je l'appellerai Emma Bovary.'[19] Whilst exploring Upper Egypt and registering scenes that were to emerge from his memory later when writing *Salammbô,* his thoughts were evidently in Normandy. According to Du Camp, Bouilhet had suggested as a theme the life of Madame Delamare, wife of a doctor practising at Ry, Normandy; a disordered life ending in suicide by poison. The similarity between the story of Delphine Delamare and Emma Bovary is evident, with Yonville-l'Abbaye for Ry. But hard on the heels of this conclusion comes another source equally convincing,

---

[12] Nr. Rouen. Bought by Dr Flaubert in 1844.   [13] Died 1872.
[14] *Par les Champs et par les Grèves* (posth. 1885).
[15] Letter to Mme Schlésinger, January 1857. *Correspondance,* Vol. 4.
[16] Letter to George Sand, March 1876. *Correspondance,* Vol. 7.
[17] *Souvenirs litt.,* Vol. I, 12.
[18] See below, pp. 286–7.   [19] R. Dumesnil, *Flaubert,* p. 136.

namely the manuscript left to Flaubert by Madame Pradier.[20] Perhaps other sources will be discovered; apart from the suicide which not all adulteresses resort to, the theme is banal enough.

A whole substructure of real events indeed seems to exist to *Madame Bovary* (1857); the same is true of *Le Rouge et le Noir*, if to a lesser extent, and no doubt of many other great works. The fact may be interesting; is it significant? Only in so far as it serves to show what an artist makes of the material life provides, how successfully he convinces the reader that underlying the events there exist a mind and heart, co-ordinating them into an understandable pattern of behaviour. That Du Camp and Bouilhet had correctly judged which way public taste was moving is independently confirmed by Baudelaire, who in a percipient and laudatory article[21] on *Madame Bovary* analyses the reasons that could have determined a choice of subject so different from the established pattern.

The public's thirst for romantic characters, charged with a dynamism beyond human measure, imposing their wills and whims upon a society decked out in a historical or contemporary setting, had been slaked. Flaubert himself in *Madame Bovary* gives an ironic commentary on the romantic tinsel with which Emma Rouault, thanks to the 'decayed gentlewoman' who mended the linen at the convent school, had adorned her imagination: 'Ce n'étaient qu'amours, amants, amantes, dames persécutées s'évanouissant dans des pavillons solitaires, postillons qu'on tue à tous les relais, chevaux qu'on crève à toutes les pages... *messieurs* [the italics are Flaubert's] braves comme des lions, doux commes des agneaux, vertueux comme on ne l'est pas, toujours bien mis et qui pleurent comme des urnes...'[22] The novel as an art-form must, if it was to recapture public favour, break new ground, search for the unheroic hero, be a mirror of the drab and even the sordid.

That adultery was scarcely a new subject, may be true from the Bible down to Balzac, Stendhal and George Sand; of Bouvard, Flaubert will later write: 'Il s'enthousiasma pour les belles adultères et les nobles amants, aurait voulu être Jacques, Simon, Bénédict, Lélio et habiter Venise!...'[23] But in all these cases the subject is really incidental, the interest is in a hero, driven by passions that defy social conventions, demand and obtain great sacrifices shown in their turn to have redemptive power. The study of adultery in itself, the mentalities and circumstances that combine to produce it, its effect on the mentalities and lives of those concerned were

[20] E. Henriot, *Réalistes et Naturalistes* (1954).
[21] *L'Artiste*, 18 October 1857.
[22] *Madame Bovary*, I, 6.
[23] *Bouvard et Pécuchet*, chap. 5. The characters are from George Sand.

new . . . and shocking. Hence the legal proceedings against Flaubert.[24]

So new was this subject that it was to attract other writers in the wake of Flaubert; two other novels on the same theme come to mind – Tolstoy's *Anna Karenina* (1873–6) and Fontane's *Effi Briest* (1895). That the author of *War and Peace* should place his heroine in a large canvas with many other characters and independent if intertwining themes is characteristic. Anna Karenina herself is a sympathetic character, generous, kind, impulsive. She and Vronsky, her lover, become progressively isolated from the society they belong to, as a result of their relationship; more and more they are compelled to look to each other for solace and comfort; nor have they the spiritual and intellectual resources to stand the test, shown as the inevitable consequence of their initial decision to flaunt society openly. Anna's suicide is seen to be grimly inevitable, her predicament is human, her fate tragic, both because the author has succeeded in showing it to be inexorable and because the reader's sympathy remains with her, against the rigid inhumanity of Karenin.

Fontane's novel scarcely compares in human or artistic value with either of the other two. The kittenish Effi, her friends, her parents, the elderly Baron von Innstetten whom she is married off to as a good match, in spite of the difference in age, are unconvincing characters. The mechanism of the story is too apparent. When early on Effi confesses to her mother that with all her admiration of the Baron something about him makes her fear him, when she admits she can put up with anything except boredom, when we then learn that she will have to live in the wilds of Pomerania, we can almost guess the rest: the lover – Crampas; the guilty secret; the letters (such a mistake to keep letters) discovered years later; the duel (exit Crampas); death of Effi.

Fontane has a moral: the effects of a rigid class code that forces Instetten to act as he does, in spite of the time lag, and that Crampas, Effi, Instetten himself and the child Annie are in their several ways all victims of. But the effects on the mental attitudes of the characters of this rigid class code are poorly studied. Effi's death-bed words to her mother are most edifying; in everything Instetten was right! – 'es tregt mir daran dass er erfährt, wie mir hier in meinen Krankheitstagen, . . . klar geworden, dass er in allem recht gehandelt.'[25] Effi speaks like a textbook, like a character from Paul Bourget or Henri Bordeaux. We know where Fontane stands, nor can we forget him to identify ourselves with the characters.

Flaubert's canvas is much smaller than Tolstoy's; unlike Anna

[24] See below, p. 280, n. 46.   [25] *Effi Briest*, chap. 36.

Karenina who is out of the story for long periods, Emma and/or
Charles seldom cease claiming the attention of the reader; hence
a concentration akin to that of a Racinian tragedy. But Emma's
fate lacks the tragic inevitability of Anna's, nor is she, as Effi is
supposed to be, the victim of a class code; she is the victim of the
petty financial operations of Lheureux, as well as of her own
romantic ideas. But for her financial ineptitude she might, as it
were, be still alive as others like her no doubt are. The plea of
defence counsel in the case brought against Flaubert, that there
was a moral lesson in Emma's fate, could apply only to the second
point, and on both, if lesson there be, the facts of the story point
to prudence and good sense, not virtue, as the essential. Flaubert's
approach to the subject, however, is neither that of a moralist like
Tolstoy nor of a moralizer like Fontane; moral issues are irrelevant.
His concern is to present facts, the sordid affairs of an adulteress in
the drab surroundings of small provincial town life, with an accom-
paniment of sordid little schemes by some, the pretentiousness of
others, the obtuse lack of imagination of the husband, the callous
egotism of most; no spark of chivalry, no more than a flicker perhaps of charity in the dog-like fidelity of Justin weeping salt tears
over the grave in the cemetery – Lestiboudois' potato patch, by the
way.[26] To crown all, the ironic contrast between the physical decline of the well-meaning Charles, undermined by grief, and the
upward progress of the worthless Homais. The heart cries out in
anguish at the devastating cruelty of it; what better proof could
there be that Flaubert has achieved his purpose of compelling the
reader's belief in a 'slice of life', objectively presented with all its
harsh reality?

He achieves it by his artistic integrity, his concern for accuracy;
the story is firmly rooted in both place and time – Normandy and
the 1840's; the care for detail compels our absorbed presence at
every scene; can we escape from any phase of Emma's slow agony
by arsenical poisoning down to the last hideous detail: 'et alors un
flot de liquides noirs sortit, comme un vomissement de sa bouche
...';[27] the portrayal of the main characters, above all the rigorous
anatomy of Emma's mentality, the emergence in her psyche of
false values and their progressive growth in a vapid personality,
barren of intellectual resources; the mechanism of her spiritual and
material degradation works with subtle precision. All the characters
live as individuals, one at least – and others might qualify: Emma
herself, Charles ... – but one has graduated to the highest level of
character creation – the type; Homais is a product of nineteenth-
century France, the archetype of the petit-bourgeois, anti-clerical,

[26] See II, 1: 'D'année en année, ... son petit champ se rétrécit ...
[27] Part III, 9.

in the first rank of the 'progressive' gadarene swine, devotee of Béranger. 'Monsieur' Homais had his living counterpart – 'Monsieur' Thiers. The comparison is unfair to Thiers who had courage, who played a historic role in the 1870's and was one of the architects of the Third Republic (quite the most successful to date); that image of him remains full of years, dignity (a little pinched perhaps) and honour. But an earlier image? The journalistic historian fighting Napoleon's battles from his study chair. If the dates were not wrong one could imagine to judge from one of his letters that Flaubert had that image of Thiers in mind when he conceived Homais: 'L'Histoire du Consulat ... je pousse des rugissements. Il n'est pas possible d'être plus foncièrement médiocre et bourgeois que ce monsieur-là. Quel style! et quelle philosophie!'[28] In the 1840's the hour of political power had not yet struck for Monsieur Homais and his kidney, but if in 1877 the famous '16 mai'[29] was to fail, it was because an army of provincial Homais ready to scatter the 'Establishment' of the day was on the march towards the citadels of power; later again that army was to find its perfect political image in the Radical-Socialist party and the masonic lodges. Yes, Monsieur Homais is indeed rooted in nineteenth-century French history, but he is more; the bulging folds of his prudential egotism and unconscious smugness cover a whole area of the human ego.

Flaubert's craftsmanship takes many other forms: the wealth of details fitting into each other like marquetry, none of them gratuitous, all contributing to the development of the story. To take but one example: Homais's explosion of wrath in Emma's presence at Justin's carelessness[30] gives Emma two bits of information that appear gratuitous at that moment: the existence of the jar of arsenic in the 'Capharnaüm'; where the key is kept. At the crisis these facts re-emerge suddenly on the conscious level of her mind, but how could she get possession of the key without the influence she wields on Justin by the distant adoration she has unintentionally inspired in him? Both facts are unimportant and are 'planted' with perfect naturalness, both are indispensable to the climax.

No author repays close textual analysis better than Flaubert – another proof of craftsmanship. A good example is the lunch-time scene at the Lion d'Or after the Bovarys' arrival at Yonville,[31] the pseudo-intellectual conversation between Emma and Léon, the verbose interruptions of Homais, the whole punctuated by the banging door and the clatter of Artémise's clogs on the tiled floor; a composite picture where the artist's every touch is important and

[28] Flaubert to E. and J. de Goncourt, May 1863; also to E. Feydeau, July 1862: 'Je lis maintenant l'Histoire du Consulat de Monsieur [sic] Thiers. Quel épicier! C'est à en vomir! ...'
[29] Constitutional crisis, 1877.   [30] III, 2.   [31] II, 2.

rich in suggestion: Emma's personality prepared to open like a flower at discovering in such an unpromising place a twin-soul able to accompany her on her pathetic flights to higher things; the different levels the participants move on in the same conversation, each according to his nature and experience.

Emma's interview with Bournisien[32] brings out, if anything more sharply, the tragic irony of a conversation where two people fail to make contact because they are not on the same wave-length. Nor should we omit the agricultural show[33] which Flaubert handles like a concerto, the speeches from the platform and the band providing the orchestra, Emma and Rodolphe the violin; nor Emma's reverie as she sits on the boulevard seat in Rouen;[34] her inner monologue provides an excellent example of Flaubert's care in composition; the 'style indirect libre', which Flaubert popularized, makes the reader move unawares from the external world: Rouen, the boulevard, the convent wall, the shade of the trees, to the internal world of Emma's nostalgic dreams and bitter sense of the vanity of it all, until suddenly both she (and he) are recalled to awareness of the surroundings by the clanging of the convent bell: 'un râle métallique...' Emma, her thoughts, her surroundings, form one whole, so skilfully are the latter presented to the reader through her experience.

Flaubert's craftsmanship is also visible by his skilful exploitation of events or objects as symbols. Far be it from him, as author, to intervene personally (as Balzac does not hesitate to do) for fear the reader has failed in attention or percipience ('Je trouve même qu'un romancier *n'a pas le droit d'exprimer son opinion* [the italics are Flaubert's] sur quoi que ce soit. Est-ce que le bon Dieu l'a jamais dite, son opinion?'[35]); instead he has recourse to symbols that are there for the reader to pick up, and drift away in reverie: the rôle of the beggar, the faded wedding bouquet consumed in the flames, its embers rising 'comme des papillons noirs',[36] the flaking plaster statue of the curé in the garden,[37] later smashed,[38] and so on.

Then there is Flaubert the master of language. To the extent that the reader himself has struggled with sentences too long, too heavy with repetitions, too laden with relative clauses divorced from their antecedents, sentences cursed with floating present participles unrelated to the subject of the verb; if he has ever groped

---

[32] II, 6.   [33] II, 8.   [34] III, 6.

[35] *Correspondance*, Vol. 5. To George Sand, 5–6 December 1866. Flaubert returns often to this idea, notably in another letter to G.S., December 1875, and in a letter to Zola, 12 December 1871. Yet any general reflection arising out of a given fact, and not ascribed to a character is, inevitably, intervention by the author; however discreet, these certainly are to be found in Flaubert.

[36] I, 9.   [37] I, 9.   [38] II, 3.

despairingly for the exact word, or sought for a metaphor to give vigour to his 'thought', or considered at all accurately his tense sequence and has then passed from a mere sentence to the relationship of sentences to each other, their rhythm, their sound, their evocative power, the length of paragraphs; to the extent that he has ever suffered under the weight of these problems he will have some measure of 'les affres de l'art',[39] 'les affres du style'[40] Flaubert groans about.

When, after a flight to nineteenth-century Normandy on Flaubert's magic carpet, the reader returns to awareness of himself and his own surroundings, he will be grateful for Flaubert's smooth perfection, for the precise word: 'il s'en allait *ruminant*[41] son bonheur...', 'Un *râle* métallique...', for the metaphors and similes: 'il se sentit triste comme une maison démeublée...', 'la conversation de Charles était plate comme un trottoir...', 'le rideau... resta droit, plus immobile qu'un mur de plâtre...', 'l'ennui, araignée silencieuse, filait sa toile...', for the use of tenses, notably the pictorial imperfect, for the rigorous avoidance of relative clauses.[42]

Flaubert's artistry in form and substance, achieved at so great a cost, has the smooth solidity of polished marble, the detached, multi-coloured, rounded perfection of a soap bubble floating in the still air.

We may admire all this and yet venture in the end to hazard one question: is Emma Bovary fully convincing as a product of her milieu, in the same way for example as Anna Karenina is of hers? The analysis of her mentality is impeccable: 'Que de fois j'ai senti à mes meilleurs moments le froid scalpel qui m'entrait dans la chair! Bovary... sera sous ce rapport la somme de ma science psychologique...'[43] Indeed, yes. We all know that her particular attitude of mind ('D'où venait donc cette insuffisance de la vie, cette pourriture instantanée des choses où elle s'appuyait...?'; 'ternissant toute félicité à la vouloir trop grande') has been isolated, docketed – le *bovarysme*, which drives its victim for ever to seek, condemns him never to find. In the critical essay already referred to, Baudelaire claims for ingenious reasons that Emma has the mentality of a man. We do not subscribe to this view; none the less, this young woman, with, as they say, ideas above her station, seems a little artificial. Can the education of the convent, which is the alleged motivation, have itself produced such a result? 'Il faut,

[39] Letter to Louise Colet, 14 January 1852. *Correspondance*, Vol. 2, Conard.
[40] Letter to George Sand, 27 November 1866, *Ibid.*, Vol. 5.
[41] 'Ruminer' and 'immense' are two of Flaubert's favourite words.
[42] Very rare in *Madame Bovary*.
[43] To Louise Colet, July 1852. *Correspondance*, Vol. 2.

par un effort d'esprit, se transporter dans ses personnages, et non les attirer à soi...'[44] Flaubert, seeker if ever there was one after a perfection he could not find, may perhaps be taxed with some infidelity to his principle; did he not after all say 'Madame Bovary, c'est moi'?[45]

From Yonville to ancient Carthage is a big leap. Several factors explain it. Ever since his childhood he had enjoyed reading history. Michelet's *Histoire romaine* had greatly impressed him; he had learnt fragments of it by heart, and in 1846 he had written to Maxime Du Camp: 'J'ai relu l'Histoire romaine de Michelet: l'Antiquité me donne le vertige... Quelque jours je m'en donnerai une saoulée...' Then there was his discouragement at the treatment *Madame Bovary* had received at the hands of government. 'On ne saura jamais ce qu'il fallut être triste pour entreprendre de ressusciter Carthage'.

The impressions of the Near East, of Egypt in particular, were vivid in his mind. Anxious as he was to avoid the sort of political interference he believed had occurred over *Madame Bovary*,[46] we can understand his welcoming the advice from his friend Gautier who himself was to turn to ancient times for inspiration, with some success: 'Prouve la variété de ta plume; ne refais pas le même roman. Va-t-en rêver sur les ruines de Troie ou sur les ruines de Carthage.'[47]

A few months after the publication of *Madame Bovary* Flaubert began sketching a plan for *Salammbô*. Not until the sixth was he satisfied; he started writing the novel on 1 September, but soon found he could make no satisfactory headway, without going to see for himself; his journey to North Africa ensued (April to June 1858), not for archaeological exploration – after Scipio's destruction of Carthage,[48] the remains of the ancient Phoenician city are vestigial – but to get visual impressions of the country, to gaze from the heights of Sidi-Bou-Saïd on the site where Hamilcar's ships were once fitted out to fight the Romans, on the rocky defiles and desert tracks he was to people with the mercenary hordes under Mathô in their struggle with the Phoenicians, destroyed in the very spot where centuries later Rommel's *Afrikakorps* was finally defeated.[49]

[44] Letter to George Sand, 5 December 1866. *Correspondance*, Vol. 5.

[45] In answer to a question about the model for Emma, Mademoiselle A. Bosquet reported Flaubert as giving this answer. Descharmes, *Flaubert, sa vie, son caractère, ses idées, avant 1857* (1909), p. 103, n. 3.

[46] Flaubert believed the case brought against him was in reality a political move against the *Revue de Paris*, where *Madame Bovary* was serialized, before publication, because the review had been a thorn in the government's side. (See letter to his brother Achille, 1 January 1857, *Correspondance*, Vol. 4.)

[47] Quoted by R. Dumesnil, 'Le centenaire de Salammbô', *Le Monde*, December 1962.   [48] 146 B.C.

[49] Le défilé de la Hache – Cap Bon. See R. Dumesnil, article cited.

As an imaginative archaeological reconstitution, *Salammbô* (1862) may be remarkable; as a novel its impact is much more debatable and Flaubert himself indirectly suggests the reason: 'Les métaphores m'inquiètent peu à vrai dire ... mais ce qui me turlupine, c'est le côté psychologique de mon histoire.'[50] The characters remain mysterious, over-simplified or lacking inner life. Salammbô herself is no more interesting as a character than the rest. With a flicker of surprise we note in her a faint resemblance to Emma: 'Alors elle examina le zaïmph;[51] et quand elle l'eut bien contemplé elle fut surprise de ne pas avoir ce bonheur qu'elle s'imaginait autrefois. Elle restait mélancolique dans son rêve accompli'.[52] Either Flaubert was so intent on giving concrete form to his vision of ancient Carthage that he lost interest in the characters, or alternatively these were too shadowy for him to penetrate the mystery time had wrapped about them; whichever is the reason they are little more than figures in a highly coloured pageant, where the dramatic interest, if such it is, is provided by no more than an adventure story, of epic proportions admittedly, but without the merit of being fast moving, and full of hideous cruelty (diverse crucifixions, the death of Mathô), dwelt upon, it seems, with delectation.

The labours of research Flaubert had undertaken could not give life to the pageant, but they at least gave Flaubert the satisfaction of being able to refute, with chapter and verse, criticisms and suggested inaccuracies misguidedly put forward by Sainte-Beuve (the opposition must oppose, the critic must criticize) who was much less competent on the matter than Flaubert.[53] Such must be the satisfaction (rare) of the scholar. Like the poems of Leconte de Lisle, which it so much resembled in spirit, *Salammbô* is the sort of book that lent itself to richly illustrated luxury editions by artists with a similarly ornate vision.[54] Composers, too, were attracted – Berlioz (1803–69), but he did not live to realize his intention, and Reyer (1823–1909). Nor were film-producers slow to appreciate the potentialities of its gorgeous pageantry.

Something of the transference of emphasis evident in *Salammbô* from character to scene occurs in the second version of *L'Education Sentimentale*, to which Flaubert was to devote over five years (April 1864–May 1869). In complexity of structure and care for

[50] Quoted by R. Dumesnil, op. cit., p. 236.
[51] The sacred veil of the Goddess Tanit.   [52] Chap. 11, 'Sous la Tente'.
[53] See letter to Sainte-Beuve, 23–24 December 1862, *Correspondance*, Vol. 5. Flaubert shows in this letter a patient deference, surprising in the circumstances. Professional critics need to be handled with care! Elsewhere Flaubert displays little love for 'l'Oncle Beuve'; in a letter to Louise Colet dated 16 February 1852 (*Correspondance*, Vol. 2) he alludes to him as 'ce lymphatique Coco'.
[54] e.g. Gustave Moreau (1826–1898).

detail Flaubert surpasses here anything he had hitherto accomplished. The 'planting of clues' which become effective later is
more subtle and more continuous than in *Madame Bovary*; like the
spectator of a 'thriller' the reader needs to be on the alert if he is
to notice a host of details that assume their full importance slowly
as the vast panorama unfolds.

There are two levels of interest, skilfully interlocked, the level of
the characters, and that of the historical events. At the centre of
the former, Frédéric Moreau, M. and Madame Arnoux. Underlying
the mysterious attitude of Marie Arnoux to Frédéric and the
cordial yet equivocal relationship between Frédéric and Arnoux,
the enterprising but in the end unsuccessful business tycoon with
artistic interests, are the vivid memories of Flaubert's relationship
with Maurice and Elisa Schlésinger.[55] Like a delicate thread now
hidden, now reappearing, the love story of Frédéric and Marie
Arnoux runs through the whole novel; full of reticence and un-
spoken thoughts, the pair never meet, as it were, on the same
emotional or spiritual plane: unfulfilment is the key-word, culminating in the auction room scene[56] where Marie's poor effects are up
for sale, and Frédéric finally breaks with Madame Dambreuse,
goaded as he is to a semblance of energetic action by the latter's
triumphant cruelty and by a nostalgic sense of 'might-have-beens'.
The story is a searing contribution, subdued yet eloquent, to the
chronicle of frustration the novel sets out to be.

Marie Arnoux has a certain remoteness throughout the novel;
perhaps this arises from the character of Elisa or from the mystery,
as yet unresolved, of her relationship with her first husband Emile
Judée and his tacit acceptance of the triangular situation with
Maurice Schlésinger. Arnoux himself is more clearly delineated and
seems to correspond closely with the reality of Maurice.[57]

What of Frédéric? If we set aside his relationship with M. and
Madame Arnoux, he seems to reflect less of Flaubert personally
than Henry Gosselin and Jules of the first version did, in whom we
have seen a record of Flaubert's intellectual development. Admittedly a Flaubertian pessimism hangs about Frédéric like a damp
mist ('Frédéric s'enfonçait dans sa tristesse...';[58] 'un matin qu'il
ruminait sa mélancolie...';[59] 'Ma vie est si triste';[60] a catena of
passages in support of that assertion is easy to make), but the reader
may justifiably derive the impression that Frédéric is observed
from the outside, that he is therefore less a projection of his crea-

[55] See above, p. 269.   [56] III, 5.
[57] See Maxime Du Camp, *Souvenirs Littéraires*, quoted by Castex, *Édu-
cation Sentimentale* in *Les Cours de Sorbonne* (Centre de Documentation
Universitaire).
[58] I, 5.
[59] II, 2. For 'ruminait' see above, p. 279, n. 41.   [60] III, 3.

tor's inner self than the 'personal' novels of the Romantic generation were of their authors, that he is a phenomenon like any other,
studied with detachment.

This novel of Flaubert's, with its theme – Romantic indeed –
sustains a note of sorrow throughout, which calls up memories of
Werther, Obermann, René, Adolphe, Amaury, Jacques, Dominique
and their like, the passive and melancholic generation of Romantics, and in a second group, the ambitious go-getters, Lucien de
Rubempré, Julien Sorel, Fabrice, Lucien Leuwen, Rastignac. But
whether the defeat that overcomes most of them arises from metaphysical anguish (e.g. Oberman, René) or is a result of energies
misdirected (e.g. Lucien de Rubempré, Julien Sorel), the overriding
impression is of vigorous characters, at least in their pride (e.g.
René, Lara, Manfred) or their thought (Obermann, Adolphe,
Amaury) or their actions (Jean Sbogar, Lucien de Rubempré,
Vautrin, Julien Sorel) – some of the 'go-getters' (Rastignac and
Co.) achieve positive results. Nor should we forget that amongst
the Romantic men of action, some, full of moral uprightness, are
out to punish wrong-doers, and thus conveniently avenge society as
well as themselves (Dumas *père*'s heroes).

Flaubert, with the strong Romantic influences of his youth,[61]
has evidently not created Frédéric and his friends without a backward look at the Romantic heroes,[62] but the impression they convey is different. Frédéric is irresolute; he has not even the energy
in despair (like Werther) to commit suicide: 'Des nues sombres
couraient sur la face de la lune. Il la contempla, en rêvant à la
grandeur des espaces, à la misère de la vie, au néant de tout! Le
jour parut; ses dents claquaient; et, à moitié endormi, mouillé par
le brouillard et tout plein de larmes, il se demanda pourquoi n'en
pas finir? Rien qu'un mouvement à faire! Le poids de son front
l'entraînait, il voyait son cadavre flottant sur l'eau; Frédéric se
pencha. Le parapet était un peu large, et ce fut par lassitude qu'il
n'essaya pas de le franchir.'[63] Deslauriers is indeed full of ambition
– a second Rastignac to the fray![64] So are others – Arnoux first and
foremost. But, one way or another, all seem to be overwhelmed by
forces too big for them: Frédéric and Deslauriers are borne down
by the flaws in their own nature: 'J'avais trop de logique, et toi de
sentiment';[65] a mysterious 'Hoodoo' brings all Arnoux's schemes
to nought; Hussonnet, the publicity man, is futile, Regimbart, the
café politician, vainly vituperative,[66] Pellerin, the artist, full of

---

[61] See particularly his Preface to Louis Bouilhet's *Derniers Poèmes*.
[62] See Castex, op. cit., chap. 6, *L'Education Sentimentale et le thème
romantique de l'échec*.
[63] I, 5.   [64] 'Rappelle-toi Rastignac...' (I, 2).   [65] III, 7.
[66] Much as Flaubert often is himself, incidentally, on politics and human
folly generally; see his letters, *passim*.

words[67] rather than performance. Dussardier, the only attractive character in the book, belongs to the group of men destined to be exploited by everyone: 'Il y a des hommes n'ayant pour mission parmi les autres que de servir d'intermédiaires; on les franchit comme des ponts et l'on va plus loin.'[68] He is killed in the end – supreme irony – by his friend, that sinister Cato, Sénécal. This little event, one of millions that add up to a fleeting moment in the life of a big city, could be taken as particularly symbolic of the whole book. Sénécal turned policeman cuts down Dussardier, in defence of order; he has abdicated his personality and acts as the blind agent of a higher power.

There is no sense in all this of fulfilment, even tragic; the key-words are abdication, frustration, hopelessness; the overriding impact, melancholy depression; and how admirably Flaubert conveys it: 'Alors, il frissonna, pris d'une tristesse glaciale comme s'il avait aperçu des mondes entiers de misère et de désespoir, un réchaud de charbon près d'un lit de sangle, et les cadavres de la Morgue en tablier de cuir, avec le robinet d'eau froide qui coule sur leurs cheveux.'[69]

The impact is all the stronger because we are not witnessing so much a series of individual defeats as the bankruptcy of a generation, irremediable, hopeless, the Romantic generation that had seen its dreams finally swept away by the 'June Days'. So much for individual hopes and desires.

The importance of contemporaneous events in *L'Education Sentimentale* (II) needs no emphasizing. In the first two parts, historical events are kept in the background, but are skilfully suggested for example by the person of M. Dambreuse; aristocrat (alias Cte d'Ambreuse) turned high bourgeois, he represents in his person the 'Establishments' of both Restoration and July Monarchy, the latter actively promoting and exploiting for its own advantage (Frédéric could have had his 'cut' too, for the asking) the industrial revolution. In Part III history comes into the foreground; as the story moves on to 1848 the individuals concerned seem dwarfed, submerged by the flood of events. At that very time Frédéric characteristically goes off to Fontainebleau with Rosanette,[70] Paris becoming the prey of the mob, vast impersonal force: 'le ciel orageux chauffait l'électricité de la multitude, elle tourbillonnait sur elle-même, indécise, avec un large balancement de houle; et

[67] He obviously speaks for Flaubert sometimes, e.g. (I, 4): 'Laissez-moi tranquille avec votre hideuse réalité...'
[68] II, 4.   [69] II, 1.
[70] See III, 1. This chapter, with its portrayal of events in Paris, the peace of Fontainebleau, the splendours of the Château, the vapid comments of Rosanette, the all-pervading melancholy of former royal palaces (un rêve des Hespérides, etc....; l'éternelle misère de tout), offers a series of ironic contrasts typical of Flaubert.

l'on sentait dans ses profondeurs une force incalculable et comme
l'énergie d'un élément.'[71] The scenes Flaubert evokes from the
euphoric February revolution to the 'June Days' are drawn from
his personal experience, from other eye-witnesses' accounts,[72] from
newspapers. In the historical frescoes Flaubert paints, one omission
is striking: the renewal of influence enjoyed by the Catholic Church
in and after 1848; what reader of L'Education Sentimentale (II)
would suspect it? Indeed, if anything, the impression would be the
other way.[73] Mere oversight? Or was it distasteful to the Voltairian
liberal that Flaubert was, to see the prestige of Rome so high, to
recall the selfless heroism of Monseigneur Affre, Archbishop of
Paris, killed by a stray bullet whilst attempting to stop the fighting?[74] If so, he missed an opportunity of bringing out the irony (so
dear to him) of events, by portraying the bourgeoisie after the
'June Days' returning to the Roman fold, as an insurance against
red revolution,[75] and more ironic still, the chorus of adulation
showered on Napoleon III by the clergy, superior and inferior.[76]
Not that irony is lacking in the kaleidoscope of events Flaubert
portrays: the tragi-comedy of the 'Clubs' with a Spanish patriot
from Barcelona as fraternal delegate addressing the unruly audience in his native tongue none can understand,[77] old Roque, to
restore his morale,[78] shooting down a helpless prisoner asking for
bread; the glistening luxury, after the troubles, of the dinner at the
Dambreuses,[79] with the guests exchanging horror stories. Flaubert
treats both sides with impartial contempt: 'le fanatisme des intérêts
équilibra les délires du besoin, l'aristocratie eut les fureurs de la
crapule et le bonnet de coton ne se montra pas moins hideux que
le bonnet rouge.'[80]

Most generations have their burden of pessimism, but its focus,
like that of optimism, tends to shift. In the Romantic generation,
pessimism was metaphysical, the individual marked out for suffering being the centre of interest; conversely the current of messianic
optimism was also a form of egotism, the individual seeing himself

---

[71] III, 1.

[72] e.g. Maxime Du Camp, Souvenirs de l'année 1848. Also Barbey
d'Aurevilly to whom Flaubert wrote (8 October 1867): 'les détails que vous
m'envoyez seront mis ... dans un livre que je fais et dont l'action se passe
de 1840 à 1852.' Correspondance, Vol. 5, Conard.

[73] e.g. at the funeral of M. Dambreuse, 'L'ignorance religieuse de tous
étaient si profonde ...' (III, 4). Admittedly the Archbishop's recognition
of the Republic is referred to (III, 1) and his death (III, 1).

[74] 'Que mon sang soit le dernier versé! ... le bon pasteur donne sa vie
pour ses brebis.'

[75] cf. Cousin's words to Rémusat, see above, p. 253.

[76] Dansette, Hist. relig. de la France contemp.e., Vol. I, Bk. VII,
chap. 1.

[77] III, 1.   [78] III, 1.
[79] III, 2.   [80] III, 1.

as the instrument of providence, as the bearer of a message of good tidings.

The pessimism that oozes from the second version of *L'Education Sentimentale* in the portrayal both of individuals and of events reflects the attitudes of the post-1848 generation as well as Flaubert's. The individual seemed no longer to hold the centre of the stage as the Romantics liked to think. Satisfaction, even of a sour kind, could no longer be obtained from the contemplation of one's own suffering, nor salvation in the expenditure of energy or the exercise of the individual will; it must be sought in knowledge. Science was the order of the day and, as in the previous generation, a conflict occurs between optimists and pessimists, the former proclaiming the inestimable benefits that science has in store, the latter, with Flaubert in the van, asking what it could teach except that man was a cog in the universal mechanism, subject to the laws of nature, which takes no notice of mice or men. Thus, bankruptcy of Romanticism and abdication of the individual, therein lies a lesson the Naturalists were to follow, and we understand what Banville meant when in reference to Flaubert's novel he claimed that from it 'tout le roman contemporain était sorti.'[81] If the first version of the novel has a clear relationship with the title, the second is more like a vast ironic commentary on the idea of education, both sentimental and political; it might more fittingly and on a different level of awareness recall Balzac's famous novel: *Illusions Perdues*.

With another set of unheroic heroes behind him, Flaubert took up again what he regarded as the central work of his life: 'Au milieu de mes chagrins,[82] j'achève mon Saint Antoine. C'est l'oeuvre de toute ma vie puisque la première idée m'en est venue en 1845 à Gênes devant un tableau de Breughel[83] et depuis... je n'ai cessé d'y songer et de faire des lectures afférentes.'[84]

He had set aside the first version (1849) in deference to the views of Maxime Du Camp and Louis Bouilhet; he had abandoned a second version (1856); the third he succeeded in completing (1872). He was free here to give rein to his powerful imagination and to portray St Anthony assailed in his desert refuge by divine temptations. For a saintly hermit, the most dangerous is that of religious doubts on the nature of God, the meaning of life and death. The devil obligingly conjures up visions before St Anthony's feverish eyes that indeed suggest a nightmare picture by Brueghel or foreshadow some surrealist canvas by Salvador Dali. In his final assaults the devil takes on two forms simultaneously, an old hag (death) and

---

[81] Obituary article in *Le National*, 17 May 1880, quoted by R. Dumesnil, op. cit., p. 263.   [82] Death of his mother (April 1872).
[83] Presumably Peter Breughel the younger (ca. 1564–1637 or 8).
[84] Letter to Mlle de Chantepie, undated. *Correspondance*, Vol. 6, Conard.

a young woman (lust), whose conflicting attractions recall passages from *Mémoires d'un fou* and *Novembre*: 'Viens', cries the old hag, 'je suis la consolation, le repos, l'oubli, l'éternelle sérénité!'; and the other: 'Je suis l'endormeuse, la joie, la vie, le bonheur inépuisable'.

But St Anthony rejects them both and seems to break through at last to the underlying and final truth: 'Encore une fois c'est le Diable, et sous son double aspect – l'esprit de formation et l'esprit de destruction. Aucun des deux ne m'épouvante. Je repousse le bonheur, et je me sens éternel.'

One question still troubles him: if there be some ultimate uniform substance of life, why the variety of ephemeral forms? The final visions are of a jumble of forms with the spirit of life pulsating through them all. The nightmare resolves itself in joy. St Anthony experiences a sense of liberation: 'O bonheur! bonheur! j'ai vu naître la vie, j'ai vu le mouvement commencer...' His concluding message appears to be that under the endless and meaningless succession of varied and ephemeral forms matter itself contains the principle of life; in a word, materialism.

The message lacks originality, perhaps importance, for anyone other than Flaubert; for him it appears to underpin the sense of the ephemeral so strongly developed in him and which on the levels of life he is concerned with as an artist, drives him on urgently to capture the fleeting moment, the fading illusion, and imprison them in formal beauty, like an insect in a crystal, for ever.

Barely two months after he finished *La Tentation de Saint Antoine*, Flaubert was writing to Madame des Genettes about his projects: 'Je vais commencer un livre qui va m'occuper pendant plusieurs années... C'est l'histoire de ces deux bonshommes qui copient une espèce d'encyclopédie critique en farce... il va me falloir étudier beaucoup de choses que j'ignore... chimie... médecine... agriculture. Je suis maintenant dans la médecine... mais il faut être fou... pour entreprendre un pareil bouquin.'[85] He was diverted from his intention by a reawakening interest in the theatre. One previous attempt in collaboration with Louis Bouilhet, *Le Château des Coeurs* (1863), had been refused by a succession of theatre managers. Louis Bouilhet had left the scenario for another play with the title of *Le Sexe Faible* which Flaubert, for the sake of Bouilhet's heir, agreed to write (1873). It was no more successful than *Le Château des Coeurs*. Undeterred, Flaubert then wrote a play of his own, *Le Candidat* (1874), which did at least get on the stage, only to be a resounding failure. At a time when politics had sprung once more into vigorous life the subject was topical enough, but Flaubert had not reckoned with political passions. His characteristically objective attitude could please no one; was the author a

[85] 18 August 1872. *Correspondance*, Vol. 6, Conard.

royalist, a Bonapartist, a republican? In the absence of a clear answer from beyond the footlights, the critics were all equally dissatisfied. Flaubert withdrew the piece after four performances. He was free to return to his 'deux bonshommes Bouvard et Pécuchet', the epitome of 'petit bourgeois' pretentiousness and stupidity.

Flaubert's natural pessimism was increased at this time by the death not only of his mother, but of a number of friends;[86] financial difficulties assailed him.[87] He who had never written with an eye for gain or popularity,[88] suddenly found himself obliged to think of both. He was only in his early fifties, but old age and certainly a real sense of solitude was seeping in on the 'hermit of Croisset'. Is there not a strong personal note in the description of the two friends' life in the country, at a particular moment of defeat: 'Donc ils vivaient dans cet ennui de la campagne, si lourd quand le ciel blanc caresse de sa monotonie un coeur sans espoir.'[89] Does not the singular here, rather than the plural – 'les coeurs', suggest that Flaubert's thought has switched from 'ces deux bonshommes' to himself? The suspicion is strengthened by the next sentence, where instead of the descriptive 'ils écoutaient', which would be natural if the writer had the image of the two friends in his mind, he writes: 'On écoute le pas d'un homme en sabots... ou les gouttes de la pluie tomber du toit par terre. De temps à autre, une feuille morte vient frôler la vitre, puis tournoie, s'en va...' Both the impersonal 'on' and the present tense lend force to the view that Flaubert's thought was turned in on himself.

If only Bouvard et Pécuchet could have afforded him some emotional relief. But Flaubert appreciated the formidable nature of his project and for the remainder of his life he was to be torn between his determination to personify his idea of the overwhelming force of human stupidity, of bourgeois mediocrity, and the difficulty of giving interest to a story that does not progress psychologically, where the responses of ardour and discouragement follow each other in regular succession. Bouvard et Pécuchet was to be the final and most eloquent orchestration of an idea which, ever since the days of his Leçon d'histoire naturelle, Genre Commis, had been a 'leitmotiv' of his novels – the efforts of Bouvard and Pécuchet to be farmers, horticulturists, chemists, archaeologists, literary and dramatic critics, amateur actors, economists, gymnasts, magnetizers, quacks, foster-parents and pedagogues get them nowhere – another tale of bankruptcy, just as Madame Bovary and L'Educa-

---

[86] Théophile Gautier (October 1872); Ernest Feydeau (1873); Louise Colet (1876); George Sand (1876).

[87] He saved his favourite niece's husband, Ernest Commanville, from bankruptcy in 1875 by sacrificing his own fortune to the creditors.

[88] Letter to Elisa Schlésinger, 14 January 1857.

[89] Bouvard et Pécuchet, 7.

tion Sentimentale (II) had been, with this difference: bankruptcy is on the plane of feeling in these two works, on the plane of intellect in *Bouvard*. The two friends are not drawn so much in hatred as with a detached contempt; their defeat is the price of their belief that knowledge and scientific skills of any kind can be acquired for the asking, without immense effort and method. Their efforts are so obviously inadequate that they are grotesque and this gives a certain vitality, the vitality of caricature. Occasional scenes reward the plodding reader, notably when the wave of euphory, moving outwards from Paris after the success of the February Revolution, hits the little village of Chavignolles where the two friends live. 'Bouffon' would doubtless have been Flaubert's word to describe the scene.

In the autumn of 1875, groaning at the difficulties of his novel,[90] he seeks relief elsewhere – *La légende de St Julien L'Hospitalier*. The contrast between this story and *Bouvard* suggests an image of Flaubert escaping to the remote solitude of a medieval church[91] from some restaurant, filled with the smell of 'caporal' tobacco, fried fat and 'pinard', the platitudes of the surfeited customers, as they sit meditatively picking their teeth, buzzing in Flaubert's ears.

From the medieval scene and mentality, Flaubert roams still further back in time to the days of Herod Antipas, and endeavours to throw some light on the psychological mechanism of that ruler, of his ageing unloved wife Herodias and Salome, her daughter.

Of the *Trois contes* (1877) the most successful is *Un Coeur Simple*, evoking his own childhood reminiscences of people and scenes from Pont-l'Evêque and Trouville. The story is a tender but unsentimentalized study of Félicité, faithful servant of Madame Aubain, whom she survives and mourns we might wonder why, but for the habit of humble souls to accept as their lot in this world the heartlessness shown to them, giving pathetic fidelity in return. Félicité recalls Catherine Leroux in *Madame Bovary*, but is a more finished portrait.

The pattern of Flaubert's mature works gave rise to the theory popularized by Émile Faguet of the two natures uneasily harnessed in him, the Romantic and the Realist, each demanding recognition and receiving it alternately, the former with *Salammbô, La Tentation, La Légende de St Julien* and *Herodias*, the latter with *Madame Bovary, L'Education Sentimentale* (II), *Bouvard et*

---

[90] To Madame des Genettes: 'B. & P. sont trop difficiles, j'y renonce...' *Correspondance*, Vol. 6, Conard.
[91] In fact, the church of Caudebec-en-Caux. For the sources of Flaubert's story see A. W. Raitt, 'Flaubert's Saint-Julien', *French Studies*, Vol. XIX, 4 October 1965.

Pécuchet, and *Un Coeur Simple*; a tidy notion, deluding in its clarity, and scarcely corresponding with the facts.[92]

In his youth Flaubert had been strongly influenced by the Romantic fashions and tastes of the time; he was the first to recognize it;[93] the early autobiographical works and in particular the analysis of Henry Gosselin and Jules in *L'Education Sentimentale* (I), mark the point where maturity for him begins; thereafter, his works should not be thought of as in two categories: Romantic and Realist, according to the time background: past or contemporary; in all of them the same attitude to art is apparent, transcending the demands of this or that literary school, rooted in an uncompromising pessimism. Various factors may have contributed to that: the Rouen hospital – grey depressing background of his formative years, the materialist ideas he imbibed in the family circle, Romantic literary influences, the tragedy of his love for Elisa Schlésinger, the epileptic condition (?) that hung over him; later, post-1848 depressions, the spiritual loneliness of this provincial 'Alceste', living in what the seventeenth century would doubtless have referred to as 'un désert', financial misfortunes, critics' attacks. But underlying all these factors, which, with the exception of the nerve malady, have their parallels in the lives of most men who do not all take the same pessimistic road, is the nature of the man; a mystery inevitably. What is not a mystery is the resultant attitude to life: 'la vie après tout n'est elle pas une indigestion continuelle?'[94] Down the years, his correspondence is studded with similar reflexions, like black pearls: 'L'homme est un composé instable, et la terre une planète bien inférieure...'[95] – ephemeral forms, with no purpose, a succession of illusions: 'Je ne crois seulement qu'à l'éternité d'une chose, c'est à celle de l'illusion, qui est la vraie vérité. Toutes les autres ne sont que relations.'[96]

The escape to art does not appear inevitable in these circumstances; fatalistic inertia might equally ensue; but for Flaubert art provided the necessary psychological compensation, the only plane where true joys are to be found, a kind of revenge perhaps, the only revenge a man can have for the hopelessness of the human situation: out of the grim non-sense of the world to build the sense, the ordered beauty of a work of art. 'C'est une chose délicieuse que d'écrire, que de ne plus être soi, mais de circuler dans toute la création dont on parle. Aujourd'hui, par exemple, homme et

[92] Admittedly Flaubert encouraged the notion: cf. letter to Louise Colet, 16 January 1852, *Correspondance*, Vol. 2: 'Il y a en moi littérairement parlant, deux bonshommes distincts: un qui est épris de gueulades...'

[93] See his preface to Bouilhet's poems.

[94] To Louise Colet, September 1847. *Correspondance*, Vol. 2, Conard.

[95] To George Sand – a quotation from *Littré*, December 1875, *ibid.*, Vol. 7.

[96] To Louise Colet, October 1847, *ibid.*, Vol. 2.

femme, tout ensemble, amant et maîtresse à la fois, je me suis promené à cheval dans une forêt par une après-midi d'automne sous les feuilles jaunes, et j'étais les chevaux, les feuilles, le vent, les paroles qu'on se disait et le soleil rouge qui faisait s'entrefermer leurs paupières noyés d'amour.'[97] At least, one joy was not denied him – artistic creation.

For Flaubert this dedication to literature implied intensity of observation,[98] historical accuracy, immense care for form, both linguistic and in plot construction. In this conjunction of qualities Realist writers and critics of the day, content to see no further than the surface of things, found their reasons for pigeon-holing him as a Realist, and Flaubert found his for rejecting that view indignantly: 'j'exècre...le réalisme';[99] to us he appears more as a high-priest of art for art's sake: 'L'homme n'est rien, l'oeuvre est tout...Je recherche par-dessus tout la *beauté*.'[100]

[97] To Louise Colet, 23 December 1853, *ibid.*, Vol. 3. The allusion here is to *Madame Bovary*, Part II, chap. 9.
[98] To Maupassant, 15 August 1878: 'les événements ne sont pas variés. Cela est une plainte de réaliste...il s'agit de les regarder de plus près...'; also Maupassant, preface to *Pierre et Jean*, see vol. V, chap. 2, iii.
[99] To George Sand, 6 February 1875, *Correspondance*, Vol. 7. See also *Education Sentimentale* (II), Part I, *passim*.
[100] To George Sand, December 1875, *ibid.*, Vol. 7 (Flaubert's italics).

Chapter 19

I. HUGO AS POET AND NOVELIST

SINCE 1857 Hugo had been in his island exile. His early royalism and Catholicism were long since behind him, the Napoleonic legend was an instrument broken in his hand; he was left to nurse his hatreds,[1] to find solace for his past sorrows as a man in conjuring up visions of the beyond,[2] and psychological compensations as a democrat in visions of a golden future for humanity, where science, democracy and liberty, having rid the peoples of Popes, clergy, kings and emperors, would combine to produce an earthly paradise informed with goodness.

These generous ideas inspired him to work on what was to be his crowning epic achievement – *La Légende des Siècles* (1859).[3]

In the preface to the first version Hugo explains what he has tried to do and reveals his further plans: *La Légende des Siècles* with its existing poems and many others that may subsequently enrich it is an epic of mankind down the ages. The poet intends to link it with two other works, nearly finished: *La Fin de Satan* and *Dieu*. Thus, though a unit in itself, the work was also to form one chapter of a yet vaster whole: 'il a esquissé dans la solitude une sorte de poème d'une certaine étendue [*sic*!] où se réverbère le problème unique, l'Etre sous sa triple face: l'Humanité, le Mal, l'Infini; le progressif, le relatif, l'absolu; en... trois chants, la Légende des Siècles, la Fin de Satan, Dieu' – a characteristic pronouncement with its promise of philosophic profundity the reader will look for in vain.

But *La Légende* grew in the intellectual climate of the day. Interest in human origins is a natural concomitant of a scientific attitude. The Christian religion may be left to ponder the destiny of the individual soul, whatever that be, to look forward with faith and hope – idle conjecture! Data are inevitably of the past, even though they may determine (in the strict sense) the future. In the world of the arts what could be more in conformity with this backward-looking attitude than epic compositions telling the story of Human development through time, much in the manner of

---

[1] *Les Châtiments.* [2] *Les Contemplations*, Bks. V and VI.
[3] Second enlarged version (1877), followed by a third, further enlarged and rearranged (1883).

Edwardian manuals for boys telling the 'story' of ships or of steam power? The scientist will piece together the evidence, the poet will give it epic form.

In so far as *La Légende des Siècles* does that, a point of contact exists here with the new scientific spirit. As the poet turns his spotlight for a while on this or that scene, characteristic in his view of a given age or civilization, a pattern of successive periods of history takes shape.

But strict conformity with the scientific attitude requires object-ivity and the suppression of value judgments. No sign of a personal attitude on the part of the poet must appear, for data leave no room for personal attitudes, even to the individuals that appear in the story, for they too are mere phenomena in a vast uninterrupted process.

Here at once Hugo parts company with the new scientific spirit, at least when the latter was being true to itself. He parts company with it in a variety of ways. Seldom for example is the reader left in doubt about the author's personal attitudes to his characters and subjects. Past history is indeed a sorry tale where, it seems, cruelty, treachery, greed, lust, oppression almost always prevail. But then what could be expected with the powers of darkness in the ascend-ant? Hugo's characters are sharply divided between the froward and the good. His Manicheism is as evident here as elsewhere and he shows himself full of moral affront and indignation at the wickedness he portrays.

Then again the conception of the work is unobjective. As Hugo points out in the preface, this vast journey through time is under-taken with the intention of drawing the appropriate lesson from history; the thread that binds the whole together is the idea of man's struggle against the powers of darkness, upwards, ever up-wards towards the light. Hugo there reflects the messianic spirit of Romanticism; the brief period between February and June 1848 was its culminating point; moral idealism and the conviction in man's fundamental goodness were strong; all that was necessary was to get rid of the oppressors – kings and priests – so that a demo-cratic republic could be established. Unfortunately, with the June reaction, confirmed and reinforced as it were by the *coup d'état*, such hopes seemed postponed *sine die*. Hugo's denunciations of the rulers, civil and ecclesiastic – and by them we must understand Napoleon III and Pio Nono – become correspondingly more shrill.

But humanity cannot live without hope; the new scientific spirit secreted its own form of Romanticism, less idealistic perhaps than the spirit of 1848 but none the less strong. The political scene might be bleak but, taking comfort from the scientific discoveries and the engineering feats of the age, men could build that smug

belief in material progress, so castigated by Baudelaire. Hugo reflects that materialistic optimism too; a remarkable flying machine,
not perhaps more airworthy than the slightly earlier model built
by the imagination of Lamartine,[4] becomes the sure sign of peace
and justice on earth in the twentieth century ('Plein Ciel').

No poet is more representative of nineteenth-century thought at
its flattest than Hugo. We can agree with the claim he himself was
to make later:[5] 'Ce siècle est à la barre et je suis son témoin'.

Yet in spite of its strongly subjective elements *La Légende des
Siècles* remains the most successful, the completest effort to give
epic form to the story of humanity. Vigny got no further than arranging his early poems by centuries and civilizations;[6] of the
grandiose vision Lamartine had had of unfolding human history he
had provided only two chapters: *Jocelyn* and *La Chute d'un Ange*.
Leconte de Lisle had more recently given a modern assessment of
ancient myths,[7] but it needed the imaginative power of Hugo to
control such a gigantic subject. When the dross of contemporaneous
enthusiasms and personal hatreds are set aside, there remains a
balance of poetic achievement that dwarfs all else in comparison;
apocalyptic visions, eventful epics, lyric pauses, with their grandeur,
their excitement, colour or tender beauty, are the fresh oases that
reward the traveller in the waste land.

The work opens abruptly, somewhat in the manner of Dante's
Inferno. 'J'eus un rêve: le mur des siècles m'apparut...'[8] The scene
that begins to unfold before the visionary's eyes is a sombre one,
nor is there any mistaking the genuine note of pity sounded here
and so often throughout the work:

> Hélas! et j'entendais sous mes pieds, dans le gouffre
> Sangloter la misère aux gémissements sourds,
> Sombre bouche incurable et qui se plaint toujours.[9]

'Bouche', 'trou', 'gouffre', 'abîme', 'ombre' – all words that recur
constantly and suggest the dark labyrinth of wickedness and suffering through which the reader will have to wander before the shades
of night are at last driven out by the vision of the future: 'éther',
'rayon', 'lumière', 'clarté', 'azur'; darkness and light are like the

---

[4] *La Chute d'un Ange*, 8ᵉ *vision*:
> Des ailes de l'oiseau le simple phénomène
> Avait servi d'exemple à la science humaine
> A leurs flancs arrondis le char était pareil;
> Dans sa concavité légère, un appareil
> Pressait à flots cachés un mystérieux fluide
> Plus léger que l'éther et flottant sur le vide:
> Du vaisseau dans les airs il élevait le poids...

[5] *L'Année Terrible*, preface, 1872.
[6] *Poèmes antiques et modernes.*   [7] *Poèmes Antiques* (1852).
[8] 'Vision d'où est sorti ce livre.'   [9] *Ibid.*

framework within which the vast drama of humanity is played out.

Amongst its numerous scenes some have evidently captured Hugo's imagination: e.g. 'Le Mariage de Roland', 'Aymerillot', 'Le Petit Roi de Galice', 'Eviradnus', 'L'Aigle du Casque', 'Le Satyre', 'Le Cimetière d'Eylau'; the tales, for that is what they really are, are drawn from periods – the early and late Middle Ages, the Renaissance, the Napoleonic Wars – that struck a sympathetic chord in the poet, now as an unrepentant Romantic in the line of Walter Scott, now as a believer in 'enlightenment' and as the poet of 'La Vache'[10] combined, now as the poet of the Napoleonic legend, who as a boy had stood on the fringe of the events that nourished it; and immediately the finest qualities of the poet respond to the touch: a child-like simplicity that believes, or at any rate can 'make believe', in the legends being evoked, that thrills at the sight of giants 'having at each other' for days on end ('Mariage de Roland'), that heaves with the appropriate emotion at the chivalrous gallantry of knights errant saving children ('Le Petit Roi de Galice') or damsels in distress ('Eviradnus'), at the cruelty of the wicked baron slaying his boy opponent ('L'Aigle du Casque'), at the devotion to duty of Napoleon's soldiers whose courage gives them the stature of giants ('Cimetière d'Eylau'), that quakes with mirth at the happy fancy of the gods discomfited by a satyr. All this has an Homeric, a Rabelaisian, Falstaffian bonhomie of the highest vein. Where history is involved it may be confused, unsound, built on fraudulent scholarship,[11] but 'what boots it?' – the story's the thing! And the stories are told with unquenchable verve; the characters are genuinely dramatic because they speak 'in character' and not as the mouthpieces (which Hugo's characters so often are) of the poet; they therefore come alive in our imagination, alive as moral beings uncomplicated in their responses to the situations they are caught up in; thanks to the great visual power of the poet, the skill with which he allies the gigantic or heroic deeds with concrete physical details and human emotions, both giants and men are related to our experience, albeit and rightly, at the upper end of the scale; Roland and Olivier are fighting on the banks of the Rhône:

> Le fleuve à grand bruit roule un flot rapide et jaune,
> Le vent trempe en sifflant les brins d'herbe dans l'eau . . .

Anyone with experience of the Mistral will evoke the scene, the intensity of colour, perhaps recall the knife-edge of the wind. Or

---

[10] *Voix Intérieures.*
[11] Hugo certainly liked giving an impression of erudition, often on flimsy foundations.

again, when Roland breaks his sword and is generously offered another by his opponent:

> Roland sourit – 'Il me suffit
> De ce bâton' – Il dit, et déracine un chêne.

The titanic struggle goes on for four days and nights; we are almost surprised to hear that beings who can sustain such a gruelling can have a merely human want such as thirst, or indulge in understatement:

> Et maintenant buvons, car l'affaire était chaude –

Skilfully, Hugo often provides us with a lyrical pause that comes as a welcome relief in the din of battle. 'Eviradnus' affords an excellent example – 'Un peu de Musique', moonlight and song in the forest:

> Et voici qu'à travers la grande forêt brune
> Qu'emplit la rêverie immense de la lune
> On entend frissonner et vibrer mollement . . .
> La guitare . . .

The last stanza is a brilliant example of Hugo's skills:

> La mélodie encore quelques instants se traîne
> Sous les arbres blêmis par la lune sereine,
> Puis tremble, puis expire, et la voix qui chantait
> S'éteint comme un oiseau se pose; tout se tait.

Visual imagery and the deliberately irregular alexandrines combine to convey the impression of snatches of song fading away in the distance, leaving us, entranced, in moonlight . . . and silence.

No reader of *La Légende des Siècles* can fail to find reminders of other works of Hugo. The situation in 'Paternité' recalls that of *Les Burgraves*; the description of the Château of Corbus ('Eviradnus') also evokes that ill-fated play, and Hugo's descriptions of the castles along the Rhine.[12] 'Montfaucon' recalls the last pages of *Notre Dame de Paris*; when Le Cid, addressing King Sancho[13], speaks of:

> Nous autres les gentilshommes
> Des bruyères et des bois,

or, better, when 'Les Chevaliers errants' are described as:

> . . . justes, bons, lugubres, ténébreux,

shades of *Hernani* arise. 'Le Bey Outragé' and 'La Chanson des Doreurs de Proues' might have found a place in *Les Orientales*. More generally the great moral ideas – pity, conscience, expiation – that preside over the fortunes and misfortunes of *La Légende*'s great epic characters and the more personal articles of Hugo's philosophic and political faith, which obtrude so often, have their

---

[12] *Le Rhin.*   [13] *La Légende, VI*, 'Romancero du Cid', 14.

parallels in earlier works and were also to be reflected in later ones.

Thus, though Hugo's work after 1850 is often referred to as his second manner, we must not be misled into expecting a great change in styles and attitude, or into thinking that in obedience to new fashions he has discovered in himself an unsuspected epic vein. It was always there; he was moving with the century; rather, the century was turning to him, to another aspect of his many-sided genius.

Yet we appreciate still more his poetic universality when we remember that in spirit or substance *La Légende* reflects not only other works of Hugo and many aspects of Romanticism, but also other moments of nineteenth-century poetic sensibility. The Parnasse was demanding plasticity, craftsmanship, above all impassibility: 'Pas de sanglots humains dans le chant du poète'.[14] What better examples than 'Booz Endormi'[15] or 'La Rose de l'Infante'?[16] In the latter, the sinister Philip II dreams of the Armada:

> Si quelqu'un pouvait voir dans l'oeil de ce fantôme...
> Ce qu'on distinguerait, c'est, mirage mouvant,
> Tout un vol de vaisseaux en fuite dans le vent...

Could this image have given Heredia the idea he so skilfully exploits in *Les Trophées* of releasing the imagination of the reader by the last line of a sonnet opening like a window on to a distant scene?[17] And lest Hugo be suspected of borrowing Parnassian principles, we may recall that he had already written a perfect example of a Parnassian poem in *Les Contemplations*.[18]

Nor is this all; the idealist Sully Prudhomme might well claim inspiration from *La Légende*, whilst poems such as 'Les Pauvres Gens' or 'Petit Paul' seem to derive from the same source as the sentimental tales portraying the virtues of humble folk from the pen of François Coppée.

Truly Hugo's dictum on Voltaire applies with equal force to himself: 'Il était plus qu'un homme, il était un siècle'.[19]

La Légende des Siècles, as Hugo points out in his preface, is linked with two other epic compositions: *La Fin de Satan* (posth. 1886) and *Dieu* (posth. 1891). The first was to show the progressive defeat of evil on earth in three stages; the first, 'Le Glaive' (1854), deals with the death of Nemrod, the giant conqueror who after conquering the earth attempts to scale the heights of heaven, the second, 'Le Gibet' (1860), portrays Christ's sacrifice, the third, 'La

---

[14] Catulle Mendès, *Légende du Parnasse Contemporain*, quoted by A. Dumas' 'Avant-Propos' to Garnier edn. of *La Légende des Siècles*.
[15] *La Légende*, II, vi. [16] *Ibid*., xxvi.
[17] See below, p. 346. [18] II, 3: 'Le rouet d'Omphale'.
[19] 1878 at Voltaire's centenary celebrations. Quoted by André Dumas, op. cit.

Prison', which remained unwritten, was to have as its subject the sack of the Bastille. We recognize the familiar pattern of Hugo's belief in progress from evil to good: war, sacrifice, liberation, enshrined in an introduction and epilogue of Miltonian grandeur dealing respectively with Satan's expulsion from heaven and, within the logic of Hugo's deistic creed, his ultimate reconciliation with God; evil is swallowed up in good.

But may not the principle of good itself be explored? Hence *Dieu*. This poem too was to have three parts: 'Ascension dans les Ténèbres' (1856), 'Dieu' (1855) and 'Le Jour' (unwritten). Like the hemisphere of the moon that remains in perpetual darkness these two poems remain in the shadows behind *La Légende*; reasonably enough, for they are cast in the same mould as the last two books of *Les Contemplations* and the visionary parts of *La Légende* itself, and though we may admire the unflagging spirit with which Hugo continues to plumb the depths of the great pit and soar to the heights of heaven, he scarcely adds anything valuable for us to his previous visions of the former or enriches our understanding of God.

More rewarding are some of Hugo's later lyrical works. With some relief, we see him set aside for a while the seer's mantle, get off his high horse of philosophy and put the steed out to grass: 'Maître, je mets Pégase au vert',[20] while he rhymes, with varying metres, the verses of *Les Chansons* (1865):

> ... rien ne maigrit
> Comme cette espèce de jeûne
> Qu'on appelle nourrir l'esprit,[21]

and so in playful and nostalgic mood once more, the poet takes us off to nature in the fields and woods, to the song of birds, sunshine and shadow, to idyllic love.

His verses have all the skill of Théophile Gautier's and call forth by their simple human feelings readier responses than those of *Emaux et Camées*. At times the rhymester of *Les Orientales* reappears and performs antics as skilful as those of Théodore de Banville on his versifying trapeze:

> La mousse des prés exhale
> Avril, qui chante drinn, drinn,
> Et met une succursale
> De Cythère à Gretna Green.[22]

But events were soon to destroy this serene interlude.

L'Année Terrible (1872), in part a verse chronicle of the dramatic events from Sedan (August 1870), through the winter siege

---

[20] *Chansons des Rues et des Bois*: 'Le Cheval'.
[21] *Ibid.*, I, iv, 11.   [22] *Ibid.*, I, iv, 10.

to the holocaust of Paris at the end of the Commune (May 1871), naturally reflects moods of sobered patriotism, mourning and exhortation to Frenchmen not to lose faith in France.

In other circumstances the collapse of the Empire which enabled Hugo to return to France would have been a moment of exultation, but the tragedy of France that saddened the patriot was further darkened by a series of personal tragedies that would have broken a lesser man: his remaining daughter, Adèle, entered an asylum in 1870; his two remaining sons,[23] Charles and François Victor, died in quick succession, the former in 1871, the latter in 1873. Having thus lost all his children, Hugo's paternal affection was concentrated on the two surviving children of Charles: Georges and Jeanne. It was for them he wrote *L'Art d'être Grand-père* (1877) which closes the cycle of Hugo's intimate lyric poetry, on a note of tenderness, recalling poems from *Les Feuilles d'Automne*[24] or *Les Voix Intérieures*.[25] The love of children is a fundamental emotion that all men can join in, yet Hugo is alone amongst nineteenth-century French poets to have sought inspiration in this theme.

The remaining volumes[26] of Hugo's lyrical poetry show him returning to familiar themes, political, social, religious, and in effect to his familiar didactic role of 'thinker-in-ordinary' to the masses.

Hugo published four novels in the latter half of his life: *Les Misérables* (1862), *Les Travailleurs de la Mer* (1866), *L'Homme qui rit* (1869), *Quatre-vingt-treize* (1874). Of these *Les Misérables* is the most important; considered as a group, however, all four novels provide a valuable insight into Hugo's ideas and genius.

Les Misérables, in its final form, consists of five parts, with one main connecting link between them – Jean Valjean. The reader falls in with him just after the latter's release in 1815 from the convict chain gangs of Toulon. From then till Jean Valjean's death in 1833 the reader is offered a series of stories: the story of the bishop's candlesticks; the story of M. Madeleine, of Fantine and of the former's great sacrifices; the stories of Cosette, of Javert, of Marius, of Gavroche and the barricades – moving stories that are in effect stages of the hero's struggle for rehabilitation in society, against fearful odds. On this guiding theme the author, as we shall see, builds a number of others.

Les Travailleurs de la Mer is much narrower in scope. The scene is Guernsey in the 1820's, the author does not specify the exact

---

[23] The eldest, Leopold, had died in infancy.
[24] e.g. 'Quand l'enfant paraît'. 'Laissez – Tous ces enfants sont bien là'
[25] 'Regarde: les enfants se sont assis en rond . . .'
[26] *Le Pape* (1878), *La Pitié Suprême* (1879), *Religions et Religion* (1880), *L'Ane* (1880), *Les Quatre Vents de l'Esprit* (1881), *Toute la Lyre* (1888–93), *Dernière Gerbe* (1902).

year in which he introduces us to his hero, the honest if taciturn Gilliatt, who loves Déruchette. Lethierry, her uncle, promises her hand in marriage to whomsoever shall salvage the engine of the s.s. *Durande,* which he owns and which has been wrecked by an act of unsuspected villainy on the part of her skipper, Sieur Clubin, on an isolated reef. At the price of immense hardship and struggles against the forces of nature (tides, storms, a giant octopus which has already accounted for Clubin but finds Gilliatt a match for him), Gilliatt carries out the hazardous operation, discovers Clubin's skeleton and his villainy, restores the stolen money to Lethierry. But Déruchette loves the Reverend Ebenezer Caudray whom she is enabled to marry thanks to Gilliatt's generosity. Whilst they sail away on the s.s. *Cashmere,* Gilliatt watches the vessel disappear as he lets the rising tide engulf him.

The scene of *L'Homme qui rit* is laid in England at the end of the seventeenth century. Of all Hugo's novels, this one has the most complicated plot woven around four exceptional characters: the mysterious Ursus and his inseparable companion, the tame wolf Homo; both are well-named, for indeed Ursus has become like an old bear in his distrust of society and Homo seems human in all but speech. Thirdly, there is Gwynplaine, kidnapped as a child by the Comprachicos[27] and victim at their hands of a surgical operation on the muscles of the face, which, as a result, has become like a mask with a fixed grin, and the beautiful but blind Dea. The reader follows the adventures of this itinerant troop of actors (which they become) until fate intervenes in the form of a storm-tossed bottle. This the reader had seen thrown overboard by the leader of a band of Comprachicos fleeing from England. The ship is lost with all hands; not so the bottle – as Vigny had rightly foretold: 'Dieu la prendra du doigt pour la conduire au port.' The document inside establishes that Gwynplaine is none other than the rightful Baron Clancharlie and Hunkerville.

In this unexpected role, but to the manner born, Gwynplaine addresses the Upper House and warns them of revolutions to come as a result of feudal oppressiveness and the people's suffering – 'Succès de scandale'; death of Dea; suicide of the heart-broken Gwynplaine by stepping into the sea from the vessel taking the four to Holland; Ursus and Homo are left to mourn; their subsequent history remains untold.

Quatre-vingt-treize promises, by its title, a story of the French Revolution, but, in fact, the main theatre of action is not Paris but Vendée. Hugo tells a story vaguely reminiscent of Balzac's *Les Chouans* but better told and better constructed. The Marquis de Lantenac lands in disguise from the British vessel the *Claymore,* to

---

[27] See Part I. Prelim., chap. 2.

direct the local revolt. After numerous adventures he is finally cornered in the Château de la Tourgue by the Republican army under the command of his nephew Gauvain. The latter is both a renegade nobleman and a sincere republican thanks to the influence of the fanatic Cimourdain, defrocked priest and commissary of the Committee of Public Safety.

The story resolves itself into a contest of self-immolation and loyalties to opposing ideals. Lantenac, who defends the château to the last and escapes, returns to save the lives of three children whom he was holding as hostage, and falls into the hands of the besiegers. Gauvain, after condemning his uncle to death, allows him to escape; Cimourdain condemns Gauvain, whom he loves as a son, to death, and when the sentence has been carried out commits suicide.

This brief recital can give only a slight idea of the complex events and adventures Hugo's characters are involved in; it will however suffice to show that a reader who expects to find in Hugo's later novels some reflection of the current trends will be disappointed. *L'Homme qui rit*, be it remembered, appeared in the same year as *l'Education Sentimental* – 1869; yet the two novels are poles apart in conception and form; the same contrast applies to the other three novels, notwithstanding that two of them are set in places and periods the author had direct experience of. In fact Hugo does draw on his own experience and observation when it suits him, apart from whether his story is modern or drawn from history.

Thus, for example, the gripping description of the storm that forms the thunderous overture of *L'Homme qui rit* is surely drawn from Hugo's observation of the sea in torment around the Channel Islands. But Hugo, in contrast to Flaubert, does not co-ordinate his great visual and imaginative gifts, for the purpose of creating an overall unity of impression and illusion, with characters, events, background fused into a well-proportioned whole. Imagination and direct experience are exploited according to the whims of the author with a view to producing some special, almost independent, effect; the magnificent description of Waterloo in *Les Misérables* is almost wholly irrelevant. The plots are indeed skilfully contrived but, like the architecture of a dream house, they are full of surprises – the real identity of Gwynplaine, the successive disguises of Jean Valjean, the real character of Clubin. The characters for the most part come on to the scene and leave it, mysteriously; Ursus is wholly unexplained, Dea is found and rescued by Gwynplaine on a night of storm and snow, beside the body of her dead mother; whence had they come, where going? Mystery! What is the background of Gilliatt, of Javert, of Fantine? Mystery! The great Jean Valjean himself, who dominates the gallery of Hugo's characters, be they drawn from the novels, the plays, or the epic parts of *La Légende des Siècles*, is more rooted in reality. We know something of his earlier background, why he was originally condemned to the chain gangs; his previous attempts to escape suggest a vigorous defiant nature, which asserts itself logically when after nineteen years he is liberated only to find that every man's hand is against him; his back-slidings over Bishop Myriel's silver candle-sticks, and in the meanest way over the young Savoyard's coin, are accountable as social or rather anti-social defence mechanisms developed by nineteen years of prison life; both incidents moreover, the former because of the Bishop's rendering good for evil, the latter because of Valjean's being unable to give the coin back, help him to dig down to the vein of pure gold in his nature and strengthen the will to expiate. Yet more powerful but well within the limits of what we accept as true of human psychology is the scene where Jean Valjean alias M. Madeleine[28] debates with himself in the manner of a hero of classical tragedy whether to disclose his real identity and give himself up to the police. Most humanly, M. Madeleine finds a host of good reasons, one of them at least (the fate of Fantine) morally compelling, not to do what he does not want to do. But the scene is more powerful than the French classical parallel usually provides because the debate soon slides from the rational level to the level of conscience where an inner voice he has no control over speaks. The hallucinatory process begins; what was at first audible only to the soul strikes his ear; for a moment the illusion is complete: 'Il crut entendre les dernières paroles si distinctement qu'il regarda dans la chambre avec une sorte de terreur. Y-a-t-il quelqu'un ici? demanda-t-il à haute voix, et tout égaré. Puis il reprit avec un rire qui ressemblait au rire d'un idiot: – Que je suis bête! Il ne peut y avoir personne.' Which of us from his own experience does not accept this as within the psychological potential; who does not believe that Macbeth really does see a dagger or the ghost of Banquo?

The scene is indeed Shakespearian, and many scenes in *Les Misérables* and the other novels are of like intensity: Cosette's fears as she goes to the well to draw water at night;[29] Valjean's midnight flight through Paris with Cosette in his arms and Javert at his heels;[30] Valjean's escape with the wounded Marius through the Paris sewers;[31] Gilliatt's struggle with the storm and later with the octopus;[32] the tarred decayed body on the gibbet performing its airy dance in the wind and moonlight before the terrified eyes of the young Gwynplaine.[33] Admittedly, in such scenes as these, Hugo

---

[28] VII, 3. 'Une tempête sous un crâne'.
[30] Part II, Bk. 5.
[32] Part II, Bks. 3 and 4.

[29] Part II, Bk. 3.
[31] Part V, Bk. 2.
[33] Part I, Bk. 1.

takes us to the outermost fringes of human experience but the fact that he forces us to accept them, at least temporarily, is testimony to his hallucinatory power which places him in this respect in the same category of visionaries as Balzac. In both cases we must usually set aside ordinary standards of reality and surrender ourselves to their imaginative world. The difference between them is that whereas Balzac's magnified characters are personifications of human passions, Hugo's are or become personifications of moral ideas: pity, expiation, duty. Valjean, well motivated at the outset, soon exchanges his human proportions for the gigantic stature of a symbol; Javert from the outset is a symbol of duty in its narrowest most unimaginative form and a dereliction of duty on his part leads to his suicide; Gavroche, dying on the barricades with a song on his lips, symbolizes the heroic spirit of Parisian youth; all these characters seem to be aware of the part they have to play in their creator's plan; they strike attitudes that seem forced. Thus the reader very soon sees, and Hugo makes sure he shall, that the characters and the novels have been created for a purpose outside themselves. *Les Travailleurs de la Mer* is an exception; the main characters are characteristically Hugo-esque by their Manichean division into creatures of light and creatures of darkness; beyond that the work cannot be said to convey a social or other message; it is a great adventure story, no more. The other three novels clearly convey a message. How often does Hugo think of some problem in the form of a trilogy? These three novels are no exception. They are like the three panels of a triptych: *L'Homme qui rit* aims to portray a society in its feudal state; Lord Clancharlie alias Gwynplaine is its prophet, necessarily without honour; *Quatre-vingt-treize* shows a society in a state of transition where the old forces (Lantenac) are struggling against the new (Cimourdain), with the unfortunate Gauvain torn between his divided loyalties. *Les Misérables* is the richest of the three in themes and substance; on the fictional level the work is an adventure story, a detective story and a love story rolled into one; on the moral level it is a social epic in a modern setting proclaiming that the spirit of revolutionary republicanism (Enjolras, Marius) is still ready to throw up the barricades in the name of suffering humanity; and, entwined with this theme, is the theme of progress, not, as in *La Légende des Siècles*, on a world stage but within a soul, moral progress by expiation and regeneration.

Les Misérables, unlike the other three novels, is not exclusively a post-exile work. It received its existing form in 1852, but Hugo had conceived the idea of writing some such novel much earlier.[34] *Le Dernier Jour d'un Condamné* and *Claude Gueux* strengthens the

[34] See Levaillant, *L'Oeuvre de Victor Hugo* (Delagrave).

links forged by those novels between Hugo and the other Romantic
writers, Lamartine, Balzac, George Sand, Eugène Sue who, either
with humanitarian notions or because of a more detached pseudo-
scientific attitude (Balzac's case), regarded the novel, and indeed
literature, as having a more serious aim than a strictly artistic one.

II. GAUTIER

The name of Théophile Gautier (1811–72) is apt to evoke two
unrelated images: a pink waistcoat and a slender volume of verse,
light equipment for the journey to posterity. Both images are connected with the history of Romanticism.

Gautier loved to recall his pink waistcoat and the event it
evokes, the euphoric moment when the Romantic wave was surging
forward with irresistible *élan* – the first night of *Hernani*, a mem-
orable performance indeed with actors and audience combining to
provide a unique example of the 'grotesque' as defined in the
Préface de Cromwell: tragedy (on the stage), comedy (in the audi-
torium) at one and the same time.

> Dans son pourpoint de satin rose...
> Terreur du bourgeois glabre et chauve
> Une chevelure à tous crins
> De roi franc ou de lion fauve
> Roule en torrent jusqu'à ses reins...
> Tel...
> Il se ruait vers le théâtre
> Quand d'Hernani sonnait le cor.

Le Château du Souvenir (1861) whence these lines come appeared
in one of the later editions of *Emaux et Camées* (1852). By then
Romanticism seemed a spent force; *Emaux et Camées*, the slender
volume referred to, is a sign-post marking a change of direction.

Artist by instinct, writer by choice, journalist of necessity, Théophile Gautier's crowded life, his tastes and distastes, may thus be
summed up. 'Si j'étais peintre, et j'ai toujours regretté de ne pas
l'être...';[35] more than once he deplored the fact;

> Ah! combien je regrette et comme je déplore
> De ne plus être peintre, en te voyant ainsi;
> A Mosé, dans ta loge, O Giulia Grisi.[36]

And he deplored it as much as the need for journalism:

> C'est un bonheur pour nous, hommes de la critique,
> Qui, le collier au cou, comme l'esclave antique,
> Sans trêve et sans repos, dans le moulin banal
> Tournons aveuglément dans un désert de plâtre...

[35] *Mademoiselle de Maupin*, V.
[36] Quoted by Judith Gautier, *Le Second Rang du Collier*.

Qu'un grand paysagiste . . .
Déchire d'un rayon la nuit qui nous inonde . . .[37]

Yet journalism at least provided him with the satisfaction of being always 'in' on events; from 1833 he never missed an exhibition of pictures; from 1837 he was a regular 'first-nighter'; as a journalist he was a power in the world of art.[38] Nor was Paris the only scene of his journalist's activity: the 'Spanish marriages' (1846) took him to Madrid; the opening of the Suez Canal (1869) gave him, at last, the long-desired opportunity of visiting Egypt;[39] Italy, Greece, Constantinople, Russia also yielded tribute to the pen of the tireless chronicler forever bringing to the mass of his readers the colours and sights that fascinated the artist's eye.[40]

The results of this ceaseless activity have no doubt sunk into oblivion; at least two contemporaries have survived better as critics: Sainte-Beuve and Baudelaire – perhaps the greatest French critic of the nineteenth century as well as its greatest poet. But from the 'dusty catacombs of journalism', Gautier's own expression,[41] we may extract at least one work, his *Histoire du Romantisme* (1874). To claim it as history is extravagant, but as a chronicle of the heroic days of Romanticism when 'les jeunes-France', the 'angry young men' of the time, won the day for *Hernani*, the work is a lively and valuable source of information.

In other fields of prose writing Gautier's work has survived better. His scenario for *Giselle* (1841), derived from Heine, has enriched the ballet repertoire with a permanent number; as short story writer and novelist he achieved considerable success in his day though the human interest of his stories is meagre. They are apt to be figments of Romantic fantasy – Fortunios, Silvios, Tiburces, Alciabiades, and the like; Tiburce, appropriately enough, is an admirer of 'Namouna';[42] even when placed against a more realistic background they mostly remain stock characters, with little in them to evoke a response in the modern reader. The constant search for the anecdote to be worked up quickly into a few columns for the next number of the paper is evident, and the stories lack the intensity so necessary if a story is to make an impact, as Mérimée knew. Perhaps the enjoyment of cruelty, detectable in the latter, was foreign to the nature of 'le bon Théo'. Even

[37] *Poésies Diverses* (1838–45); 'A Trois Paysagistes'.
[38] See J. Gautier, op. cit. 'Quand approchait le printemps, époque des expositions, les peintres affluaient à la maison . . . les articles du grand critique faisaient mieux que tous autres, les réputations.'
[39] A fall on board ship during the crossing of the Mediterranean restricted him to Cairo.
[40] *Tra los montes* (1843); *Italia* (1852); *Constantinople* (1853); *Voyage en Russie* (1867).
[41] *Histoire du Romantisme*.   [42] cf. 'La Toison d'Or'.

when he exploits the fantastic vein in the manner of Hoffmann[43] the effect is muted.

Of the short stories mention may be made of the following: *Omphale* (1834), *La Chaîne d'Or* (1837), *Une Nuit de Cléopâtre* (1838), *Le Roi Candaule* (1844), *Arria Marcella* (1852), *Jettatura* (1856), *Avatar* (1856), *Spirite* (1866); the three novels finally, *Mademoiselle de Maupin* (1835), *Le Roman de la Momie* (1858), *Le Capitaine Fracasse* (1863).

In some of these, the author has at least partially succeeded in overcoming the defects mentioned. In *Le Roi Candaule*, Gautier, in the footsteps of Herodotus, imbues the characters with authentic human traits; as a result, a sense of passionate conflict and dramatic development is created; the 'ennui' that weighs so heavily on Cleopatra (*Une Nuit de Cléopâtre*) seems out of historical context; but in *Le Roman de la Momie*, with the Bible as his guide, Gautier has imparted a suggestion of a human attitude to the granite-like Pharaoh, driven in spite of his obstinacy to release the Israelites from bondage, thinking better of it, giving chase only to be engulfed within sight of his prey, leaving Tahoser, whose feelings towards her late spouse remain as mysteriously remote to us as to Lord Evandale, discoverer of her tomb, to reign alone.

From ancient Egypt, Gautier takes the reader in *Arria Marcella* to Pompeii. The impact of Pompeii on a modern visitor is due in part to its immediacy; everywhere the visitor gets a sense of arrested movement: the meal being prepared, the banquet in full swing, the tavern talk, the play announced for the morrow – surely these and countless other activities, proof of which he sees around him, will spring into life and fulfil their unresolved promise? Here is a rich source of fascination and although the story, like the one about ancient Egypt, is burdened with much carefully drawn but gratuitous archaeological detail, Gautier persuades the reader to go along with Octavien as the latter wanders in the moonlight from his hostelry into the ancient world; the very name of the young man seems appropriate. Of the three young travellers Max is too down to earth, Fabio, though interested in what he sees, lacks poetic insight, only Octavien seems predestined by name and nature for the experience that comes to him. But the vision of ancient Pompeii, Arria Marcella and all, fades. In contrast with Hugo's *Notre Dame de Paris*, the final impression is not of a mysterious life that informs all but of death that engulfs all; the reader is left as though with a handful of ashes.

Probably the best known of Gautier's stories is *Le Capitaine Fracasse*. From the ancient world we are translated into the seventeenth century, into the baroque picaresque world of itinerant

---

[43] e.g. *Jettatura, Avatar, Spirite.*

actors Paul Scarron depicted in *Le Roman Comique*; a breathless
succession of scenes, truculence and flashing sword play, a second
d'Artagnan to the fight. The tempo of the story masks the weaknesses of characterization and makes the work not unworthy to
stand beside *The Three Musketeers*; indeed the brilliant evocation
of period is superior in detail to the work of Dumas; Gautier's
Baron de Sigognac is like a connecting link between the irrepressible d'Artagnan and Rostand's Cyrano de Bergerac flanked by his
'cadets de Gascoigne'; the duel between Sigognac and the rascally
Lampourde, in which the latter, artist that he is, carries on a running commentary on his adversary's skill, as they jab and lunge at
each other, has a parallel in *Cyrano* where the hero accompanies
his sword play with the composition of rhyming couplets.[44] But unlike d'Artagnan, Sigognac has a strong air of melancholy and,
though this too has an echo in Cyrano, it recalls much more the
spirit of certain heroes of Romantic drama, Didier and Ruy Blas,
and when in a letter to his faithful old retainer Pierre, Sigognac
writes: 'Si je dois être le dernier des Sigognac que la volonté de
Dieu s'accomplisse! Il y a encore pour moi une place dans le
caveau de mes pères', we detect echoes of Chateaubriand.

The interest of Gautier's stories and novels taken as a whole is
less in their intrinsic merits, where these exist, than in the light
they throw on Gautier's attitudes and development as an artist.
Just as in his pen-portrait of Saint-Clair,[45] Mérimée lifts for a
moment the veil of discretion he usually hides behind, so in *Spirite*
there are a few pages[46] where the reader may suspect Guy de Mali-
vert, the hero, to be Théophile Gautier himself: 'Il est moins difficile de connaître un auteur subjectif qu'un auteur objectif: le
premier exprime ses sentiments ... et juge la société et la création
en vertu d'un idéal; le second présente les objets tels que les offre
la nature; il procède par image, par descriptions; il amène les
choses sous les yeux du lecteur; il dessine, habille et colore exacte-
ment ses personnages, leur met dans la bouche les mots qu'ils ont
dû dire et réserve son opinion.' 'Leur met dans la bouche, etc.', on
that claim we may have reservations, for if it were true the characters in his stories would have more life, but we may accept the rest
of the claim he makes for the objective writer as a fair statement
of his own endeavours, although he does in fact reveal his own
ideals and tastes indirectly by the choices he makes; in *Mademoiselle de Maupin*, moreover, he had not only revealed himself in the
character of d'Albert, but he had written an aggressive preface in
his own name. Novel and preface are important in the development of Gautier's aesthetic ideas. The preface is a vigorous and

---

[44] Act I, Cyrano: 'A la fin de l'envoi je touche ... !'
[45] *Le Vase etrusque*, see above, p. 220.   [46] chap. 8.

entertaining diatribe against the moralizers in art and literature. We may feel tempted to demur when the author puts forward as an argument that everything useful is ugly and that since moralizing literature is useful, it must be bad; 'tout ce qui est utile est laid, car c'est l'expression de quelque besoin, et ceux de l'homme sont ignobles et dégoûtants, comme sa pauvre et infirme nature. – L'endroit le plus utile d'une maison, ce sont les latrines.' Any object well designed to meet a need has a beauty derived from its functional quality. But we may cordially agree with Gautier's fundamental thesis that didactic or moralizing literature is bad; against such a prostitution of art Gautier proclaims the useless alone to be beautiful: 'Il n'y a de vraiment beau que ce qui ne sert a rien.' Art must have no end but itself – art for art's sake.

That principle does not necessarily uproot literature from its essential soil – human life. But that was the interpretation Gautier put on it, rejecting thereby certain tendencies in the nature of Romanticism, obeying some in his own. We have had occasion before now to emphasize an essential trait in the Romantic – the conviction of being the chosen vessel of some mysterious force with the consequent alternative results on the same psychological plane: preoccupation with self, or messianism. Both attitudes provoked a release of energy, passion, emotion. In spite of his loyal friendship for Hugo and other contemporaries, Gautier turned his face against both attitudes, thus showing himself not to be a Romantic in the profoundest sense. He reflects only a small aspect of it, with which his own nature had affinities. On a less deep level, Romanticism means awareness of the unique characteristics that distinguish individuals from each other, country from country, periods in history from other periods; 'local colour' was an effort to place a story or drama in the appropriate setting either of time or place. In this respect it leads to observation of external detail; Gautier with his painter's instinct naturally responded to this aspect of Romanticism as much as he rejected the deeper. Thus it was natural for Gautier to interpret his doctrine of art for art's sake in literature as a pursuit of an impersonal, plastic ideal of beauty. D'Albert, evidently speaking for Gautier, proclaims his ideal of art:[47] 'Au reste, je ne circonscris point la beauté dans telle ou telle sinuosité de lignes – l'air, le geste, la démarche, le souffle, la couleur, le son, le parfum, tout ce qui est la vie entre pour moi dans la composition de la beauté; tout ce qui embaume, chante ou rayonne y revient de droit – j'aime les riches brocarts, les splendides étoffes ... les larges fleurs et les cassolettes, la transparence des eaux vives et l'éclat miroitant des belles armes, les chevaux de race et ces grands chiens blancs

[47] *Mademoiselle de Maupin*, chap. 5.

comme on en voit dans les tableaux de Paul Veronese – je suis un vrai païen de ce côté et je n'adore point les dieux qui sont mal faits...'. There speaks a disciple of Chénier, a forerunner of Leconte de Lisle and Pierre Loüys. 'Tout ce qui est la vie...' in another context might naturally include human passions, but here it as clearly sums up a host of details all appealing to the senses, mostly visual.

An unrewarding novel, *Mademoiselle de Maupin* shows Gautier's ideal of beauty, plastic, pagan, combining masculine strength and feminine grace in the hermaphrodite personality of the heroine.

Gautier's pessimism also responded to this ideal. Throughout his work, poetry and prose, the ephemeral nature of life, the fragility of human things, the idea of death as final are very marked; hence his striving after a form of beauty that would resist the erosion of time.

Gautier's superficial Romanticism did not interfere with his ideal of plastic beauty. He very soon abandoned the cardboard medievalism so much in fashion in the 1820's, and though, on the other hand, he responded both to the call of Hoffmann and the supernatural (*Jettatura, Avatar, Spirite*), and to the picaresque in the vein of Dumas (*Fracasse*), this did not interfere with his *fugue* to antiquity, from the ugliness of the utilitarian modern world, to Greece (*La Chaîne d'Or*), to Ancient Rome (*Arria Marcella*), above all to Egypt, which had been a subject of great interest and study since the days when Bonaparte had taken a group of scholars with him on his expedition (1798), since Champollion had found the key to hieroglyphic writing (1822), Egypt, which his friends Nerval, Flaubert, Du Camp, saw, which he was to see so late in life and which in the meantime, from documents and illustrations,[48] seemed to combine all the qualities of his ideal: formal perfection, dazzling light, brilliant colour.

Gautier's poetic works show much the same pattern of development as his stories, from the early *Poésies* (1830), republished in 1832 with *Albertus ou l'Ame et le Péché*, to the triumphant affirmation of his ideal of beauty in *Emaux et Camées*, which from 1852 to 1872 was to be re-edited six times during the poet's lifetime, carrying the number of poems from the original eighteen to the forty-seven of the definitive edition.

The *Poésies* exploit typical Romantic themes – the Middle Ages ('Moyen Age'), Orientalism ('Les Souhaits'), the fugacity of time ('Tête de Mort', 'Souvenirs'), horror ('Tête de Mort', 'Cauchemar'), earthly love as the way to God: 'Et comment croire en Dieu quand on n'est pas aimé!' (Sonnet vi).

[48] e.g. the work of his friend Ernest Feydeau (1821–73).

Reminiscences of Byron:

> Avant cet heureux jour, j'étais sombre et farouche,
> – Mon sourcil se tordait sur mon front soucieux . . .,
>
> (Sonnet vi)

of Lamartine:

> Et le poète, assis près des flots, sur la grève
> Ecoute les accents fugitifs comme un rêve . . .   (Sonnet i)

of the poet of *Les Orientales*, of the author of 'Namouna' and 'Rolla' are obvious – a collection of borrowed attitudes, in fact, rather than genuine personal emotion. Most of the poems have an epigraph, which underlines that they are largely poetic exercises on given themes, often skilful; with what rhythmical cunning, for example, does the metre and the very disjointedness of the lines suggest the darting flight of the dragon-fly:

> Sur la bruyère arrosée
> De rosée;
> Sur le buisson d'églantine;
> Sur les ombreuses futaies.
> Sur les haies . . .   ('La Demoiselle')

'Albertus', too, is full of literary affiliations: sardonic Byronism, Rolla's impertinence; a witches' broomstick ride in the style of Bürger – withal an occasional glimpse of a personal note:

> Tout autre amour en moi s'est tû . . .
> Excepté le tien, O Poésie . . .
> . . . et toi, sa soeur jumelle,
> Peinture, la rivale et l'égale de Dieu
> Déception sublime, admirable imposture,
> Qui redonnes la vie et doubles la nature,
> Je ne vous ai pas dit adieu!
>
> (From stanzas lvii and lviii)

The *Poésies Diverses* (1833–8) and the Second Collection with the same title (1838–48)[49] add little to the area of experience the poet has already explored; the same delight in the 'fugitive piece' on a given theme, largely provided by 1830 tastes and attitudes: Byronic despair and disbelief ('Ténèbres'), Orientalism and dagger play ('Le Nuage'); occasionally, that typical formula of Romantic poetry – the image which after its description is seen to be the symbol of the author's own attitudes, beliefs or feelings ('Les Colombes', 'Le Pot de Fleurs', 'L'Hippopotame').

La Comédie de la Mort (1838) is characteristic of the author in that under the light and, in the strict sense, impertinent tone the idea of the physical destruction of death provides a hackneyed theme; the poem is superficial in treatment and lacks any indica-

---

[49] *Poésie. Complètes*, Charpentier edn. (1877).

tion that the poet is emotionally committed. Dryness, astringency,
these words come easily to mind in reading Gautier's poetry. Both
before and after the full emotional potential of Romanticism had
been orchestrated in Musset's *Nuits*, Gautier remains unmoved,
as emotionally dry as the Spanish sierras and deserts he recalls in
España:[50]

> Les pitons des Sierras, les dunes du désert . . .
> Sont moins secs et moins morts aux végétations
> Que le roc de mon coeur ne l'est aux passions.
>
> ('In Deserto')

But at least the reader is from time to time stimulated by an effective image:

> La rosée arrondie en perles,
> Scintille aux pointes du gazon,
> Les chardonnerets et les merles
> Chantent à l'envi leur chanson.
>
> ('Promenade Nocturne')

The strong contrast here in value between the first two lines and
the second two, between the sparkling dew-drops, set with all the
precision of a jewel, in their linguistic mounting, and the drab
'chantent à l'envi' which calls forth no sensuous response, serves
to underline that Gautier was as insensitive to music as he was sensitive to visual beauty. The relation between music and verse will
have to wait for Verlaine and the Symbolists. Evident in *España*
is Gautier's delighted response to colour and harshness of outline
or spirit, to anything in fact that by its intensity or hardness seems
to resist the erosion of time and belongs to eternity: 'L'Escurial',
'Deux Tableaux de Valdés Leal', 'A Zurbarán'; Delacroix derived
inspiration from literature for some of his great compositions;
Gautier often reverses the process, *España* contains poems inspired
by pictures; so do *Emaux et Camées*.

In *Emaux et Camées*, Gautier was to achieve his highest poetic
potential; in form and substance they are the epitome of Gautier's
artistic ideals and they have a representative quality for the time,
which gives them a particular interest. Gautier's skill in handling
intricate metres and verse forms, is obvious enough from his early
poetry; his ardour in pursuit of rare and difficult rhymes would
have done honour to a champion of 'bouts rimés'. Sometimes he
had used the octosyllabic metre; in *Emaux et Camées* he was to
reveal his mastery of that difficult verse form, difficult because it
fits so tightly over the matter that it gives the poet little elbow-
room, demands descriptive precision, a concentration of form
where every syllable is essential to the sense and stimulative quality
of the poem, and leaves little or no room for conjunctions, relative

[50] *Ibid.*

pronouns or any of the air-cushions of vocabulary that may occasionally help the poet in search of an extra syllable or two for his alexandrine. These are virtues indeed, but in cultivating them the poet's skill may fall down on the other side of the peak he has been ascending; linguistic concentration may result in a rhythmical stress as monotonous as a metronome; and, avoiding that danger, may bring the poet too close to a series of unstressed lines, much resembling prose, saved only by the rhyme. Sometimes perhaps Gautier falls short of his own high standards:

> Le son en est si faux, si tendre,
> Si moqueur, si doux, si cruel,
> Si froid, si brûlant, qu'à l'entendre
> On ressent un plaisir mortel
>
> ('Carnival de Venise', iv)

Are not these lines dangerously near prose? The rhyme, tendre/entendre, scarcely saves them.

Sometimes the reader's imagination is ready to take wing but is immediately brought down to earth again by an obtrusive rhyme:

> Tous les vices avec leurs griffes
> Ont, dans les plis de cette peau
> Tracé d'affreux hiéroglyphes,
> Lus couramment par le bourreau.

The vices take on the shape of hideous monsters, the image is powerful but is at once destroyed by the very ingenuity of the rhyme and the laboured ingenuity of the metaphor. Every reader will decide for himself how far or how little Gautier has been victim of the difficulties of his chosen metre, but in general from the purely technical point of view *Emaux et Camées* is a remarkable achievement. Later poets – Mallarmé, Valéry – will achieve greater degrees of concentration – compression would be a better term – but in them we shall find a system of poetics that has evolved much further in its exploration of the psychological responses that words and groups of words may achieve by the tricks of substitutions of meaning, symbols, labyrinthine thought, suggestion. In 1852 the time had not come for poetry to move on to this quintessential plane. We remain on a level where linguistically the poetic norm is still that of prose, from which it differs by its verse forms, metres, rhythms, rhyme and the sensuous stimulus it may provide by its imagery. With no other means than these at his disposal Gautier's skill is prodigious: ingenuity of metrical design, rhythms and rhyme, descriptive skills that by their evocation of form or colour stimulate responses usually provided by painting – 'transpositions d'art'; not for nothing had Gautier the journalist laboured for years to convey in prose to his readers the responses he had experienced at countless exhibitions. All this, however, is a closed form of poetry, that imprisons rather than releases the imagination, like drawings that define rather than suggest.

Is there in *Emaux et Camées* something for the emotions? In truth very little: love is reduced to the level of sensual excitement ('Le Poème de la Femme'; 'Coquetterie Posthume'; 'A une Robe Rose'), the familiar theme of the ephemeral nature of things reappears here and there ('Affinités Secrètes', 'L'Art'); otherwise this feast for the eye provides as little nourishment to the hungry soul as a coloured photograph of good food to a hungry man, though an occasional tit-bit of humour or agreeable fantasy may sustain him for a moment.

After practising various types, Gautier was wise to choose the octosyllabic metre as his special domain. The alexandrine is doubtless more supple but it requires some emotional or intellectual vibration to sustain it all along its length. Between it and Gautier's peculiar skills there were no 'Affinités Secrètes'; the octosyllabic metre conferred upon his vision of beauty the crystalline angularity of a precious stone, the bright surface of enamel:

> Que ton rêve flottant
> se celle
> Dans le bloc résistant.   ('L'Art')

'Si j'étais peintre (et j'ai toujours regretté ne pas l'être)' – pathetic, the idea of a man bound all his life by a wrong choice, but perhaps after all Gautier was more fortunate than he knew. Had he in fact become a painter he might well have been one of that crowd of painters, mercifully out of fashion, who combined Realist detail with evocations of antiquity, a French counterpart of Alma Tadema or Lord Leighton, whereas by his constant striving to make poetry evoke what painting can depict (if it must) he has an assured place in French literature.

III. BAUDELAIRE

From his early youth Charles Baudelaire (1821–65) felt himself predestined to isolation[51] and he was soon to show how incapable he was of adjusting himself to ordinary life. With such predispositions, Baudelaire would surely have built a dark spiritual home whatever materials life provided, even without the very genuine pretext, afforded by his mother's remarriage, soon after his father's death, for disenchantment, for Hamlet-like revolt, even without

---

[51] *Journaux Intimes*; *Mon coeur mis à nu*, VII. *Oeuvres Posthumes*, 2, p. 90, Conard. 'Sentiment de *solitude* [B.'s italics] dès mon enfance. Malgré la famille – et au milieu des camarades, surtout – sentiment de destinée éternellement solitaire . . .'

the incompatibility of character that made conflict with his step-father inevitable.[52]

Certain facts, however, have a direct bearing on his work: his being packed off on a sea voyage to the Far East,[53] when his family could bear no longer the scandal of his behaviour. As an effort to bring some order into his life and peace in his family rela-tionships the voyage was a failure, but it was an experience that enriched his imagination as *Les Fleurs du Mal* were to show. Or again, his literary apprenticeship; for all Baudelaire's apparent idle-ness, he knew well the immense value for a poet of a well-stocked treasure-house of knowledge; the classics,[54] the early Church Fathers, French literature from the sixteenth century, the English Romantics, he read or re-read them all; certain writers especially called forth vigorous responses from his nature: the intransigent and high Catholic Joseph de Maistre, the truculent Petrus Borel, the rugged and individualistic Carlyle, the moralist Emerson, later, Edgar Allan Poe.[55]

Nor were Baudelaire's scholarly activities exclusively literary; he was as often in the Paris picture galleries as in its libraries and some of his writings show that his interest in painting, derived perhaps from his father – that most mediocre amateur artist, according to Baudelaire, was as carefully fostered by him as his love of literature.

As part of his apprenticeship must also be reckoned his early ex-perience of Parisian life, literary circles, cafés, drugs, prostitutes, a life of apparent idle luxury, at the price of half his modest patri-mony; during it Baudelaire was able to realize his own ideal of dandyism[56] – a style in dress that was the outward sign of an aristocratic, unflinching, discerning attitude towards life; no affect-ation of flamboyance; on the contrary, for him the key-note was elegance in studied simplicity. Thereafter, financial eclipse, a 'con-seil judiciaire'[57] imposed by his family, a brief attack of democratic enthusiasms in 1848 – like many other writers, but for less hu-manitarian and more personal reasons,[58] debts and poverty, com-plicated in the closing years by the relentless advance of disease that carried him off, prematurely aged by syphilis and drugs, at forty-four.

Baudelaire's critical and poetic work were carried on together during his most creative period – 1845 to 1865 – although a few of the poems of *Les Fleurs du Mal* are of an earlier date.

[52] Major, later General Aupick.
[53] He went as far as L'Ile Maurice and L'Ile Bourbon, 1841.
[54] He had been a brilliant classic at school.
[55] 'De Maistre et Edgar Poe m'ont appris à raisonner': *Mon coeur mis à nu*, CXI. *Journaux Intimes*.
[56] *L'Art Romantique*, III, 9, Conard edn.
[57] M. Ancelle, appointed in September 1844.
[58] e.g. his hatred of his step-father.

The critical articles, of which the earliest was his 'Salon de 1845', were collected and published posthumously in two volumes: *Curiosités Esthétiques* (1868) and *L'Art Romantique* (1869). Baudelaire's reputation as a critic has not ceased to grow; some would acclaim him as not only the greatest French poet but also the greatest French critic of the nineteenth century. Sainte-Beuve's literary range may be greater, yet, in comparison with Baudelaire's percipient mind, he seems pedestrian. His literary range is greater, because as a professional critic he must needs deal with everything that came his way; to that should be added his scholarly or academic criticism.[59] Baudelaire, on the other hand, confined himself mostly to artists, writers and even a musician in whom he saw either some affinity with his own aesthetic ideas or, alternatively, the negation of these: for Edgar Allan Poe,[60] Flaubert, Gautier, Delacroix, Constantin Guys, Wagner, he is full of admiration; but 'Les Drames et les Romans Honnêtes', 'L'Ecole Païenne', Horace Vernet, Hégésippe Moreau he trenchantly condemned. Baudelaire's luminous intelligence and his capacity to get into the minds of other writers[61] – poets for the most part – and artists, thereby enriching progressively his own aesthetic ideas, is what makes his criticism so stimulating; he is passionately concerned to defend a point of view: 'pour être juste [i.e., right], c'est à dire pour avoir sa raison d'être, la critique doit être partiale, passionnée, politique, c'est à dire faite à un point de vue exclusif, mais au point de vue qui ouvre le plus d'horizon.'[62]

Probably the three most valuable sources of enrichment Baudelaire found for his own aesthetic theories were Eugène Delacroix, Edgar Allan Poe and Constantin Guys. From his first article on the Salon of 1845 to his obituary article[63] on the great Romantic painter, Baudelaire often returned[64] to the subject of Delacroix. He begins with a sweeping claim: 'Monsieur Delacroix est décidément le peintre le plus original des temps anciens et des temps modernes. Cela est ainsi, qu'y faire...' Never thereafter does his admiration abate; it merely becomes more discerning. Anyone interested in painting would derive benefit from Baudelaire's analysis of the born colorist (Delacroix) and the born draughtsman (Ingres);

[59] See below, pp. 357 *et seq.*

[60] The two critical studies on Poe do not as a matter of fact figure in either of the two volumes mentioned here. They appeared as prefaces, the first to Baudelaire's translation, *Histoires Extraordinaires* (1856), the second to the translation *Nouvelles Histoires Extraordinaires* (1857).

[61] The most striking example of this is provided by his article on *Madame Bovary*, 1857.

[62] *Salon de 1846.*

[63] Published in three instalments, in *L'Opinion Nationale*, 2 and 14 September, and 22 November 1863.

[64] *Salon de 1846, Exposition Universelle,* 1855, *Salon de 1859.*

all his studies of Delacroix are full of pregnant and stimulating reflections that go beyond painting into the domain of aesthetic
theory, applicable whatever the medium, and by their penetration
seem to have an almost tonic moral effect.[65]

To summarize them is to sacrifice many valuable details,[66] but
Baudelaire goes to the heart of the matter when he quotes Delacroix himself on the attitude both of them believed the artist should
have towards nature:[67] 'La nature n'est qu'un dictionnaire, répé-
tait-il fréquement. Pour bien comprendre l'étendue du sens impli-
qué dans cette phrase, il faut se figurer les usages nombreux et
ordinaires du dictionnaire. On y cherche le sens des mots, la génération des mots...on en extrait tous les éléments qui composent
une phrase et un récit; mais personne n'a jamais considéré le
dictionnaire comme une composition dans le sens poétique du mot.'

Artists, continues Baudelaire, that are content to copy nature
fall into the commonplace. How then shall they avoid this pitfall?
What indispensable quality do they need for penetrating beneath
the surface of things, apprehending their subtle relationships –
'correspondances' is Baudelaire's word – for attaining the inner
core of spiritual reality hidden within the coarse external envelope,
for creating from natural chaos the ordered unity of a work of art,
which, by its very 'artificiality' (the hallmark of beauty in Baudelaire's view because opposed to nature) could call forth deeper
responses from viewer, reader or listener, release them from the
bonds tying them down to one point in space and time, send
them soaring on the wings of reverie? Not the least of Delacroix's
merits, incidentally, in Baudelaire's view, was his power to produce
that effect even when his subjects were taken from history, tied
down to earth, in fact, and imprisoned in time: 'Que nous donne-t-
il de plus que le passé? Aussi grand que les grands, aussi habile que
les habiles, pourquoi nous plaît-il davantage? On pourrait dire que
doué d'une plus riche imagination, il exprime surtout l'intime du
cerveau, l'aspect étonnant des choses...C'est l'infini dans le fini.
C'est le rêve et je n'entends pas par ce mot les capharnäums de la
nuit, mais la vision produite par une intense méditation, ou, dans
les cerveaux moins fertiles, par un excitant artificiel...'[68]

The quotation in fact gives the answer to the question: how to
avoid the commonplace? Imagination is the precious, the essential
quality, imagination 'Reine des facultés'. Baudelaire had already
discussed this quality in the second of his two critical studies on
Poe.

[65] *Salon de 1846*, i–v inc. and vii, and *Salon de 1859*, i–v inc. are
especially important.
[66] See also D. Parmée's admirable synthesis in his Introduction to his
Selected Critical Studies of Baudelaire (C.U.P., 1949). [68] *Salon de 1859*, v.
[67] *Salon de 1859*, iv.

The word enrichment, used earlier to describe the nature of Delacroix's and Poe's influence on Baudelaire, is particularly justified in the latter's case. Poe's impact on Baudelaire, whose interest in the American dates from about 1847,[69] was immense but 'precisely because for Baudelaire Poe was a twin soul...',[70] just as unhappy in his relations with society, believing, as Baudelaire did, in original sin, in spiritual values and beauty whilst the world lusted after material progress; a twin soul too in his ideas on art and the artist.

The second of Baudelaire's two articles on Poe is the more important here. Not only do we find there the analysis just referred to of imagination, but a host of other ideas that reflect Baudelaire's beliefs and poetic practice as well as Poe's: the need, given the innate poetic disposition and inspiration, for knowledge, hard work, skilful poetic construction; brevity as the hall-mark of a great poem – for the test of great poetry is its power to stimulate, uplift the soul, but this emotional excitement is, by psychological necessity, transitory, thus: 'un long poème n'existe pas; ce qu'on entend par un long poème est une parfaite contradiction de termes'; the heresy of didactic or moralizing poetry – for poetry can have no aim but itself and only by the joy of its creation can it hope to create joy by beauty and thus, indirectly, contribute to morality; virtue, morality are a form of harmonious beauty, vice is a moral deformity that offends the sense of harmonious and rhythmical beauty; the immortal instinct for beauty is what leads us to see in the beauties of this world 'comme un aperçu, comme une correspondance du ciel'; through poetry and through music the soul may win a glimpse of the splendours that lie beyond death. Apart from the obituary on Delacroix, *L'Art Romantique* contains a number of articles both illuminating on the writers or subjects chosen and full of ideas interesting in themselves or in relation to *Les Fleurs du Mal*: the theory of beauty compounded of eternal and period elements, and the theory of dandyism;[71] the idea of 'la consolation par les arts';[72] the sensuous wealth of Wagner's music,[73] where colour, sound, ideas blend, 'correspond' in fact; the value of favourite words as a guide to a poet's mentality.[74]

Baudelaire's other prose works are also important. *La Fanfarlo* (1847) is one of Baudelaire's rare excursions into fiction, his first published work apart from the *Salons* of 1845 and 1846. He was

---

[69] His first published translation of Poe – 1848. *Oeuvres*, Conard. *Histoires Extraordinaires*, p. 387.
[70] See Parmée, op. cit.
[71] Essay on Constantin Guys, *L'Art Romantique*, iii.
[72] Essay on Théophile Gautier, op. cit., vii.
[73] 'Richard Wagner et Tannhäuser à Paris', op. cit., ix.
[74] Essay on Théodore de Banville, op. cit., xiv.

twenty-two when he wrote it and still under the influence of Balzac whom he never ceased to admire; anyone who, unaware of the real author, ascribed the story to the author of *La Fille aux Yeux d'Or*, could be forgiven. *La Fanfarlo* has considerable merit as a short story in its own right; the plot is skilfully developed, the four characters credible. None the less, the main interest of the work is probably its autobiographical aspects, at any rate so far as the sparkling Samuel Cramer, author of a book of poems, *Les Orfraies*, is concerned, evidently modelled on Baudelaire as he saw himself in the early twenties: dashing, sardonic, voluptuous. Madame de Cosmelly may have been inspired by his half-brother's wife,[75] La Fanfarlo[76] by Marie Danbrun, the actress, transformed into a dancer in the story.[77] Further, there are evident links with *Les Fleurs du Mal*,[78] and what better suggestion of Baudelaire's style both in prose and poetry than the description of Samuel's: 'Cette parole tantôt brutale comme un chiffre, tantôt délicate et parfumée comme une fleur ou un sachet...'

Les Paradis Artificiels consist of two separate essays: 'Le Poème du Haschisch', derived from an earlier essay entitled 'Du Vin et du Haschisch', and translated extracts from de Quincey's *Confessions of an Opium Eater*. Baudelaire's personal experience of hashish probably dates from the years 1843 to 1847.[79] Nor was his experience limited to hashish; opium was not unknown to him; thus he could both appreciate the authenticity of de Quincey's *Confessions* and link his extracts from them together by his own penetrating commentary, to produce an investigation reminiscent of Nerval's *Aurélia* by its objective, almost clinical, examination of the hashish and opium eaters' mental and moral states, their joys, terrors and progressive enslavement. Like some magic key, these drugs unlock the door to the mysterious kingdom lying beyond the fringe of normal experience and before the addict's spell-bound gaze are revealed, to a degree of intensity the uninitiated cannot know, the beauties inherent in all phenomena.

Like other drug takers, Baudelaire had presumably been tempted at the outset by the lure of curiosity[80] and by man's constant need of 'escape' to some kind of beatitude: 'il (l'homme) a, sans s'inquiéter de violer les lois de sa constitution, cherché dans la science physique, dans la pharmaceutique, dans les plus grossières liqueurs,

[75] See *La Fanfarlo*, edited by Claude Pichois; edn. du Rocher, 1957.
[76] The name was perhaps imitated from a dancer, well-known during the July Monarchy, la Fanfarnou.
[77] *Ibid.* But another model has been suggested for la Fanfarlo, Elise Sergent, known as la Pomaré. See Gustave Kahn, preface, *F. du M.*; Flammarion.
[78] e.g. 'elle osait marcher en dansant', and *F. du M.*, xxvii, 'Le temps était noir comme la tombe... pluie', and *F. du M.*, lxxv, cv, and cxiii.
[79] See Conard edn., iv, p. 285.   [80] *Paradis*, iii.

dans les parfums les plus subtils, sous tous les climats et dans tous les temps, les moyens de fuir, ne fût-ce que pour quelques heures, son habitacle de fange...'[81]

But also, at the price of little effort, the drugs gave him the power to extend his sensuous experience, intensify the acuteness of his vision, accelerate his mental mechanisms, in short achieve the sense of 'correspondances': 'puis arrivent les équivoques, les méprises et les transpositions d'idées. Les sons se revêtent de couleurs, et les couleurs contiennent une musique... tout cerveau poétique dans son état sain et normal, conçoit facilement ces analogies... seulement, ces analogies revêtent alors [i.e. with hashish] une vivacité inaccoutumée; elles pénètrent, elles envahissent, elles accablent l'esprit de leur caractère despotique.'[82]

Whether or not his experience of drugs gave him the initial idea of 'correspondances', he found it confirmed by Poe and Hoffmann;[83] for him it was present in all art he termed 'modern' and personally responded to vigorously – e.g. Poe, Delacroix, Wagner; it inspires his own poetic conception.

Most of the poems of *Les Fleurs du Mal* (1857) were written between 1840 and 1850,[84] but Baudelaire was constantly revising, adding or eliminating.

The second edition (1861) contained 127 poems as against the 101 poems of the first edition, and that despite the six poems he had had to cut out after the famous prosecution and condemnation the first edition had led to. These 'pièces condamnées' were published with divers other poems in *Les Epaves* (1866).

Les Fleurs du Mal are not a mere collection of isolated poems, they have something of the ordered structure of a book with the poems placed in a thematic pattern, that has nothing to do with the chronological order of their composition.

The Preface communicates at once what was to be one of the constants of the work – the poet's overwhelming sense of the sin in the world, and crowning sin of all – 'ennui':

> Dans la ménagerie infâme de nos vices,...
> Il en est un plus laid, plus méchant, plus immonde...
> C'est l'ennui!

By 'ennui' we must understand boredom raised to a metaphysical pitch of anguish at the purposelessness of life and linked with 'spleen', the outward moroseness, it causes. In the poet's view that sense is familiar to us all:

> Tu le connais, lecteur, ce monstre délicat
> Hypocrite lecteur – mon semblable – mon frère!

[81] *Ibid.*, i.   [82] *Ibid.*, iii.
[83] See *Salon de 1846*, quotation from Hoffmann's *Kreisleriana*.
[84] See *Fleurs du Mal*, Conard edn., p. 298.

In claiming to speak for Everyman, the poet assumes almost a moralist's role, but, be that as it may, with 'ennui' as the major spiritual torment of life, the various sections *Les Fleurs du Mal* are divided into, record the types of experience whereby the poet seeks escape: the quest of beauty in the arts, love, Paris life, wine and tobacco, vice, revolt.[85] But all types of experience in this life offer no more than a temporary opiate (to speak as Baudelaire might) and so in the last section, 'La Mort', the poet invokes death.[86]

The last poem of all, 'Le Voyage', is one of the longest poems in the book, perhaps because it is like a final summing up of life; we start out with hope:

> Pour l'enfant, amoureux de cartes et d'estampes,
> L'univers est égal à son vaste appétit.
> Ah! que le monde est grand à la clarté des lampes!

but we end with an overwhelming sense of bankruptcy, of the dreary sameness and permanence of sin:

> Pour ne pas oublier la chose capitale,
> Nous avons vu partout, et sans l'avoir cherché,
> Du haut jusques en bas de l'échelle fatale
> Le spectacle ennuyeux de l'immortel peché . . .

Thus Baudelaire turns to death:

> O Mort, vieux capitaine . . .

The image of a ship, so familiar in *Les Fleurs du Mal*, is suggested with powerful effect:

> . . . il est temps! levons l'ancre!
> Ce pays nous ennuie, O Mort! Appareillons!

Sky and sea may be as black as ink, but:

> Nos coeurs que tu connais sont remplis de rayons

We sail out of the book, as it were, on this triumphant image; death will bring an experience that cannot be worse, may be better, and in any case – Oh joy! – will be new.

Within the longest section of the book – 'Spleen et Idéal' – three cycles of love poems form an inner pattern; of these, the largest number are inspired by Jeanne Duval, the mulatto with whom Baudelaire's relationship over the years was a mixture of sensual love, hatred and jealousy (a fact that some of the poems bear eloquent witness to), a smaller number[87] by Madame Sabatier,

85 Parmée, *Twelve French Poets*, introduction.
86 *Ibid.*
87 'Tout entière', 'Que diras-tu ce soir', 'Le Flambeau Vivant', 'Réversibilité', 'Confession', 'L'Aube Spirituelle', 'Harmonie du Soir', 'Le Flacon', 'A celle qui est trop gaie', 'Hymne' and perhaps also 'Semper Eadem'.

la Présidente, and another small group by Marie Danbrun.[88] Within this inner pattern, like a box within a box, is yet another series of patterns: the theme of bodily beauty in 'Les Bijoux'[89] (for Jeanne), 'Tout Entière' (for Madame Sabatier) and 'Le Beau Navire' (for Marie Danbrun perhaps?) – of the three 'Les Bijoux', as could be expected, is the most sensual; the theme of intercession: 'De Profundis' (for Jeanne), 'Réversibilité' (for Madame Sabatier), 'L'Irréparable' (for Marie). Other themes have been suggested.[90]

This complex design – an example Mallarmé was to follow in *Poésies* – may owe its existence to Delacroix's dictum about Nature's being merely a dictionary, and Baudelaire's consequent intention to construct a significant unity from the variety of his experience. But the idea of what has been called its inner 'architecture'[91] must not be exaggerated, if by the term be meant a rigorous uniformity of attitude either overall or even within each section. Baudelaire claimed for himself the right of any man to contradiction. Thus within 'Spleen et Idéal' the theme of love gives rise to different orientations, some of them contradictory; the visions of Paris in *Tableaux Parisiens* are diverse, the same may be said of 'Le Vin'; the tone of hatred and revolt in the three poems of 'Révolte' is very different from the quasi-mystical attitude towards death of the last section; within the last section, finally, the ideas about death vary, having in common only the notions of deliverance and final joy, but there too 'Le Rêve d'un Curieux' is an exception,[92] echoing the theme that death may deceive, already expressed for example in 'Le squelette laboureur' (*Tableaux Parisiens*).

An immediate formal impression provided by *Les Fleurs du Mal* is the relative shortness of the poems; many are sonnets; we are reminded that Baudelaire, like Poe, condemned 'l'hérésie de la longueur ou de la dimension, la valeur absurde attribuée aux gros poèmes';[93] the value of a poem lies in its power to excite the soul, but that excitement is fleeting; if it has subsided before the reader has finished reading the poem, the poem is by that much too long.

This shows that a poem in Baudelaire's view is not merely a vehicle for the expression of *his* sufferings, a release for *his* emotions and therefore an intimate link between poet and reader – as the Romantics thought a poem should be – but an objective entity,

---

[88] 'L'Irréparable', 'Causerie', 'Chant d'Automne', 'A une Madonne', 'Sonnet d'Automne', and perhaps 'Le beau Navire' and 'L'Invitation au Voyage'.
[89] One of the 'pièces condamnés'.
[90] See on these points, C.-E. Magny: 'Ce grand bélier: Baudelaire', in *Preuves*, No. 57 (March 1959).
[91] Barbey d'Aurevilly.
[92] See on these points, C.-E. Magny, op. cit.
[93] *Notes Nouvelles sur Edgar Poe.*

designed to make an independent impact. It will also affect the whole conception of poetry, the choice of subject; anything that suggests a development in time, an action, a story, any kind of discursive movement by way of moral exposition or argument, will be eschewed. This lack of progression leads Baudelaire to reintroduce into French poetry the traditional song technique:[94] refrains (e.g. 'L'Invitation au Voyage'[95]) and recurring lines in a variety of rhyme schemes (e.g. 'Le Balcon', 'Réversibilité', 'Harmonie du Soir', etc.), thus turning the poem back on itself. The poet must capture the fleeting moment of his exhilaration, register the crisis point of his experience and imprison it, as a fly in amber, and, as it were, hand the poem over to the reader as a thing of beauty, something static but at the same time a small power unit capable of developing a tremendous potential of suggestion like the old scent bottle . . .

> D'où jaillit toute vive une âme qui revient . . .
> Voilà le souvenir enivrant qui voltige
> Dans l'air troublé; les yeux se ferment; le vertige
> Saisit l'âme vaincue . . .   ('Le Flacon')

A poem like a drug must first subjugate the reader by its impact, the result of its emotional intensity, or of the force, the crudity, the horror (e.g. 'La Charogne', 'Voyage à Cythère') of the images, or of that mixture it evokes, of the eternal and the relative or circumstantial,[96] without which no true beauty exists. When the reader is conditioned, the poem must induce reverie; and what is reverie, if not a chain of silent images or more precisely (to keep within the static idea) a palimpsest[97] of images, each, as it fades, revealing the one beneath; a poem must be like a dark glassy pool we peer into, deeper and deeper. 'La plus grande nouveauté de son art n'a-t-elle pas été précisément d'immobiliser ses poèmes, de les développer en profondeur?'[98] Force of impact, deliberate lack of movement allowing, instead, development in depth, reverie at different levels – 'La Chevelure' affords one amongst numerous examples of these essential elements of Baudelaire's technique:

> O toison, moutonnant jusque sur l'encolure!
> O boucles!

Like an artist suggesting an object with a few significant strokes, the poet provides the minimum physical notations.

[94] See C.-E. Magny, op. cit.
[95] Is the sound of the word 'luxe' not a blemish though, in this poem?
[96] Baudelaire's essay on Constantin Guys, 'Peintre de la vie moderne'.
[97] Baudelaire himself uses the word in speaking of the brain: 'Qu'est-ce que le cerveau humain, sinon un palimpseste immense et naturel'? Paradis Artificiels; 'Un Mangeur d'Opium', viii.
[98] Gide, Nouveaux Prétextes.

The physical image at once gives way to a sensuous suggestion: 'O parfum . . .', the poet, be it noted, makes no effort to describe the scent; the word 'parfum' is merely a visual or auditive signal to switch the readers' attention, and immediately we pass to the effect of the scent on us: 'O parfum chargé de nonchaloir!' Immediately before his ecstatic gaze a host of faint and distant memories that are in reality deep down in his own consciousness seem to appear in the dark scented forest of tresses:

> Tout un monde lointain, absent, presque défunt,
> Vit dans tes profondeurs, forêt aromatique!

The vision changes:

> Fortes tresses, soyez la houle qui m'enlève . . .
> mer d'ébène . . .
> . . . noir océan . . .

The poet's liberated spirit embarks on the ocean of his dreams. The poem is entirely subjective – experience is bound to be – and in that forms no exception in *Les Fleurs du Mal*, but such is its evocative power of tropical sights, sounds, colour and smell that the reader unconsciously identifies himself with the poet, enters into the 'je' of the poem and shares the nostalgic flight to the Isles.

Another striking example of how the subjective experience of the poet achieves general symbolic value is provided by 'La Musique'. 'La Musique souvent me prend comme une mer'. In this and the succeeding lines a series of words and ideas gradually brings into the reader's mind the image of a ship in full sail. Not until the tenth line does the word 'vaisseau' confirm the image the reader has been led to create for himself and which is all the more firmly fixed in consequence; that the ship, now struggling in the storm, now mirrored in the flat calm, symbolizes the poet's experience under the inspiration of music is secondary, for it has become, if not the symbol of our own experience, at least one we can accept as valid for men generally.

In contrast[99] with Baudelaire's skilful creation of the symbol in this poem may be cited Hugo's introductory poem of *Les Contemplations*:

> Un jour je vis, debout au bord des flots mouvants . . .
> Passer, gonflant ses voiles, un rapide navire . . .

The ship is placed before the reader's eye in the first stanza; at once the lesson follows:

> Et j'entendis, penché sur l'abîme des cieux . . .
> Me parler à l'oreille une voix . . .
> Poète, tu fais bien!

[99] G. Michaud, *L'Oeuvre et ses Techniques*, Nizet (1957).

The image, the idea directly communicated by the Almighty to Hugo, and Hugo, chosen to communicate it thus, all remain separate; clear-cut, didactic, orotund ... and tiresome. There is no chance of a communication or fusion of experience because on the poet's side no experience, no deeply felt experience at any rate, exists to communicate; merely some visual impressions suggesting an idea (if it may be called such).

The reader of *Les Fleurs du Mal*, on the other hand, although he knows the poems to be deeply rooted in the poet's personal experience, to have no point of reference other than the poet's own emotion, none the less loses sight, at any rate in the most successful poems, of the poet's personality and sufferings because of the symbols the poet has created for him, nay, led him to create for himself.

It should be noted too that these are not usually the result of 'word-painting' in the manner of Leconte de Lisle, whose aim is essentially descriptive, who uses adjectives or adjectival phrases to create before the reader's inner eye whatever object or scene the poet has in mind; the adjectives therefore accurately describe the object. In Baudelaire they are connected more with the emotion of the poet or the emotional state he desires to excite in the reader: 'un ciel chagrin' ('Les Phares') ... 'le soir charmant' ('Crépuscule du Soir') ... 'aimable soir' ('Crépuscule du Soir') ... 'O parfum, chargé de nonchaloir!' ('La Chevelure'). The images become symbols charged with emotional content.

In all these ways the poet creates that 'sorcellerie évocatoire' he speaks of in 'Fusée',[100] thus does he distil from the words of Nature's dictionary their inner spiritual content, that quintessence he refers to in the oft-quoted lines:

> Car j'ai de chaque chose extrait la quintessence
> Tu m'as donné ta boue, j'en ai fait de l'or[101]

In a letter (25 April 1857) to Poulet-Malassis, Baudelaire refers to '*les poèmes nocturnes*' (his italics); here is the first mention of the idea that was to ripen into that collection of fifty fugitive prose pieces, only some of which under varying titles appeared during Baudelaire's lifetime; ill-luck and review editors' misgivings were the cause. The complete collection with the dual title of *Petits Poèmes en Prose* (*Le Spleen de Paris*) were published only two years after his death, in the first full edition of his works (1869).

In abandoning verse forms, Baudelaire was sacrificing great advantages: rhyme, rhythm, varieties of verse structure, concentration, all the advantages that confer upon a poem its closed independent

---

[100] No. xvii, *Journaux Intimes*.
[101] 'Epilogue adressé à la ville de Paris', from *Fragments inemployés* of *F. du M.* See Conard, 'Juvenilia', *Oeuvres Posthumes*.

unity. To the question: what was he hoping to get in return? an answer is suggested in section three of the *Notes Nouvelles sur Edgar Poe* where he analyzes the advantages of the short story, of which Poe was, in his view, a master, both over the novel and over the poem.

The short story, we are told, leaves a much more powerful impression on the mind than the novel, because of its beauty; the effect is concentrated, not dispersed; the author, instead of being obliged to fit his thought to a broad series of events, can *ab initio* decide what effect he wishes to produce and then build up a rapidly developing incident to achieve it; from the beginning to the end he remains in control; he can, if skilful, find a perfect equation between means and purpose. Over the poem, the short story has the advantage of suppleness. A poem's aim is beauty; rhythm is a valuable factor but may be an obstacle to the untrammelled development of thought which is the aim of the short story; a lesser aim perhaps, but with greater variety, more easily communicable to the reader, disposing of a greater range of tone and shades of language.

The craft of the novel is not applicable here; but the rest of this passage, where Baudelaire speaks both from experience (*La Fanfarlo*) and as the admiring and penetrating critic of Poe, applies closely to what he aimed at in the *Petits Poèmes en Prose*. He has in a sense taken on a wager, that of retaining the interest and attention of the reader, without exploiting the advantages of poetry, nor yet acquiring the advantages of the short story; he hovers between the two, endeavouring to combine the merits of both; the lyrical beauty of the poem, the vigorous impact of the short story, reinforced by the suppleness of prose. The treatment varies according to the incident, object or idea that inspires him at the moment; at times he seems on the very edge of a poem (e.g. Nos. i, vii, xxxiv, xlv), at others he comes very near to the short story, reaping the advantage of a rapidly developing and dramatic narrative in the Maupassant manner (e.g. Nos. ix, xxx, xlvii); at others again the story in miniature is very like an apologue (e.g. Nos. xix, xx). With the variety of treatment goes the great range of attitudes from pity (e.g. Nos. ii, xiv) to a savage irony or sardonic humour, (e.g. Nos. ix, xv, xxx, xlvii, xlix) which hovers over so many of the pieces, with such virulent effect – particularly noteworthy perhaps because so evidently a part of Baudelaire's nature:

> Ne suis-je pas un faux accord
> Dans la divine symphonie
> Grâce à la vorace Ironie
> Qui me secoue et qui me mord?[102]

[102] *Fleurs du Mal*: 'l'Héautontimorouménos'.

In *Les Fleurs du Mal* the irony is under control; in the prose poems it has free rein. A number of parallels exist between the prose poems and poems in *Les Fleurs du Mal*,[103] themes that are typical of the latter recur constantly in the former: the nostalgia of seas and harbours, of travel and escape, Paris solitude and crowds, the pathos of aged women and widows, the fatal attraction of woman's beauty, feminine cruelty and, often, vacuity ('sot comme une lorette'), dandyism; at every turn the reader of the *Petits Poèmes* . . . will find some reminder, not only of *Les Fleurs du Mal*, but of Baudelaire's other works: *Les Paradis Artificiels*, the critical essays, even *La Fanfarlo*. Thus the *Petits Poèmes* . . . are like a final welling-up of the Baudelairian springs of poetry, a triumphant re-assertion in prose form of the aesthetic formula that Baudelaire had built up for himself from his experience and his studies of Delacroix, Poe and, last but not least, Constantin Guys; nature as the dictionary, the spiritual beauty hidden within external reality, the ambivalent 'beau moderne' compounded of the eternal and the contemporary, the diurnal motley astringently distilled.

In a letter to Sainte-Beuve (15 January 1866) Baudelaire, refer-ring to what was then still no more than an idea, speaks of 'l'espoir de pouvoir montrer un de ces jours un nouveau Joseph Delorme, accrochant sa pensée rapsodique à chaque accident de sa flânerie et tirant de chaque objet une moralité désagréable'. The quotation brings out three points: the lyrical element of the *Petits Poèmes*: 'sa pensée rapsodique . . .'; the trivial and often sordid scene that inspires most of them: 'chaque accident de sa flânerie . . .'; and finally the moral aspect. Some of the prose poems tend indeed to become apologues, as though, by setting aside poetry in favour of prose, Baudelaire becomes less inward-looking; by developing scenes in a narrative way, in contrast to what he does in *Les Fleurs du Mal*, he is often less concerned to define his own attitude than to reflect on the general significance: 'Leur moralité désagréable'. The prose poems taken separately make less impact than poems from *Les Fleurs du Mal*; each is less detachable from the whole group because it lacks the advantage of verse form, but cumula-tively their effect is powerful; they are like a summing up of the whole Baudelairian matter.

No less significant in their own way are the *Journaux Intimes*. Published posthumously (1887) they comprise two parts: *Fusées* and *Mon coeur mis à nu*, the former dating from not later than 1857,

---

[103] e.g. *P.P. en P.*, Nos. ii, xiii, xxv, and *F. du M.*, 'Les Petites Vieilles'; *P.P. en P.*, No. iii and *F. du M.*, 'Chant d'Automne'; *P.P. en P.*, Nos. xvii, xxxi and *F. du M.*, 'Parfum Exotique', 'Le Fantôme', 'La Chevelure'; *P.P. en P.*, No. xviii and *F. du M.*, 'L'Invitation au Voyage'.

N.B. 'L'Horloge' (*P.P. en P.*, No. xvi) has no connection with the poem of that name in *F. du M.*

the latter belonging for the most part to 1862.[104] Both consist of a series of reflections, some reduced to mere jottings, others more fully worked out. They are an illuminating commentary on his work, both creative and critical; they are like a prism splitting up the rays of his genius: his attitude towards society, politics, progress and the like; the satanist, the aesthete, the hedonist, the aristocratic dandy, the moralist and judge of his generation, the latter-day René,[105] sharing his spiritual forbear's moral vertigo – 'la sensation du gouffre... de l'action, du rêve, du souvenir...'[106] – with the same sense of being marked out by destiny for isolation,[107] all are there. Not the least moving is Baudelaire's courageous recognition that he was on the verge of paying the price of deliberately fostering mental excitement for the sake of poetry: 'J'ai cultivé mon hystérie avec jouissance et terreur. Maintenant, j'ai toujours le vertige, et aujourd'hui 23 janvier 1862 j'ai subi un singulier avertissement, j'ai senti passer sur moi le vent de l'aile de l'imbécilité.'[108]

The presentiment of the lurking tragedy, like the fleeting moment of 'L'Horloge'[109] (... avec sa voix d'insecte), drove him on: 'A Honfleur! le plus tôt possible, avant de tomber plus bas. Que de pressentiments... envoyés par Dieu, qu'il est *grandement temps* d'agir, de considérer la minute présente comme la plus importante des minutes et de faire ma *perpétuelle volupté*[110] de mon tourment ordinaire, c'est à dire du travail.'[111]

That the public of Baudelaire's generation, with little to guide them but the malevolence of Sainte-Beuve,[112] the Olympian condescension of the Guernsey exile and his 'frisson nouveau',[113] not to mention the hostile rabble of lesser critics, should have seen in the poet of *Les Fleurs du Mal* the deliberate intention to shock and scandalize, that the next generation should in particular have seen in his cult of beauty the reflection of their own aesthetic delights,

[104] See *Journaux Intimes*, Crès edn., 1920. Note pp. 138, 139.
[105] He was a great admirer of Chateaubriand. See Crès, op. cit. Note p. 147.
[106] *Mon cœur mis à nu*, No. cix.
[107] *Ibid.*, No. xxxiv.
[108] *Ibid.*, No. cix.
[109] *Les Fleurs du Mal*, No. cvii.
[110] His italics in both cases.
[111] *Fusées*, No. xvi.
[112] 'Il n'est pas si aisé qu'on le croirait de prouver à des académiciens ...comme quoi il y a, dans *Les Fleurs du Mal*, des pièces très remarquables vraiment pour le talent et pour l'art; de leur expliquer... qu'en somme M. Baudelaire a trouvé moyen de bâtir, à l'extrémité d'une langue de terre réputée inhabitable... un kiosque bizarre... Ce singulier kiosque...qui depuis quelque temps attire les regards à la pointe extrême du Kamtchatka romantique, j'appelle cela *la folie Baudelaire*'. (S-B.'s italics.) See Sainte-Beuve, 'Des prochaines elections de l'Académie', 20 January 1862, *Nouveau Lundis*, Vol. I.
[113] 'Que faites-vous quand vous écrivez ces vers saisissants: "Les Sept Vieillards" et "Les Petites Vieilles" que vous me dédiez, et dont je vous remercie?... Vous dotez le ciel de l'art d'on ne sait quel rayon macabre. Vous créez un frisson nouveau?' Letter to Baudelaire, 6 October 1859.

all that is understandable. To-day with all the other works at our disposal besides *Les Fleurs du Mal – La Fanfarlo, Les Paradis Artificiels, Les Curiosités Esthétiques, L'Art Romantique, Les Petits Poèmes en Prose* and *Les Journaux Intimes* – we are in a better position to understand him, to see how with all his Romanticism, he was both a man of his own literary generation ('la consolation par les arts'[114]) rejecting the materialism of his day and a forerunner of the Symbolists;[115] in fine, the greatest French poet of the nineteenth century.

IV. NERVAL

Translator of Goethe's *Faust*[116] and of poems[117] by Heine, occasional light opera librettist,[118] dramatic critic and peripatetic journalist, Gerard de Nerval[119] (1808–55) was all of these; but the voluminous writings that resulted could scarcely justify the radiant reputation that is his today; this rests on the small collection of sonnets entitled *Les Chimères* (1854) and, amongst the prose works, on *Les Filles du Feu* (1854), with particular emphasis on *Sylvie*. Other important prose writings are: *Les Illuminés* (1852), *Les Petits Châteaux de Bohême* (1853), *Aurélia* (1854) and *Voyage en Orient* (1851).

None of these works is directly autobiographical but in one way or another they are intimately connected with Nerval's tragic spiritual adventure, tragic and mysterious. The aura of mystery that hangs about Nerval brings his personality and work into sharp relief, the esoteric mystery of the sonnets, the mystery of Nerval's occultism, the mystery that attaches inevitably to insanity, deepened in his case by the alternating periods of madness and lucidity, darkened by his suicide.

Nerval's mother died in 1810. A child of two may have learnt to know his mother; that he can acutely feel her loss at the time or that her memory can have anything but a shadowy reality is doubtful; such a loss at such an age need be followed by no inevitable consequences.

Yet the very shadowiness of the memory may explain its power in some cases of which Nerval's appears to be one. A child, deprived of protective maternal affection, may, as he slowly becomes aware of what he lacks, build up for himself both as a bulwark

[114] e.g. Huysmans, *A Rebours*.
[115] Notably in the sonnet 'Correspondances'.
[116] *Faust I* (1827); *Faust II* (1840).
[117] Translations published in *Revue des Deux Mondes* (1848).
[118] *Piquillo* (1837), *Léo Burckhart* (1838), *Les Monténégrins* (1846), *Le Chariot d'Enfant* (1850), *L'Imagier de Haarlem* (1851); also eight scenes from *Faust* to the music of Berlioz.
[119] Real name Gérard Labrunie.

of security and as an emotional compensation, a dream that becomes rooted in his mind as firmly, more firmly than any images
derived from day to day experience. These crowd in upon him
jostling one another, and in their haste for recognition drive each
other out before they have time to make any deep impression; the
dream is a personal creation of his own, an intimate sanctuary in
his being, grows with him like lettering on the bark of a tree,
invites the habit of sliding into a dream world, may become obsessive. Nerval's capacity for marrying dream and reality is marked –
'l'épanchement du songe dans la vie réelle, to quote his own
words.[120] The initial lack of security as a distant result of his
mother's death may account for the all-pervading sense of quest
both in his life and writings, a quest that takes two forms, often
merging into each other: the pursuit of an ideal love, both protective and tender, and the search for a firm pattern of belief; a dual
quest that, if successful, could provide the stability or security he
lacked.

The quest for a belief is reflected in both *Les Illuminés* and
Voyage en Orient.

After his mother's death, Nerval had been entrusted to the care
of a great-uncle, Antoine Boucher, at Mortefontaine. Here, in the
heart of the wooded and soft misty landscapes of the Valois, still
fresh with the memories of Rousseau,[121] Nerval spent much of his
boyhood, here he acquired his interest in the rich store of local
legends,[122] and from his uncle's library his first acquaintance with
the writings of the eighteenth-century mystical philosophers and
free-masons. The kind of knowledge Nerval later acquired of esoteric writers has its source in that library; *Les Illuminés* are evidence of it but again the significance of this work in relation to
Nerval himself extends beyond a matter of erudition in by-ways of
history: the origins of free-masonry are connected with the secret
mysteries of antiquity. Thus Nerval's interest in the subject becomes part of his quest for the sources of esotericism; in addition,
he evidently thought of the eccentric characters he studies in some
way as kindred spirits: Nicolas pursuing an ideal love in a succession of women,[123] Raoul Spifame whose dream becomes reality –
for him, and Cazotte, with much the same experience of precognition.[124] 'L'intérêt des mémoires, des confessions, des auto-
biographies, des voyages même', he writes in his study of Restif,[125]

---

[120] *Aurélia, Oeuvres*, Garnier edn., Vol. I, p. 760.
[121] Ermenonville was close by.
[122] cf. 'Chansons et Légendes du Valois' in *Les Filles du Feu*.
[123] 'Cette femme, il l'avait vue autrefois, mais non pas telle qu'elle lui
apparaissait maintenant ... rêve.' *Oeuvres*, Vol. I, p. 173.
[124] '... le narrateur qui croit à sa légende ...' *Oeuvres*, Vol. I, p. 272.
[125] *Les Confidences de Nicolas.*

'tient à ce que la vie de chaque homme devient ainsi un miroir où chacun peut s'étudier, dans une partie du moins de ses qualités ou de ses défauts.'[126] Restif's voluminous series of novels are shown to be chapters, as it were, of his personal experience, just as Nerval's own writings are chapters of his.

Voyage en Orient is in the first instance a record of Nerval's journey to the Levant (1843) which took him to Malta, Egypt, Syria, Cyprus, Constantinople and Naples.[127] Nerval, an entertaining and skilful journalist, an acute observer, relates his day-to-day travel experience. This aspect of the *Voyage* accords well with a period when travel was no longer an idea or even a practice lying beyond the ordinary man's ken, and when the interest in foreign lands was rapidly being disseminated by printed and pictorial means: paintings, lithographs, engravings. Particularly was this true of the Near East; since the days of Chateaubriand and Byron what Romantic had not felt, even if he had not always obeyed, its lure? Lamartine, Hugo, Musset, Gautier, Flaubert, Delacroix, Decamps, Fromentin. Nerval was no exception.

Yet the attraction for him lay not, as for so many of his contemporaries, in the sights, ruins and colour of the East, not primarily at least, but in its legends and lore, which might provide a unifying pattern for the different religions of the world and reveal the secret of life and death. This intimate personal aspect, which was the reason why he undertook the journey in the first place, is reflected particularly in the two long tales interpolated into the travelogue much in the manner of *The Arabian Nights* or *The Decameron*: *Histoire du Calife Hakem* and *Histoire de la Reine du Matin et de Soliman, Prince des Génies*.

The sense of a quest in the *Voyage* is insistent. 'Ne suis-je pas toujours, hélas!', he writes, 'le fils d'un siècle déshérité d'illusions, qui a besoin de toucher pour croire, et de rêver le passé . . . sur ses débris.'[128] The Near East appears to him as 'ce sol sacré qui est notre première patrie à tous . . .', he feels the need to refresh himself: 'à ces sources vivifiantes de l'humanité, d'où ont découlé la poésie et les croyances de nos pères.'[129] Hakem, the God of the Druses and Adoniram,[130] the mysterious descendant of the sons of Cain, the sons of fire, for both Nerval feels a secret affinity. Both have dream-experiences similar to those of the author of *Aurélia*. Tubal-Kaïn appears in a vision to Adoniram and encourages him:

[126] Nerval's letter to Alexandre Dumas, which stands as an introduction to *Les Filles du Feu*, gives a valuable insight into Nerval's mentality and his capacity to identify himself with the experience of others.
[127] The introduction entitled 'Vers l'Orient', where the author speaks of Germany and Austria, relates in reality to an earlier journey. His trip to the Levant began and ended at Marseilles.
[128] *Oeuvres*, Vol. II, p. 77, Garnier.
[129] *Ibid.*, p. 378.   [130] In *Histoire de la Reine du Matin*.

'Fils de Kaïn! subis ta destinée...Les Génies du feu viendront à ton aide...'[131] Perhaps Nerval, with his profound knowledge of cabalistic writings and his capacity for identifying himself with characters in history and legend, may have derived strength and encouragement from the message. The mystical fire, controlled by the sons of Cain, the source of their power in their struggle against the sons of earth under the leadership of Adonaïs, is also the fire of the title, *Les Filles du Feu*, and the dream figures of that work are, in Nerval's belief, of the race of Cain, as he felt himself to be.

Nerval's tour in the Levant was not the only journey he under-took; he travelled extensively in Europe: Italy, Belgium, Germany, Austria, Holland, England; a nomadic instinct seems to beckon him. Germany, Austria and Italy had particular significance for him; his mother was buried in Silesia.[132] This fact served in the first instance to draw his gaze across the Rhine and to make of him the translator of Goethe and Heine, but Germany also provided him with inspiration and spiritual comfort;[133] Germany and Austria gradually became associated in his mind with the East, to which they become a gateway; the *Voyage en Orient* purports to start in Germany and Austria, and that section of the work is en-titled 'Vers l'Orient'. By its strong links with antiquity, the south-ern part of the Italian peninsula also becomes a portal to the world of Pythagorean, cabalistic and Isiac mysteries, wherein he sought to find the underlying pattern of human life and history.

Les Petits Châteaux de Bohème recall scenes and episodes in Nerval's life during the early 1830's. The reminiscences here are on the plane of reality, the dream-like nostalgia is no more than suggested by the title: memories as frail as a house of cards and suffused with the romantic aura of Bohemian life. Yet for Nerval the word 'Châteaux' probably had a symbolic significance, con-nected with the distant adoration he had felt in childhood for Sophie Dawes, Baroness de Feuchères, châtelaine of Mortefontaine. The suggestion gains strength from one of the 'Odelettes' incorpor-ated in the work. 'Fantaisie',[134] the poem in question, evoked: 'un château de brique à coins de pierre' and a lady at her casement window: 'une dame à sa haute fenêtre, Blonde aux yeux noirs...' This dream castle recurs in the more important and more character-istically Nervalian work *Sylvie*,[135] woven from reminiscences of his childhood. The constant shift from the present of the narrator

[131] *Oeuvres*, Vol. II, p. 633.
[132] Gross Glogau, whither she had gone to join her husband, an army doctor, in charge of a hospital there.
[133] By the writings of the German mystics in which he was interested: Boehme, Mesmer, Gall; also Swedenborg – by extension northwards.
[134] Originally published in 1832.
[135] chap. 2, 'Adrienne', *Oeuvres*, Vol. I., p. 594.

(Nerval himself) to his own childhood, which is therefore at a double-remove from the reader, is at the source of this work's dream-like quality, much more than the fact that some sections of the story are in fact dreams. Yet the shift is neither jerky nor sudden. This too is a detail which our own experience of dreams will confirm. Just as in our dreams we float effortlessly from place to place without reference to time or space, so do some of the characters in *Sylvie*. At the same time the scenes depicted are firm and clear cut; the crystalline precision of the scenes, their arbitrary yet smooth succession and the simplicity of the prose make of this work a clear forerunner of Alain-Fournier's *Le Grand Meaulnes*.[136]

Sophie Dawes reappears in the pages of *Sylvie* in the shadowy figure of Adrienne; in addition there is Sylvie the peasant girl of Mortefontaine, a memory of Nerval's youth, and under the name of Aurélia, the actress Jenny Colon, idealized figures, all of them, forming part of the gallery of *Les Filles du Feu*.

There is a suggestion of arbitrarily chosen material to fill out a slender volume in *Les Filles du Feu*: a romantic tale from the seventeenth century ('Angélique'), personal reminiscences ('Sylvie', 'Octavie'), a folkloric story ('Chansons et légendes du Valois'), reflections about the ancient cult of Isis, arising from a visit to Pompeii ('Isis'), a dramatic sketch faintly reminiscent of Musset ('Corilla'); a literary patchwork indeed, but the stories are like cameos of his feminine ideal of love, tenderness and beauty, derived from Nerval's direct experience in childhood and early maturity, partly from his researches in the byways of history and in the secret religions.

For all the delicate charm of *Sylvie*, the highest point of Nerval's achievement is *Les Chimères*. Often the lines have an arresting beauty irrespective of their contribution to the underlying meaning of the sonnet:

> Toujours, sous les rameaux du laurier de Virgile,
> Le pâle hortensia s'unit au myrte vert   ('Myrtho')
> La déese avait fui sur sa conque dorée,
> La mer nous renvoyait son image adorée
> Et les cieux rayonnaient sous l'écharpe d'Iris   ('Horus')
> La connais-tu, Dafne, cette ancienne romance,
> Au pied du sycomore, ou sous les lauriers blancs
> Sous l'olivier, le myrte, ou les saules tremblants,
> Cette chanson d'amour qui toujours recommence?   ('Delfica')

Such lines by their visual or rhythmical qualities call forth an immediate response; they are incantatory.

The same may be said with greater force of the best known sonnet of the collection, 'El Desdichado', for here there is more than

---

[136] See vol. V, chap. 4, iv.

a response to the detached beauty of the lines; we can share the poet's mood. There is a wealth of suggestion in the title – the disinherited[137] – and in the first stanza, 'le ténébreux', a physical description conveying the idea of a moral attitude; 'le veuf' – strengthening the sense of loss inherent in the title; 'l'inconsolé' – an emotional condition; 'le prince d'Aquitaine à la tour abolie' – evoking a vaguely historical figure against a background of ruin; the sense of despair is strengthened in the third line by the physical image, of the star's light put out, the whole culminating in the image of the last line: 'Le soleil noir de la mélancolie', so powerful that it forces the attention and stimulates our visual imagination into creating a vision that corresponds to no physical experience, but enables us to feel the poem's mood of spiritual anguish.

But can we be content to remain on this superficial level of appreciation? The least inaccessible sonnets of *Les Chimères* are the five grouped together under the title of *Le Christ aux Oliviers*;[138] they are earlier in date than the remainder and for that reason perhaps less tightly packed with recondite and apparently unrelated allusions. In contrast to Vigny's grievance[139] against God for not revealing the divine plan in the Universe, thereby implying that the plan exists, Nerval's Christ is in despair at finding no creator, his death is part of no divine purpose, Pilate's action was fortuitous, all is chaos:

> Enfin Pilate seul...
> Sentant quelque pitié, se tourna par hasard:
> 'Allez chercher ce fou...'   (*Le Christ aux Oliviers*, iv)

But in the last sonnet Christ is revealed as one in the long chain of victims, whose sacrifice leads to resurrection:[140]

> C'était bien lui, ce fou cet insensé sublime...
> Cet Icare oublié qui remontait les cieux
> Ce Phaéton perdu...
> Ce bel Atys meurtri que Cybèle ranime!

Death and rebirth for ever renewed, a cycle, a recognizable pattern; thus what seemed chaos is shown to have an ordered movement, whence comes security and renewed confidence.[141]

Esoteric poetry may arise from a skilful distillation of sensuous experiences; the result will be a concentration of meaning as powerful as a concentrated scent; alternatively it may arise from an intense absorption of the poet in his own spiritual experience. His eye is turned inwards: his poetry is then likely to be packed with

---

[137] From Scott's *Ivanhoe*.
[138] See A. Fairlie, 'An Approach to Nerval' (*Studies in Modern French Literature*, M.U.P., 1961).
[139] *Le Mont des Oliviers*.
[140] A. Fairlie, op. cit.   [141] A. Fairlie, op. cit.

allusions culled from many sources, physical and intellectual, obscure for the reader, full of light for the poet; they take on something of the character of mystic formulae destined to release the poet's emotive tensions.

Les Chimères have all the signs of both forms of esotericism; an intense inner experience begun in darkest anguish, moving towards the light, with a wealth of symbolic associations drawn now from Nerval's knowledge of the classics, of ancient religious cults and cabalistic interpretations, of necromancy, now from nostalgic memories of his Mediterranean travels – and all on their own levels supporting by their parallelisms the central 'shift of mood from chaos to pattern, from terror to consolation';[142] the whole merged into a complex but organic whole triumphantly controlled within the narrow limits of the sonnet form by the consummate and deliberate artist Nerval was. 'La dernière folie qui me restera probablement', he writes to Alexandre Dumas, 'ce sera de me croire poète...'[143]

Nerval's tendency to carry over his dream-states into daily life had more than once assumed its most acute form, where dream and reality become one. These moments were his 'descentes en enfer',[144] to use his own expression, and there is an evident allusion to them in 'El Desdichado': 'Et j'ai deux fois vainqueur traversé l'Achéron'. *Aurélia* is the compressed chronicle of these recurrent attacks. It is an arresting document which places its author in the long line of visionaries, from St John of Patmos and Dante to Milton and Blake, to whom is given the power of gazing so intently on their visions that they can set them down in clear-cut outline and detail.

The endless chain of dreams merging into each other are recorded with hallucinatory precision; the themes that nourish his other works and some of the dominating experiences of his life, notably his love for Jenny Colon and her death, all recur. *Aurélia* is thus a kind of Nervalian testament, tragic in the light of Nerval's suicide, but having also a significance that extends beyond Nerval. It is an early exploration of the full potential of the human psyche and points the way to a new source of artistic inspiration subsequently to be exploited by Lautréamont,[145] the painter Odilon Redon (1840–1916) and in this century by the Surrealists.

[142] A. Fairlie, op. cit.; see also her analysis of 'El Desdichado' from this point of view and its parallel associations.
[143] A. Dumas, *Les Filles du Feu.*
[144] *Aurélia.*   [145] See below, pp. 348–50.

V. BANVILLE

The cult of form is nowhere better shown than in the work of Théodore de Banville (1823–91). *Les Cariatides* (1842), *Les Stalactites* (1846), *Odes Funambulesques* (1857), to quote the best known, evoke images that symbolize the author's poetic ideals: purity of form, hardness, balance; other titles also carry their message: *Améthystes* (1856) – the brilliance of precious stones; *Odelettes* (1857), *Ballades Joyeuses* (1873), *Rondels* (1875) all recall Banville's delight in reviving ancient French verse forms from Charles d'Orléans to Villon, from Marot to the Pléiade;[146] *Les Occidentales* (1875) are an indirect compliment to Victor Hugo whom he set above all other French poets, with Gautier and Leconte de Lisle in second place:

> Gautier parmi ces joailliers,
> Est prince, et Leconte de l'Isle (*sic*)
> Forge l'or dans ses ateliers;
> Mais le père est là-bas, dans l'île.[147]

Banville's ideas on poetry are summed up in his *Petit Traité de Poésie Française* (1872), where incidentally he salutes the author of *La Légende des Siècles* as the chief architect of modern French prosody.[148] Characteristically Banville uses the word 'poésie' in the title, where we could have expected 'versification', but Banville sees no difference; poetry, of all the arts, is the most arduous, he tells us, its victories are achieved only at the price of the strictest discipline from the poet, of his refusal to compromise with poetic licence – 'il n'y en a pas' – [149] of his skilful handling of rhyme, in particular 'la rime riche'.

Banville's example is as good as his precept; his skill in versification is impeccable; who better than he handles his rhythms to strengthen the image he wishes to create – the jumping clown for example: 'Plus haut! plus loin! de l'air! du bleu!'[150] Rather in the manner of the 'Père de tous les Rimeurs'[151] he rhymes his own achievements:

> ... j'ai tenu bien haut dans ma main
> Le glaive éclatant de la Rime[152]

But what has he to say? In truth, very little. Whatever human emotion he touches on quickly evaporates: the theme of human pity ('Le Paria'[153]) is no more than a versification exercise in 'dizains' (poems of ten decasyllabic verses) in the manner of

---

146 See Prefaces to *Odelettes* and *Ballades Joyeuses*.
147 *Ballades de Victor Hugo, Père de tous les Rimeurs*.
148 See Introduction.   149 See op. cit., chap. 4.
150 'Le Saut du Tremplin' (*Odes Funamb.*).
151 In 'Réponse à un acte d'accusation' (*Contemplations*, Bk. I).
152 'Ma Biographie' (*Odes Funamb.*).   153 *Cariatides*.

Clément Marot, nostalgia, momentarily awakened ('Nous n'irons plus au bois, les lauriers sont coupés[154]), is quickly hustled out to make way for a plastic image:

> Les Amours des bassins, les Naïades en groupe
> Voient reluire au soleil en cristaux découpés
> Les flots silencieux qui coulaient de leur coupe.

The patriotic chord[155] vibrates in 1870 but the theme lacks originality. Like his clown who jumps to the stars Banville feels what he calls 'l'attrait du gouffre d'en haut'[156] but tells us little about his idealism except to register his dislike of realism[157] and the vulgar herd – 'Ces épiciers et ces notaires'[158] – and to take refuge[159] in the sort of romantic fantasy or fairyland, e.g. *Gringoire* (1866), *Riquet à la Houppe* (1884), that we shall find again in Rostand.

The emotional content of Banville's poetry is negligible, the ideas shallow. A little less than the equal of Gautier in the impact of his visual and colour impressions, he is perhaps superior in variety of rhythms and verse forms, in rhyming skill; he contents himself essentially with verbal jugglery. Nonetheless, alongside Gautier's, his technical perfection was to be an inspiration for the Parnassians; later the Symbolists were to fasten on the value of varied metres and the tonal effects of 'rime riche'.

'L'Art pour l'Art' and 'le Parnasse', the two seem to merge into each other and yet the background of each is different. The former, as we have seen, is a refinement of one aspect of Romanticism at the expense of others, a flight from personal emotion, from any subservience of art to other ends, especially moral or political, into the cult of beauty, the contemplation of the lily:

> Et je n'ai jamais plus filé
> Qu'un lys au bord des eaux courantes[160]

Banville clearly belongs to that school; with his loyalties to Hugo and Gautier, he has a small but ornate niche in the temple of Romanticism, rather than in the new age's palace of science, scholarship and the arts, which was to be the spiritual home of the Parnassian poets.

The background is different, but much of what Gautier and Banville stood for was accepted by the Parnassians: the rejection of personal emotion and anything savouring of a direct personal confession, technical perfection, plasticity.

The fusion of the ideals of 'art for art's sake', with belief in scholarship and knowledge as an indispensable basis of poetry, was achieved by Leconte de Lisle.

---

[154] *Stalactites.*
[155] *Idylles Prussiennes.*   [156] Commentaire (*Odes Funamb.*).
[157] 'Le Réalisme' (*Odes Funamb.*).   [158] 'Saut du Tremplin'.
[159] See his plays.   [160] *Odes Funambulesques*, 'Ma biographie'.

VI. LECONTE DE LISLE

Leconte de Lisle (1818–94) made three declarations of artistic faith:[161] the preface to the *Poèmes Antiques* (1852), the preface to *Poèmes et Poésies*[162] (1855) and the foreword to *Les Poètes Contemporains* (1864). The first is a strong attack on all modern poetry inspired by the personal emotions of the poet. This vein is exhausted; its excessive exploitation explains public indifference and lack of interest in poetry; it explains why poets have forfeited the position of authority as teachers, theirs in ancient times: 'l'époque ne vous entend plus parce que vous l'avez importuné de vos plaintes stériles...' The modern age, the author goes on, is an age of knowledge: 'Nous sommes une génération savante'. Thus if poetry is to regain its position, poets must accept the discipline of scholarship with all it means in abnegation and solitude, for it alone will provide the key to the proper understanding of the ancient world, the basis the modern world is built on: 'le génie et la tâche de ce siècle sont de retrouver et de réunir les titres de famille de l'intelligence humaine'. The accompanying collection of poems – *Poèmes Antiques* – is accordingly described as a series of 'studies' bearing little trace of personal emotion and no relation with the passions and the events of the day.

That this manifesto did not pass without hostile comment is evident from the preface to *Poèmes et Poésies*. The poet joyfully accepts the taunt of antiquarianism and the hatred of his own day: 'Plût aux Dieux, en effet, que je me fusse retiré au fond des antres de Samothrace ou des sanctuaires de l'Inde...' He turns with loathing from the modern scene... the coal smoke... the industrial pandemonium; he can see no relation between poetry and modern inventions: 'Les hymnes et les odes inspirées par la vapeur et la télégraphie électrique m'émeuvent médiocrement et toutes ces périphrases didactiques n'ayant rien de commun avec l'art, me démontreraient plutôt que les poètes deviennent d'heure en heure plus inutiles aux sociétés modernes.' Follows a panegyric of the Greek world, the moral value of its polytheism not only in the social and religious domains but also in art. In the two great Ionian epics, in the legends of Prometheus, Oedipus, Antigone and Phaedra, is to be found expressed in the most beautiful form the whole range of emotions the human soul is capable of. The author would extend his praise also to the Hindu 'Itihaças',[163] so closely linked to

[161] All are to be found in *Derniers Poèmes* (posth., 1895).

[162] The poems in this collection were republished either in *Poèmes Barbares* or in the later editions of *Poèmes Antiques*.

[163] '... an event of olden time, conjoined with a tale and provided with a demonstration of duty, profit, love and final emancipation (the four objects of human existence) is termed "itihāsa"'. (Hastings, *Encyclopaedia of Religion and Ethics*, Vol. VII, p. 461.)

the Homeric legend by common traditions, if they displayed to the same extent the three great qualities of the Greeks – order, clarity, harmony – and he concludes by reaffirming the belief, inherent in the first manifesto, that subject to equivalent genius, works that evoke historical origins, and are inspired by ancient traditions, works that carry the modern reader back to the times when man and the world were in the first bloom of strength and beauty, will always excite more interest than what he refers to as: 'le tableau daguerréotypé des moeurs et des faits contemporains.'

The foreword to his studies on contemporary poets is an aristocratic declaration of faith in the doctrine of 'L'Art pour l'Art'. Art, of which poetry is the most brilliant expression, is inaccessible to the vulgar crowd; its exclusive domain is beauty: 'Le monde du Beau, l'unique domaine de l'Art est en soi un infini sans contact possible avec toute autre conception inférieure que ce soit.

'Le Beau n'est pas le serviteur du Vrai, car il contient la vérité divine et humaine. Il est le sommet commun où aboutissent les voies de l'esprit. Le reste se meut dans le tourbillon illusoire des apparences.'

To this high ideal the poet must bend all his powers of emotion, thought, knowledge and imagination; anything less than this total dedication will not only fail in its object but also be a betrayal: 'une mauvaise action, une lâcheté, un crime, quelque chose de honteusement et d'irrévocablement immoral'.

The critical studies the foreword introduces confirm the uncompromising attitudes of the preface; Béranger, poet of the vulgar herd, deserves none of the extravagant praise that has been lavished on him; Lamartine, great poet that he is, fails in one respect: 'Il lui a manqué l'amour et le respect religieux de l'art.' Criticism has no hold on that force of nature, Hugo. Vigny is praised for his majestic aloofness and cult of poetry, but in a poem like 'Moïse' he fails to recreate, as scholarship demands, the true Moses of history: 'rien ne rappelle dans le Moïse du poète le chef sacerdotal et autocratique de six cent mille nomades féroces errant dans le désert de Sinaï, convaincu de la sainteté de sa mission et de la légitimité des implacables châtiments qu'il inflige...' Auguste Barbier (strange to find him and Béranger in this exalted company) has not the lyrical or intellectual powers to make him the great satirical poet he wanted to be; the moderate praise he none the less receives must be ascribed to the bond of sympathy Leconte de Lisle may have felt for a man who looked for inspiration from the sort of social and humanitarian aspirations he himself had espoused before 1848.[164] The last essay is devoted to Baudelaire in

[164] There is an interesting echo in the essay on Barbier of Flaubert's aristocratic attitude, so similar to Leconte de Lisle's own. The first sentence

whom Leconte de Lisle praises the poet dedicated, like himself, to beauty.

None of this doctrine seems reconcilable with the enthusiastic Fourierism of the young law student at Rennes Leconte de Lisle had been (1836), of the republican intellectual he became after his return from two years' sojourn in his native Réunion (1845), writing in the Fourierist journals of the capital,[165] and of the aspiring politician, welcoming the February Revolution as the dawn of a universal republic. His enthusiasm for Ancient Greece was indeed already vigorous but it mingled with his political interests; the Greek myths were nothing less than republican or even socialist symbols.

Leconte de Lisle, however, shared with many other writers the sense of complete spiritual bankruptcy, after the failure of the 1848 revolution and the *coup d'état* of 1851. His political enthusiasms and Fourierist 'mystique' fall away; the cult for Ancient Greece remains pruned of its contemporary symbolic message, that cult and, it may be added, the phobic hatred – an inevitable concomitant of republican ideas at that time – of Christianity. Though his political abdication, his aloofness from the modern world remain constant, Leconte de Lisle will be the dedicated poet seeking to establish poetry on new and, as he thought, indestructible foundations, and within the intellectual structure of the Positivist era: elimination of the personal element; knowledge as the indispensable condition of any ultimate re-establishment of the poet's ancient authoritative position of teacher; severance of the poet's contacts with contemporaneous events and politics; the contribution he can make to society by scholarly evocations of ancient civilizations in their historical reality, notably the civilization of Greece, supreme in beauty, and the civilization of the Hindus, supreme in wisdom; cult of beauty, aloof, cold and resting on the twin pillars of knowledge and impeccable form.

Leconte de Lisle's three great collections of poems: *Poèmes Antiques* (1852), *Poèmes Barbares* (1862), *Poèmes Tragiques* (1884), to which must be added the posthumous *Derniers Poèmes* (1895), seem on the surface at least to be faithful reflections of these ideas, both intellectual and aesthetic. The poems in each collection can be grouped according to certain distinct themes. In *Poèmes Antiques* the emphasis, as the title indicates, is on ancient Greek civilization (e.g. 'Hélène', 'Niobé', 'Khiron', 'Les Plaintes du Cyclope', 'Héraklès au Taureau', 'Pan'), but in addition the

---

seems a direct reminder of the famous Comice speech in *Madame Bovary*, when it refers to: '... recettes destinées à l'amélioration des espèces bovine ovine, chevaline et humaine.'

[165] *La Phalange, La Démocratie pacifique.*

significant theme, to which the poet draws attention in his preface, of ancient Hindu religious legends (e.g. 'Bhagavat', 'La Vision de Brahma', 'Çunacépa'). A small group of descriptive poems ('Juin', 'Midi', 'Nox') indicates a theme that was to become much more important in *Poèmes Barbares*: aspects of nature. One or two poems, finally, though not directly personal, betray attitudes, e.g. to the Christian religion ('Hypatie', 'Hypatie et Cyrille') or to where true wisdom lies ('Dies Irae').

Poèmes Barbares pursues the investigation of ancient civilizations. With Greece, as the hub of his world, the poet pushes into the non-Greek world; northwards to the Germanic world (e.g. 'La Mort de Sigurd'), to the Nordic (e.g. 'La Légende des Nornes', 'L'Epée d'Angantyr', 'Le Coeur de Hialmar', 'Le Runoïa'); westwards to the Celtic (e.g. 'Le Barde de Temrah', 'Le Massacre de Mona'); southwards to the Egyptian ('Néférou-Ra'); eastwards to the Jewish ('La Vigne de Naboth'), the Persian (e.g. 'La Vérandah') and as far east as the Polynesian ('La Genèse Polynésienne'). The poems suggest a series of illustrations in a great book of world civilizations, albeit with omissions[166] – China, Japan, the Aztecs, the Incas; none the less the poet pays his tribute to the never-ending scientific enquiry, which was particularly active in his day, into the origins of man and his beliefs, a vital factor in moulding civilizations.

Some of the poems in both *Poèmes Antiques* and *Poèmes Barbares* (e.g. 'Hélène', 'Niobé', 'Khiron', 'Bhagavat', 'Çunacépa', 'La Légende des Nornes', 'Le Runoïa') have an epic quality, very different in spirit, be it noted, from Hugo's *Légende des Siècles*. The attitude is more akin to that of another work, the foundations of which were being laid at that time, on religious origins; Renan's *Les Origines du Christianisme*.[167]

The second theme of *Poèmes Barbares*, much more important here than in *Poèmes Antiques*, is provided by the world of exotic nature and wild animals: 'Les Eléphants', 'Le Sommeil du Condor', 'La Panthère Noire', 'Les Jungles', 'Le Jaguar', 'Le Rêve du Jaguar'. A third group of poems reflects personal attitudes, e.g. to Christianity ('Qaïn'), to his own time ('Aux Modernes'), to life ('Les Montreurs'), to death the deliverer ('Fiat Nox', 'Solvet Seclum').

A very similar pattern is to be found in *Poèmes Tragiques*: ancient civilizations, Moslem, Celtic, Persian, Greek; exotic nature and the zoological kingdom; a number of poems show the spell exercised on the poet by the wisdom of the East (e.g. 'La Maya'),

---

[166] Some slight compensation in the sonnet 'L'Orient', *Derniers Poèmes*. The Aztec religion is given a passing mention in 'La Paix des Dieux', *ibid*.
[167] See below, p. 364.

or conversely his hatred of Christianity (e.g. 'L'Holocaust', 'Les Siècles Maudits'), or again his attitude to life and death (e.g. 'Le Secret de la Vie', 'L'Illusion Suprême'). *Derniers Poèmes* contain at least three significant poems: 'La Paix des Dieux', which provides a summing up of Leconte de Lisle's attitude to the numerous and successive religious systems that have possessed men's minds, 'Les Raisons du Saint-Père', which directs a final shaft at Christianity and more particularly at the Catholic Church, and 'Soleils! Poussière d'Or', which throws some further light on Leconte de Lisle's 'philosophy'.

A constant return to certain well-established themes, that impression comes very clearly across from Leconte de Lisle's poetry considered as a whole. The idea that life is suffering:

> Sombre douleur de l'homme, O voix triste et profonde
> Cri de l'âme, sanglot du coeur supplicié..., ('Bhagavat', *P.A.*)

that the modern world is hideous:

> Oui! le mal éternel est dans sa plénitude
> L'air du siècle est mauvais aux esprits ulcérés...
> ('Dies Irae', *P.A.*)

that man is odious and materialistic:

> Noyés dans le néant des suprêmes ennuis,
> Vous mourrez bêtement en emplissant vos poches.
> ('Aux Modernes', *P.A.*)

that man cannot seek consolation in religion, for religions are ephemeral human creations:

> ...anciens songes de l'Homme,
> Qu'il a conçus, créés, adorés et maudits...
> ('La Paix des Dieux', *D.P.*)

not excluding Christianity:

> Grâce à nous, pour jamais, tu resteras O Maître,
> Un Dieu, le dernier que l'homme aura rêvé.
> ('Les Raisons du Saint-Père', *D.P.*)

Christianity is peculiarly odious because of the cruelty for which it has been responsible ('L'Holocauste', 'Les Siècles Maudits', *P.T.*) and – supreme crime – because it has destroyed Ancient Greek polytheism whence flowed all beauty:

> Le vil Galiléen t'a frappée et maudite ('Hypatie', *P.A.*)

But Christianity is also subject to the inevitable cycle of birth and decay:

> ...Tu mourras à ton tour
> Tu mourras comme moi, Dieu des âmes nouvelles...
> ('Le Runoïa', *P.B.*)

Nor does nature provide what formal religions cannot, for with all its beauty and luxuriance, nature is an impassive setting (scarcely an original thought) for the human tragedy:

> La nature se rit des souffrances humaines;
> Ne contemplant jamais que sa propre grandeur . . .
>
> ('La Fontaine aux lianes', *P.B.*)

In the beautiful blue waters of the lake lies the suicide's corpse and the woods remain indifferent:

> . . . Les bois, sous leur ombre odorante, . . .
> . . . berçaient leur gloire indifférente
> Ignorant que l'on souffre et qu'on puisse en mourir (*Ibid.*)

The teeming life in nature is like a prodigious mechanism that obeys the law of hunger:

> La Faim sacrée est un long meurtre légitime
>
> ('Sacra Fames', *P.T.*)

The whole thing is as meaningless as the train of elephants that comes from the distant horizon and vanishes into it again ('Les Eléphants', *P.B.*).

The wisdom of Buddha provides the only acceptable interpretation of life. Throughout the poems Leconte de Lisle returns again and again to Buddhist themes: life is like the rings that form when a stone breaks the surface of a pool, a momentary disturbance that slowly merges once more into the even suface of eternity ('Çunacépa, *P.A.*), the things of this world are but a dream ('La Vision de Brahma', *P.A.*), life is an illusion ('La Maya', *P.T.*), death is the deliverer ('Dies Irae', *P.A.*; 'Solvet Seclum', *P.B.*; 'L'Illusion Suprême', *P.T.*).

Illusion, dream, such metaphors of life seem to come naturally from lands where the opium poppy grows, as Leconte de Lisle might have observed, though the opiate he turned to was not drugs but the pursuit of beauty. If we were tempted to ask why, since all is illusion, beauty is an aim more worth pursuing than, for example, the Indian Fakir's effort to merge with Nirvana by total physical inertia and one-pointed mental concentration, Leconte de Lisle would presumably reply that the ephemeral nature of life makes beauty the more precious and that in the scales of value the intensity of human experience, which beauty can alone provide, outweighs any futile religious belief in individual survival.

> Soleils, Mondes! si tout est éphémère et vain
> Dans nos coeurs aussi bien qu'en vos profonds abîmes
> Votre instant est sacré, votre rêve est divin, . . .
>
> ('Soleils! Poussière d'Or', *D.P.*)

Why sacred? Why divine? Of great price, we understand, but, like his contemporary Renan,[168] Leconte de Lisle uses the word 'divine' and allied concepts in the loosest way.

To speak of Leconte de Lisle's 'Enigma Variations' on life as though they were a well co-ordinated philosophy is excessive; rather are they a series of well-entrenched attitudes, in alignment with philosophic ideas of the day, produced perhaps by personal sorrows, of which there are echoes in the poems, and by political disappointments. Nor are they necessarily pessimist. Leconte de Lisle may despair of life as he saw it about him, but he appears to look with hope or at least with relief towards the final absorption of all things into the 'divine (*sic*) nothingness'.

The insistence Leconte de Lisle brings to the themes outlined above suggests not only conviction, but also the determination to communicate it to others. He seems indeed as eager as any of the messianic writers of an earlier generation to hammer home a 'message' and we, in our generation, as eager to look elsewhere in him for our enjoyment of poetic experience. No poet before him in the nineteenth century provides more intense sensuous impressions: heat and cold, colour, sunlight and moonlight, tropical luxuriance and aridity, polar ice and gloom. Where are we given a finer gallery of birds and beasts of prey than in *Poèmes Barbares*, evoked with a precision of detail that recalls the sculpture of Antoine-Louis Barye?[169]

The impact of all this is powerful, although admittedly the rigorous correspondence between intention and effect ties the reader down to what is stated or described. Like drawings that define rather than suggest, Leconte de Lisle's poetry rarely contains an imaginative potential or that 'iridescent suggestion of an idea', that stimulates the reader's own imaginative power. There are exceptions: 'Pan' (*Poèmes Antiques*) for example, where the poet, with an emotional response to his own ideals apparently, conjures up a scene of Greek mythology that foretells Mallarmé's *Après-Midi d'un Faune*, and is rich with Mediterranean allusion:

> Pan d'Arcadie...
> Emplit les verts roseaux d'une amoureuse haleine...

Occasionally too, the reader detects a tremor of what the poet most condemns – a personal emotion:

> Tu t'en venais aussi, par ces matins si doux...
> Dans ta grâce naïve et ta rose jeunesse... ('Le Manchy', *P.B.*)

---

[168] See J. Lemaitre, *Les Contemporains*, 1e série: 'Il serait intéressant... de dresser la liste des contradictions de M. Renan. Son Dieu tour à tour existe ou n'existe pas, est personnel ou impersonnel...'
[169] 1796–1875.

At such moments, rare but all the more refreshing, the poet escapes and we with him from his self-imposed discipline or objective erudition and cold plasticity of form.

VII. THE PARNASSIANS AND HEREDIA

Three efforts at least were made in the early 1860's to build a new literary school round a critical review: Catulle Mendès launched the *Revue fantaisiste* in February 1861; it survived till November. Louis Xavier de Rizard founded the *Revue du progrès moral, littéraire, scientifique* in March 1863; its title at least reflects the new intellectual orientation, the desire to harness literature to social progress and science; it lasted a year. Another review, *L'Art*, owed its short existence (November 1865–January 1866) to the same founder.

The sense of a certain community of attitudes promoted by these 'ephemera' was also promoted by what may be regarded as the first 'Naturalist' play – though the term had not yet been coined – *Henriette Maréchal*.[170] The performances, which faintly echoed the 'battle of Hernani', brought the partisans of the new ideas closer together, but in the absence of public interest and funds to establish on a firm basis a critical review as a rallying ground, the idea of a volume of contemporary poetry was born in the mind of the publisher Lemerre. Though lacking the character of an aggressive literary manifesto, *Le Parnasse contemporain, recueil de vers nouveaux* (1866) has given its name to a generation rather than a school of poets; amongst the contributors – some forty in all – figured poets as diverse as Baudelaire and Heredia, Mallarmé and Verlaine. The watchwords were craftsmanship, plasticity, objectivity; at least they could share their admiration for a trinity of poets – Gautier, Leconte de Lisle, Banville, and their dislike of much Romantic poetry, especially the sentimentalism of Lamartine and Musset.

Of all the poets who contributed to the *Parnasse contemporain* the most representative is José Maria de Heredia (1842–1905). By 1866 he was already the acknowledged master of the sonnet; *Les Trophées* (1893) contains the full collection of 118 sonnets, composed with splendid craftsmanship over the previous thirty years, 'Romancero', a ballad in Romantic vein on the 'Cid', and a minor epic, 'Les Conquérants de l'or', saga of Pizarro, the Spanish Conquistador.

With this apparently modest baggage Heredia has an assured place in French literature, showing thereby with another poet of his day, though only remotely of his persuasion,[171] that concentra-

[170] See vol. V, chap. 2, i.   [171] Mallarmé.

tion and quality are more important than the dispersal and quantity that come from the outpourings of Romantic emotion.

The sonnet form is usually associated with love poetry – Petrarch, Ronsard, Du Bellay, Shakespeare. Heredia's own master, Leconte de Lisle, uses the sonnet only rarely; his themes – e.g. the legends of primitive peoples on man's origins, the horrors of modern materialism and more generally of this life, the peace of Nirvana, the cruelties of nature in exotic climes – seemed too copious a draught for so small a vessel, designed to contain only the fragrant essence of love or some other lyrical mood; the few sonnets in *Poèmes Barbares* suggest that he chose the sonnet when passion – love, hatred, contempt – welled up in him and needed to be communicated in a discreetly personal but not dispassionate form: e.g. 'Le Colibri', 'Les Montreurs', 'Le Voeu suprême', 'Aux Modernes'.

Heredia's most successful sonnets, in contrast, have no appeal to the emotions. The ephemeral nature of things admittedly recurs often:

> La vie O Sextius est brève. Hâtons-nous
> De vivre . . . ('A Sextius')

> Tout meurt . . .
> Les roses et les lys n'ont pas de lendemain
> ('Sur le livre des Amours')

> Le temps passe. Tout meurt. Le marbre même s'use
> ('Médaille Antique')

But even if this theme represents the poet's own pessimism, its purpose in the sonnets concerned is not to reveal his mood, it is to evoke the ethos or fit into the picture of a period: Rome, the Renaissance, Sicily. In none of the sonnets concerned is the reader allowed to dwell on the idea of the fugacity of things and give it personal lyrical importance by an inward look on himself. This is particularly true in the last case where the attention is at once fastened on history and concrete details:

> Agrigente n'est plus qu'une ombre, et Syracuse
> Dort sous le bleu linceul de son ciel indulgent.

In short, Heredia as a good Parnassian transposes emotion from a personal to an aesthetic key. This is well brought out by comparing his sonnet 'Soir de Bataille', with Leconte de Lisle's poem 'Le Soir d'une Bataille'. The slight difference in the title has its importance; Leconte de Lisle's battle has substantival and therefore greater force than the adjectival force of Heredia's. From the outset therefore we are warned that Leconte de Lisle is going to evoke the horrific aftermath of a specific battle and make a direct impact on the reader's emotion, whereas Heredia intends to take advantage of battle effects in general, to make an aesthetic impact. The absence in Heredia's title of the definite article reinforces this impression, by giving it general significance, which in its turn seems to remove the horror from close proximity to our personal experience.

These impressions are confirmed by the contents of the poems themselves. Leconte de Lisle's, a modern battle,[172] something close to the reader's experience therefore, or at any rate only a short remove from it by imagination, the whole ending on a political note – the value of the sacrifice in the name of liberty; Heredia's, on the other hand, far removed in time. We can therefore imagine the scene with as little personal emotion as though we were watching it through a telescope on the moon; distance in space or time transforms emotion into intellectual interest or curiosity. Here, perhaps, lies the explanation why Heredia's evocations of past situations come no nearer to us than the Renaissance. He then veers to the East – distance in space. Any attempt to capture the spirit of the modern age might have meant a departure from the objectivity Heredia cultivated. Only in the last section, 'La Nature et le Rêve', does the poet allow a personal element to creep in, but this section which, save in the pen pictures of Brittany, lacks a theme like those that give unity to each of the other sections, is not the most characteristic or satisfying of *Les Trophées*.

At their best Heredia's sonnets are like microcosms of a given age or civilization; references that invoke the reader's own framework of knowledge:

> La terre maternelle et douce aux anciens Dieux.   ('L'Oubli'.)

Vivid sensuous impressions:

> Le ciel vert, au couchant, de pourpre et d'or se frange ('Le Prisonnier')

rhythms that create the desired image:

> La houle s'enfle, court, se dresse comme un mur
> Et déferle . . .[173]   ('Le Bain')

and above all the technique Heredia made all his own – the last line that releases the reader's imagination from the narrow confines of the sonnet and gives the miniature the dimensions of a large canvas. Examples of this abound, but the classic case occurs in 'Antoine et Cléopâtre':

> Et sur elle courbé, l'ardent Imperator
> Vit dans ses larges yeux étoilés de point d'or
> Toute une mer immense où fuyaient des galères.

Here two factors combine to produce a maximum effect: the physical images conveyed by the lines and the knowledge the framework

---

[172] Solferino or Magenta?
[173] The 'rejet' conveys the crash of the breaking wave splendidly.

provides. The qualifying phrase – 'étoilès de point d'or' – retains our attention for a moment longer on Cleopatra's eyes and then they, like a 'fading' on the films, merge into the vast horizon of the sea; but what strengthens the impact of the latter is our realization that the allusion is to Actium, seen as in a convex mirror endowed with the magic power of reflecting the future; references, sensuous impressions, skilful techniques all are tightly packed within the narrow confines of Heredia's sonnets, like 'Le combat des Titans au pommeau d'une dague'.[174]

When the *Parnasse Contemporain* was published the intention was to follow it up with other similar collections. A second volume appeared in 1871, a third in 1876. By then the character, in so far as it existed, of the first volume had disappeared. Time had revealed that the three collections were no more than anthologies, and that Parnassianism, since affecting the form rather than the substance of poetry, could cover a diversity of attitudes; there are the poets who, with Heredia, followed closely in the line of Leconte de Lisle: Louis Bouilhet (1828–69), the friend of Flaubert, Léon Dierx (1838–1912) – a native of Réunion like the master – Catulle Mendès (1842–1909); though scholar, painter, teacher and even scientist more than poet, Louis Ménard (1822–1901) belongs to this group by his enthusiastic Hellenism; Sully Prudhomme (1839–1907) veers towards philosophic Parnassianism, as does Madame Ackermann (1813–90); François Coppée (1842–1908) found a fruitful and successful vein of poetic inspiration in the virtues of the humble poor; Albert Glatigny (1839–73) remained in the strict obedience of Théodore de Banville.

With all their skills and contemporary successes their originality was not strong enough to ensure their literary survival, except as names or anthology poets. Not even the Nobel Prize for literature (1907) and 'Le Vase brisé'[175] has saved Sully Prudhomme. Time soon betrays the facile or the derivative, in poetry perhaps even more quickly than in any other art form. To read these poets nowadays is to be overcome with a paralyzing sense of sameness and boredom.

But there were two poets amongst the early Parnassians whose powerful originality was to launch them on a different poetic trajectory: Mallarmé and Verlaine, who will be discussed later.

In the meantime a word must be said about an isolated figure who is totally out of place in the Parnassian age and yet whose short life falls wholly within it, the 'Comte de Lautréamont'.

[174] 'Sur le Pont-Vieux'.   [175] *Stances*, 'La Vie intérieure'.

VIII. THE 'COMTE DE LAUTRÉAMONT'

The 'Comte de Lautréamont' – the romantic pseudonym con-
ceals the more prosaic name of Isidore Ducasse (1846–70), which
suggests – Isidore anyway – a valet from a comedy by Labiche.
But the phenomenon Ducasse-Lautréamont is anything but prosaic.
Ducasse is shrouded in mystery. He was born in Montevideo of
French parents. At the age of fourteen he was sent to France to
complete his schooling at Tarbes and then at Pau. His gift for
mathematics pointed to the Ecole Polytechnique and accordingly
in 1867 he went to Paris where, with little money, he lived a solitary
life, in one hotel after another. Then suddenly in November 1870
he was dead. How? The death certificate which, with a few letters,
is one of the few extant documents relating to Ducasse is uncom-
municative on the point: '... décédé ce matin à 8 heures ... sans
autres renseignements ...' Could the revolutionary anarchist that
Ducasse was supposed to be have been the victim of the police as
a defence measure on the eve of the siege of Paris?[176] How else is
the discreet silence on the cause of his death to be explained?
Whatever be the truth, the mysterious, isolated being left an
equally mysterious legacy: *Les Chants de Maldoror* (Canto i, 1868;
Cantos i–vi, 1869) and *Poésies* i and ii (1870).

'Monsieur, j'ai une prière à vous faire', writes Ducasse in a
polite note to his banker. 'Si mon père envoyait d'autres fonds
avant le 1 septembre, époque à laquelle mon corps fera une apparition devant la porte de votre banque, vous aurez la bonté de me le
faire savoir...' 'Mon corps fera...', the expression could be no
more than an example of 'student's humour' that likes to say
things ... differently, but equally it could be a fortuitous piece of
evidence in support of the view so strongly suggested by the
Chants, that Lautréamont was much more to Ducasse than a mere
pen name. Like that of the worthy Chrysalde in *Les Femmes
Savantes* Ducasse's body is in need of sustenance, but, as his body
seems to infer, the mind appears to be elsewhere.

The 'Comte de Lautréamont'[177] takes charge in the silent sleep-
less watches of the night. The theme of sleeplessness is strongly
emphasized: 'Voilà plus de trente ans que je n'ai pas encore dormi
... Quand la nuit obscurcit le cours des heures quel est celui qui
n'a pas combattu contre l'influence du sommeil, dans sa couche
mouillée d'une glaciale sueur.'[178]

---

[176] cf. *Chants de Maldoror*, Canto vi, Corti, p. 324. 'Il savait que la
police, ce bouclier de la civilisation, le recherchait avec persévérance...'

[177] It has been suggested that Ducasse invented the name from Sue's
novel on the seventeenth-century adventurer Latréaumont; an alternative
suggestion is 'l'autre mont', i.e. Montevideo whence he hailed.

[178] Canto v, Corti, p. 295.

The scene is Faustian: a top floor room, a single candle flickering in the shadows, silence, broken only when the figure at the table strides to the piano and strikes a few cacophonic chords expressing the disharmony of his mood; the visions begin: 'Sur le mur de ma chambre, quelle ombre dessine, avec une puissance incomparable, la fantasmagorique projection de sa silhouette racornie...'[179]

The first impact of the *Chants* is likely to produce horrified astonishment. Are these the disordered imaginings of a madman? Critics have not been wanting from Léon Bloy to Thibaudet who say they are. Certainly the sombre hallucinations that follow each other in bewildering and hypnotic succession lie (fortunately) outside normal experience. Yet there is every evidence of a coherent intention, of a powerful and brilliant mind in control, from the opening page, where he warns off the lily-livered reader with cries of woe, 'Par conséquent, âme timide, avant de pénétrer plus loin dans de pareilles landes inexplorées, dirige tes talons en arrière et non en avant...', knowing well that this is the surest way of attracting him; from the opening page to the last section of Canto vi where Lautréamont shows his understanding of the technique of visionary literature and has been deliberately following it: 'Pour construire mécaniquement la cervelle d'un conte somnifère il ne suffit pas de disséquer des bêtises...'. The reader must be reduced to a state of hypnosis which will render him powerless and force him to admit, of the author: 'il m'a beaucoup crétinisé. Que n'aurait-il pas fait, s'il eût pu vivre davantage.'

Throughout, Lautréamont pursues his course down the dark labyrinth of his mind with lucid deliberation, often borrowing from the experience of Ducasse – his love of the sea, for example,[180] and of mathematics.[181] Lautréamont is constantly at the reader's elbow, as the narrator, the 'je' of the text, but he also projects himself into the character of Maldoror whose experiences in the narrator's visionary world the latter relates. The effect of sleeplessness, similar to that of certain drugs, enables the narrator to be both subject and object. We are reminded of some painter, in the grip of hypnosis, expressing on his canvas, with figurative accuracy and coherence, a series of nightmarish scenes projected on the screen of his imagination – a Hieronymus Bosch, a Pieter Brueghel. Now with sardonic humour, now with savage irony, the narrator evokes before the reader's eyes a lurid kaleidoscope of horror, cruelty or mere fantasy. The theme running through

[179] Canto iv, Corti, p. 267.
[180] e.g. the splendid meditation on the ocean: 'Vieil Océan... etc.' in Canto i, Corti, p. 136, also Canto iv, pp. 250 and 256: the shark and the tunny fish on deck. Ducasse may have witnessed such an incident crossing the Atlantic.
[181] Canto ii, Corti, p. 194.

Maldoror's adventures and the narrator's commentary is hatred of God and man: 'Race stupide et idiote! Ma poésie ne consistera qu'à attaquer, par tous les moyens, l'homme cette bête fauve, et le créateur qui n'aurait pas dû engendrer une pareille vermine...'[182] In Canto vi the narrator explains that this long journey in depth, through evil, has been nothing but a foundation for his work: 'les cinq premiers récits... étaient le frontispice de mon ouvrage... l'explication préalable de ma poétique future...'[183]

What the future work was to be remains, like so much else in Lautréamont, a mystery. The *Poésies* I and II, which, no more than the *Chants de Maldoror*, are not poetry in the technical sense of being in verse, provide no solution. They too are called a preface in which the author with some pertinent reflexions on nineteenth-century poetry seems at pains to refute Maldoror's message of despair. As in Beethoven's Pastoral Symphony, after the storm comes peace. But again we are left with a question-mark. Is this the schizophrenic passing from his evil to his good self, from Mr Hyde to Dr Jekyll?

The answer matters little; the significant point is that at a time when poetry was dying under marmoreal weight of unimaginative Parnassianism, Lautréamont was not so much writing poetry, which he did not do, as finding new sources. His long cry of hatred against God and man may give him the appearance of yet another Romantic rebel enjoying his isolation, but his revolt led him to investigate Freudian levels. No wonder the Surrealists were to claim him as one of themselves.[184]

[182] *Ibid.*, p. 170.   [183] Corti, p. 322.   [184] See vol. V, chap. 10.

Chapter 20

THE DRAMA

DUMAS *FILS*, AUGIER, SARDOU, LABICHE

POSITIVISM was to make itself felt in the theatre no less than in other forms of literature. Even if Ponsard had had more talent, a return to neo-classical tragedy was not within the context of the new age where an interest in society rather than individuals had been implanted. The social drama of Alexandre Dumas *fils* (1824–95) and Emile Augier (1820–89) was to meet the need, though neither had begun as a dramatist.

Dumas *fils*' first important work was a novel, *La Dame aux Camélias* (1848), the embellished story of his attachment for Alphonsine Plessis, or Marie Duplessis as she styled herself.[1] Need of money, so he tells us,[2] was the spur that made him carve a play out of the novel in the space of eight days[3] – eight days that transformed a character who would probably have been forgotten with the novel she figured in, into one of the great romantic heroines of the French stage.

The word 'romantic' may seem paradoxical in reference to Dumas *fils*, but it applies here; the courtesan redeemed by a pure love is a theme recalling *Marion Delorme*; indeed the theme is greatly accentuated both because in Dumas' play Marguerite occupies the centre of the stage, whereas in Hugo's, Marion plays second fiddle to Didier, and because the details of Marguerite's sacrifice are much more specific: fortune, Armand's love as a result of M. Duval's appeal, life itself. The bitter-sweet pathos of the final reconciliation, too late for happiness, has not lost its impact. Dumas, in the manner of the Romantics, had, as it were, secreted his novel, and by extension the play, from a personal sorrow, but both novel and play contained elements pointing the way to social drama: the contemporaneous courtesans' environment and especially M. Duval senior's intervention (Act III). The former, with glimpses of the underlying sordidness of prostitution appearing through its gaiety and luxury, gives the play all the air of a play of

---

[1] A noted courtesan; died 1847, aged 23.
[2] 'Préface Générale' (1867) to his works.   [3] Ditto.

manners, the latter opens the way to the play with a thesis. When Dumas wrote the preface (1867) his art had developed strongly in the latter direction; the preface shows he had appreciated the thesis-potential of the play; *La Dame aux Camélias* from a romantic play is transformed into a presentation of a problem: the prostitute's position in society. M. Duval's significance is thereby increased; instead of being a means of emphasizing the great-heartedness of Marguerite, he becomes the defender of morality and the play a kind of preface to *Les Idées de Madame Aubray* (1867) where the question of marriage and the problem of divorce is ventilated.

Dumas' second play, *Diane de Lys* (1851), provides a situation resolved by a pistol shot; a symmetrical variant on Dumas *père*'s *Antony* must have attracted Dumas *fils*: Antony kills his mistress; the Comte de Lys kills the lover. Like *La Dame aux Camélias*, *Diane de Lys* has its source in the author's personal experience;[4] it is a high-tension drama in the manner of Victorien Sardou. Not until *Le Demi-Monde* (1855) does Dumas *fils* achieve the play of manners proper.

Dumas presents a social set – the *'Demi-Monde'*[5] – which appears to belong and yet does not belong to high society; to the untutored eye no more difference appears than between two baskets of peaches that look identical in quality and yet have a different price.[6] Pick up one of the cheaper peaches from the bed of wadding it nestles in and behold the explanation – the bruise on the other side. By the same token, the *'Demi-Monde'* is composed of women who have all the airs of high society but who have something to hide; they are 'women with a past'.

In Dumas *fils*, at any rate, the line between the comedy of manners and the play with a thesis is tenuous. Despite the title which suggests as the main intention that of painting a given society, the *'Demi-Monde'* has its thesis: 'Let the uninitiated [e.g. Nanjac] beware!' 'On n'épouse pas Mme d'Ange ... Il faut arriver d'Afrique pour avoir cette idée-là,[7] and by skilful manoeuvring and at some personal risk Olivier de Jalin saves his friend from the wiles of the enchantress, to whom he declares at the end:

> Ce n'est pas moi qui empêche votre mariage. C'est la raison ... la justice ... la loi sociale qui veut qu'un honnête homme n'épouse qu'une honnête femme.[8]

But if we may hesitate what label to give *Le Demi-Monde* no doubt remains about the group of plays that follows: *La Question d'Argent* (1857), *Le Fils Naturel* (1858), *L'Ami des Femmes* (1864),

[4] His love for Ctsse Lydie Nesselrode.
[5] Dumas created the expression, which does not denote the world of courtesans or prostitutes.
[6] *Le Demi-Monde*, II, 8.   [7] Op. cit., III, 5.   [8] Op. cit., V, 5.

Les Idées de Mme Aubray (1867). If there were any doubt the preface to the plays would dispel it.[9] Dumas has become the moralist preoccupied with social problems: money, the fate of illegitimate children, marriage and divorce. The series continues with the post-war plays: e.g. *La Princesse Georges* (1871), *La Femme de Claude* (1873), *L'Etrangère* (1876), *Denise* (1885), *Francillon* (1887). In these the zeal of the reforming moralist burns fiercely, the message becomes more emphatic: the Prince de Birac is rightly forgiven by his wife for his infidelity *(Princesse Georges)*; Césarine *(Femme de Claude)* is rightly shot dead for trying to sell her husband's new secret weapon to the enemy; the Duc de Septmonts *(L'Etrangère)* is rightly dispatched in a duel by Mr Clarkson; Denise, despite an early lapse, is rightly forgiven by the Comte de Bardannes who loves and marries her. Marriage is a contract equally binding on both parties; Francillon is fully justified in her attitude to her husband Lucien de Riverolles' infidelity.

The extent to which, in this last group of plays, Dumas emphasizes the moral ideas at the expense of his previous social realism is brought out by comparing *Le Demi-Monde* with *Denise*. In the former La Baronne d'Ange's efforts to rehabilitate herself by getting an honest man to marry her are condemned and she gets no pity when she fails; her efforts are shown as nothing but a sordid intrigue society punishes; Denise's rehabilitation, on the other hand, is shown to be in line with a generous moral code.

Augier's development as a dramatist offers some parallel with that of Dumas. As a member of 'L'Ecole du Bon Sens' Augier's early plays appeared before those of Dumas: e.g. *La Ciguë* (1844), *L'Aventurière* (1848), *Gabrielle* (1849), verse comedies, in the classical tradition, of which the latter two already reflect their author as defender of the family and the sanctity of marriage.

Dumas' success with *La Dame aux Camélias* – romantic in inspiration perhaps, but realist in form – encouraged Augier to abandon his efforts to revive classical comedy and to express his social and moral attitudes in a series of plays, similar in form to those of Dumas *fils*.

Broadly they fall into three categories: comedies of manners: e.g. *Le Gendre de M. Poirier* (1854), *Le Mariage d'Olympe* (1855), *Les Lionnes Pauvres* (1858); social comedies: e.g. *Ceinture Dorée* (1855), *Les Effrontés* (1861), *Le Fils de Giboyer* (1862), *Me. Guérin* (1864), *La Contagion* (1866), *Lions et Renards* (1869); plays with a thesis: e.g. *Jean de Thommeray* (1873), *Mme Caverlet* (1876), *Les Fourchambault* (1878).

The three plays mentioned in the first category all deal with some aspect of marriage: conflict arising between son-in-law (im-

---

[9] Especially the preface (1868) of *Le Fils Naturel*.

poverished nobleman) and wealthy father-in-law (bourgeois parvenu), owing to different codes of value (*Gendre de Monsieur
Poirier*); the dangers of a marriage between honest man and courtesan (*Mariage d'Olympe*); venal adultery (*Les Lionnes Pauvres*).
In the social comedies Augier enlarges his canvas; from personal
relationships he passes to questions such as the impact of money on
happiness and marriage (*Ceinture Dorée*), the attitudes of Press
and finance magnates (*Les Effrontés*), clericalism in high society
(*Le Fils de Giboyer*), the sinister influence of the Jesuits (*Lions et
Renards*), class enmity (*La Contagion*), dishonest lawyers (*M^e.
Guérin*); in the thesis plays patriotism (*Jean de Thommeray*), divorce (*Mme Caverlet*), illegitimacy (*Les Fourchambault*) are the
subjects chosen.

Augier's plays from *Le Gendre de Monsieur Poirier* onwards are
not only similar in form to those of Dumas *fils* but, naturally
enough, often touch on the same questions. The attitudes of the
two dramatists are not dissimilar in some respects, e.g. on marriages
for money, illegitimacy, divorce, adultery, patriotism, but whereas
Dumas tends, as his art develops, to treat his ideas of right and
wrong from a more abstract point of view, irrespective of social
contingencies, Augier stands firmly in defence of the bourgeois
citadel. The author of *L'Aventurière* was unlikely to take a charitable view of Marguerite Gautier and her kind; his reply to *La
Dame aux Camélias* is the odious Olympe Taverny who sows disaster in the honest family she marries into; the aristocracy are on
the whole shown in an unfavourable light: either cynically aware
of their own social exile since the Revolution and watching with
amusement the race by the ambitious bourgeois for money and
power (e.g. Marquis d'Auberive in *Les Effrontés* and *Le Fils de
Giboyer*), or as adventurers (e.g. Baron d'Estrigaud in *La Contagion* and *Lions et Renards*). Nor could the grandson of Pigault-
Lebrun, that most Voltairian of bourgeois, be expected to look with
favour on Catholic influence; hence the anti-clericalism of *Le Fils
de Giboyer* and the hostility to the Jesuit machinations of M. de
Sainte-Agathe (*Lions et Renards*).

These differences of approach account for differences of style
and performance; while both Dumas and Augier are masters of
plot construction, Dumas launches easily into the brilliant tirade
(e.g. Olivier de Jalin in *Le Demi-Monde*, Mistress Clarkson in
L'Etrangère); he is remembered, less for his characters – apart from
Marguerite Gautier, what character of Dumas survives? – than for
his types – notably his *raisonneurs* (e.g. Olivier de Jalin, des Ryons),
for his brilliant style, his vigorous quips (again, des Ryons in
L'Ami des Femmes), his prefaces. Augier, more down to earth,
more objective in his observation, is better remembered for his

gallery of characters than for the theses he defends: Séraphine Pommeau is better remembered as a character vaguely reminiscent of Emma Bovary than the play she figures in – *Les Lionnes Pauvres*; the same applies to Poirier and his daughter Antoinette,[10] his son-in-law Gaston de Presles; Vernouillet and Charrier, d'Auberive and d'Estrigaud, Olympe.

Of Dumas *fils*'s many prefaces, the one most pertinent to the conception he and Augier put into practice is the preface to *Un Père Prodigue* (1859).[11] In it occurs this passage: 'L'auteur dramatique qui connaîtrait l'homme comme Balzac et le théâtre comme Scribe serait le plus grand auteur dramatique qui aurait jamais existé.' Here we have the heart of the matter; Scribe provides the mould the dramatists under the Second Empire and early Third Republic will use; into it Dumas *fils* and Augier were to pour their respective mixtures of social and psychological observations laced with a moral message. Contemporaneous dramatists have other mixtures to use, the mould remains the same.

Eugène Labiche (1815–88), fecund author, with many collaborators, fills the mould now with a gaiety, forgotten since the days of Beaumarchais, in farces such as *Le Chapeau de Paille d'Italie* (1851), *La Cagnotte* (1864), *La Grammaire* (1867), now with a spirit of non-corrosive satirical comedy that has not lost its savour. *Le Voyage de Monsieur Perrichon* (1860) and *La Poudre aux Yeux* (1862), full length comedies, have a germ of human truth – the difficulty of gratitude (*Perrichon*); the value and the risks of appearing richer than one is (*Poudre aux Yeux*) – that give the main characters enough humanity to enrich the comedy derived from their foibles and absurdities. Théodore Barrière (1823–77) is remembered for one play at least, *Les Filles de Marbre* (1853), where responding, like Augier later,[12] to the challenge of *La Dame aux Camélias*, he shows that courtesans have no heart, only a stone or a money bag; again the Scribian formula with a dash of social observation.

At the highest level of structural skill stands Victorien Sardou (1831–1908). *Les Pattes de Mouche* (1860), *Dora* (1877),[13] offer admirable examples of Sardou's theatrical skill, of the dramatic suspense to be extracted from compromising letters, which should never have been, but always do get written, should have been, but never are, destroyed, and may at any moment, but never do, fall

---

[10] Remembered particularly for the masterly 'coup de théâtre': 'Et maintenant, va te battre, va!' (*Gendre de M. Poirier*, IV, 4).

[11] The play itself is more an act of piety from son to father than anything else. The uncalculating generosity of Dumas *père* inspires the Comte de la Rivonnière. André, his son, is a self-portrait.

[12] *Mariage d'Olympe*.   [13] Renamed *L'Espionne*, when revived (1905).

into wrong hands. In *La Famille Benoîton* (1865) the formula is the same but Sardou has endeavoured to inject an element of social satire in the manner of Augier; the picture he paints, however, of a family of enriched bourgeois, father, mother (in the wings), three daughters and two sons, is caricature rather than true observation.

More typical of the time than any other writers are Henri Meilhac (1831–97) and Ludovic Halévy (1834–1908), joint authors of the sentimental comedy *Frou-Frou* (1869) and a series of light operas, to the music of Offenbach, which breathe the spirit of 'la fête impériale': *La Belle Hélène* (1865), *La Vie Parisienne* (1866), *La Grande-Duchesse de Gérolstein* (1867), *La Périchole* (1868), *Le Petit Duc* (1878).

Chapter 21

CRITICS AND HISTORIANS

SAINTE-BEUVE,

TAINE, RENAN, FUSTEL DE COULANGES

'THE prince of French critics', as Amiel called Charles Augustin Sainte-Beuve (1804–69) on hearing of his death, had begun by studying medicine (1823) but Dubois (1793–1874), joint-founder with Pierre Leroux (1797–1871) of *Le Globe*, recruited him into journalism (1824) and, although he did not immediately forsake medicine, the literary world now beckoned him, in those early days of the Romantic movement with Charles Nodier enthroned at the Arsenal, surrounded by the eager young men of the Cénacles.

In thrall to Hugo, Sainte-Beuve published in book form a collection of his articles, championing the Romantic cause, under the title *Tableau historique et critique de la Poésie française au seizième siècle* (1828): 'En secouant le joug des deux derniers siècles', he writes, 'la nouvelle école française ... a dû s'inquiéter de ce qui s'est fait auparavant et chercher dans nos origines quelque chose de national à quoi se rattacher...'[1]

A series of volumes gathered in thereafter a harvest of current (mostly review) articles. *Critiques et Portraits Littéraires*, six volumes (1832–39), *Portraits de Femmes* (1844), *Portraits Contemporains*, three volumes (1846), *Derniers Portraits Littéraires* (1852).

In addition to his critical articles, Sainte-Beuve made two important excursions into academe; in the academic year 1837–8 he gave a course of lectures at Lausanne on Port-Royal; in 1848–9 a course on Chateaubriand and his friends at Liège; *Port-Royal* had three editions during Sainte-Beuve's lifetime, the third and definitive edition, loaded with notes – scholarly additions and occasional reservations on his religious inclinations of the 'thirties,[2] appeared in 1867 (seven volumes); *Chateaubriand et son groupe littéraire sous l'Empire* in 1861. A third course of lectures on Virgil was to have

---

[1] *Tableau*, last chap.
[2] For a good example see Bk. iii, chap. 2 (p. 419, n. 2, 1888 edn.): 'Allons plus au fond ... chrétien'.

been given at the Collège de France, but student hostility to the lecturer for political reasons as a result of his perfidious article *Regrets*,[3] frustrated his intention; this appeared with the title *Etude sur Virgile* in 1857. Masterpieces of academic criticism, these, or at any rate the first two, are what remains most living of Sainte-Beuve's work.

Sainte-Beuve the journalist as opposed to the review critic[4] is revealed in *Les Causeries du Lundi* (fifteen volumes, 1849–61) and *Les Nouveaux Lundis* (thirteen volumes, 1861–6). Posthumous works include his *Correspondance Générale*, 1935—[5]), his *Cahiers* (1876) and his *Chroniques Parisiennes* (1876), a series of articles published in *La Revue Suisse* (1843–5).

Criticism is a house with many mansions, but a percipient critic of recent date has distinguished three broad types:[6] 'spontaneous criticism', ranging from the conversation of informed (or merely pretentious) laymen to the newspaper article; this deals usually with new works or new writers: 'professional criticism', extending from longer studies in reviews and learned periodicals to literary history; this aims at discerning evolutionary trends of literature, establishing relationships and categories, mapping out large areas of the literary scene in a form the reader can take possession of and store away neatly in his mind: finally, the criticism of the artists who from Chateaubriand to Baudelaire and on to Proust have meditated on their art. Proust for one holds[7] that this form of criticism precedes rather than follows artistic creation, is not judgment but the self-examining creative impulse; it is in any case concerned with aesthetics.

Sainte-Beuve, whose pretentions to creative art are slim, figures in the latter category only to a small extent,[8] but the catalogue of his work shows him as a wide-ranging critic equally at home in the other two. Nineteenth-century precursors and contemporaries of Sainte-Beuve adopt distinctive attitudes: the relativism of Madame de Staël and later, Villemain (1790–1870),[9] the traditional dogmatism of Nisard (1806–88),[10] the moralism of Saint-Marc Girardin (1801–73),[11] hostile like Nizard to Romanticism, the determinism of Taine.[12]

The image Sainte-Beuve evokes is that of the liberal impressionistic humanist of criticism, yet for a critical career extending over

[3] See below, p. 360.
[4] First in *Le Constitutionnel* and *Le Moniteur* (1849–61), later in *Le Temps* (1861–69).
[5] Editor, J. Bonnerot.   [6] Thibaudet, *Physiologie de la Critique*.
[7] *Contre Sainte-Beuve*. See Vol. V, chap. 9, iv.
[8] e.g. his 'intimiste' conception of poetry.
[9] e.g. *Tableau de la littérature au dix-huitième siècle*, 1828–9.
[10] e.g. *Histoire de la Littérature française*, 1844–9.
[11] e.g. *Cours de littérature dramatique*, 1843.   [12] See below, pp 360–2.

forty years to show no trends, no variation of attitude would be strange. As already indicated, his early years dominated by Hugo saw him campaigning under the Romantic banner. If *Le Tableau Historique*, where he is at pains to emphasize affinities between the reformers of the 'Pléiade' and the Romantics, is the culminating point of this trend, many of his early *Portraits Littéraires* are well in line; the reservations he added later in the form of notes or postscripts,[13] when his Romantic fever had abated and given way to jealousies or enmities, underline the fact.

New interests drew his attention in the early 'thirties: the ideas of Saint-Simon, the liberal Catholicism of Lamennais; echoes of his religious explorations are to be found in *Volupté*, and *Les Consolations*; his visit to Lausanne brought him, under the influence of Vinet, the Swiss critic and moralist, to the fringes of Calvinism. Only momentarily, however; in none of these intellectual positions did he more than briefly sojourn. 'Dans toutes ces traversées je n'ai jamais aliéné ma volonté et mon jugement... engagé ma croyance, mais je comprenais si bien les choses et les gens, que je donnais les plus grandes espérances aux sincères qui voulaient me convertir et qui me croyaient déjà à eux...'[14]

On his return from Lausanne his religious moods were over, he had returned to his fundamental scepticism which goes well with the liberal attitude in criticism already clearly stated in an article on 'Bayle et l'Esprit critique'[15] (1835). Although his break with Romanticism was not to be absolute until 'Dix ans en littérature' (1840),[16] the article on Bayle is a disengagement operation, a milestone marking the second and most characteristic phase in Beuvian criticism – the attitude of neutral guide in the literary domain. This remains, but a further trend is discernible around 1850.

On the one hand, the course of lectures he gave at Liège (1848–9) on Chateaubriand enabled him to administer a few digs at the father of Romanticism; on the other, the trend toward Realism in literature has his sympathy: 'en bien des endroits et sous des formes diverses, je crois reconnaître des signes littéraires nouveaux ...'[17] Sainte-Beuve rejects, albeit politely, Positivist methods in criticism; Taine's dogmatism in scientific guise fails in the essential question, that is the individual genius, criticism has to deal with.[18] In opposition to Taine, Sainte-Beuve is almost forced to show that he too after all has his method,[19] is no mere superficial rhetorician

---

[13] e.g. *Portraits Litt.*, Vol. I, article on Boileau. Here in a postscript he corrects his earlier hostile attitude to the old classical writer.
[14] *Causeries du Lundi*, xi; 'Notes et Pensées'.
[15] *Portraits Littéraires*, I.   [16] *Portraits Contemporains*, I.
[17] *Causeries du Lundi*, xiii; see also above, p. 256.
[18] *Causeries du Lundi*, xiii; also *Nouveaux Lundis*, viii.
[19] *Nouveaux Lundis*, iii, 'Causerie sur Chateaubriand' (1862).

but 'une espèce de naturaliste des esprits tâchant de comprendre et de décrire le plus de groupes possible, en vue d'une science plus haute qu'il appartiendra à d'autres d'organiser. J'avoue qu'en mes jours de grand sérieux, c'est là ma prétention et comme ma chimère'. This pronouncement, the passage whence it comes, are characteristic of the man: a categorical statement to begin with: 'Je suis non pas...mais...', then a series of attenuating touches: 'tâchant de comprendre...', 'en vue d'une science plus haute...' The sort of science Taine claims is relegated to an indefinite future: 'J'avoue . . .' – apologetic, 'en mes jours de grand sérieux . . .' – jocund! Such gravity is evidently infrequent; 'ma prétention... ma chimère' – a claim, nay, an illusion! Sainte-Beuve, 'naturaliste des esprits' (the phrase has stuck), but with characteristic skill he leaves us in doubt whether or not he means it.

Sainte-Beuve was nothing if not perfidious and feline, as some of his contemporaries whom he misjudged or of whom he was jealous learned to their cost: Chateaubriand,[20] Balzac,[21] Baudelaire,[22] especially Baudelaire, Stendhal,[23] Vigny.[24] Notable amongst his perfidies, though here the matter is political rather than literary, is the article entitled *Regrets* (1852)[25] in which he railed at his former Orléanist friends for not rallying to Louis Napoleon as he had done.

Sainte-Beuve scarcely shows to advantage in such cases. On the other hand, where personal relationships or feelings did not enter in – or indeed if they did – what a model of scholarship (e.g. *Port-Royal* and *Chateaubriand*), what an inexhaustible mine of information (e.g. *Lundis* and *Nouveaux Lundis*), and praiseworthy, if not always discriminating curiosity, what moral finesse and sureness of judgment. He does not go very deep in his exploration of the psyche, but his literary portraits (excluding contemporaries) are excellent, and in relating a writer to the society of his day or a work to its author ('tel arbre tel fruit') he excelled. The *Lundis* and the *Nouveaux Lundis*, but especially *Port-Royal* and *Chateaubriand et son groupe*, are Sainte-Beuve's greatest achievement: yet, though at the height of his powers, he was not entirely at home in the intellectual climate of the post-1848 generation, in pursuit, under the impulse of Auguste Comte, of scientific certainties, beyond the limits Sainte-Beuve was prepared to accept in the critical field, for there the search implied establishing objective norms.

Sainte-Beuve veered skilfully away from them. Hippolyte Taine (1828–93), on the other hand, is the critic of the hour, although he came to literary criticism only by accident. Philosophy was his aim,

<hr>

[20] *Les Grands écrivains français par Sainte-Beuve*, 1927.   [21] *Ibid.*
[22] *Ibid.*   [23] *Ibid.*   [24] *Ibid.*   [25] *Causeries du Lundi*, vi.

Hegel the philosopher of his choice, but the authorities were suspicious of philosophy.[26] Taine, as a future teacher, was obliged to fall back on a literary subject – La Fontaine – for his degree thesis. Driven to the study of literature against his inclinations, Taine none the less saw that it offered him a vast testing ground for his philosophical ideas, derived from Hegel. The universe is a vast indivisible mechanism; experimental method is capable of discovering the intermeshed complex of forces controlling it.[27] This is true on every level and in every field, literature included, 'on peut faire de la critique littéraire une recherche philosophique.'[28] He writes and proceeds to use La Fontaine as a means of isolating the aesthetic laws of the beautiful. All his essays and studies of this period reveal the same systematic approach, the search for what he calls, in the preface to his *Essai sur Tite Live* (1856), 'la faculté maîtresse'. 'Y a-t-il en nous', he asks in a style that clearly reveals his deterministic belief, 'une faculté maîtresse dont l'action uniforme se communique différemment à nos différents rouages et imprime à notre machine un système nécessaire de mouvements prévus? J'essaye de répondre oui, et par un exemple'. But what conditions this controlling cause? Taine gives a partial answer in his *Voyage aux Pyrénées* (1854): 'Le climat façonne et produit les bêtes aussi bien que les plantes ... Le sol, la lumière, la végétation, les animaux, l'homme, sont autant de livres où la nature écrit en caractères différents la même pensée'.[29] The complete theory is expounded in the preface to his *Histoire de la littérature anglaise* (1864) where we are shown that three factors operate: 'la race, le milieu et le moment' (i.e. momentum). Taine was convinced he held the key that unlocks the mystery of national and individual psychology, that literature provided an inexhaustible store of documents for that purpose. The ardour of his faith at times bursts out in lyrical passages: 'La science approche enfin, et approche de l'homme; on a dépassé le monde visible et palpable des astres, des pierres, des plantes où dédaigneusement, on la confinait; c'est à l'âme qu'elle se prend, munie des instruments exact et perçants dont trois cents ans d'expérience ont prouvé la justesse et mesurée la portée...'[30]

Taine's dogmatic pronouncements, like those of Comte, reflect the spirit of his Positivist generation. We may question whether his theories do anything to solve the mystery of the individual creative power and genius. On the other hand, his impact on the Naturalist school, his contribution to its ideas, are beyond doubt. The

[26] Abolition of the 'Agrégation de Philosophie', December 1851.
[27] See Preface to *Les Philosophes Classiques du XIXe siècle* (1857).
[28] *Essai sur les fables de La Fontaine* (1853), republished as *La Fontaine et ses Fables* (1861).
[29] *Voyage aux Pyrénées*, Part III: *Plantes et Bêtes*.
[30] *Histoire de la littérature anglaise*, Bk. IV, chap. ii, sec. 6.

only difference between the literary critic and the novelist is that the former works on the 'dead' document, the latter studies the living 'document'; both are concerned with man considered as a physiological mechanism and society, that vast organism determined by stable, measurable forces: 'L'un et l'autre (criticism and novel), sont maintenant une grande enquête sur l'homme ... toutes les floraisons, toutes les dégénérescences de la nature humaine.'[31]

In 1864 Taine was appointed lecturer in the history of art at L'Ecole des Beaux Arts, Paris, and was thus provided with an opportunity to apply his method to another field. The results are to be found in: *Philosophie de l'art* (1865), *Philosophie de l'Art en Italie* (1866); *De l'idéal dans l'Art* (1867); *Philosophie de l'art dans les Pays-Bas* (1868); *Philosophie de l'art en Grèce* (1869). Apart from the application of the system, these works provide an interesting sidelight on Taine as a man; the erudite scholar has an evident preference in art for periods that are full of life and colour – fifteenth-century Florentine carnivals, or Flemish fairs, for eruptive geniuses – Rubens, Benvenuto Cellini; the latter he regards as 'un abrégé en haut relief des passions violentes des vies hasardeuses, des génies spontanés et puissants, des riches et dangereuses facultés qui ont fait la Renaissance et qui en ravageant la société ont produits les arts.'[32] Such Romantic amoralism might have been from the pen of Stendhal or Nietzsche.

Taine had travelled widely in Europe to see the works he was to lecture on; his journey to Italy was duly chronicled, as his journey to the Pyrenees had been and as his second journey to England was to be a few years later.[33] Striking in his *Voyage en Italie*, apart from the descriptions that reveal Taine as a fine stylist, is the occasional note of pessimism; a magnificent soliloquy on the inhumanity of nature escapes him, as he gazes on the statue of Niobe at Florence: 'Que de ruines, et quel cimetière que l'histoire! ... Quel sourire indifférent que celui du ciel pacifique et quelle cruauté dans cette coupole lumineuse étendue tour à tour sur les générations qui tombent comme le dais d'un enterrement banal ...'

The optimistic Hegelian of the earlier years is less in evidence. The war of 1870 and the Commune inevitably darkened his pessimism, and gave a new direction to his studies.[34]

Taine treated the study of literature as a branch of experimental psychology; Ernest Renan (1823–92) decided to become the historian of the origins of the Christian religion because he saw in its

---

[31] *Essais de critique et d'histoire*, 2nd edn., 1865.
[32] *Philosophie de l'Art en Italie*, chap. V, 3.
[33] *Notes sur l'Angleterre* (1872); his first journey to England was in 1858. For his travels in France, see also his *Carnets de voyages*.
[34] See Vol. V, chap. 1.

birth and early growth a moment of vital importance in the development of the human mind; the intellectual climate of the Positivist age is evident in both though neither was to remain at ease
within it.

Renan was destined to the priesthood from his early years; he
persisted in that path from the days when his intellectual promise
at the school of his native Tréguier had won him a scholarship to
the 'petit séminaire'[35] of St Nicholas du Chardonnet (1838), directed by l'Abbé Dupanloup (1803–78), future bishop of Orléans;
thence to the theological seminary of Issy, and thence to St Sulpice
(1843). Not until the end of the academic year 1845, when Renan
was on the threshold of the priesthood, did the serious questionings
that had been growing in his mind make him hesitate, and finally
refuse to take the irrevocable step. *Souvenirs d'Enfance et de Jeunesse*, that impeccable book[36] (1883), describes, *inter alia*, the agonies
of soul attending his decision, the sadness he felt at parting from
the masters at St Sulpice whom he regarded with affectionate
respect and the generosity of mind with which they on their side
respected a decision taken with such transparent sincerity and sorrow. Renan's years of cloistered study for the priesthood marked
him for life; the direction of his adoration changes, his religious
attitudes remain and often the style expressing them. His mind has
been compared to 'une cathédrale désaffectée'.[37]

Renan's life after his spiritual crisis was to be dedicated to
scholarship. *L'Avenir de la Science* (1848–9, published 1890) proclaims his new faith in science. Though reflecting the new scientific
enthusiasms in France after 1848, the search for a new faith to replace Christianity, destined to inevitable destruction, it remained
unknown because Renan on his return from Rome[38] (1850) decided not to publish it. Its interest therefore derives mainly from
the light it throws on the author himself, the breadth and brilliance
of his mind, the fervent optimism of the convert (or renegade,
whichever way you look at it), the able apologia for the branch of
knowledge he had made his own – philology ('science exacte des
choses de l'esprit. Elle est aux sciences de l'humanité ce que la
physique et la chimie sont à la science philosophique des corps');[39]

[35] Schools run by the Church for boys intending to take orders.
[36] Largely written at Ischia, 1875. 'La Prière sur l'Acropole', *Souvenirs*,
chap. 2, that magnificent soliloquy where Renan describes the impact upon
him of classical beauty, was not, as the context suggests, a lyrical flash of
inspiration that came to him on the Acropolis (1865), but a carefully
composed piece written at Fontainebleau (1876). H. Psichari, *La Prière
sur l'Acropole et ses Mystères*, 1956.
[37] A Daudet; see J. Lemaitre, *Les Contemporains*, Vol. I, p. 204.
[38] He went there (1849) with his friend Charles Daremberg, with the
approval of the Minister of Public Instruction, Cte de Falloux, to explore
the wealth of MSS. in the Vatican library during the occupation of Rome
by French troops under Oudinot. [39] Chap. viii.

his plea for an enlarged conception of psychology: 'Du moment que l'humanité est conçue comme une conscience qui se fait et se développe, il y a une psychologie de l'humanité comme il y a une psychologie de l'individu';[40] his suggestion of the value in this new psychology of a study of the origins of Christianity.[41] Here are the seeds of the project he was soon to embark on: *L'Histoire des Origines du Christianisme* (1863–81).[42] Christianity having its roots in Judaism, Renan then wrote his *Histoire du Peuple d'Israël* (1887–93). These two works, to which may be added as a prepara- tory work of erudition his philological treatise, *Histoire générale des langues sémitiques* (1855), constitute Renan's major contribu- tion to the scholarship of his day. They show that throughout his life as a scholar he remained faithful to the aims he had set himself in *L'Avenir de la Science*.

The early history of Christianity is in the life of its founder, in the lives of the men who preached it, carried it overseas, strength- ened it by suffering persecution, gave it its dogma. Thus, Renan's work is studded with biographical and character studies, outstand- ing amongst them that of Jesus, which raised storms of protest, created a European reputation for its author and led to his losing his professorial chair at the Collège de France (1864).

The fascination for Renan of Jesus the man is not difficult to understand; a man who in the short space of his ministry made an impact on the world as much by his personality as by his teaching, that has not lost its power down the centuries, a man of whose life only a small part is known and then only through the writings of men fallen under his spell, a figure distorted perhaps by hearsay and centuries of pious legends about miracles. Here was a challenge to a Positivist historian.

Renan in one of his pessimistic or sceptical or merely modest moods treats history as 'petites sciences conjecturales, qui se défont sans cesse après s'être faites. . . .'.[43] In another he says of Christi- anity, 'c'est par les sciences historiques qu'on peut établir (et selon moi, d'une manière péremptoire) que ce fait n'a pas été surnaturel . . .'[44] This is surely the mood in which he approached his problem, determined, albeit with veneration for the perfect man he believed Jesus to be, to strip away all legend, explain (away) all miracles, direct the rays of research as far as possible into the darkness and illumine Jesus the man. We may respect the sincerity of Renan's intentions without regarding the image of the Jesus of history that emerges from *La vie de Jésus* as more than partially convincing.

---

[40] Chap. x.   [41] *Ibid.*
[42] *La Vie de Jésus*, 1863; *Les Apôtres*, 1866; *Saint Paul*, 1869; *l'Anté- christ*, 1873; *Les Evangiles*, 1877; *L'Eglise chrétienne*, 1879; *Marc Aurèle et la fin du monde antique*, 1881.
[43] *Souvenirs D'Enfance Et De Jeunesse*, chap. iv.   [44] *Ibid.*, chap. iv.

The enchanting words, the irresistible smile, the tenderness and melancholy suggest a Winterhalter portrait rather than the reality; they are projections of Renan's own personality.

Much the same may be said of others of his portraits, notably St Paul, the fanatical man of action, so lacking in that quality Renan prized – scepticism: 'nous ne comprenons pas le galant homme sans un peu de scepticisme...';[45] and by contrast Marcus Aurelius detached from the vanities of this world – Renan's ideal.

The subjective intrusions are strong in the objective historian Renan aimed to be and even some of the principles that guided him are surprising: 'Dans les parties où le pied glisse entre l'histoire et la légende, c'est l'effet général seul qu'il faut poursuivre.'[46] The Venus of Milo has no arms; would Renan, one wonders, have liked to see a pair added in the position, from an intelligent guess, the sculptor may have had in mind?

In spite of criticisms, Renan's history is a great work. After Renan, the Church could no longer afford to rely, as it had tended to do before him in the nineteenth century, on its charity, pastoral good works and sentimental faith; Renan was a more dangerous enemy than Voltaire and his spiritual descendants; he was almost like a thief carrying away the treasure of Christian virtues the Church had implanted in him, and, by his learning, undermining the whole structure of belief. The Church would have to look to its defences, recast its seminary teaching, call Biblical scholars to her aid.

Renan was not content with pure scholarship and he turned away from the materialism of his age, engendered by Positivism; he needed a faith to bring light into his 'disaffected cathedral'. Its elements are to be found scattered in e.g. *La Métaphysique et son Avenir* (1860), and *Dialogues et Fragments Philosophiques* (1876).[47]

Renan retains the idea of progress, but, as might be expected, he is concerned with the progress of man towards moral perfection which is God, not existing but always becoming. The Christian idea of a personal God has disappeared; Renan substitutes a high if cold idealism delighting to express itself in Christian terms.

The scholar, and the philosopher in the broadest sense, are the two constants in Renan; there is a third aspect – the publicist and commentator on current affairs, political and other. It was in this role that Renan created the best known image of himself, but that was to be after 1870.[48]

.   .   .

[45] *L'Antéchrist*, chap. iv. Some highly characteristic pages.
[46] *Les Apôtres*, introduction, vii.
[47] *Inter alia*, the letter (1863) to his friend Berthelot on the natural and historical sciences.   [48] See Vol. V, chap. 1.

An exact contemporary of Taine and Renan, Fustel de Coulanges (1830–89) represents, better than either, the scientific temper
of the age in its impact on scholarship.

From his thesis on Polybius (1858) to *La Cité antique* (1864) and
on to *L'Histoire des Institutions politiques de l'ancienne France*
(six volumes, 1888–92), the most rigorous and objective discipline
is applied. The thesis on Polybius is a study on the nature of
patriotism in the second century B.C. and its decay under the influence of factions; in *La Cité antique* the study of the city-state
in the Ancient World, already in embryo in the thesis on Polybius,
is worked out in great detail. In a rigorous chain of argument relying solely on the evidence provided by language, literature, customs
and laws, Fustel shows each family tightly-knit by the cult of their
own dead and the families forming tightly-knit groups united in
the cult of the Olympian Gods. At this stage of the city-states'
evolution, other factors leading ultimately to their decline begin to
operate: wealth in the hands of the few, the formation of the
'plebs' excluded from citizenship; the final stage of the cycle is
reached when the city-states are absorbed into the Empire, and the
Universalist cults – stoicism, Christianity – replacing the animist
cults transform the whole structure of the family and therefore of
society.

In Fustel's other great work, that on the institutions of the
Ancient French Monarchy, the theme is the emergence of the
feudal world during the eight centuries that separate the Roman
conquest of Gaul from the last Carolingians; Fustel examines in
detail the origins and growth of the feudal institutions, extracting
from the original sources every shred of evidence they can properly
be made to yield. The subject here does not lend itself to the same
tight organisation as in *La Cité antique* but both works have the
same characteristics; each is the study of a society in growth and
decay; events and individuals have almost no part, only institutions, laws, customs, all things that mould societies; Fustel looks
back to Guizot and Tocqueville, but the sociologist's concern with
laws and processes, the search, at least in *La Cité antique*, for the
original impulse that sets the machinery in motion, much as Taine
looked for 'la faculté maîtresse', are even more pronounced; individuals, however important, fade into mere social units. 'L'histoire',
he explains, 'n'est pas l'accumulation des événements de toute
nature qui se sont produits. Elle est la science des sociétés humaines.'[49] What could reflect better the spirit of Positivism?

[49] *Histoire des Institutions*, Vol. IV, introduction.

Bibliography

BIBLIOGRAPHY

1. *Histories of Literature*

Castex, P.-G. and Surer, P., *Manuel des Etudes Littéraires Françaises, XIXe siècle* (1 vol.), 1960.
Chassang, A. and Senniger, C., *Recueil de Textes Littéraires Français, XIXe siècle* (1 vol.), 1966.
Clouard, H., *Petite Histoire de la Littérature Française*, 1966.
Lagarde and Michaud, *Collection Textes et Littérature, XIXe siècle* (1 vol.), 1964.
Thibaudet, A., *Histoire de la Littérature Française de 1789 à nos Jours*, 1936.

2. *Political and Social History*

Bury, J. P. T., *France 1814–1940*, 3rd edn. revised, 1954.
Napoleon III and the Second Empire, 1964.
Champion, E., *La France d'après les Cahiers de 1789*, 1897.
Elton, Lord, *The Revolutionary Idea in France 1789–1878*, 1923, 2nd edn. 1931.
Gaxotte, P., *Histoire des Français* (2 vols.), 1951.
Howarth, T. E. B., *Citizen King*, 1961.
Lucas-Dubreton, J., *La Restauration et La Monarchie Libérale*, 1926.
Madaule, J., *Histoire de France* (2 vols.), 1945-7.
Rémond, R., *La Droite en France de 1815 à nos Jours*, 1954.
Siegfried, A., *Tableau des Partis en France*, 1930.
Simpson, F. A., *The Rise of Louis Napoleon*, 3rd edn., 1950.
Louis Napoleon and the Recovery of France, 3rd edn., 1951.
Thibaudet, A., *Les Idées Politiques de la France*, 1932.

3. *Religion and the Church*

Dansette, A., *Histoire religieuse de la France Contemporaine* (2 vols.), 1948-51, vol. I.
Phillips, C. S., *The Church in France: A Study in Revival*, 1929.

Weil, G., *Histoire de l'Idée Laïque en France au dix-neuvième siècle*, 1925.

4. Intellectual Background

Barrière, P., *La Vie intellectuelle en France du seizième siècle à l'époque contemporaine*, 1961.

Charlton, D. G., *Secular Religions in France, 1815–1870*, 1963.

Earle, E. M., *Modern France. Problems of the Third and Fourth Republics*, edited by E. M. Earle, 1951.

Faguet, E., *Politiques et Moralistes du dix-neuvième siècle* (3 vols.), 1891–9.

Manuel, F. E., *The Prophets of Paris*, 1962.

Raitt, A. W., *Life and Letters in France. The Nineteenth Century*, 1966.

Simon, P. H., *Le Domaine héroïque des Lettres Françaises du dixième au dix-neuvième siècles*, 1963.

Wright, C. H. C., *The Background of Modern French Literature*, 1926.

5. Literary Movements

a. Romanticism:

Gautier, Th., *Histoire du Romantisme*, 1874.

George, A. J., *The Development of French Romanticism: the Impact of the Industrial Revolution on Literature*, 1955.

Giraud, J., *L'Ecole Romantique Française; les Doctrines et les Hommes*, 6th edn., 1953.

Maigron, L., *Le Romantisme et les Moeurs*, 1910.

Le Romantisme et la Mode, 1911.

Marsan, J., *La Bataille Romantique* (2 vols.), 1912, 1924.

Praz, M., *The Romantic Agony*, translated from the Italian by A. Davidson, 1933.

Reynaud, L., *Le Romantisme*, 1926.

Shroder, M. Z., *Icarus. The Image of the Artist in French Romanticism*, 1961.

Souriau, M., *Histoire du Romantisme* (2 vols.), 1927.

b. Realism:

Dumesnil, R., *L'Epoque Réaliste et Naturaliste*, 1945.

Le Réalisme et le Naturalisme, 1955.

Henriot, E., *Réalistes et Naturalistes*, 1954.

Maynial, E., *L'Epoque Réaliste avec Florilège des Auteurs cités*, 1931.

c. *Parnasse:*

Martino, P., *Parnasse et Symbolisme, 1850–1900,* 9th edn., 1954.
Souriau, M., *Histoire du Parnasse,* 1929.

6. *The Novel*

Le Breton, A., *Le Roman Français au dix-neuvième siècle,* 1905.
Martino, P., *Le Roman Réaliste sous le Second Empire,* 1913.
Merlant, J., *Le Roman Personnel de Rousseau à Fromentin,* 1905.
Rousset, J., *Forme et Signification. Essais sur les Structures Littér-
aires de Corneille à Claudel,* 1962.

7. *The Drama*

Latreille, C., *La Fin du Théâtre Romantique et François Ponsard,*
1899.
Le Breton, A., *Le Théâtre Romantique,* 1923.
Lénient, L., *La Comédie en France au dix-neuvième siècle* (2 vols.),
1898.
Le Roy, A., *L'Aube du Théâtre Romantique,* 2nd edn., 1904.
Lintilhac, E., *Histoire Générale du Théâtre en France,* Vol. V, n.d.
Nebout, P., *Le Drame Romantique,* 1899.

8. *Poetry*

Banville, Th. de, *Petit Traité de Poésie Française,* 1872.
Brandin, L., and Hartog, W., *A Book of French Prosody,* n.d.
Brunetière, F., *L'Evolution de la Poésie Lyrique en France au dix-
neuvième siècle* (2 vols.), 1894.
Hackett, C. A., *Anthology of Modern French Poetry from Baude-
laire to the Present Day,* 2nd edn., 1964.
Hartley, A., *The Penguin Book of French Verse,* ed. A. Hartley,
1957.
Mansell Jones, P., *The Oxford Book of French Verse XIII–XXth
Century,* 2nd edn. ed. P. Mansell Jones, 1957.
Mansell Jones, P., and Richardson, G., *A Book of French Verse.
Lamartine to Eluard,* edited with Introduction and Notes by P.
Mansell Jones and G. Richardson.
Parmée, D., *Twelve French Poets 1820–1900,* Introduction and
Notes by Douglas Parmée, 1957.

9. *Criticism*

Belis, A., *La Critique Française à la fin du dix-neuvième siècle,*
1926.

Brunetière, F., *L'Evolution de la Critique*, 1890.

Carloni, J.-C., and Filloux, J.-C., *La Critique Littéraire*, 1955.

Giraud, V., *La Critique Littéraire; le Problème, les Théories, les Méthodes*, 1946.

Michaud, G., *L'Oeuvre et ses Techniques*, 1957.

Peyre, H., *Essais de Méthode de Critique et d'Histoire Littéraire de G. Lanson, présentés par*, H. Peyre, 1966.

Thibaudet, A., *Physiologie de la Critique*, 1930.

10. *Miscellaneous*

Bourget, P., *Essais de Psychologie Contemporaine*, 1883–5.

Carré, J.-M., *Les Ecrivains Français et le Mirage Allemand, 1800–1940*, 1947.

France, A., *La Vie Littéraire* (4 vols.), 1895–7.

Gourmont, R. de, *Promenades Littéraires* (7 vols.), 1904–28.

Parmée, D., *Baudelaire. Critical Studies selected from L'Art Romantique*, with an essay on Baudelaire's Aesthetics by D. Parmée, 1949.

Sainte-Beuve, C.-A., *Causeries du Lundi* (14 vols.), 1868–70. *Nouveaux Lundis* (13 vols.), 1865–9.

Tieghem, P. van, *Les Influences Etrangères sur la Littérature Française 1550–1880*, 1961.

Select Bibliography for Chapter 3

Bingham, A. J., *Marie-Joseph Chénier, Early Political Life and Ideas (1789–1794)*, 1939.

Bouissounouse, J., *Condorcet. Le Philosophe dans la Révolution*, 1962.

Dumay, R., *Joubert. Pensées et Lettres, présentées par R. Dumay*, 1954.

Hartog, W. G., *Guilbert de Pixérécourt. Sa Vie, son Mélodrame, sa Technique et son Influence*, 1913.

Sainte-Beuve, C.-A., *Chateaubriand et son Groupe Littéraire sous l'Empire. Cours professé à Liège en 1848–49*, 1948 edn.

Scarfe, F., *André Chénier*. Poems selected and edited by Francis Scarfe, 1961. *André Chénier. His Life And Work 1762–1794*, 1965.

Tessonneau, R., *Joseph Joubert, Educateur. D'après des documents inédits (1754–1824)*, 1944.

Wilson, A., *Fontanes. 1757–1821. Essai biographique et littéraire*, 1928.

Select Bibliography for Chapter 4

Du Bos, C., *Grandeur et Misère de Benjamin Constant*, 1946.
Guillemin, H., *Benjamin Constant, Muscadin 1795–1799*, 1958.
Herold, J. C., *Mistress to an Age. A Life of Madame de Staël*, 1959.
Holdheim, W. W., *Benjamin Constant*, 1961.
Jasinski, Mme B., *Madame de Staël. Correspondance Générale. Texte établi et présenté par* Beatrice W. Jasinski (Vols. I and II to date), 1960–2.
Larg, D. G., *Madame de Staël; la Vie dans l'Oeuvre, 1766–1800*, 1924.
Madame de Staël; la seconde Vie, 1800–1807, 1928.
Pozzo Di Borgo, O., *Ecrits et Discours Politiques par Benjamin Constant. Présentation, Notes et Commentaires par* O. Pozzo Di Borgo (2 vols.), 1964.
Souriau, M., *Les Idées morales de Madame de Staël*, 1910.

Select Bibliography for Chapter 5

Buche, J., *L'Ecole Mystique de Lyon, 1776–1847*, 1935.
Debidour, V.-H., *Rivarol. Ecrits Politiques et Littéraires Choisis et présentés par* V.-H. Debidour, 1956.
Le Breton, A., *Rivarol. Sa Vie, ses Idées, son Talent*, 1895.
Levaillant, M., *Chateaubriand, Madame Récamier et les Mémoires d'Outre-Tombe*, 1936.
Merlant, J., *Senancour. 1770–1846. Sa Vie, son Oeuvre, son Influence*, 1907.
Michaut, G., *Senancour. Ses Amis et ses Ennemis*, 1909.
Mongland, A., *Le Journal Intime d'Obermann*, 1947.
Moreau, P., *Chateaubriand. L'Homme et la Vie*, 1927.
Sainte-Beuve, C.-A., *Chateaubriand et son Groupe Littéraire sous l'Empire*, 1948 edn.
Ubrich, O., *Charles de Villers, Sein Leben und seine Schriften*, 1899.
Vial, A., *Chateaubriand et le Temps Perdu*, 1963.

Select Bibliography for Chapter 6

Berthier, A., *Xavier de Maistre. Etude biographique et littéraire*, 1918.
Kimstedt, C., *Frau von Charrière, 1740–1805; ihre Gedankenwelt und ihre Beziehungen zur französischen u. deutschen Literatur. (Romanische Studien*, 48), 1938.
Ley, F., *Madame de Krüdener et son Temps 1764–1824*, 1961.
Sykes, L. C., *Madame Cottin*, 1949.

Select Bibliography for Chapter 7

Bayle, F., *Les Idées Politiques de Joseph de Maistre*, 1945.

Cioran, E. M., *Joseph de Maistre. Textes Choisis et présentés par E. M. Cioran*, 1957.

Margerie, A. de, *Le Comte J. de Maistre, sa Vie, ses Ecrits, ses Doctrines; avec des documents inédits*, 1882.

Moulinié, H., *De Bonald*, 1915.

Spaemann, R., *Der Ursprung der Soziologie aus dem Geist der Restauration. Studien über L. G. A. de Bonald*, 1959.

Select Bibliography for Chapter 8 (I)

Castex, P.-G., *Charles Nodier: Contes avec des Textes et des Documents inédits. Introduction, Notices etc. par* P.-G. Castex, 1961.

Held, M., *Charles Nodier et le Romantisme*, 1949.

Lebois, A., *Un Bréviaire du Compagnonnage. La Fée aux Miettes*, 1961.

Oliver, A. R., *Charles Nodier, Pilot of Romanticism*, 1964.

Select Bibliography for Chapter 8 (II)

Citoleux, M., *La Poésie Philosophique au dix-neuvième siècle. Lamartine*, 1906.

Doumic, R., *Lamartine*, 1912.

Fréjaville, G., *Les Méditations de Lamartine*, 1931.

Guillemin, H., *Lamartine, L'Homme et l'Oeuvre*, 1940.

Le Jocelyn de Lamartine, 1936.

Levaillant, M., *Lamartine. Oeuvres choisies ... avec Biographie, Notes Critiques ... par* M. Levaillant, 1949.

Guyard, M.-F., *Oeuvres poétiques complètes. Texte établi annoté et présenté par* M.-F. Guyard, 1963.

Select Bibliography for Chapter 9

Desternes, L., *Paul-Louis Courier et les Bourbons. Le Pamphlet et l'Histoire*, 1962.

Duine, F., *La Mennais. Sa Vie, ses Idées, ses Ouvrages*, 1922.

Jasenas, E., *Marceline Desbordes-Valmore devant la Critique*, 1962.

Gurvich, G., *Les Fondateurs Français de la Sociologie Contemporaine: Saint-Simon et P. J. Proudhon* (Centre De Documentation Universitaire), 1955.

Samie, Mme P. de, *A l'aube du Romantisme. Chênedollé 1769–1833. Essai biographique et littéraire*, 1922.

Simon, J., *Thiers, Guizot, Rémusat*, 1885.

Select Bibliography for Chapter 10

Barrère, J. B. M., *Hugo. L'Homme et l'Oeuvre*, 1959.
Billy, A., *Sainte-Beuve. Sa Vie et son Temps* (2 vols.), 1952.
Castex, P.-G., *Vigny. L'Homme et l'Oeuvre*, 1952.
Choisy, L.-F., *Sainte-Beuve. L'Homme et le Poète*, 1921.
Combe, T. G. S., *Sainte-Beuve Poète et les Poètes Anglais*, 1937.
Estève, E., *Alfred de Vigny. Sa Pensée et son Art*, 1923.
Flottes, P., *La Pensée Politique et Sociale d'Alfred de Vigny*, 1927.
Gastinel, P., *Le Romantisme d'Alfred de Musset*, 1933.
Gregh, F., *L'Oeuvre de Victor Hugo*, 1933.
Roos, J., *Les Idées Philosophiques de Victor Hugo. Ballanche et Victor Hugo*, 1958.
Tieghem, P. van, *Musset. L'Homme et l'Oeuvre*, 1944.

Select Bibliography for Chapter 11

Arvin, N. C., *Eugène Scribe and the French Theatre*, 1924.
Barrère, J. B. M., op. cit. above.
Castex, P.-G., op. cit. above.
Clouard, H., *Alexandre Dumas*, 1955.
Glachant, P. et V., *Essai Critique sur le Théâtre de Victor Hugo* (2 vols.), 1902.
Gregh, F., op. cit. above.
Lafoscade, L., *Le Théâtre d'Alfred de Musset*, 1901.
Petroni, L., *Alfred de Vigny. Chatterton* Edition Critique publiée par Liano Petroni, 1962.
Pommier, J., *Variétés sur Alfred de Musset et son Théâtre*, n.d.
Schorr, T., *Über Casimir Delavigne* (Giessener Beiträge zur Philologie), 1926.

Select Bibliography for Chapter 12

Allem, M., *Sainte-Beuve et Volupté*, 1935.
Bory, J. L., *Eugène Sue. Le Roi du Roman Populaire*, 1962.
Castex, P.-G., op. cit. above.
Clouard, H., op. cit. above.
Doumic, R., *George Sand*, 1909.
Gregh, F., op. cit. above.
Salomon, P., *George Sand*, 1953.
Thibaudet, A., *Intérieurs – Baudelaire – Fromentin – Amiel*, 1924.
Vier, J., *Pour l'étude du Dominique de Fromentin*, 1958.

Select Bibliography for Chapter 13

Albérès, F. M., *Le Naturel chez Stendhal*, 1956.
Atherton, J., *Stendhal*, 1965.
Bardèche, M., *Stendhal Romancier*, 1947.
Baschet, R., *Du Romantisme au Second Empire. Mérimée (1803–1870)*, 1959.
Hemmings, F. W., *Stendhal. A Study of his Novels*, 1964.
Jourda, P., *Stendhal. L'Homme et l'Oeuvre*, 1934.
Léon, P., *Mérimée et son Temps*, 1962.
Martineau, H., *L'Oeuvre de Stendhal . . . Histoire de ses Livres et de sa Pensée*, 1945.
Trahard, P., *La Jeunesse de Prosper Mérimée*, 1924.
   Prosper Mérimée de 1834 à 1853, 1928.
   Prosper Mérimée et l'Art de la Nouvelle, 3rd edn., 1952.

Appendix to Chapter 14

La Comédie Humaine (Selection)

A. *Etudes De Moeurs*

   I. *Scènes de la Vie Privée:*

   La Maison du Chat-Qui-Pelote (1830).
   Le Bal de Sceaux (1830).
   Modeste Mignon (1844).
   Albert Savarus (1842).
   Madame Firmiani (1832).
   La Femme Abandonnée (1832).
   Gobseck (1830).
   La Femme de Trente Ans (1831–44).
   Le Père Goriot (1834–5).
   Le Colonel Chabert (1832).
   La Messe de l'Athée (1836).

   II. *Scènes de la Vie de Province:*

   Ursule Mirouët (1841).
   Eugénie Grandet (1833).

   Les Célibataires:
      (Part 2) *Le Curé de Tours* (1832).
      (Part 3) *La Rabouilleuse* (1841–2).
   Illusions Perdues (3 Parts, 1837, '39, '43).

III. *Scènes de la Vie Parisienne:*

> *Histoire des Treize:*
>> (Part 2) *La Duchesse de Langeais* (1833–4).
>> (Part 3) *La Fille aux Yeux d'Or* (1834–5).

> *Histoire de la Grandeur et de la Décadence
> de César Birotteau* (1837).
> *Splendeurs et Misères des Courtisanes* (4 Parts, 1839–47).
> *Facino Cane* (1836).

> *Les Parents Pauvres:*
>> (Part 1) *La Cousine Bette* (1846).
>> (Part 2) *Le Cousin Pons* (1847).

IV. *Scènes de la Vie Politique:*

> *Le Député d'Arcis* (1847).

V. *Scènes de la Vie Militaire:*

> *Les Chouans* (1829).

VI. *Scènes de la Vie de Campagne:*

> *Les Paysans* (1844).
> *Le Médecin de Campagne* (1833).
> *Le Curé de Village* (1839).
> *Le Lys dans la Vallée* (1835).

B. *Etudes Philosophiques*

> *La Peau de Chagrin* (1831).
> *Jésus-Christ en Flandre* (1831).
> *Melmoth Réconcilié* (1835).
> *Le Chef-d'Oeuvre Inconnu* (1831).
> *Gambara* (1837).
> *La Recherche de l'Absolu* (1834).
> *Les Marana* (1832).
> *El Verdugo* (1830).
> *L'Auberge Rouge* (1831).
> *Louis Lambert* (1832–3).
> *Séraphita* (1835).

C. *Etudes Analytiques*

> Nil.

Select Bibliography for Chapter 14

Bardèche, M., *Balzac Romancier*, 1940.

Bertault, P., *Balzac*, 1962.

Guyon, B., *La Pensée Politique et Sociale de Balzac*, 1947.

Hunt, H. J., *Honoré de Balzac. A Biography*, 1957.

Balzac's Comédie Humaine, 1959.

Lotte, F., *Dictionnaire Biographique des Personnages Fictifs de la Comédie Humaine*, 1952.

Pradalie, G., *Balzac Historien. La Société de la Restauration*, 1955.

Pierrot, R., *H. de Balzac: Correspondance. Textes réunis, classés et annotés par* R. Pierrot (3 vols. to date), 1960–4.

Select Bibliography for Chapter 15

Carré, J.-M., *Michelet et sons Temps*, 1926.

Jullian, C., *Extraits des Historiens Français du XIXe Siècle .. Précédés d'une Introduction sur l'Histoire en France par* Camille Jullian, 1910.

Lively, J., *The Social and Political Thought of Alexis de Tocqueville*, 1962.

Mayer, J. P., *Prophet of the Mass Age*, 1939.

Monod, G., *La Vie et la Pensée de Jules Michelet 1798–1852* (2 vols.), 1923.

Simon, J., op. cit., see p. 374.

Herr, R., *Tocqueville and the Old Régime*, 1962.

Select Bibliography for Chapter 17

Baldick, R., *The First Bohemian. The Life of Henry Murger*, 1961.

Benoit-Guyod, G., *La Vie et l'Oeuvre D'Erckmann-Chatrian*, 1963.

Bésus, R., *Barbey d'Aurevilly*, 1958.

Bonnes, J. P., *Le Bonheur du Masque. Petite Introduction aux Romans de Barbey D'Aurevilly*, 1947.

Bornecque, J.-H., *Barbey D'Aurevilly, Les Diaboliques ... Introduction ... par* J.-H. Bornecque, 1963.

Bouvier, E., *La Bataille Réaliste*, n.d.

Crouzet, M., *Un Méconnu du Réalisme: Duranty 1833–1880*, 1964.

Evans, I. O., *Jules Verne and his Work*, 1965.

Lange, M., *Le Comte Arthur de Gobineau. Etude biographique et critique*, 1924.

Marash, J. G., *Henry Monnier. Chronicler of the Bourgeoisie*, 1951.

Tabary, L. E., *Duranty (1833–1880). Etude biographique et critique*, 1954.

Nouvelle Revue Française, 1 February 1934. Special Number on *Gobineau et le Gobinisme*.

Select Bibliography for Chapter 18

Bollème, G., *La Leçon de Flaubert*, 1964.
Bruneau, J., *Les Débuts littéraires de Gustave Flaubert, 1831–1845*, 1962.
Descharmes, R., *Flaubert, sa Vie, son Caractère, ses Idées avant 1857*, 1909.
Dumesnil, R., *Gustave Flaubert. L'Homme et l'Oeuvre*, 3rd edn., 1947.
Fairlie, A., *Flaubert: Madame Bovary*, 1962.
Thibaudet, A., *Gustave Flaubert, 1821–1880. Sa Vie. Ses Romans. Son Style*, 1922.
Spencer, P., *Flaubert. A Biography*, 1952.

Select Bibliography for Chapter 19

Albérès, R-M., *Gérard de Nerval*, 1955.
Austin, L. J., *L'Univers poétique de Baudelaire*, 1956.
Blanchot, M., *Lautréamont et Sade*, 1949.
Blin, G., *Baudelaire*, 1939.
    Le Sadisme de Baudelaire, 1948.
Borgal, C., *Baudelaire*, 1961.
Boschot, A., *Théophile Gautier. Emaux et Camées . . . avec une Esquisse biographique . . . par* Adolph Boschot, 1954.
Cellier, L., *Gérard de Nerval. L'Homme et l'Oeuvre*, 1956.
Charpentier, J., *Théodore de Banville. L'Homme et son Oeuvre*, 1925.
Estève, E., *Leconte de Lisle. L'Homme et l'Oeuvre*, n.d.
Fairlie, A., *Leconte de Lisle's Poems on the Barbarian Races*, 1947.
    Baudelaire. Les Fleurs Du Mal, 1960.
Flottes, P., *Leconte de Lisle. L'Homme et l'Oeuvre*, 1954.
Ibrovac, M., *José-Maria de Heredia. Sa Vie. Son Oeuvre*, 1923.
Jasinski, R., *Les Années romantiques de Théophile Gautier*, 1929.
Jean, M., and Mezei, A., *Maldoror. Essai sur Lautréamont et son Oeuvre*, 1947.
Marie, A., *Gérard de Nerval. Le Poète et l'Homme*, 1955.
Porché, F., *Baudelaire. Histoire d'une Ame*, 1944.
Putter, I., *The Pessimism of Leconte de Lisle* (2 vols.), 1954, 1961.
Quennell, P., *Baudelaire and the Symbolists*.
Rigal, E., *Victor Hugo, Poète épique*, 1900.
Ruff, *Baudelaire. L'Homme et l'Oeuvre*, 1955.
Starkie, E., *Baudelaire*, 1957.

Simaika, R., *L'Inspiration épique dans les romans de Victor Hugo*, 1962.
Turnell, M., *Baudelaire. A Study of his Poetry*, 1953.
Vianey, J., *Les Poèmes Barbares de Leconte de Lisle*, 1955.
Fairlie, A., 'An Approach To Nerval', *Studies in Modern French Literature*, M.U.P., 1961.

Select Bibliography for Chapter 20

Carton, P., *Meilhac et Halévy. Théâtre. Préface et Notes de P. Carton*, 1955.
Gaillard de Champris, H., *Emile Augier et la Comédie Sociale*, 1910.
Hart, J. A., *Sardou and the Sardou Plays*, 1913.
Lamy, P., *Le Théâtre de Dumas Fils*, 1928.
Soupault, P., *Eugène Labiche. Sa Vie, son Oeuvre*, 1964.
Taylor, F. A., *The Theatre of Alexandre Dumas Fils*, 1937.

Select Bibliography for Chapter 21

Chadbourne, R. M., *Ernest Renan as an Essayist*, 1957.
Cresson, A., *Hippolyte Taine. Sa Vie, son Oeuvre*, 1951.
Kahn, S. J., *Science and Aesthetic Judgment. A Study in Taine's Critical Method*, 1953.
Lehmann, A. G., *Sainte-Beuve. A Portrait of the Critic, 1804–1842*, 1962.
Leroy, M., *La Pensée de Sainte-Beuve*, 1940.
Michaut, G., *Sainte-Beuve avant les Lundis*, 1906.
Nicolson, H., *Sainte-Beuve*, 1957.
Tourneur-Aumont, J.-M., *Fustel de Coulanges, 1830–1889*, 1931.
Wardman, H. W., *Ernest Renan. A Critical Biography*, 1964.

Index

Printed in Great Britain
by Western Printing Services Ltd
Bristol